THE EXCLUDED AMERICANS

HOMELESSNESS
AND
HOUSING
POLICIES

THE EXCLUDED AMERICANS

WILLIAM TUCKER

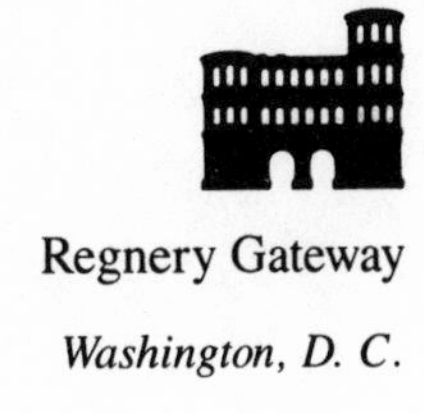

Regnery Gateway

Washington, D. C.

Library of Congress Cataloging-in-Publication Data

Tucker, William, 1942–
The excluded Americans : homelessness and housing policies / William Tucker.
p. cm.
Includes bibliographical references.
ISBN 0-89526-551-6
1. Housing policy—United States. 2. Homelessness—United States. 3. Rent control—United States. 4. Zoning—United States. 5. Housing—New York (N.Y.) I. Title.
HD7293.T77 1989
363.5′8′0973—dc20 89-10769
CIP

Published in the United States by
Regnery Gateway
1130 17th Street, NW
Washington, D.C. 20036

In cooperation with
Cato Institute
224 Second Street, SE
Washington, DC 20003

Distributed to the trade by
National Book Network
4720-A Boston Way
Lanham, MD 20706

Manufactured in the United States of America

10 9 8 7 6 5 4 3 2

This book is dedicated to a man I never knew,
my grandfather, Thomas Gorman.
He owned a building.

Acknowledgments

For a book that has turned out to be such a long project, stretching both backward and forward into former careers and unanticipated efforts, it is difficult to begin making the proper acknowledgments.

I first became interested in planning and zoning matters while working at *The Rockland Journal-News* in the 1970s. My education there was begun under editor Dennis Murray and continued under Stephen Hesse, Grant Jobson, Arthur Gunther, and the late Janet Fisch. At *The Bergen Record*, I continued my apprenticeship under the late Bob King and Tom Koyce. All of these helped in my initiation to the reporting trade. Paul Lieberman enhanced my enjoyment and understanding of the profession at both newspapers. The late Sylvan Davis gave me the opportunity to expand in many new directions at *The Haverstraw Times.* Both William Chase and Dan Fried at the Rockland County Planning Board gave me my first introduction to the endlessly fascinating subject of municipal policies.

At *The New York Times*, my understanding of the world of real estate was permanently enhanced by Alan S. Oser, editor of the real-estate page. Jon Storm also offered good editorial direction and Carter Horsley provided good companionship.

Once the undertaking of this book was begun, the list of people who have been helpful grows to impossible lengths. To name only a few, I would like to thank Louis Winnick, Dan Rose, Charles Urstadt, Elizabeth Ivory Greene, George Sternlieb, Helen Barrera, Philip Rudd, Juliette McGinnis-Nelson, Roberta Bernstein, Anthony Gliedman, John Gilbert, Jack Froines, Gwen Wunder, Nancy Pakes, Cathy Young, Chris Alexis, Richard Boodman, Frank Ricci, Loren Renz, Janet Bulen, Wilbur Bascomb, Helen Daniels, Joan Dawson, Winifred Dozier, Linda Eskanas, Aeolus and Shirley Green, the Rev. Dale Hanson, the Rev. James Harris, Stanley Hawkins, Sid Kirshnet, Steve Lande, Molly and Bill Lairamore, Miriam Lee, James Lioi, Grace Liota, Jeffrey Manocherian, Roger Meltzer, Pat Nash, Christine Pirakowski, Jack Richman, Carol Rogers, Norman Romney, Helen Rowland, Helen Sadlowska, Judy Seigel, Jimmy Silber, Howard Smallowitz, Yvonne Stafford, Michael Stewart, Isabelle Tuit, Flossie Turner, Mariel Uttmark, Eleanor Vail, Ming Wang, Bruce Wittenburg, Susan Wolf, David Yallich, David Yannick, Arthur Zabarkas, and David Zincovage.

I would like to thank Michael McKee of the New York State Tenant and Neighborhood Coalition and Anne Pasmanick, of the People's Firehouse, for their kind cooperation. Also, I would like to express my appreciation to Jane Benedict and the Metropolitan Council on Housing for being gracious enough to allow me to attend their annual meeting even though they knew we differed on many issues.

Early funding for this book was provided by both the Manhattan Institute and the Cato Institute, which have been equally helpful in bringing this effort to fruition. I would like to thank both William Hammett, of the Manhattan Institute, and David Boaz, of the Cato Institute, for their advice and their unusual patience in waiting for the final product to emerge. Peter Salins and Gerald Mildner at the Manhattan Institute also offered important assistance. The Hoover Institution also gave me the time and place to put the final pieces together. I would like to thank Tom Henriksen and the entire Hoover staff, plus the Stanford Library and its remarkable facilities, for their invaluable assistance.

Portions of this book have appeared in *The American Spectator, The New Republic, Reason,* and *National Review.* I would like to thank editors Vlad Pleszczynski and Andy Ferguson at *The American Spectator*, Michael Kinsley and Dorothy Wickenden at *The New Republic*, Virginia Postrel and Bob Poole at

Reason, and Richard Vigilante and Maggie Gallagher at *National Review*, for their comments and criticism in shaping the material. Cassandra Moore, former director of the Interagency Council on the Homeless, also read the manuscript.

Bonnie Goldman and William Millard provided invaluable assistance in researching the libraries and tracking down odd facts and statistics. Goldman also edited the manuscript and did some excellent reporting on housing issues in New York. Pamela Dillon helped in investigating the world of Mitchell-Lama housing and Michael Meer offered an endless series of leads and anecdotes.

The statistical work on the analysis of the homelessness was done by Dr. Jeffrey Simonoff, of New York University. He has been especially knowledgeable and patient in leading me through a difficult subject.

At Regnery Gateway, Harry Crocker has been an excellent and efficient editor.

I would also like to thank my parents, William and Grace Tucker, for their untiring efforts in culling the newspapers and for their usual support.

In writing a book that says a few kind words about landlords, I have often been confronted with the question, "Who's paying you to do this?" With the publication of this book, I would like to reveal the secret. This book has been underwritten almost entirely by my wife, Sarah Greene, whose financial and emotional support has been the only thing that made it possible for me to continue so long in the essentially charitable undertaking of writing a book. It has been a long effort and only she knows the true meaning of it.

Finally, to the many landlords who have been willing to sit down and tell me their stories, often in the midst of great emotional anguish, I would like to remind them that this too is their book.

Contents

In America, it is indispensable that every well wisher of true liberty should understand that acts of tyranny can only proceed from the publick. The publick, then, is to be watched, in this country, as, in other countries kings and aristocrats are to be watched. . . . [T]he man who would dare to resist a monarch, shrinks from opposing an entire community.

—James Fenimore Cooper,
The American Democrat.

Preface

Grand Central Station, February 28, 1987

After midnight, New York's Grand Central Station essentially belongs to the homeless. The cavernous waiting room, normally filled with the bustle of commuters, is now nearly empty. The stragglers who remain seem incongruously glamorous. A 50-year-old man with a fur coat and a suntan appears to have stepped out of a television ad as he hustles to make the last train. A leggy blonde, sucking voraciously on a cigarette, seems bent upon some mysterious midnight assignation.

What makes these ordinary New Yorkers seem suddenly so elevated, perhaps, is the mute Greek chorus in front of whom they perform. Propped up against every wall, spread out across waiting-room benches, sprawled in front of shuttered boutiques, squirreled into every dark corner, lies the human wreckage that has washed up on the shores of American life—the homeless.

Not all are stumblebums and bag-ladies. One young waif, almost pretty, wanders across the waiting room holding a paper cup. Approaching each stray party of travellers, she is at first taken for an ingénue asking directions. Only after a moment do they recoil in horror as they realize she is begging for money.

On the whole, though, few of the homeless are so energetic. Mostly they are the old, the spent, the disturbed. Some talk to themselves, others sip wine or lie scratching their bloated bodies. Most have sought some forgotten corner. In an arcade of telephone booths, every third cubicle contains a disheveled occupant propped up asleep. An elderly black man sits in a wheelchair, snoring. Along the rows of shuttered stores a gang of black teenagers in high-school jackets cavort loudly. One young woman drops into an agile karate stance and laughingly challenges her boyfriend to a fight. Presiding over this entire panorama, knots of boyish policemen absentmindedly slap their nightsticks against their palms.

At age 44, I admit, I am getting a little old for adventures. In wintertime, I do go for an occasional midnight ski in Brooklyn's nearby Prospect Park, but it has been a long time since I hopped a freight or hitched a ride. One thing I've learned is that as you get older and dress more respectably, you become an ever-more inviting target.

The last time I hitched a ride, for example, I was in Houston and had missed the last bus back to my motel. After 20 minutes, a car with two Mexicans in the front seat finally stopped. I probably wouldn't have gotten in except in the back sat a long-haired blonde girl. Although a bit strange, it didn't seem too threatening.

The blonde girl turned out to be a sinister-looking teenage boy. Between us sat a huge stereo system, obviously just stolen. The Mexicans couldn't speak English and in their confusion were nice enough to drive me almost all the way to my motel before the kid pulled a .22 and shoved it in my face. I dove out the door as he shot three times, close enough so I could smell the gunpowder. I didn't even know whether I was hit until I found myself standing 30 yards down the road, shaking but still in one piece. After that, I decided to take cabs.

With a wife and two kids, I am much more cautious about taking risks. Still, to write about anything you have to be there. Besides, with so many reporters, politicians, and movie actors spending nights with the homeless, it almost seemed obligatory. Only recently, Mayor Andrew Young of Atlanta had wandered unrecognized for several nights among the homeless. In New York, TV anchorwoman Pat Harper painted her teeth yellow and spent a week on the streets, causing some critics to charge she was turning the homeless into an entertainment.

And so, one night late in February, after everyone was asleep, when the television news announced the temperature would be dropping to near-zero, I suddenly realized this might be my last chance to spend a night in Grand Central Station. Putting on my long underwear and gathering some stale bread, I wrote an elaborate note to my wife promising to call at 6 A.M., then set off to explore that most puzzling of all American paradoxes—homelessness in the midst of a well-housed, affluent society.

After an hour of wandering Grand Central, I still hadn't quite decided what to do. Dressed in jeans and an old parka, I was a bit too disheveled to pass for a reporter, yet too well-dressed to look really homeless. Besides, the homeless talked so little among themselves that striking up a conversation seemed a rude invasion of their privacy. Most of them obviously wanted to be left alone.

Generally, there seemed to be two categories of homeless. The first was the old, the disheveled, the crazed. A few were women, but most were men. They generally dressed in pants that were too big or shoes that didn't match. Although most were asleep or in a stupor, a few wandered aimlessly through the station.

The second group—scattered in loud clumps, laughing and talking—was a sizable population of young black men. Generally appearing sound of mind and able of body, they wore flashy shirts, shiny maroon pants, and other shopworn statements of forgotten fashion. In pondering the black welfare culture of single mothers and children, people have often wondered what has happened to the "missing men" of that society. Now, at midnight, in Grand Central Station, I was beginning to get the idea that some of them might be right here. Although distinctly set apart from the downtrodden, drunk, and crazy, they seemed to be a permanent part of the scenery.

A tour of the station turned up few approachable people. One gray-haired woman sitting beneath a row of shuttered ticket windows seemed fairly normal as she smoked and stared into space. Everyone else was either asleep, deranged, or fairly sinister.

As I began a second tour, a young black kid motioned me over to a gated newsstand. It was the kind of gesture you ignore three times a day in New York, but now I went over to see what he wanted. Giving me his hostile-teenager's stare, he asked for a cigarette. I said I didn't have one. Then I hunched my shoulders and asked what time the station closed. His face softened a bit.

"Two o'clock, man," he said.

"Do the cops kick you out?"

"Yeah, man."

I hunched my shoulders again, thanked him, and walked off.

"Good luck, man," he called after me.

By the time I returned to the main waiting room, the gray-haired woman beneath the ticket windows had disappeared. I chose a spot for myself against the wall and sat down to survey the huge ceiling. Across the beautiful pale blue vault, tiny lights twinkled as stars, while faint, luminescent diagrams outlined the constellations. Perhaps the cold was already beginning to shape my mood, but even with its legs and claws neatly illustrated, Cancer still looked like just a bunch of stars.

So there we sat, an expectant audience of 100 or so, facing our huge amphitheater-in-the-round, the main waiting room. It seemed as if anything might happen—a murder, a police chase, even a scrimmage by the New York Giants football team, whose recent Super Bowl victory was celebrated on a 50-foot Kodacolor mural covering one wall. Far above in another corner, Pat Harper's face smiled down on us all.

Yet nothing happened. And after a while, I realized nothing was going to happen, either. The journey from expectation to resignation can be a long one, sometimes covering an entire lifetime. But without a bed to sleep on, it can be traversed in a single night. Like everyone else, I soon found myself staring into space.

Somehow I had gotten the impression that city vans would soon be arriving to herd us all off to one of the shelters that have been established by a Federal court order. I half-expected that, after convincing some psychiatrist of my sanity or insanity (whichever seemed more appropriate), I would be trundled off to a lice-infested armory in the Bronx. Now I remembered that the practice had been discontinued. The vans were only taking people off the streets.

In 15 minutes Grand Central would close. The temperature outside was below ten degrees. It was already too late to ride home on the subways, which become progressively more dangerous as the night wears on. I had two dollars in my pocket. The floor beneath me was a block of ice. It looked as if I might be in for the duration.

Once again I decided to explore smaller waiting rooms. Like traces of some forgotten civilization, huge plaster statues stood forgotten in the corners. The stench of urine was everywhere. On each wooden bench, neat as church cushions, lay rows of bodies hidden under piles of blankets, coats, sleeping bags. At least I assumed there were bodies in there. Not an inch of flesh was visible anywhere.

Wandering downstairs I was attracted by the sound of voices. All at once, I found myself looking through a folding iron gate. On the other side, not six feet away, a dozen black men and women stood unpacking shopping carts. Behind them, a long exit ramp rose to the outside doors. On the floor, scattered everywhere, lay bodies buried in blankets.

The grating was like a prison bar—wide enough to shake hands through yet confining enough to keep someone from putting a knife to your throat. As I stood watching the little troop set up camp, I realized their efforts were all being directed by one intelligent-looking man in his 30s.

"Whatta we gonna do with this, Bullet? Whatta we gonna do with that?" The questions kept coming and the man fielded each one with nothing more than his good judgment. "Put it over here. Put it over there," he directed them casually.

Bullet had a sidekick, a short, wiry man with a knot of boyish hair and a lopsided grin—a perfect Hollywood wiseguy. After every third or fourth directive, he would challenge Bullet's authority. They would square off in mock confrontation, until Bullet tousled the wiseguy's hair and sent him back to work. The women were laughing and joking—all except one, already bedded down, whose tubercular cough wracked through three blankets. Much of the activity centered around making her comfortable.

"What's the rent in this place?" I asked as Bullet passed in front of me for the third time.

"Oh, not bad," he said. "You get heat, light, and a bed, all for nothing. Here, you wanna come in? Just go up the stairs and come down again. This is considered outside the station. The cops won't bother you here."

As I stood debating, Bullet pulled a last blanket out of his shopping cart, revealing a worn copy of *Coming of Age in Samoa*.

"How do you like Margaret Mead?" I asked.

"Oh, not bad," he said, thumbing the pages with some embarrassment. "I think I liked some of her other books better, though."

I decided to join them.

When I found the top of the ramp, I suddenly realized it was a place Pat Harper had encountered in her wanderings. Harper had been terrified by the hordes of young black men perched like vultures on the overhanging railings. Expecting they would swoop down on the sleeping homeless during the night, she had opted for the streets instead. Yet Bullet's group didn't seem entirely defenseless. I walked down and joined them.

At the bottom, where the little band had assembled, an overhanging enclosure with overhead lights promised some warmth. Most of the places there were already taken. Back up the ramp, things got quickly colder. At the top were the outside doors, and every time they opened, a gust of arctic air blew in. I took an open space as far down the ramp as possible. Over my head, a sign advertised the Oyster Bar.

Of the dozen-or-more bodies on the floor, most were sleeping peacefully. Only the one right next to me thrashed away in the obvious throes of a nightmare. After a while, a pale hand appeared from beneath the blankets. As seems common in these scenes at the bottom of American life, most of the black people were normal while the whites were somewhat disturbed.

Just above me on the ramp was another woman whom I soon realized was also connected to the group. She was a black dwarf, no more than four feet tall, wearing red jogging pants and aviator glasses. Around her sat a whole inventory of shopping bags. She was proud of her association with the group and kept calling to Bullet on seemingly inconsequential matters.

"Bullet, do you think I should leave these bags out? Bullet, do you think John's going to find enough boxes? He's been gone over an hour, do you think I should go look for him?"

"Don't worry, Evelyn, he'll be back."

Now I realized why the business of boxes was so important. The floor beneath me was cold as a gravestone and everyone had two or three boxes broken into mattresses. One young man had even built himself a little house with several empty cartons. When he disappeared into his makeshift tent for the night, everyone applauded.

Shortly after, John returned with six beautiful boxes. Although she barely came to his waist, Evelyn immediately began chiding him for taking so long. A small man in his 30s with a knock-kneed look that suggested something wrong with his legs, John obediently endured Evelyn's lecture.

Bullet finally walked by and we acknowledged each other again. "You want some bread?" I asked, offering the little I had brought.

"No, we got plenty," he said. He probably wasn't all that happy I had asked, but I fell in beside him anyway.

"My name's Bill," I said, shaking hands.

"Bullet," he said. We headed up the ramp.

"How long you been out here?"

"Oh, about four years. We've been out to the West Coast, Las Vegas, everywhere."

"This whole group?"

"Most of 'em."

"What's it like out West?"

"Beautiful. Lots of sun, you can live outdoors, really enjoy yourself."

"What made you come back to all this freezing cold?"

He shrugged and surveyed the scene for a moment. "This is my home." He lit a cigarette. "This isn't what I really want to do," he went on. "My dream is to get a big trailer and take my wife and kids on a trip all around the country."

"Is that your wife down there?"

"No, she's back home."

"Where's home."

"Brooklyn. I was born there."

"That's where I lived, too."

"Is that right? So what brings you out here on such a cold night."

I had prepared a story about my wife kicking me out of the house but I didn't think it would ring true. "Temporarily displaced," I said, smiling with embarrassment.

"Temporarily displaced," he echoed. I had no idea what he was thinking.

"Where'd you get your education?" I asked.

"I was in the Job Corps. I finished high school but I never did go to college," he said. "I should have done what my brother did and gone in the Navy. He's a drill sergeant in the Marines now. He's a big success. Not like me."

"It might not be too late for you."

"It is," he said, crushing his cigarette.

"It's not easy finding a place to live in New York these days, is it?"

"Look at all this," he said, surveying the bodies all around us.

"Well, good luck," I said, shaking hands.

"Good luck to you too, man."

I went back to my place next to the wall.

Evelyn and John were still struggling with the boxes so I offered to help. "That's all right, we're fine," she said, not unfriendly. Every time she bent down her sweatpants slipped down over her hips and she had to struggle to pull them up again. Eventually, she and John laid a mattress three boxes thick and then lined up three more empty cartons as a headboard. They began stuffing their shopping bags inside.

The station was closing down. Upstairs the police rattled another grating shut, noisily evicting a few stragglers. Cleaning equipment began to whir and buzz. Behind our gate, the police rolled past on an electric baggage cart, shouting at people to leave the station. Despite their incessant patrols, dozens of people eluded them. All night long, wraithlike shadows padded back and forth before us, like ghosts flitting through a haunted house.

Next to me the writhing body shouted, "I got you! I got you both!" Tubercular coughs were everywhere. Upstairs a man intoned, "If you wanna play baseball, go t' the park. If you wanna play baseball, go t' the park." At one point, a dazed Puerto Rican wandered into our midst asking for drugs. When no one responded, he stood statue-like for 15 minutes with his hand stretched out before departing. At least four times during the night, a well-dressed, late-night traveller burst through the outer doors, strode confidently down the walkway, and recoiled in horror as he found himself facing a locked gate and a floor filled with homeless people. Each turned and fled back up the ramp.

After a while everyone in Bullet's group bedded down. One man in a blue knit cap propped up his head and spent half an hour reading *The Daily News'* story about Sir Rudolph Bing and his delinquent new wife. Two men fervently argued basketball. I found it impossible to sleep while sitting on the cold floor and wondering if someone upstairs might drop a brick on my head.

Suddenly, a loud confrontation erupted at the outside doors. "Get the fuck outta my way, you stupid motherfucker!" someone shouted. A tall, wiry black man with eight shopping bags strung over a long shoulder pole disentangled himself from a terrified white teenager. As the kid flew out the door, the man marched straight down toward us. He was about 50, gaunt and undernourished, his body bristling with pent-up anger.

"What the fuck, we got white boys down here now?" he proclaimed, heading straight for me. "Look at this motherfucker. What are you doing, working undercover or somethin'?" Like children and others outside the bounds of convention, he had no trouble seeing through my pretense. "Get the fuck out of here, will you? I want to lie down." He stood directly over me.

I suppose in the grand scheme of things, I probably should have given him my space. After all, he was in it for life, while I was only pretending. Still, there was a long, cold night ahead and for some reason I didn't feel like moving. I edged over a bit toward the sleeping lunatic next to me and tried to ignore him.

The man plopped his things down in the small space between me and Evelyn. Now she took offense. "What the fuck you trying to move in here for?" she said. "Why don't you go someplace where you got room."

"Listen, little lady, you give me any trouble and I'll throw you right out of this goddamn building." It was an exquisitely cruel insult. She barely came up to his thighs.

"Then what you gonna do about me?" said knock-kneed John. It was the first word I had heard him utter all night.

"I'll throw you outta here, too," said the man and undoubtedly he could have. But heads were beginning to pop up everywhere and the man sensed the tide turning against him. "Well, why don't you tell this ofay boy to get outta my way?" he said. ("Ofay"—"foe" in pig latin—is an old black hipster term for whites.) Once again I tried to ignore him. Quietly, he picked up his belongings and moved farther up the ramp.

Evelyn and John crawled into bed under a heavy burlap blanket. The headboard, I realized, made a nice windbreak against the cold air. As they settled down, Evelyn took off her glasses, laid them on the headboard, and said, "Now dear, try not to break these tonight, will you?" Then they burrowed under the covers, giggling and talking like newlyweds.

For a while, I had fretted about having my pocket picked, even though I only had a few dollars. Now I decided there was nothing much to worry about. The bonds of civilization asserted themselves, even here in the bowels of Grand Central Station. Among these bedraggled and broken souls, the rules of ordinary behavior still applied. As the man in the knit cap finished reading his *Daily News,* he smiled and handed it over to me. I thanked him profusely and carefully spread it on the floor for a mattress.

Around four o'clock, an entire airline crew came clattering out of the station. A mini-skirted stewardess shrieked as the cold air hit her legs. Later, the man in the wheelchair came down and parked right next to me. In a minute, he was asleep again. Then I noticed the gray-haired woman, whom I had seen earlier beneath the shuttered ticket windows, had taken up roost near the top of the ramp. I went and bummed a cigarette, thinking to start a conversation. "I'll give you one if you get out of here and leave me alone," she said. That was the end of our interview.

At six o'clock I went outside and called my wife. She wasn't nearly as worried as I had feared—although she had missed my note at first and spent an anxious half-hour assuming I was lying unconscious on skis in Prospect Park.

Back on the floor again I started shivering uncontrollably. The cold had finally gone through me. Up to this point, I had survived by letting my hands and feet get cold while trying to keep my chest warm. Now the cold was *inside* me and there was nowhere to retreat. I breathed slowly, ate some bread, and tried to stop shaking. A shot of whiskey would have been perfect.

Half an hour later the station attendants clanked the gate open and shooed us away. Although it felt like an eviction, I soon realized it was our moment of deliverance. By twos and threes, everyone began filtering back into the station, looking for a warm place to catch a few hours' sleep before the commuters arrived.

I wandered around a bit, then decided to head home. Dawn was breaking and it was still frightfully cold. At the corner, a carload of suburban teenagers pulled up and yelled to a newsstand dealer, "Hey, you know where we can find any girls around here?"

The cold wave was on the front page. The temperature had dropped to four degrees, the lowest in two years. Two homeless men had frozen to death and two others were murdered. A gang of teenagers had jumped out of a car and knifed them as they slept in a doorway.

I got on a subway and headed home, my little piece of investigative reporting done. A nice warm bed waiting for me. I would probably sleep half the day.

For those with whom I had spent the night, and would probably never see again, there would be many more cold nights ahead in Homeless America.

PART I

HOMELESSNESS AND THE SATISFIED MAJORITY

"Don't put it in my backyard."
—Anonymous

Chapter 1

The Paradox of Homelessness (I)

Homelessness has become both a national disgrace and a national paradox—poverty in the midst of plenty. In 1988, America still had the highest standard of living of any industrial country. Unemployment had receded to a 15-year low and more people were working than ever before. Americans were so well housed that—as one pair of experts pointed out—there is now one bedroom for every American.[1] Yet in the midst of all this, in city after city, the number of people who cannot find anyplace to live continues to grow.

In Miami, Latin immigrants have set up large tent cities beneath highway underpasses. In response, the city council has adopted a law allowing the police to arrest homeless people. In Washington, the homeless regularly camp out in Lafayette Park, right across from the White House. When the city forbade them to sleep in subway stations, widespread protests ensued. In New York, bus stations, subway stations, and railroad terminals often resemble YMCAs, with scores of homeless people bedded down in neat, dormitory rows. Panhandlers are everywhere and subway signs carry instructions on how to deal with beggars.

Though the East Coast media capitals have garnered most of the attention, the problem is actually worse in the Far West. Estimates made by the U.S. Conference of Mayors in 1988 showed that, after Miami, San Francisco and Los Angeles had the highest rates of homelessness in the country.[2] A study by *The Los Angeles Times* estimated that 40,000 people are living illegally in garages around the city. "These are places with one fire exit, no toilet and extension cords hanging from ceilings with a hot plate at the other end," said Gary Squier, the city's housing coordinator. "They're very substandard units."[3]

While early estimates of the national homeless population at 2 to 3 million were probably exaggerated, by the end of the decade these figures were beginning to seem more realistic. By 1988, even the most optimistic assessments put the population at nearly one million. A 1988 study by the U.S. Conference of Mayors noted that although the growth of homelessness had slowed a bit—up 13 percent in 1988 rather than the 21 percent of the previous year—the trend was still upward.[4]

What has caused this strikingly visible new upsurge of poverty in the last decade? Of the many explanations put forth, most fell into four major categories:

1. the incomes theory: homelessness has been caused by deteriorating incomes, the result of rising unemployment and poverty.
2. the government-cutback theory: homelessness is the result of Federal cutbacks in welfare, social security benefits, and above all, the construction and maintenance of public housing.
3. the affordable housing theory: homelessness is the result of a lack of housing around the country, particularly "affordable" housing, accessible to low-income people.
4. the personal-pathologies theory: homelessness is due to individual inabilities to function, whether because of mental illness, substance abuse, or lack of personal organization.

These arguments are by no means mutually exclusive and most people embrace at least two or three of them. But the choice of emphasis is important, since each leads to a different strategy for dealing with the homeless.

Let us begin by examining the theories to see how they measure up against each other.

The Incomes Theory

This theory says that homelessness has been the result of general underlying economic weaknesses of the economy, mainly as reflected in rising unemployment and poverty rates. Testifying before Congress in 1986, Governor Mario Cuomo of New York probably summed up the case when he argued: "The nature of our homeless population is largely misunderstood. They are the people we all know in our families and our communities, homeless only because they are unemployed, because of chronic poverty, or simply because of the nationwide shortage of affordable housing." In other words, the homeless are basically victims of hard times.

At first, the argument seems compelling. After a long post-war period in which unemployment rarely rose above five percent, it jumped to the six to eight point range in the 1970s, then peaked at ten percent in 1982 during the Reagan recession, before sliding downward since then.[5]

FIGURE 1–1
Unemployment Rates 1930–1989

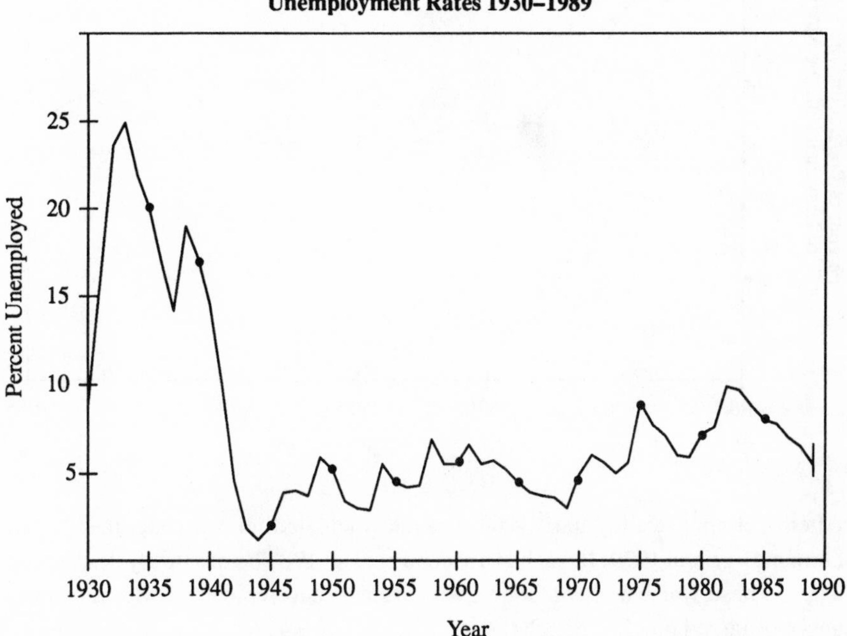

During the early 1980s, whole Midwestern industries closed down, leaving miles of abandoned factories in their wake. Cleveland saw unemployment reach 20 percent. Houston newspapers were sold on the streets of Detroit as discharged auto workers looked to the Sunbelt for jobs. From 1980 to 1985, Detroit lost 20 percent of its population, the result of declining employment.

Even when migrating Midwesterners drove their campers and station wagons to Dallas and New Orleans, they encountered more adversity. Hard upon the Rust Belt followed the Oil Bust, which left much of Texas, Oklahoma, and Louisiana in a regional recession. By 1985, unemployment in New Orleans and Houston had climbed to double digits, leaving incoming migrants without jobs or opportunity.

Poverty rates—measured by the percent of the population with incomes of less than half the median—also reflected the economic hardships of the early 1980s.[6]

FIGURE 1–2
Poverty Rates 1960–1988

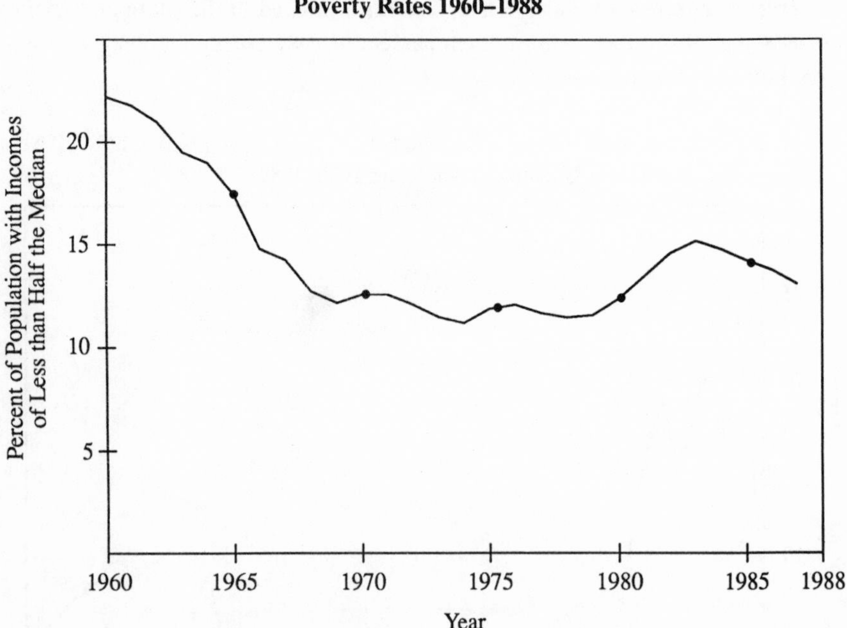

After declining steadily until 1969, the rate vacillated for a decade, then began climbing again in 1979. It reached a second peak in 1983 before slowly descending again. These worsening conditions, it is argued, have coincided with the emergence of large homeless populations.

Obviously, unemployment and poverty have led to homelessness. Most homeless people are, almost by definition, poor and unemployed. Yet there are also arguments against this analysis. The nation, after all, had endured other postwar recessions without experiencing homelessness. The recession of 1958–59 lifted unemployment to 6.9 percent, the highest rates in almost two decades. The Oil Shock of 1973 produced a recession in which unemployment neared nine percent and housing starts, always a leading economic indicator, fell to less than half their 1972 level. Yet in neither instance did homelessness begin to appear. In addition, although unemployment rates were high in the early 1980s, by 1989 they had declined to 5.5 percent, a level that would have been considered reasonable in the 1950s.

Interestingly enough, homeless shelters around the country often report that a surprisingly large portion of their residents are regularly employed. When the Conference of Mayors surveyed shelters in 27 major cities in 1988, it found that an average of 23 percent of the homeless had jobs.[7] In New York, Mayor Edward Koch asked people in the city's shelter system to start paying rent after discovering that some residents were making as much as $14,000 a year in wages.

If poverty were the cause of homelessness, we might have expected homelessness in the early 1960s, when poverty rates were much higher. Yet that did not occur. The steady ascent of poverty since 1978 does indeed coincide closely with the rise of homelessness. Yet by the same measure, we should have expected the number of homeless to decline when the poverty rates declined again after 1983.

Although poverty and unemployment are obviously playing a part, there are probably other important factors as well. As Kim Hopper and Jill Hamberg, of the Community Service Society in New York, note:

> [Poverty and unemployment] have occurred at various times in the postwar era and did not produce the level of homelessness we see today. Indeed, if widespread poverty, hunger, unemployment, deinstitutionalization, and migration were invariably linked with homelessness, we would expect to have seen much more of it at other times during the postwar period.[8]

While the vast majority of the homeless are poor and unemployed, the vast majority of the poor and unemployed are not homeless. In fact, 37 percent of the people in poverty *own* their own homes. These are usually elderly people with assets but very little income (poverty rates only measure income). Thus, while poverty and unemployment are obviously contributing factors, they may not be the whole story.

This is an important distinction to make. No one would argue that creating jobs and reducing poverty cannot improve the general welfare. But we must not necessarily assume that it will reduce homelessness. If the principal cause lies elsewhere—in the release of mental patients or in the availability of housing—then we can work very hard at reducing poverty and unemployment and still have large homeless populations.

The Government-Cutback Theory

Many critics of the Reagan administration have argued that it has not been simply adverse economic conditions but specific cutbacks of the social safety net that have led to homelessness. Frequently cited are cutbacks in social security disability payments, welfare benefits, and housing-assistance programs.

"In late 1983, in the wake of widespread protests," wrote Hopper and Hamberg, "the Social Security Administration curtailed its practice of terminating disability benefits to those it considered no longer unable to work—but not before almost half a million of the disabled (nearly a sixth of the total) had been dropped from the rolls."[9] These policies undoubtedly left a residue of poor or disabled people without incomes. Yet there is little indication that these people were a significant fraction of the homeless. Even Hopper and Hamberg admit their numbers are not very large.

Another factor commonly cited is the gradual erosion of welfare benefits, particularly Aid to Families with Dependent Children (AFDC). Peter Rossi, author of *Without Shelter: Homelessness in the 1980s,* notes that by 1985, AFDC payments were worth only 63 percent of their value in 1968. Most of this erosion took place during the period from 1975 to 1980, when the benefits were ravaged by inflation.[10]

The rise of the welfare family—most often a minority woman and her children—has indeed been one of the significant social developments of the last 15 years. As early as 1981, in their book, *The Future of Rental Housing,* George Sternlieb and James Hughes, of the Urban Policy Research Center at Rutgers University, noted that the only social group that showed any significant deterioration of income versus rent over the previous decade was the female-headed household:[11]

MEDIAN ANNUAL RENT AS A PERCENT OF MEDIAN ANNUAL INCOME

	Total U.S. Renters		**Black Central City Renters**	
	1973	*1978*	*1973*	*1978*
Two or More Person Households	19.6	23.8	21.8	27.5
Male Head, Wife present	18.2	19.4	18.1	18.2
Other Male Head	21.0	27.8	24.2	23.7
Female Head	*26.9*	*35.8*	*24.9*	*34.1*
One Person Households	30.7	30.3	31.9	30.6

"What appears to be certain levels of degeneration in the rental housing market may not be indicative of a rent housing problem *per se,* but a symbol of much more significant problems of American society," concluded Sternlieb and Hughes.[12]

The situation of single-parent households has continued to deteriorate. In 1987,

46 percent of single mothers with one child had incomes below the poverty level of $7,800 and the percentage was higher for mothers with more children.[13] Young single mothers paid an average of 58.4 percent of their income in rent, while two parent families of the same age group paid only 25.4 percent.[14]

This failure of family formation is a grave social problem in and of itself. Peter Rossi notes that women now form 25 percent of the homeless population, whereas several studies of homeless populations in the 1950s and 1960s showed their numbers were insignificant.[15] This could mean that deteriorating welfare benefits have been a contributing factor. But then again, the welfare family itself was not nearly as common then as it is now. Whether the growing number of homeless women represents lowered benefits, the growing number of single-parent households, or some other factor common to both men and women, is still an open question.

Perhaps the most passionate criticisms have been raised over the alleged cutbacks in Federal housing programs run by the Department of Housing and Urban Development (HUD). "Since 1981, Budget Authority for all federal housing assistance programs has been cut 75 percent—from $32 billion to $5.7 billion a year," says a fund-raising letter from Mitch Snyder's Community for Creative Non-Violence in Washington, D.C., one of the nation's best-known homeless advocacy groups. These figures are constantly cited in homeless debates and are said to illustrate "the federal government's abdication of responsibility for creating or maintaining low-cost housing."[16]

The numbers seem to create a *prima facie* case that the social cutbacks of the administration of President Ronald Reagan have been the principal cause of homelessness. Yet strangely enough, there are people who will argue that there have been no real budget cutbacks and that Federal housing aid to the poor actually *increased* during the Reagan administration. Writing in *The Wall Street Journal* in December 1988, Edgar Olsen, professor of economics at the University of Virginia, argued:

> You would never know it from reading the popular press, but the Reagan administration has made considerable headway in eliminating the inefficiencies and inequalities that have plagued housing subsidies to low-income households for more than 50 years. . . . In fact, total outlays on housing subsidies of low-income households rose from $5.7 billion in fiscal 1980 to $13.8 billion in 1988. During this same period, the Bureau of Labor Statistics' residential rent index rose only 60 percent. So even after correcting for inflation, housing subsidies to low-income families have increased more than 50 percent during the past eight years. Furthermore, the number of low-income households receiving housing subsidies has increased by about one-third over this period to 4.2 million.[17]

Who is telling the truth here? In fact, both parties are correct in what they are saying. It is just that they are talking about two different things. Subtleties of language—and budgeting practices—confuse the issue.

The important thing to note is that when Mitch Snyder talks about budget cuts, he is referring to spending *authority.* Always and ever, in the criticisms of the Reagan administration's housing programs, it is *authorizations* for HUD's housing assistance programs that are cited as proof of reduced spending for the poor. Yet *authorizations are not spending*. They are only *commitments* to spend money at some future date.

When we look at the amount of money actually spent for housing assistance programs, the figures look like this:[18]

FIGURE 1–3

Housing Assistance Payments As a Percentage of Total Budget Outlays (1962–1985)

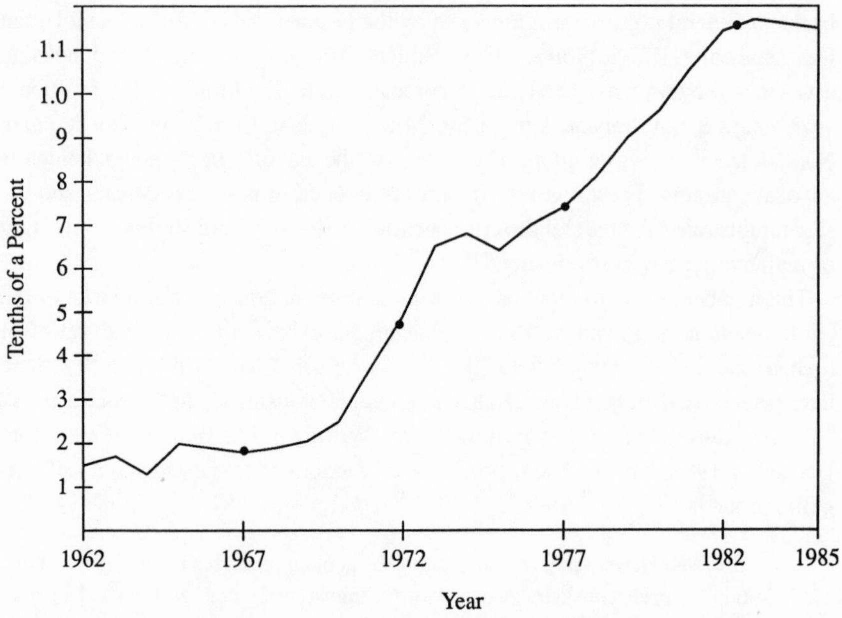

Perhaps the best way to sort out the confusion is to consider the "housing vouchers" and "housing certificates," both issued under section 8 of the Housing and Community Development Act of 1974. Vouchers and certificates are, in effect, "rent stamps" that the Federal government issues to poor people to help them pay their rent. Certificates are contracted for a fifteen-year basis, whereas vouchers have a life of only five years. The Carter administration issued section-8 certificates. After 1984, the Reagan administration shifted its emphasis to housing vouchers.

According to Federal budget practices, however, *all* the money that will be spent on a certificate *over the next 15 years* is credited to the single year in which Congress authorizes the spending. Thus, Congress can "triple authorizations" by switching from 5-year vouchers to 15-year certificates, or "cut authorizations 67 percent" by going the other way. Yet the amount of money spent—and the number of poor people actually assisted—will be exactly the same.

This confusing terminology also carries over into the construction of public housing. A new unit of public housing is paid for by bonds that will be retired over 40 years. Yet once again, the whole 40-year authorization is credited to the first year. As a result, the authorization of public housing units greatly overstates the immediate commitment of funds—and does not even indicate that any funds have been spent at all.

In addition, it may be 10 to 15 years after authorization before a unit of public housing is actually brought on line. (Vouchers and certificates, on the other hand, become available immediately.) There are still some public housing units in the pipeline from the Ford administration. Here is the number of public housing units *authorized* each year by Congress over the last decade compared to the number of units actually *brought on line:*[19]

Year	*New Units Authorized*	*New Units Brought on Line*
1977	31,764	5,192
1978	56,245	10,134
1979	54,914	10,763
1980	36,677	15,109
1981	35,921	32,485
1982	12,099	27,611
1983	2,740	27,041
1984	0	24,058
1985	7,312	19,093
1986	5,314	14,897
1987	9,801	10,415
1988	7,000	9,146

Despite the large cutbacks in authorizations, the 1980s have actually been boom years for public housing. All this cannot be credited to the Reagan administration, which worked to get the government out of the business of building public housing. But it completely undercuts the argument that a slackening effort in public housing has been the cause of homelessness.

Another issue on which the Reagan administration has been faulted is the deteriorating condition of many public housing units. Once again, this is commonly attributed to "sharp budget cuts," as in this report from *The Wall Street Journal:*

> [P]rojects in many larger cities are crumbling, and federal budget cuts are a major factor. Under the Reagan administration, authorized funds for housing programs fell to about $8 billion in fiscal 1986, down 70 percent from the $30 billion authorized in 1981, according to the council of Large Public Housing Authorities.[20]

Yet once again, there have been no budget cuts. HUD's appropriations to local housing authorities for both short-term maintenance and long-term "modernization" have undergone regular increases:[21]

Year	*Operating Funds ($ million)*	*Modernization Funds ($ million)*
1977	592	324
1978	662	448
1979	726	544
1980	755	545
1981	1,067	927
1982	1,494	855
1983	1,154	1,260
1984	1,203	787
1985	1,494	823
1986	1,421	707
1987	1,458	1,438
1988	1,515	1,691

All this does not mean there have not been maintenance problems in public housing. In fact, many units are deteriorating badly and projects in many cities are now being torn down. But it is hard to blame any lack of effort at the Federal level. In fact, the problems lie elsewhere.

As we shall explore at greater length in chapters 11 and 12, public housing has always had a very ambiguous role. When first undertaken in 1937, public housing was conceived as temporary shelter for the "submerged middle class" of the Depression. It would help this group save its money for homeownership. Projects had *minimum* income standards and were often run as a training ground for middle-class behavior. Only during the 1950s, when large high-rise projects were undertaken, did public housing become "poor people's housing."

As a result, public housing was never built to very high standards. As temporary housing, it was not expected to last long. When it became poor people's housing, it wasn't expected to be built very well, either. Consequently, while most ordinary buildings can be expected to last about 75 years, public housing projects are often worn out after only 20 years. The wear and tear inflicted by low-income tenants and their children does not help.

As originally conceived, public housing tenants were supposed to pay the operation and maintenance costs of their buildings, with the Federal contribution covering only long-term construction and financing costs. In practice, however, most public housing residents no longer even pay their own heating bills, as can be seen from the balance sheet of the 4,300-unit Robert Taylor Homes in Chicago:[22]

1985 Expenditures ($1,000)		*1985 Income ($1,000)*	
Gas	$ 5,052	Rent	$3,768
Electric	897	Other	76
Water	608		
Maintenance	4,350		
Vandalism	1,560		
TOTAL	$12,467	TOTAL	$3,844
1985 operating loss			$8,623

Even this does not state the full magnitude of the shortfall, since collecting rent has become a major problem in public housing. The District of Columbia Housing Authority, for example, now fails to collect $6 million in rents a year—32 percent of its entire rent roll. In 1987, a special Blue Ribbon Commission on Public Housing found that one-quarter of the city's tenants were at least three months behind in their rent.[23] In St. Louis, tenants' accounts receivable was 25 percent of the annual rent roll.

Corruption, theft, and mismanagement within the housing authorities are also staggering. In Washington, Alphonso Jackson, former director of the D.C. Housing Authority, told the 1987 Blue Ribbon Commission that $7,000 worth of stoves, refrigerators, and maintenance materials disappeared from the authority's warehouses every *week*. Even the security cameras guarding the warehouses had been stolen.[24]

Faced with all these overwhelming difficulties, many public housing authorities have begun to tear down their most unmanageable projects. In 1987, Dallas demolished 2,600 units in the West Dallas complex—almost one-third of the city's public housing units. Newark, Kansas City, Houston, Pittsburgh, Jacksonville, and Bridgeport, Connecticut, have done the same. Altogether, 12,856 of the nation's 1.3 million public housing units—one out of a hundred—were razed or scheduled for demolition from 1980 to 1987.[25]

The trend actually began in 1972 when St. Louis decided to dynamite the 3,000-unit Pruitt-Igoe complex, which had won a national design award when it opened only 15 years earlier. In fact, almost from the moment the construction of new high-rises began in the 1950s, these projects were being criticized in some quarters as "institutionalized ghettoes." The outcry finally climaxed in 1968 when Congress outlawed the construction of housing projects higher than six stories, except in a few large cities.

Since then, the nation's 3,100 public housing authorities have been concentrating on low-rise, "scatter-site" projects designed to disperse the poor among the middle class. Yet this scatter-site strategy has aroused its own opposition from neighborhoods that do not want public housing. A great deal of the slowdown in construction over the last 15 years has been due to these siting difficulties.

Thus, once again, budget cuts have not been the source of the dilemma of public housing. Despite *increasing* spending efforts at the Federal level, the program has continued to suffer from internal difficulties. While public housing has worked in providing housing for the elderly, it has not proven capable of handling the low-income families—particularly single-parent welfare families—that have become its principal inhabitants.

Since the Nixon administration, there has been a broad sea-change in the philosophy of public housing, away from large construction projects and toward giving the poor vouchers and certificates that would allow them to find their own accommodations in the private market. The Nixon and Carter administrations concentrated on section-8 certificates, which now pay the landlord the difference between 30 percent of the tenant's income and the market rent in a housing unit approved by the government. The Reagan administration, on the other hand, has switched to housing vouchers, which give a monthly rent supplement to tenants and allow them to spend it wherever they want.

Vouchers are easier to administer than certificates and cost less than half of what it takes to build and maintain a unit of public housing. In addition, vouchers can be easily targeted for the poorest of the poor, while public housing has often been occupied by the "aristocrats of the poor"—the highest reaches of the low-income population. One of the most interesting effects of section 8 of the Housing and Community Development Act of 1974 has been the remarkable improvement in delivering housing aid to people with the lowest incomes, while moving subsidies away from tenants with higher incomes.[26]

FIGURE 1–4
Rental Assistance by Household Income
(As Percent of Rental Households)

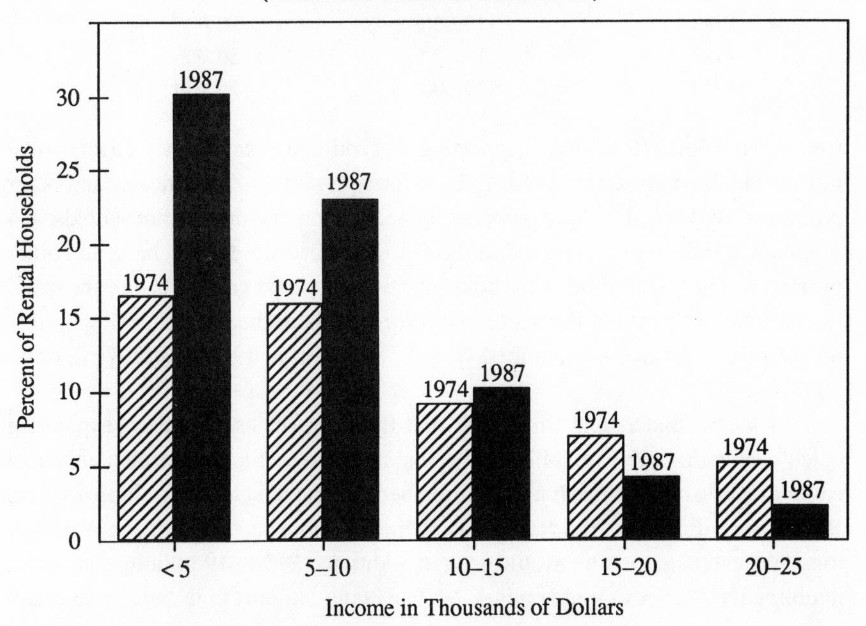

SOURCE: Joint Center tabulation of 1974 Annual Housing Survey and 1987 Current Population Survey data

Hence, the alleged budget cuts of the Reagan years have actually been nothing more than a changeover in the methods of reaching the poor. Government ownership of housing and long-term certificates (which, as we shall see, have often been used by local governments for political purposes) have gradually been replaced by a system of highly flexible, tenant-oriented vouchers. (See table on next page.)[27]

The rate at which new vouchers are issued has not yet reached the rate at which certificates were issued in 1979. Yet the certificates issued in 1979 will still be operating in 1994. The housing assistance program has been constantly expanding over the last decade, it has just been expanding at a slightly lower rate.

By any measure, then, housing assistance increased under the Reagan adminis-

Year	*New Certificates Issued*	*New Vouchers Issued*
1979	125,000	—
1980	76,000	—
1981	110,000	—
1982	105,000	—
1983	53,000	—
1984	55,000	14,000
1985	36,000	38,000
1986	10,000	50,000
1987	10,000	50,000
1988	10,000	50,000

tration. In 1980, HUD was supporting 3.1 million low-income tenants—1.2 million in public housing and 1.9 million through section-8 certificates and other programs. By 1988, HUD was supporting 4.2 million low-income households, 1.4 million in public housing and 2.8 million through certificates, vouchers, and other programs. The 4.2 million households represent 11.8 percent of the entire rental market and 28 percent of the nation's poverty-level households.[28] HUD's spending on housing assistance has climbed from $5.6 billion in 1980 to $13.8 billion in 1988.

Critics who understand this argue that the program has not been expanding quickly enough. "We would like to see vouchers and certificates made a universal entitlement that would reach all 7 million people who are currently eligible," said Barry Zigas, director of the National Low Income Housing Coalition, in Washington. "We estimate that this would cost an additional $15 to 19 billion, essentially doubling HUD's housing-aid budget."[29] The home-building industries, which also have a vested interest in expanding the voucher program, have often complained that it remains only an experiment. Yet it is just such open-ended entitlement programs—the costs of which can never be predicted but always seem to outrun original estimates—that both Congress and the President have been trying to avoid in recent years.

Thus, there has been no withdrawal from the business of housing assistance under the Reagan and Bush administrations. In *The Report of the President's Commission on Housing* (1982), the Reagan administration made an early determination that housing *supplies* were essentially sufficient. There was no great need for the government to go on building public housing—which is by far the most expensive way to serve the poor. Instead, there would be a policy change toward getting more *income* in the hands of housing consumers.[30] This policy has been pursued through the voucher program. Where both administrations may have failed is in underestimating the difficulties that *local* government housing policies would place in the way of the voucher program.

Every housing expert agrees that vouchers can work only as long as housing supplies can respond to increased demand. In most cities, they have been successful. In Chicago, for example, apartment listings frequently carry the notice, "section-8 recipients welcome." But in cities with tight housing markets—Boston, New York, and San Francisco—vouchers have not fared well at all. In Boston, 35 percent of vouchers are being returned because tenants cannot find anywhere to spend them. In New York the figure is 60 percent. Not incidentally, these cities also have notably high rates of homelessness.

Expansion of the voucher program remains an area where increased Federal spending could bring quick results to ease homelessness. Yet the question remains, why has the voucher program worked in some cities but not others? *Something* is obviously going on that has frustrated the Federal effort.

Chapter 2

The Paradox of Homelessness (II)

Beyond the incomes theory and the government-cutback theory, we also have the affordable-housing and personal-pathologies theory. Let us examine each of these in turn.

The Affordable-Housing Theory

If a slackened effort in Federal housing assistance cannot be blamed for the homeless problem, it may still be possible to argue that the overall supply of housing is at fault.

Perhaps the foremost exponent of this school has been Robert Hayes, the former Wall Street attorney who brought the landmark lawsuit against New York City on behalf of the homeless (*Callahan vs. Carey,* 1979) and who headed the Coalition for the Homeless until 1989.

"There is a three-word solution to the homeless problem," said Hayes: " 'Housing, housing, and housing.' " Individual homeless people may have personal pathologies, said Hayes. They may be unemployed, mentally disturbed, or impoverished. But homelessness comes from lack of housing.

"The mentally ill cannot begin to cope with their disease until they have a place to live," he argued. "The unemployed person cannot begin to look for work until he or she has a place to change their clothes and sleep at night. Housing is the one indispensable starting point in solving homelessness." (Hayes recently modified this viewpoint, however, admitting that he and other homeless advocates had shied away from discussing the drug problem because they feared losing public sympathy. "The bottom line is that we have to tell the truth," he said.)[1]

One difficulty with this argument is that, on a nationwide scale at least, there has been plenty of housing available. Writing in 1984, Hopper and Hamberg worried that:

> Annual vacancy rates hovered nationally between 5.0 and 5.4 percent from 1979 to 1982, far below the rates typical during recessions. By the end of 1983 rental vacancy rates were 3.7 percent in the Northeast and 4.4 percent in the West. In specific markets vacancies were even scarcer, with rates averaging between 1 and 2 percent in such cities as New York, San Francisco, and Boston.[2]

Yet national vacancy rates of 5.0 to 5.4 percent were not unusually low, since economists consider a 6 percent vacancy rate to be normal. Moreover, vacancies have since climbed steadily, reaching a national level of 7.8 percent in 1988, the highest levels since World War II. Vacancies soared above 10 percent in cities like Houston, Phoenix, and New Orleans by the mid-1980s. Even as the homeless problem was emerging as a national issue, the construction and housing finance industries were worried about a "housing glut."

In fact, all along, there has been a steady drumbeat of expert opinion that there is really no "housing crisis" in America. "[A]s the nation moved deeper into the second half of the 1980s, America's housing barometers began to indicate market conditions thought to be relics of the past," wrote George Sternlieb—generally considered one of the country's leading housing experts—and James Hughes, both of the Center for Urban Policy Research at Rutgers:

> National rental vacancy rates began to approach double-digit levels, mortgage rates trended into single-digit ranges, and homeownership affordability thresholds again began to include the majority of American families.[3]

The percentage of income required from married couples age 25 to 29 to buy their first home rose sharply from 1975 to 1982, but has since descended again:[4]

FIGURE 2–1
Percent of Income Required to Buy First Home

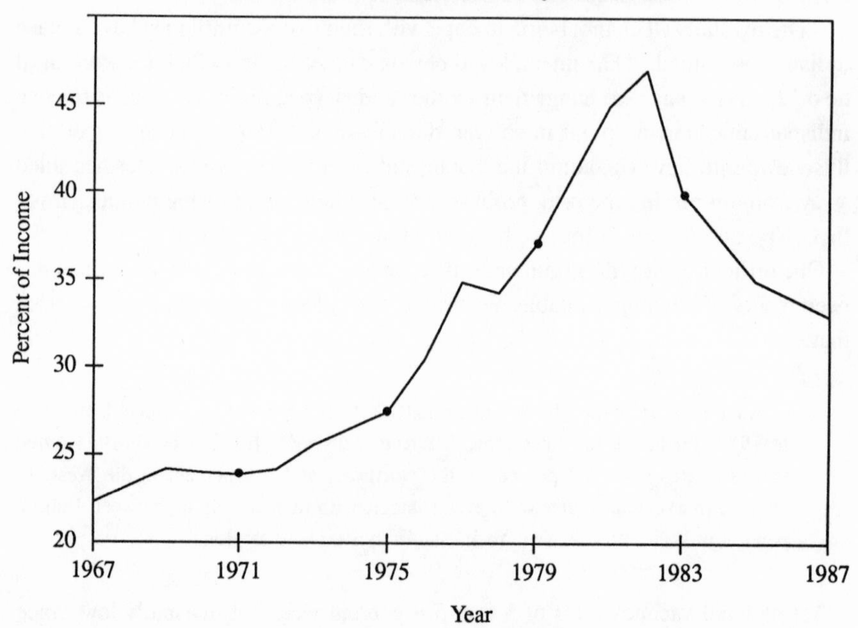

In order to try to sort out these conflicting views, let us begin by looking at the most obvious statistics—the number of new housing units begun each year since 1960:[5]

FIGURE 2–2
Housing Starts 1960–1989

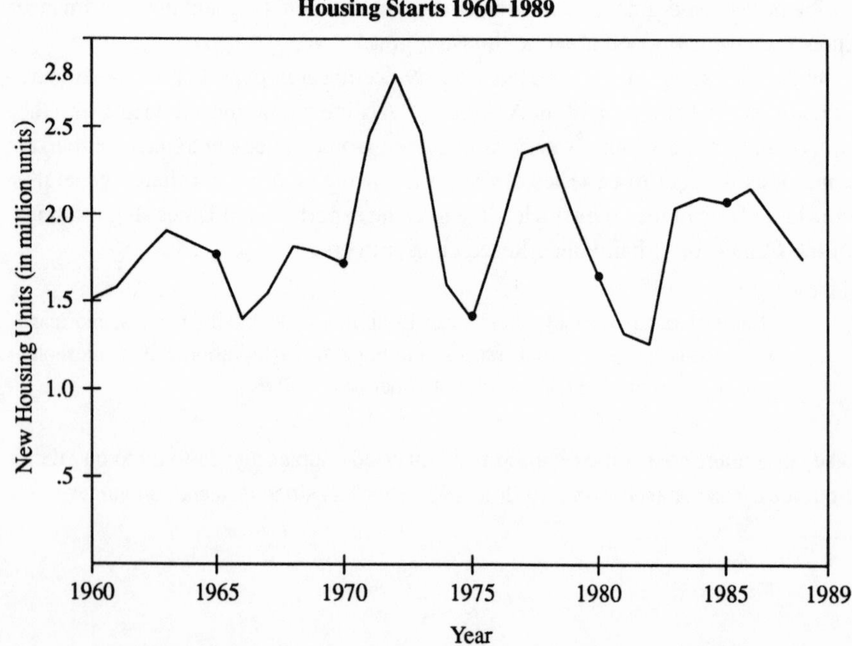

Housing starts have gone through a fairly cyclical pattern. They boomed just before the Arab Oil Embargo, then fell back abruptly to 1964 levels. There was a recovery in the late 1970s, then another trough in the early 1980s. The mid-1980s recovery was fairly strong, but has since slackened off a bit.

Altogether, though, housing starts have never quite returned to the heights they attained in 1972 and 1973. The industry is obviously cyclical, but the peaks have been diminishing. Whether this is because of a slackening demand for housing or because of increasing impediments to supply is something that is not yet entirely clear.

Once again, what these national figures tend to mask is an astonishing range of conditions in different parts of the country. Here, for example, are the figures for average annual housing starts per capita in seven major cities, compared with their most recent rental vacancy figures:[6]

City	*Multi-Family Housing Starts Per 1,000 1981–1986*	*Vacancy Rates (1984)*
San Diego	7.8	6.2
Phoenix	5.8	11.2
Seattle	2.9	5.5
Atlanta	2.4	9.0
Boston	1.7	2.8
Newark	1.4	2.3
Washington	1.3	2.0
San Francisco	1.3	1.6

Looking at these figures, one might conclude that builders like to put up houses where there is already enough housing and don't like to build where it is needed. In one way, the numbers make sense. Phoenix, Atlanta, and San Diego have high vacancies precisely because they have been adding new construction. Yet why doesn't some intelligent person go and build apartments in San Francisco and Boston where they would be more in demand?

Even homeless advocates recognize this paradox. "What good are empty apartments in Houston and Dallas to people who are living in New York?" complain Hopper and Hamberg. John I. Gilderbloom and Richard P. Appelbaum, authors of *Rethinking Rental Housing*, argue that overall demand—the desire of people to live in a few major cities on the East and West Coasts—has been responsible for driving up housing prices.[7] Yet in theory, at least, it is just as easy to pour concrete and nail boards together in San Francisco as it is in Houston. Why is housing so plentiful in some cities and so scarce in others?

Faced with the dilemma of a general glut of housing in the face of homelessness, many people have argued instead that it is not just housing, but "affordable housing," that is the problem. In a way, the argument begs the question. Housing is housing and the only thing that makes it affordable is if there is plenty of it. Where there is ample housing, as in Phoenix, for example, it is likely to be relatively cheap, even when it is brand-new. Where housing is scarce, on the other hand, as in New York, people will pay remarkably high prices for accommodations that are often remarkably dilapidated.

Thus, to argue that it is not housing but only "affordable housing" that is the core of the dilemma is a bit like arguing that the poor can't get major loans from banks because there is a shortage of "affordable money." Let us follow the argument a bit further, though, and see what it is about.

In the 1988 report, "The State of the Nation's Housing," William C. Apgar and H. James Brown, of the Joint Center for Housing Studies of Harvard University argued that a crisis in affordable housing was turning America into a "nation of housing haves and have-nots."

> Homeownership costs have eased somewhat since the early 1980s but remain high by historical standards. Young households find purchasing a first home especially difficult, as housing costs remain high relative to income. Unable to secure a home of their own, these persons remain renters and bid up the price of rental housing.
>
> Despite five years of strong construction activity and rising vacancies, the supply of low-cost rental housing continues to shrink as units are lost to abandonment or are upgraded for higher-income occupants. Having lagged inflation in the 1970s, real rents (measured in constant 1986 dollars) have moved up sharply since 1981 and now stand at their highest level in over two decades. Rising rents have led to an increasing share of households paying 30, 40, or even 50 percent of their incomes for rents, if they can secure housing at all.[8]

The Harvard authors offer the following charts to buttress their conclusions:[9]

FIGURE 2–3
Rental Costs

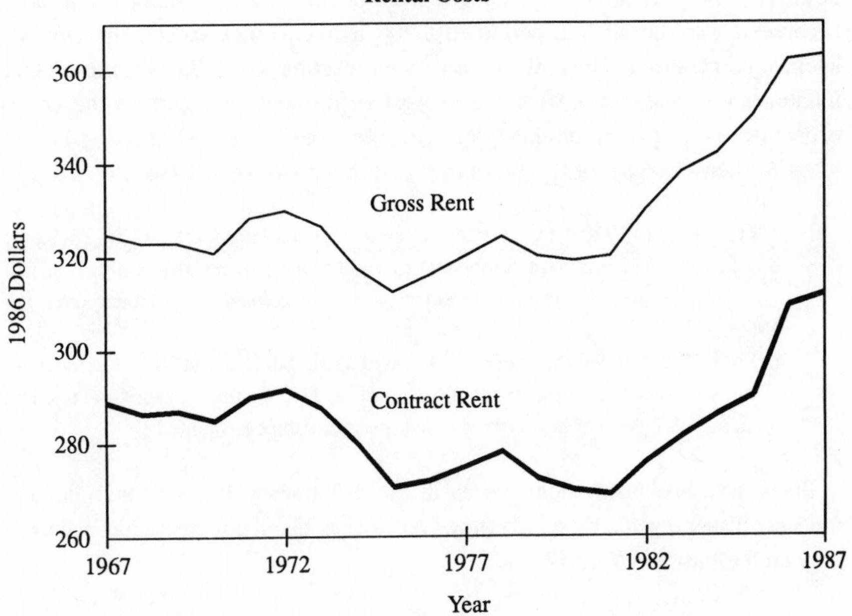

FIGURE 2–4
Rental Cost Burden

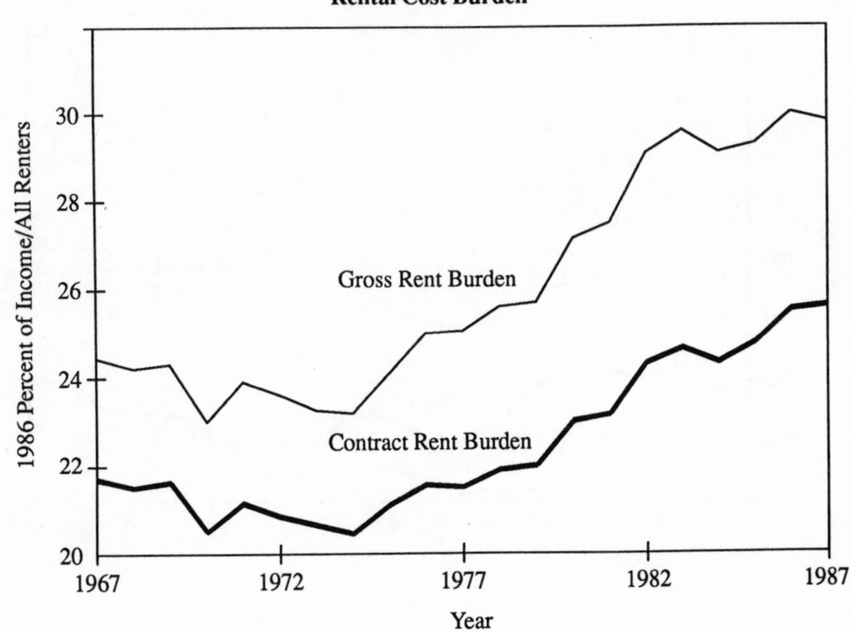

Rents have clearly risen sharply since 1981. The period from 1967 to 1980, however, was marked by stability and even decline. This is important to note because it was during this period that 200 municipalities around the country adopted rent controls, allegedly to curb "skyrocketing rents." In fact, during that inflationary period, rents were the slowest rising consumer item in the entire economy. (Home prices, on the other hand, were one of the fastest rising.)

As Anthony Downs, of the Brookings Institution, wrote in 1984:

> From 1960 to 1970 the Consumer Price Index for all items increased 31.1 percent, but the CPI residential rent component rose only 20.1 percent, or two-thirds as fast . . . [Thus,] the real level of residential rents *declined* 8.4 percent over the 1960s. . . .
>
> From 1970 to 1980 the overall CPI soared 112.2 percent, but its rent component went up 74.0 percent—again about two-thirds as fast. By this measure real resident rents fell *18.2* percent in this eleven-year period. [Emphasis added.][10]

Rents have taken a definite upturn in the deflationary 1980s. When national rents are disaggregated by region, however, we see that the increase has occurred only on the East and West Coasts.[11]

FIGURE 2–5
Regional Gross Rentals

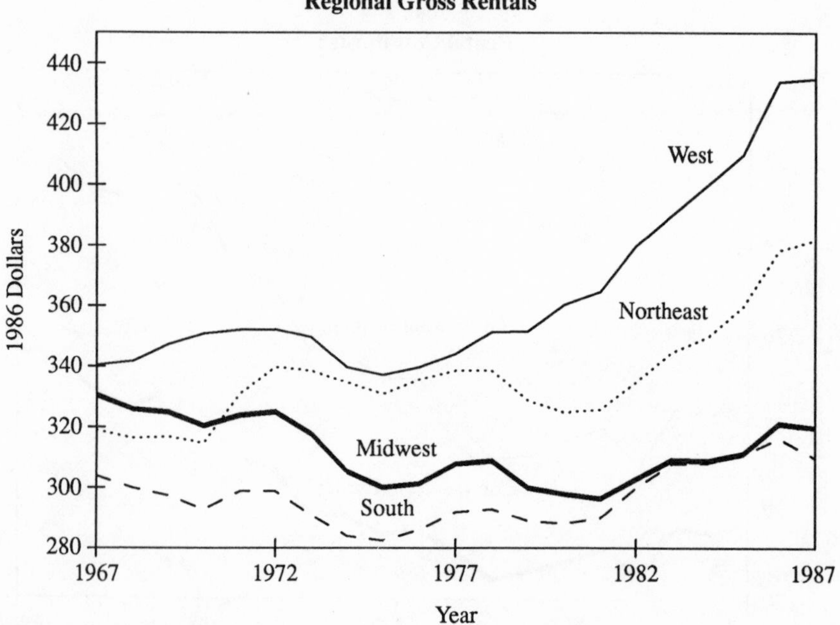

Remarkably, rental costs in the Midwest and South are still barely above their 1967 levels. Only in the Northeast and the Far West have rents pushed to new heights. Since the homeless problem is known to be heavily concentrated in these two regions, it appears we may be finally on the trail of something that is important to homelessness.

Along with the figures for rising rents, Apgar and Brown point out that tenants have been becoming poorer.[12]

FIGURE 2–6
Household Income of Owners and Renters (In 1986 dollars)

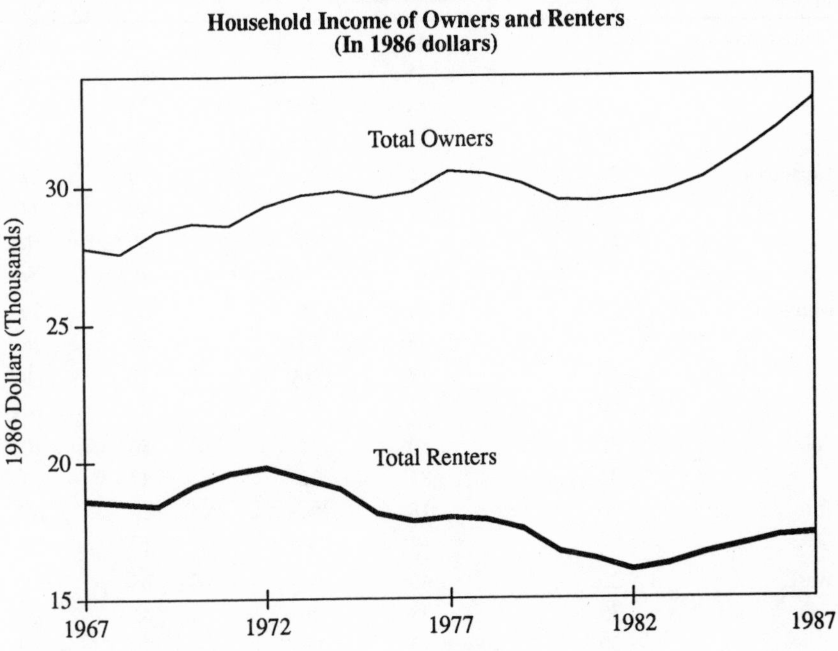

The decline, however, does not necessarily mean that individual tenants have lost income. Instead, the numbers show a process known as "creaming," wherein the wealthiest tenants are constantly moving up to homeownership, leaving the remaining pool of tenants poorer and poorer. Creaming has been a steady pattern over the decades. In fact, the recent *increase* in tenant income may reflect the shrinking rate of homeownership, which has declined from 66 percent in 1980 to 64 percent in 1988.

Nevertheless, it is clear that tenants—particularly those at the lower end of the scale—have come under increasing rental pressures in the last decade. The rental cost burden has risen steadily since 1974 and took its biggest jumps during the 1981–82 recession. Moreover, as Gilderbloom and Appelbaum illustrate, this trend has fallen most heavily on the poor, who now pay a much larger fraction of their income in rent than in 1970:[13]

PERCENTAGE OF HOUSEHOLDS THAT PAY EXCESSIVE RENTS, 1983 AND 1970

Region	*Excessiveness of Rent*	1983 *Total*	1970 *Total*	1983 *Central City*	1970 *Central City*
United States	25*	55	36	60	40
	35*	35	23	40	26
	50	22	NA	25	NA
	60	16	NA	19	NA
Northeast	25	56	36	59	37
	35	37	23	40	24
	50	23	NA	26	NA
	60	17	NA	19	NA
Midwest	25	54	36	60	39
	35	35	23	41	26
	50	22	NA	27	NA
	60	17	NA	21	NA
South	25	50	35	56	40
	35	31	22	37	25
	50	18	NA	22	NA
	60	14	NA	17	NA
West	25	60	41	65	45
	35	38	26	41	29
	50	23	NA	26	NA
	60	17	NA	20	NA

* 25 corresponds to percentage of households that pay 25 percent or more of their income into rent; 35 corresponds to percentage paying 35 percent or more of their income into rent; etc.
Source: U.S. Department of Housing and Urban Development (1983a: tables A-2, D-2, A-10, B-2, E-2, F-10, C-2, A-8, F-4, F-5, F-8).

Still, we do not know why rents suddenly started rising after a two-decade period of stability and even decline. And why has the pattern been so uneven? Here is a comparison of rent rises since 1967 in fourteen major cities.[14] The figures do not compare rent levels, but only the *increase* over the last 20 years. Once again, we are struck with the regional variations.

GROSS RENT INCREASES, 1967–1987 (1967 = 100)

City	*1987 figure*	*City*	*1987 figure*
San Francisco	378.6	Detroit	273.1
Los Angeles	362.5	Baltimore	271.8
Boston	341.3	Pittsburgh	263.9
Philadelphia	322.9	Chicago	261.4
New York	318.8	St. Louis	247.3
Washington	317.7	Cleveland	235.7
(U.S.A.)	293.1	Houston	211.2
Dallas	275.6		

The largest increases have been concentrated in a few major cities on the East and West Coasts, while rents have remained much more level in the demographically similar Midwestern cities like Chicago, Dallas, and Houston.

Thus, while housing is definitely becoming unaffordable in some areas of the country, it remains relatively affordable in others. Why is this so? Although the phenomenon may be the key to understanding homelessness, we have not yet pinpointed exactly what has created this pattern.

Personal Pathologies

One final theory of homelessness is that some people suffer such severe personal disabilities that they are unable to find housing in any market. These disabilities include mental illness or drug and alcohol dependencies.

In an extensive study of the homeless population, the Urban Institute has suggested that homelessness can be broken into three roughly equal categories. One-third are released mental patients, one-third are substance abusers (drugs and alcohol), and one-third are "economically homeless" (homeless because of economic conditions).[15]

The population of mental patients is most easily traced. In the 1950s, there were 500,000 patients in state mental hospitals. Today there are only 150,000. Some of these releasees have found shelter in half-way houses and other institutions, but others have obviously fallen through the cracks.

In a scathing history of deinstitutionalization, Dr. E. Fuller Torrey, former assistant to the director of the National Institute of Mental Health, has reviewed the history of the whole tragic episode.[16] Torrey lays the blame at the feet of the psychiatric profession itself.

The old state mental hospitals, he notes, came under criticism as "snake pits" during the 1940s, after they were staffed by conscientious objectors during World War II. During the 1950s, the psychiatric profession, now organized around the new National Institute of Mental Health, proposed transferring mental patients to a series of new "community mental health centers" to be established around the country. The program received Congressional funding in the 1960s when it was adopted by President John Kennedy (whose sister had suffered a schizophrenic breakdown, although the Kennedy family kept it well hidden).

By the late 1960s, the transfer had begun. State mental hospitals, denied Federal Medicare and Medicaid funding for their inmates, finally began to disgorge their patients. Yet the community mental health centers were not prepared to receive them. Doctors running these centers had decided to turn them into all-purpose psychiatric clinics for the "worried well." Tired of dealing with the severely mentally ill, they did not make any serious effort to recruit the former hospital patients. Court decisions allowing disturbed people to reject confinement only made things worse.

In the end, only a few former inmates from the state hospitals ended up in community mental health centers. "Halfway houses" that were supposed to pick up the slack never materialized on any appreciable scale. As a result, large numbers of former mental patients ended up in the streets.

Critics who argue that homelessness is *not* a housing problem often cite the case of Joyce Brown, a.k.a. "Billie Boggs," a "bag lady" and diagnosed schizophrenic who lived on a Manhattan street corner for more than a year until she was forcibly confined to Bellevue Hospital in 1987. Brown was taken in by the American Civil Liberties Union, spoke at Harvard, and became a minor talk-show celebrity. Yet within a year she had again deteriorated, lost her city-paid motel room, and ended up on the same street corner, shouting obscenities at passers-by.

"The mentally ill who live in utter degradation on our streets are not there by choice," argued columnist Charles Krauthammer, who holds a degree in psychiatry. "They are there because we have almost totally dismantled the mental health system that used to care for them and we have so expanded the limits of their pseudo-liberty that society is prevented at every turn from intervening to help."[17] Added *New York Post* columnist Eric Breindel, "Housing would not have saved Billie Boggs."

While arguments over the homeless are often pictured as a traditional liberal-conservative debate—liberals anxious to be of help, conservatives worried about spending money—an equally important division in the debate is between those who believe homelessness is a *housing* problem and those who believe it is one of *personal pathologies.*

Writing in *Scientific American,* in 1984, Ellen Bassuck, associate professor of psychiatry at Harvard Medical School and member of the Committee on Health Care for Homeless People, made a strong case for mental illness as the root of homelessness:

> [M]y own experience as a psychiatrist working with homeless people in Boston leads me to believe [that] an increasing number—I would say a large majority—of the homeless suffer from mental illness, ranging from schizophrenia to severe personality disorders. . . . Shelters have been saddled with the impossible task of replacing not only the almshouses of the past but also the large state mental institutions[18]

Other observers have downplayed the clinical pathologies of the homeless and concentrated more on their social isolation.

"The homeless antidote prescribed by some advocates—'housing, housing, and housing'—is mistaken," declared David Whitman, in a cover story for *U.S. News and World Report.*

> What is now clear is that if every homeless person were put in an affordable low-income apartment tomorrow, many would be back on the street several weeks later. The reason, as study after study has shown, is that the homeless are different from other poor people in one crucial respect: They are profoundly alone.[19]

In a 1986 study of people receiving free meals in Chicago homeless shelters, Professor Michael R. Sosin, of the School of Social Service Administration at the University of Chicago, reached a similar conclusion.

"[R]ising rents do not explain all aspects of homelessness," wrote Sosin. Rather, "[t]he homeless generally have problems in their interaction with other social institutions, such as the family or the welfare system," plus "characteristics . . . that might make it difficult for them to live with others in a dwelling or to maintain relations with landlords."[20]

Sosin found that the homeless had been paying, on average, only $168 a month in rent at their last dwelling. "Most sample members report some reasonable work experience, but that the cycle has been downward for a long period. The best job an individual had obtained paid about $234 per month in 1977 (standard dollars) on average, or $169 at the median." Available rents, then, would absorb nearly all their income.

But other people in similar circumstances were still able to find shelter with family or friends. What differentiates the homeless, said Sosin, is a series of personal qualities:

> Mental hospital experience within the entire sample appears to be greater than one might expect . . . The extent of family formation and the nature of family composition also show differences from the norm. Only 44.8 percent . . . had married, as opposed to 67 percent of adult males and 74 percent of adult females in Chicago. . . . Only 9 percent of individuals are currently married, compared with the figure for Chicago of over 50 percent of adults. . . . If anything, one-parent families are slightly

> underrepresented in this sample: they make up only 17.8 percent of the sample, but represent about 27 percent of all Chicago households.[21]

Although often eligible for welfare benefits, homeless people were far less likely to be receiving them.

Homelessness, Sosin concluded, "may be a function of the lack of the economic supports families provide, such as the ability to share costs of food or to borrow money, when crises occur."

> [I]ndividuals . . . might not become homeless if jobs for the least skilled were more plentiful or welfare benefits were high and stable. Nevertheless, the results of this study strongly suggest that some group members have a special lack of cash or other tangible supports that greatly complicates finding and then maintaining a home.[22]

In *Without Shelter: Homelessness in the 1980s,* (1989), Peter Rossi reached almost identical conclusions. Looking for a similar group of indigents who were not homeless, Rossi selected the Chicago recipients of "general assistance" (sometimes called "home relief"), a form of welfare available in most states to any adult in difficult circumstances. (General assistance is not supported by the Federal government and constitutes only about one percent of all welfare payments.)

Rossi found that in most respects, general assistance recipients were very similar to the homeless. They were predominantly male (68 percent), black (76 percent), and unmarried (92 percent). Income levels were also almost identical. Although both groups were generally unemployed, the homeless had been without jobs longer (four years as opposed to only one year).

What differentiated the homeless was, once again, their personal qualities:

> Very few (1 percent) of the GA clients had ever been hospitalized for mental illness, compared to 23 percent of the homeless. Fewer were afflicted by alcoholism: 2 percent of the GA recipients mentioned alcohol problems as a reason for being unable to work, compared to 20 percent of the homeless. The GA recipients also appeared to have less contact with the criminal justice system. . . .[23]

The major difference seemed to be, not that general assistance recipients were able to care better for themselves, but that *they were able to rely more on relatives and friends* for housing and income.

> Most (67 percent) of the GA recipients were living in households (as opposed to living by themselves), *predominantly in their parents' households.* Among the one in three who lived by themselves, more than half reported that they received financial support from families, friends, and relatives; the remainder managed to survive by adding earnings from part-time, intermittent employment to their GA benefits. [Emphasis added.][24]

One remarkable trend Rossi noted is the increasing tendency for young black males to remain in their parental homes long after they have reached maturity. Whereas in 1970, 39 percent of black and white males between the ages of 20 and 29 lived with their parents, today 54 percent of these black males live with their parents as opposed to 41 percent of whites.[25] Rossi speculates that the increasing failure to form families among blacks has led to an increase in both male and female homelessness.

The profile developed by Rossi appears quite accurate from anecdotal experience. The homeless, he said, are people who have exhausted the patience and resources of family and friends, either through their long dependency or antisocial behavior. Family break-up and high levels of drug use and alcoholism among low-income blacks have also obviously played a part.

Yet at the same time, it is difficult to believe that *all* the upsurge of homelessness in the last decade can be attributed to a rise in pathological behavior. Just what the relation is to other factors remains an unanswered question.

Homelessness as a Non-Problem

There is one more theory about homelessness, usually emanating from the conservative end of the spectrum, that is probably worth mentioning. This is that the homeless problem really does not exist at all or has been highly exaggerated. Instead, it is the invention of public figures like Mitch Synder, of Washington's Community for Creative Non-Violence, and Robert Hayes, former director of New York's Coalition for the Homeless—aided and abetted by a gullible media. Or, alternately, it is a perverse result of the public services that have been set up to help the homeless.

Writing in *Reason* magazine in 1987, Martin Morse Wooster argued, "Ten years ago there were homeless in America. Twenty years ago there were homeless. How is it that in the 1980s there is a *homeless crisis?* A close look at what statistics there are reveals that nobody really knows how much—or even whether—the number of homeless is increasing." (Emphasis in original.) Wooster goes on to argue that the homeless crisis is really "an adman's dream . . . the issue by which the champions of the welfare state hope to regain lost ground."[26]

A second argument is that the very attractions of services offered in cities like New York, Washington, Boston, and San Francisco, have drawn people out of marginal living arrangements and into the shelter system. Surveying New York's homeless shelters, Thomas Main, writing in *The Public Interest,* noted that 33 percent of the residents were "able-bodied young males" who had been living with a friend or relative—or even in their own apartment—before coming to the shelters. He argued that New York City's "right to shelter" policy, the result of

Robert Hayes' 1979 court suit, is pulling marginal people into the system. "The important question," said Main, "is, why are these higher-functioning young men in the shelter system at all?"[27]

There is no question that homelessness has been around for much longer than most people realize. Prior to 1980, every city had its "Skid Row" (originally named after a street in Seattle's lumber district) where middle-aged men, most of them alcoholics, congregated to live in cheap housing and do day labor. Studies of The Bowery district of New York in 1949 found 14,000 men living in flophouses and other fragile accommodations in 1949, although the population had dropped to 8,000 in 1964.[28]

Anna Kondratas, formerly of the Heritage Foundation and now an assistant secretary of HUD, offers the following passage from a 1911 publication, *One Thousand Homeless Men,* to illustrate the timelessness of the problem:

> [T]hough the beggar and tramp are not peculiar in our own time and nation, it is nonetheless true that there has been a remarkable increase in the number of these men in the United States during the past two decades. Twenty years ago, a few cheap lodging houses built for the accommodation of the homeless working men might have been found in some half dozen of our larger cities. Today, there are a number of such lodging houses in every large city, in every county. They house not only hundreds and thousands of homeless working men, but also a large number of tramps and beggars in America. Various methods for solving the problems due to this increase have been suggested, none of which have been generally adopted, or have proved strikingly successful.[29]

Yet as Peter Rossi points out, the drunks and stumblebums of the old Skid Rows were generally considered "homeless," not because they did not have homes but because they did not have *families.* Most had some kind of accommodations, no matter how tenuous. As late as the 1960s, most downtowns had hotels that offered partitioned cubicles containing no more than a bed for as little as $2 a night.

> Whatever the faults of the cubicle hotels . . . they at least provided more acceptable accommodations than the dormitory arrangements characteristic of today's shelters and were certainly preferable to sleeping in the streets. What is striking is that homelessness today is a more severe condition of housing deprivation than in decades past.[30]

Ultimately, the arguments that the increase in homelessness is illusory defy both common sense and everyday experience. Many things can be said about homeless shelters around the country, but one thing that cannot be said is that they are very appealing, even to a person who has few other alternatives. In many cities, homeless shelters have become centers of crime and violence and are feared by other homeless people almost as much as the rain and cold.

Likewise, few people exposed to any large city on the East or West Coast would argue that the homeless situation has not become dramatically worse in recent years. Bus terminals and railroad stations in New York City were not overrun with homeless people ten years ago. The "beach people" of Santa Monica (often called the "homeless capital of the West Coast") were not there at the beginning of the decade. There is plenty of room for argument about why things are getting worse, but almost no one doubts that major cities around the country are facing an increasingly serious problem. Anecdotal evidence can often be misleading, but anyone who has walked the streets of New York or San Francisco over the last ten years knows that things have gotten much worse. The question is, why?

When many plausible explanations are offered for a single phenomenon, scientists often try to sort them out using a mathematical tool called "multiple regression analysis."

The technique is basically very simple. We take a single phenomenon like homelessness and measure how often it occurs in combination with any of the possible explanations—unemployment, poverty, or lack of public housing. The more often a possible explanation coincides with the target phenomenon, the more likely it is that the two are somehow related. This establishes what is called a "correlation."

A frequent correlation suggests that the two are somehow related. A weak or non-existent correlation suggests they are unrelated. At the same time, regression analysis does *not* prove cause and effect. It only measures coincidence. If two factors occur together frequently, we can infer that there is some kind of causal relation between the two. But we cannot say which is causing the other. We must first frame an hypothesis and then offer some kind of verifiable experiment to prove causality.

In 1986, I set out to examine homelessness by using regression analysis. I gathered data on the comparative size of the homeless populations in 50 cities. Then I ran a regression analysis, looking for correlations between homelessness and a dozen possible explanatory factors: local unemployment rates, poverty rates, the availability of public housing, the size of the city, its growth rate over the last 15 years, the annual mean temperature, the annual rainfall, the size of its minority population, the price of homes in the metropolitan area, the rental vacancy rate, and the presence or absence of rent control.

The results offer a starting point in helping us understand the problem of homelessness.

Chapter 3

What Causes Homelessness?

In comparing homelessness from city to city in order to try to identify causes, the first problem is to come up with reliable numbers. This is not easy. The debate over the figures has raged for almost a decade.

When homelessness first surfaced in the early 1980s, much of the public dialogue was dominated by Mitch Snyder, the Washington, D.C., activist. Snyder is a rather peculiar, charismatic figure. A former advertising executive who once spent time in a Connecticut jail for car theft, Snyder left his wife and children in the early 1970s to found the Community for Creative Non-Violence (CCNV), which was dedicated toward ending the Vietnam War.

When the war ended, Snyder cast around for other causes and discovered the homeless. He set up a tent city in Lafayette Park, went on hunger strikes, and recently led violent efforts to break into locked subway stations so the homeless could sleep in them at night.

Testifying before Congress in 1980, Snyder declared flatly that there were 2.2 million homeless in the United States—one out of every 100 people. (Once he declared there were 250,000 homeless in Chicago, which would mean one out of every eight city residents.) When Congressmen asked for the source of his estimates, Snyder criticized their "gnawing curiosity for a number," criticizing them as "Americans with little Western minds that have to quantify everything in sight." Nevertheless, CCNV went on quantifying things itself, pushing the figure up to 2 to 3 million in its book, *Homelessness in America,* published two years later.[1]

Snyder is obviously picking numbers out of the air, yet the figure of "2 to 3 million homeless" has become a kind of shibboleth in newspaper stories. It is repeated over and over and rarely challenged. Interestingly enough, despite the growth in homelessness, CCNV has not raised the figure since 1982, but still talks about "an estimated 2 to 3 million homeless Americans." The organization does predict that the homeless population will reach 18 million by the year 2005.[2]

Part of the problem obviously lies in definition. When most people think of the homeless, they think of someone living on the street or in a homeless shelter. Homeless advocates have often found this definition far too confining. They like to include the "hidden homeless," people who are sleeping on couches, staying with relatives, or even generally dissatisfied with their circumstances.

"I consider everyone in prison or in an institution to be homeless because if they were released tomorrow they wouldn't have anyplace to live," said Sister Mary, director of the Amos House shelter in Providence, R.I., founded in 1973. Larry Rice, director of the New Life Evangelical Center's shelter in St. Louis, told me that the homeless should include "all those women who are forced to live with a man when they don't want to and sell their bodies to him because they don't have anyplace else to live." These circumstances, regrettable though they may be, probably do not constitute the average person's definition of homelessness.[3]

Perhaps the most rigorous attempt to define the problem has been made by Peter Rossi, professor of sociology at the University of Massachusetts. In his 1989 book, *Without Shelter: Homelessness in the 1980s,* Rossi offered the following definition:

> [P]ersons are classified as homeless if they are living outside conventional dwellings, either spending nights in shelters for homeless persons or in locations that are not intended for dwelling—on the street, in abandoned houses, or in public places such as bus stations or hospital waiting rooms.[4]

Using this definition, Rossi and his colleagues at the Social and Demographic Research Institute of the University of Massachusetts spent two nights in 1985 and 1986 conducting a block-by-block survey of downtown Chicago, counting homeless people with the help of policemen and social workers. Arguing that this constituted "the first scientifically defensible estimates of the size and composition of the homeless population in any city," Rossi and his colleagues reported "a final estimate of 2,722 persons literally homeless in Chicago on an average night."[5]

The figure, of course, is far below estimates that would satisfy most homeless advocates. Even leaving aside Snyder's figure of 250,000, most estimates of Chicago's homeless population have ranged from 17,000 to 26,000. On the other hand, Rossi's figures constitute a far more rigorous study than anything ever attempted before.

For the purposes of my study, however, I decided to use the estimates of shelter operators and public officials, which are embodied in the equally controversial 1984 *Report to the Secretary of Housing and Urban Development on Emergency Shelters and Homeless Populations.*[6] In that report, using information from these presumably reliable sources, HUD compiled estimates for homeless populations in 60 cities—20 large cities, 20 medium-sized, and 20 small.

HUD's method was to ask municipal and volunteer organizations providing shelter to make estimates of the homeless population. To these figures, HUD added other estimates from academic studies. It also commissioned a few body-counts of its own, in order to have an independent standard. From all these estimates, HUD compiled two sets of numbers—the range of *all* estimates, which often differed by tens of thousands, and a "most reliable range," within which HUD believed the true figure to lie. The "most-reliable" range usually spread over only a few thousand.

For my study, I used the midpoint of the most-reliable range for 34 of the 40 largest cities (except for three cities, New York, Baltimore, and Cleveland, where I took a figure slightly above the midpoint but below the highest estimate). I eliminated six smaller cities—Baton Rouge, Colorado Springs, Davenport, Dayton, Charlotte, and Scranton—where vacancies figures were difficulty to obtain and where homelessness was close to the median. I then added 16 cities that HUD had not sampled—major metropolitan areas like Dallas, Denver, Atlanta, San Diego, Milwaukee, Newark, New Orleans, and St. Louis, plus two smaller cities, Yonkers and Santa Monica, that practice rent control.[7]

When first published in 1984, the HUD *Report* was excoriated by homeless advocates for "whitewashing" the problem. The basis of their criticism was the *Report*'s estimate that the nation's entire homeless population numbered 350,000. This was, of course, far below the figure of 2 to 3 million that had become the commonly adopted standard.

The main criticism of HUD's method was that it counted the homeless in the downtown areas and then projected this number as the homeless population for the entire Standard Metropolitan Statistical Area (SMSA). Homeless advocate Chester Hartman, testifying before Congress in 1984, argued cogently that the SMSAs often include other sizable cities where more homeless should have been counted. New York's SMSA, for example, includes both Yonkers and Newark, which have their own sizable homeless populations.

In order to correct this problem, I used only the city population itself, instead of the SMSA, as the denominator for the per-capita figure. This created a few minor problems of its own. "City limits" vary widely around the country. Cities like Houston and Phoenix have incorporated huge outlying areas, while cities like St. Louis and Richmond have remained little islands in a sea of independent suburban municipalities. Using only the city populations as the denominator would make homelessness look far more serious in Richmond than in Houston. Of the two methods, however, using city populations seemed to provide a more realistic picture.

What was most important for my purposes was that HUD used a reasonably consistent method from city to city. If HUD had over- or underestimated the problem in one city, it probably did the same for the others. Since my purpose was only to compare relative rates of homelessness, rather than worry about absolute numbers, the HUD *Report* seemed like a legitimate place to start.

When drawn together, the figures for homelessness looked like this:

City	*Homeless Population*	*Total Population*	*Homeless Per 1,000*
Miami	5,590	372,000	15.9
St. Louis	5,000	429,000	11.6
San Francisco	8,250	712,000	11.5
Worcester	1,700	160,000	10.6
Los Angeles	32,600	3,097,000	10.5
Santa Monica	900	88,000	10.2
Newark	3,000	314,000	9.5
Hartford	1,200	136,000	8.8
Washington	4,700	623,000	7.5
Detroit	7,500	1,088,000	6.8
Yonkers	1,300	191,000	6.8
Chicago	19,800	2,992,000	6.6
Seattle	3,200	488,000	6.5
Las Vegas	1,100	183,000	6.0
Boston	3,200	571,000	5.6
Richmond	1,175	219,000	5.3
New York	36,000	7,165,000	5.0
Dallas–Ft. W.	7,000	1,388,000	5.0
Denver	2,500	504,000	4.9
Charleston, W.V.	300	63,000	4.7

City	*Homeless Population*	*Total Population*	*Homeless Per 1,000*
Atlanta	2,000	426,000	4.6
Ft. Wayne	725	165,000	4.3
Portland	1,550	366,000	4.2
Houston	6,400	1,706,000	3.7
San Diego	3,000	960,000	3.1
Salt Lake City	525	165,000	3.1
Little Rock	500	170,000	2.9
New Orleans	1,600	559,000	2.8
Charleston, S.C.	200	69,000	2.8
Albuquerque	1,000	315,000	2.8
Tucson	1,000	365,000	2.7
Burlington	100	37,000	2.7
Baltimore	1,900	763,000	2.4
Cincinnati	875	370,000	2.3
Syracuse	380	164,000	2.3
Tampa	650	275,000	2.3
Pittsburgh	900	403,000	2.2
Philadelphia	3,600	1,646,000	2.2
Birmingham	584	280,000	2.0
Louisville	575	290,000	1.9
Grand Rapids	350	183,000	1.9
Minn.–St. Paul	1,000	624,000	1.6
Milwaukee	1,000	621,000	1.6
Providence	250	156,000	1.6
Cleveland	800	547,000	1.4
Phoenix	1,050	853,000	1.2
Kansas City	400	443,000	0.9
Charlotte	275	331,000	0.8
Lincoln	135	180,000	0.7
Rochester	150	243,000	0.6

The national median is 3.1, a figure achieved in San Diego and Salt Lake City. Spread evenly across the country, this would translate into a national homeless population of 880,000, a not unreasonable figure. The eighteen cities with homeless rates of over 5.0 are generally known to be places with serious homeless problems. The ones at the bottom of the scale, on the other hand, have not been regarded as having serious problems. If the numbers seem small in certain cities, it should be remembered that these are conservative estimates and 1984 figures.

As mentioned earlier, the highest concentrations are in cities in the Far West.

Surprisingly, the figures are generally low in the Northeast, with the exception of several large cities—Boston, Washington, Newark, and New York. On the West Coast, San Francisco, Los Angeles, and Santa Monica have similar rates. When broken out by region, (but without weighting the different cities by population) the figures look as follows:

Northeast	2.5
Upper Midwest	2.9
South	4.3
(without Miami)	3.2
Southwest	3.5
West	8.2

To use regression analysis, we plot a "dependent variable" (in this case, homelessness) against a series of "independent variables" (the possible causes) to see how frequently they coincide. Homelessness is plotted on the vertical axis, while the independent variables are on the horizontal axis. Each city is represented by a single "datapoint," which plots its position in relation to homelessness and the other variable. When large numbers of these datapoints are plotted, they eventually form a kind of cloud. A straight line is then calculated that best represents the general pattern formed by the datapoints. This is called the "trendline."

If there is no correlation between the two variables, the line will be perfectly flat. This means that, as unemployment (for example) rises and falls, homelessness stays exactly the same. If there is some correlation, on the other hand, the line will tilt either left or right. The steeper the slope, the stronger the correlation. This is expressed by the "R-factor," a number between 0 and 1. "R-squared" gives the strength of the correlation. If homelessness and unemployment show an R-factor of .5, then R-squared = .25. This means that 25 percent of the variation in homelessness between cities can be accounted for by the differences in unemployment between cities. In sciences like physics and chemistry, R-factors run as high as .999. In the social sciences, a correlation over .50 would be considered highly respectable.

Correlations are also measured by their "P-factor," which indicates how closely the pattern of datapoints conforms to the trendline. There will always be some trendline that best expresses the pattern, but if the great mass of datapoints are far from the line, the match is not considered reliable. P-factors are measured in numbers from 1 to 0. A P-factor must be below .1 to be considered significant. Anything below .01 is highly reliable.

Just to show how difficult it is to get a significant correlation in a regression analysis, let us start with a nonsense factor. Let us suppose, absurdly, that the rate of homelessness may depend on a city's place in alphabetical order. The following graph plots homeless rates against a city's position among the 26 letters of the alphabet:

FIGURE 3–1
Alphabetical Order

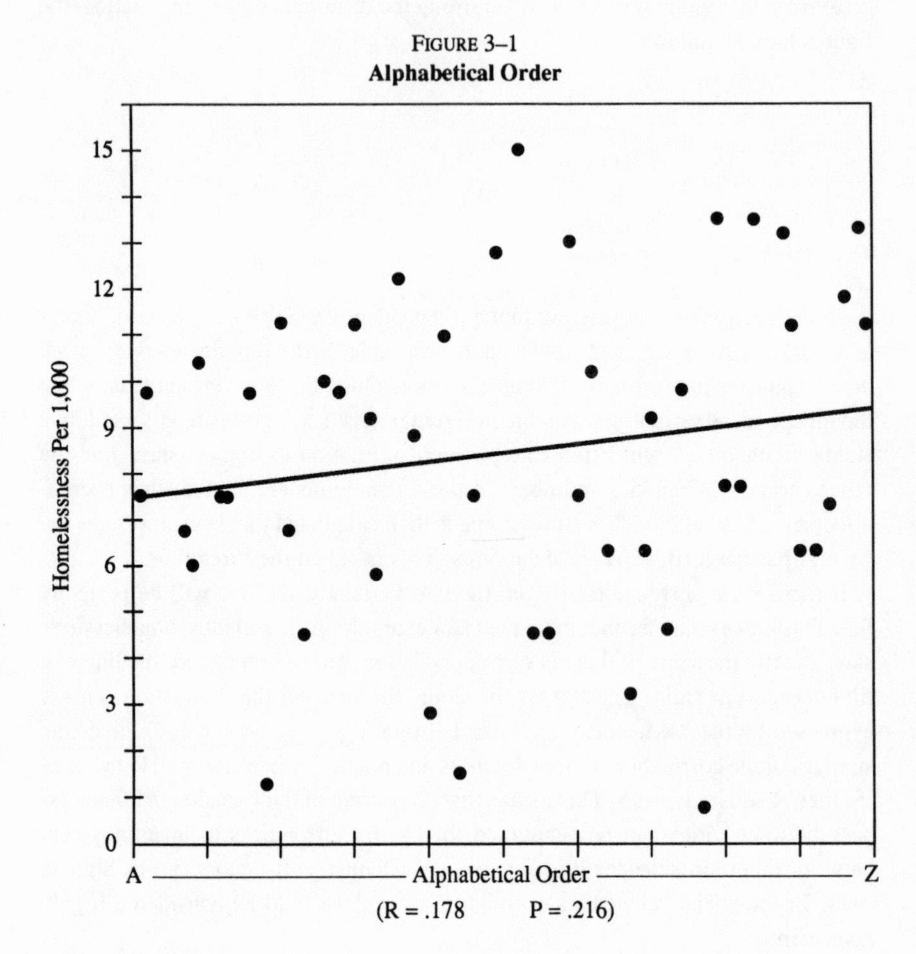

As would be expected, the datapoints are a random jumble. The trendline actually slopes slightly upward, meaning cities toward the end of the alphabet have higher homelessness. But the R-factor of .178 is very small and the P-factor of .216 indicates the correlation is meaningless.

Now let us try an assumption that is at least debatable. Eleven of the cities are state capitals and one is the national capital. Let us see if this makes any difference. The hypothesis might be that politicians are embarrassed by large numbers of homeless people and spend more money to solve the problem, or, conversely, that homeless people migrate to state or national capitals, expecting greater services there. Rather than a continuous scale, the cities will be plotted on an either/or basis, with non-capital cities on the left and capital cities on the right:

FIGURE 3–2
State Capital

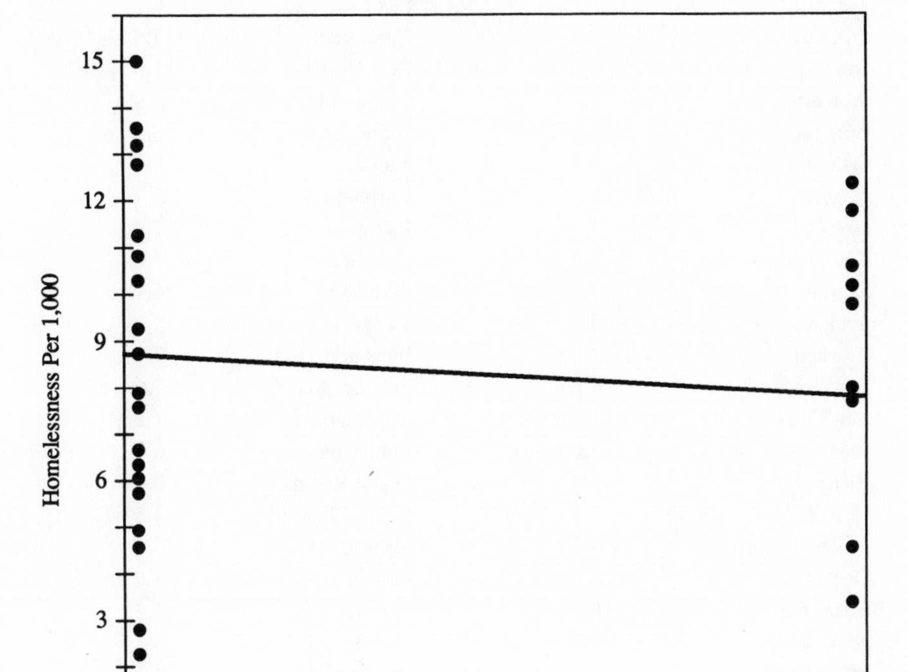

(R = .065 P = .655)

Once again, the trendline has a slight tilt, suggesting that capital cities have slightly less homelessness. But the R-coefficient (.065) is actually lower than it was in the alphabetical hypothesis and the P-factor of .655 indicates the results are meaningless. Homelessness does not relate to whether or not a city is the state or national capital.

Now let us try some more serious presumptions.

Unemployment is often cited as a cause of homelessness. At the same time, unemployment rates vary widely from city to city. Here are the unemployment rates in the 50 cities as they stood in 1984, the year the HUD survey was made:

City	*Unemployment Rates (percent)*	*City*	*Unemployment Rates (percent)*
Miami	7.5	Salt Lake City	6.3
St. Louis	8.4	Little Rock	5.8
San Francisco	6.0	New Orleans	11.0
Worcester	3.7	Charleston, S.C.	4.4
Los Angeles	7.9	Albuquerque	6.3
Santa Monica	7.0	Tucson	5.3
Newark	5.9	Burlington	3.4
Hartford	7.1	Baltimore	7.0
Washington	8.4	Cincinnati	7.2
Detroit	9.1	Syracuse	6.7
Yonkers	4.9	Tampa	5.0
Chicago	8.3	Pittsburgh	9.4
Seattle	6.6	Philadelphia	7.0
Las Vegas	8.9	Birmingham	7.2
Boston	4.6	Louisville	6.7
Richmond	5.3	Grand Rapids	8.6
New York	7.4	Minn.–St. Paul	4.5
Dallas–Ft. Worth	4.7	Milwaukee	6.4
Denver	5.0	Providence	4.9
Charleston, W.V.	10.7	Cleveland	12.4
Atlanta	5.0	Phoenix	5.1
Fort Wayne	6.3	Kansas City	4.6
Portland	7.4	Charlotte	3.7
Houston	8.4	Lincoln	3.6
San Diego	5.3	Rochester	7.0

Here is what unemployment figures look like when plotted against the rates of homelessness:

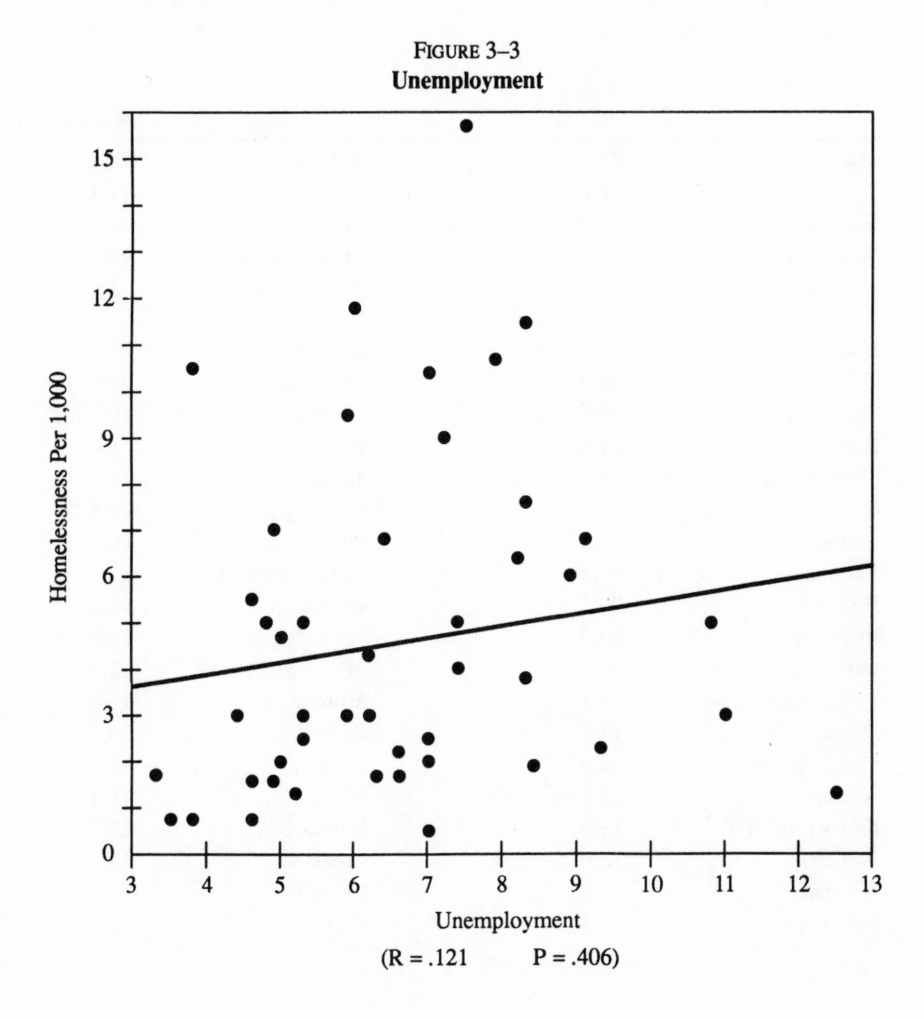

The datapoints form a random jumble, very similar to what we got when we plotted the cities in alphabetical order. The trendline has a slight upward tilt. But the R-factor is .121 (explaining less than 2 percent of the variation between cities) and the P-factor is .406. The results are statistically insignificant. There is no correlation between unemployment rates and homelessness.

Poverty is another factor often cited as a cause of homelessness. The most recent breakdown for poverty rates by cities is from the 1980 census. Although slightly outdated by 1984, they are the best figures available:

City	*% Pop. in Poverty*	*City*	*% Pop. in Poverty*
Miami	24.5	Salt Lake City	14.2
St. Louis	21.8	Little Rock	14.1
San Francisco	13.7	New Orleans	26.4
Worcester	14.4	Charleston, S.C.	14.1
Los Angeles	16.4	Albuquerque	12.4
Santa Monica	9.9	Tucson	14.7
Newark	32.8	Burlington	11.3
Hartford	25.2	Baltimore	22.9
Washington	18.6	Cincinnati	19.7
Detroit	21.9	Syracuse	18.4
Yonkers	9.8	Tampa	18.7
Chicago	20.3	Pittsburgh	16.5
Seattle	11.2	Philadelphia	20.6
Las Vegas	10.5	Birmingham	22.0
Boston	20.2	Louisville	19.3
Richmond	19.2	Grand Rapids	13.5
New York	20.0	Minn.–St. Paul	12.4
Dallas–Ft. Worth	14.1	Milwaukee	13.8
Denver	13.7	Providence	20.4
Charleston, W.V.	12.6	Cleveland	22.1
Atlanta	27.5	Phoenix	11.1
Fort Wayne	11.0	Kansas City	17.5
Portland	13.0	Charlotte	13.2
Houston	12.7	Lincoln	12.4
San Diego	12.4	Rochester	8.9

Here is what the figures look like when plotted against per-capita homelessness:

FIGURE 3–4
Poverty

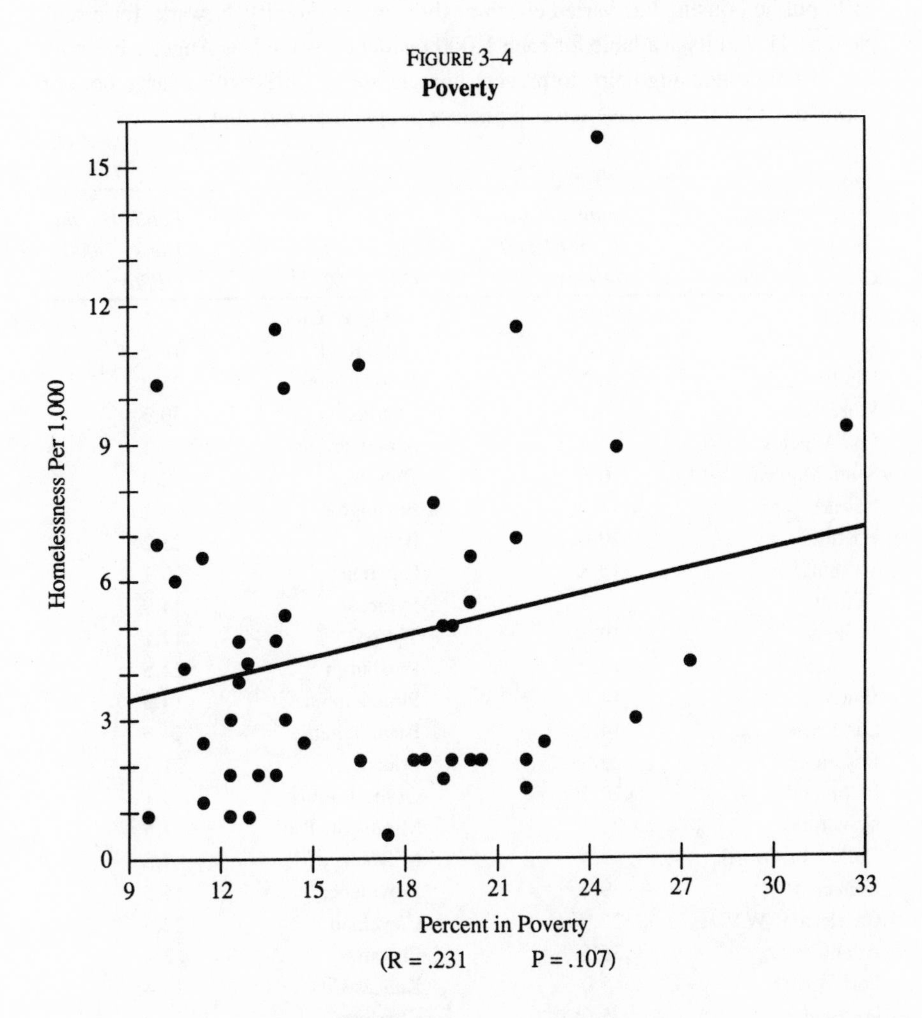

Again, there is a slight upward tilt to the line, indicating a small correlation between homelessness and higher poverty rates. But the correlation is only .231, accounting for about 5 percent of the variation, and the P-factor is .107, a little too high for the results to be meaningful. The results are statistically insignificant.

Let us try a third hypothesis—the availability of public housing. The effort to build public housing has varied enormously from city to city. Newark, for example, has 41.7 units available for each 1,000 residents, while Los Angeles has only 2.8. If public housing helps to prevent homelessness, cities with a large pool of public housing should have fewer homeless people than the others.

City	*Public Housing Units / 1,000 (1986)*	*City*	*Public Housing Units / 1,000 (1986)*
Miami	29.8	Salt Lake City	6.5
St. Louis	14.0	Little Rock	16.8
San Francisco	10.2	New Orleans	25.2
Worcester	14.1	Charleston, S.C.	30.6
Los Angeles	2.8	Albuquerque	3.1
Santa Monica	0.8	Tucson	2.4
Newark	41.7	Burlington	9.1
Hartford	20.0	Baltimore	23.2
Washington	19.8	Cincinnati	20.1
Detroit	9.7	Syracuse	14.9
Yonkers	10.7	Tampa	17.1
Chicago	13.0	Pittsburgh	24.5
Seattle	14.6	Philadelphia	14.3
Las Vegas	14.2	Birmingham	24.3
Boston	25.3	Louisville	21.3
Richmond	20.5	Grand Rapids	5.1
New York	21.5	Minn.–St. Paul	17.9
Dallas–Ft. Worth	5.9	Milwaukee	7.5
Denver	9.0	Providence	15.5
Charleston, W.V.	22.9	Cleveland	22.5
Atlanta	35.5	Phoenix	2.4
Fort Wayne	5.0	Kansas City	10.4
Portland	5.0	Charlotte	6.0
Houston	1.9	Lincoln	12.7
San Diego	1.1	Rochester	1.4

FIGURE 3–5
Public Housing

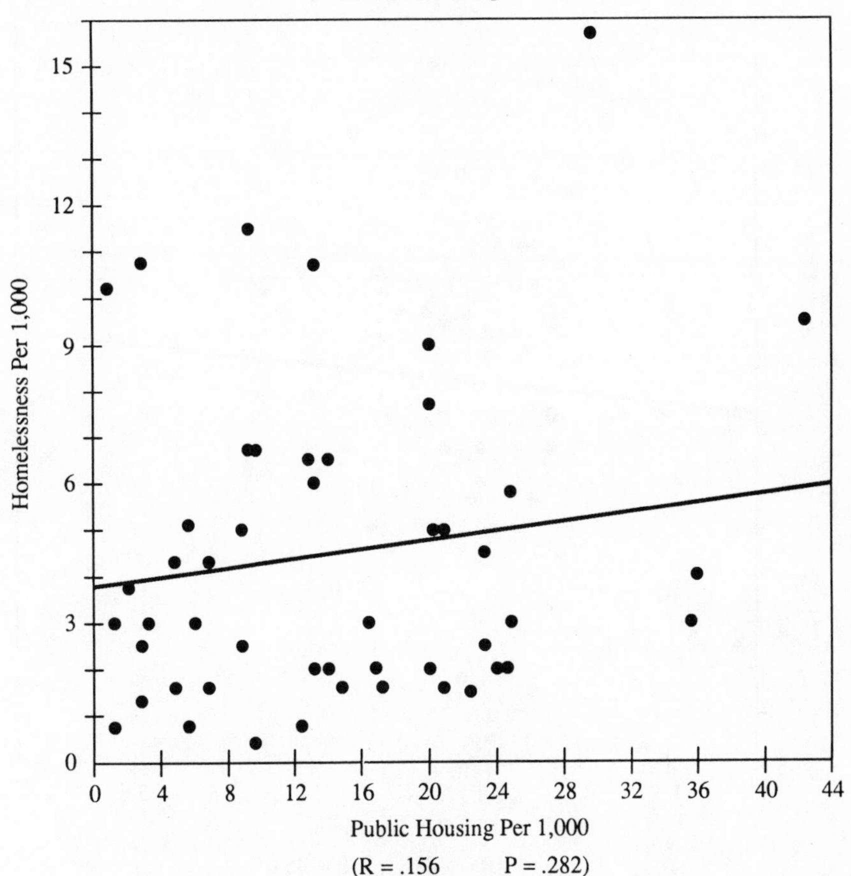

(R = .156 P = .282)

Once again, however, there is no statistically significant correlation. The availability of public housing does not seem to have any influence on homelessness.

Another common explanation about homelessness relates to the size of the city itself. It has often been hypothesized that homeless people migrate to large cities in search of jobs and housing. Thus, we might expect larger cities to have more homelessness. Graphing this factor produces the following results:

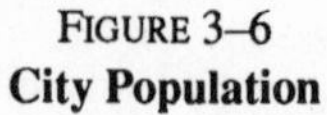

FIGURE 3–6
City Population

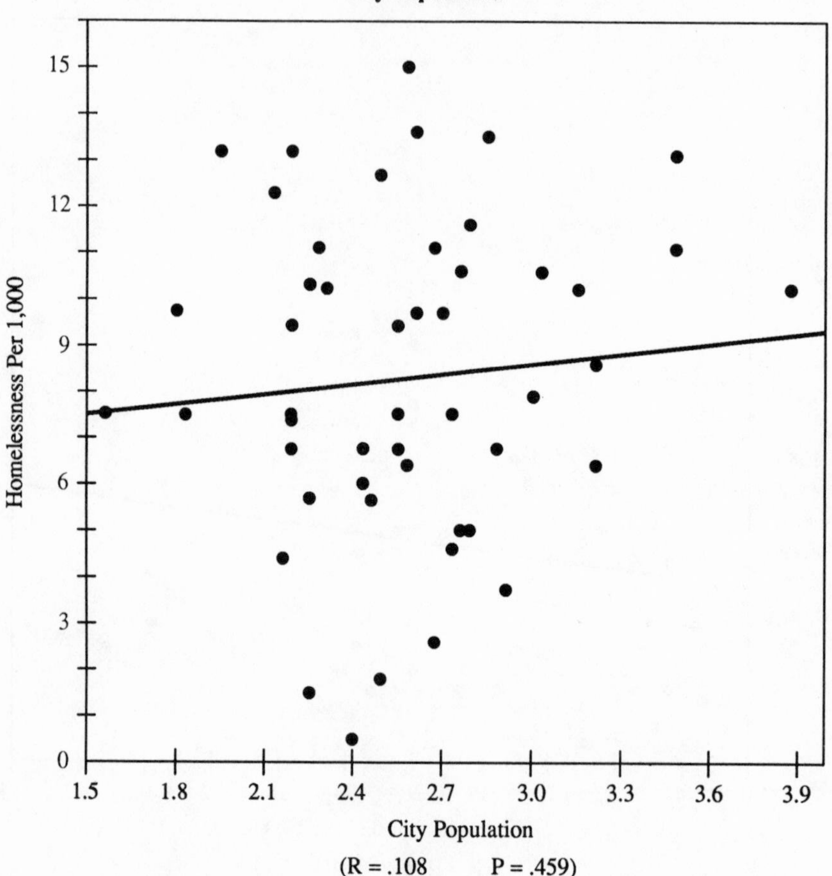

(R = .108 P = .459)

Once again, there is no significant correlation.

Let us try another hypothesis. It is often said that homelessness is aggravated by economic boom-and-bust cycles in the local economy. An expanding job market, so the argument goes, first attracts a large in-migration, then collapses, leaving large numbers of people stranded. The 1980s "oil bust" in Texas and Louisiana is often cited. Alternately, a rapid in-migration could outstrip the capacities of the local homebuilding industry, making housing scarce and producing homelessness.

The best way to separate "boom-towns" from stagnant or declining cities is to measure their population growth or decline over the last 15 years. Here are the figures:

City	*Percent Growth 1970–1985*	*City*	*Percent Growth 1970–1985*
Miami	11	Salt Lake City	6
St. Louis	−31	Little Rock	29
San Francisco	− 1	New Orleans	− 6
Worcester	− 9	Charleston, S.C.	3
Los Angeles	10	Albuquerque	43
Santa Monica	0	Tucson	39
Newark	−18	Burlington	5
Hartford	−14	Baltimore	−16
Washington	−17	Cincinnati	−19
Detroit	−28	Syracuse	−17
Yonkers	− 6	Tampa	− 1
Chicago	−11	Pittsburgh	−22
Seattle	− 8	Philadelphia	−16
Las Vegas	46	Birmingham	− 8
Boston	−11	Louisville	−20
Richmond	−12	Grand Rapids	− 7
New York	− 9	Minn.–St. Paul	−11
Dallas–Ft. Worth	9	Milwaukee	−13
Denver	− 2	Providence	−13
Charleston, W.V.	−12	Cleveland	−27
Atlanta	−14	Phoenix	46
Fort Wayne	− 8	Kansas City	−18
Portland	− 3	Charlotte	−13
Houston	39	Lincoln	37
San Diego	52	Rochester	21

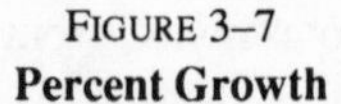

FIGURE 3–7
Percent Growth

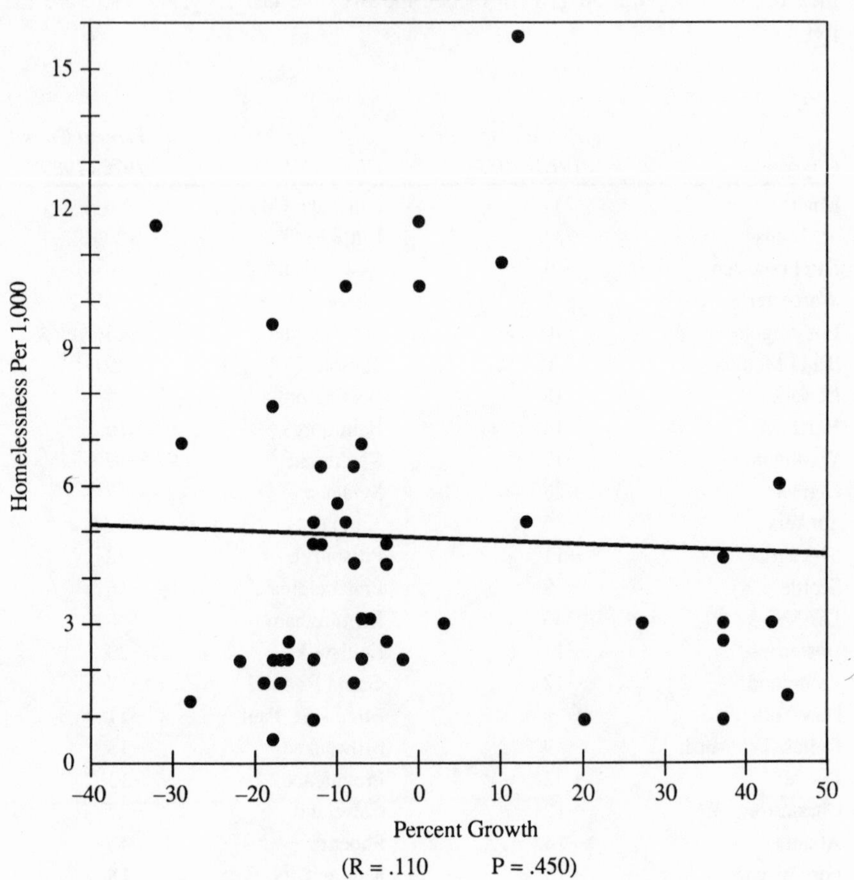

The line actually slopes downward, suggesting, if anything, that declining cities have more homelessness. But the correlation is very small and the P-factor too high. Once again, the results are statistically insignificant.

Since none of the conventional hypotheses have worked so far, let us try one that common sense tells us might affect homelessness—the weather. All things being equal, the choice between doubling up with a relative and living in the street could be influenced—if ever so slightly—by local weather conditions. This is not to suggest that people are homeless "by choice." But there might be certain marginal effects that make people more desperate to get inside during inclement weather.

Let us first try average annual rainfall and snowfall in the 50 cities:

City	*Annual Precipitation*	*City*	*Annual Precipitation*
Miami	57.55	Salt Lake City	15.31
St. Louis	33.91	Little Rock	49.20
San Francisco	19.71	New Orleans	59.74
Worcester	43.84	Charleston, S.C.	51.59
Los Angeles	14.85	Albuquerque	8.12
Santa Monica	14.85	Tucson	7.11
Newark	42.56	Burlington	33.69
Hartford	44.39	Baltimore	41.84
Washington	39.00	Cincinnati	40.14
Detroit	30.97	Syracuse	35.74
Yonkers	42.82	Tampa	55.42
Chicago	33.34	Pittsburgh	39.09
Seattle	38.60	Philadelphia	41.42
Las Vegas	7.87	Birmingham	15.31
Boston	43.84	Louisville	43.56
Richmond	45.92	Grand Rapids	32.72
New York	42.82	Minn.–St. Paul	26.36
Dallas–Ft. Worth	23.15	Milwaukee	30.94
Denver	15.31	Providence	41.91
Charleston, W.V.	40.74	Cleveland	35.20
Atlanta	48.61	Phoenix	7.11
Fort Wayne	39.12	Kansas City	31.13
Portland	37.39	Charlotte	43.16
Houston	44.76	Lincoln	30.34
San Diego	12.48	Rochester	35.74

FIGURE 3–8
Annual Precipitation

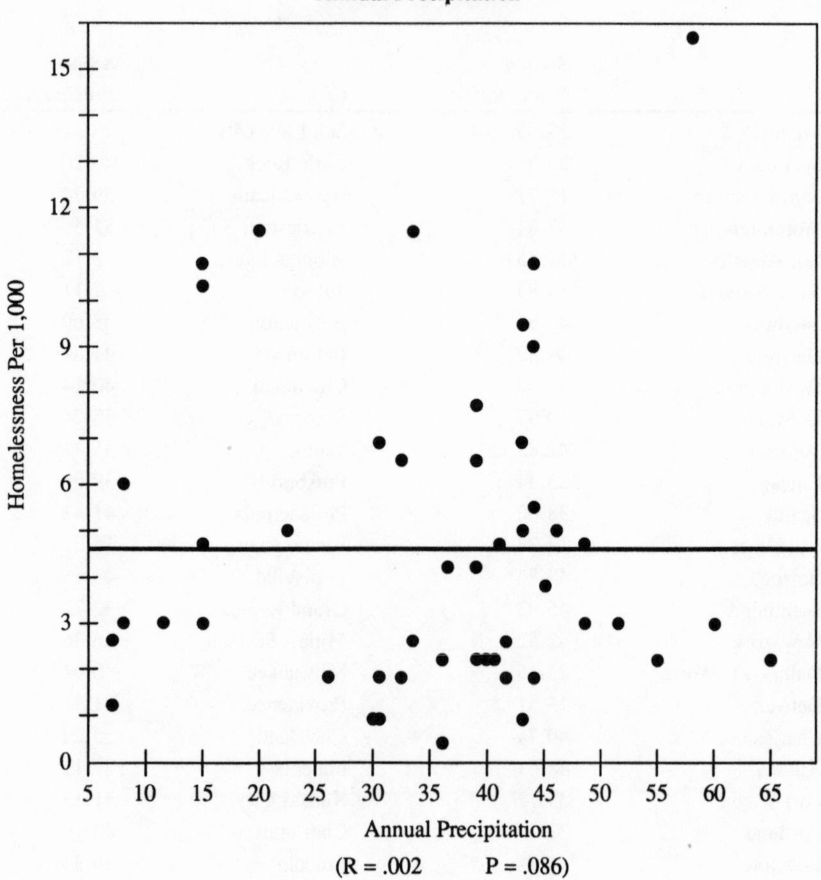

The trendline is perfectly flat. There is no correlation.

Now let us try the same thing with annual average temperature:

City	*Average Annual Temperature*	*City*	*Average Annual Temperature*
Miami	74	Salt Lake City	57
St. Louis	55	Little Rock	62
San Francisco	57	New Orleans	67
Worcester	52	Charleston, S.C.	63
Los Angeles	66	Albuquerque	63
Santa Monica	66	Tucson	73
Newark	54	Burlington	45
Hartford	49	Baltimore	55
Washington	58	Cincinnati	53
Detroit	50	Syracuse	47
Yonkers	54	Tampa	67
Chicago	49	Pittsburgh	54
Seattle	55	Philadelphia	55
Las Vegas	59	Birmingham	66
Boston	52	Louisville	55
Richmond	61	Grand Rapids	47
New York	55	Minn.–St. Paul	42
Dallas–Ft. Worth	67	Milwaukee	45
Denver	52	Providence	51
Charleston, W.V.	56	Cleveland	50
Atlanta	61	Phoenix	72
Fort Wayne	52	Kansas City	55
Portland	57	Charlotte	59
Houston	67	Lincoln	50
San Diego	68	Rochester	48

FIGURE 3–9
Temperature

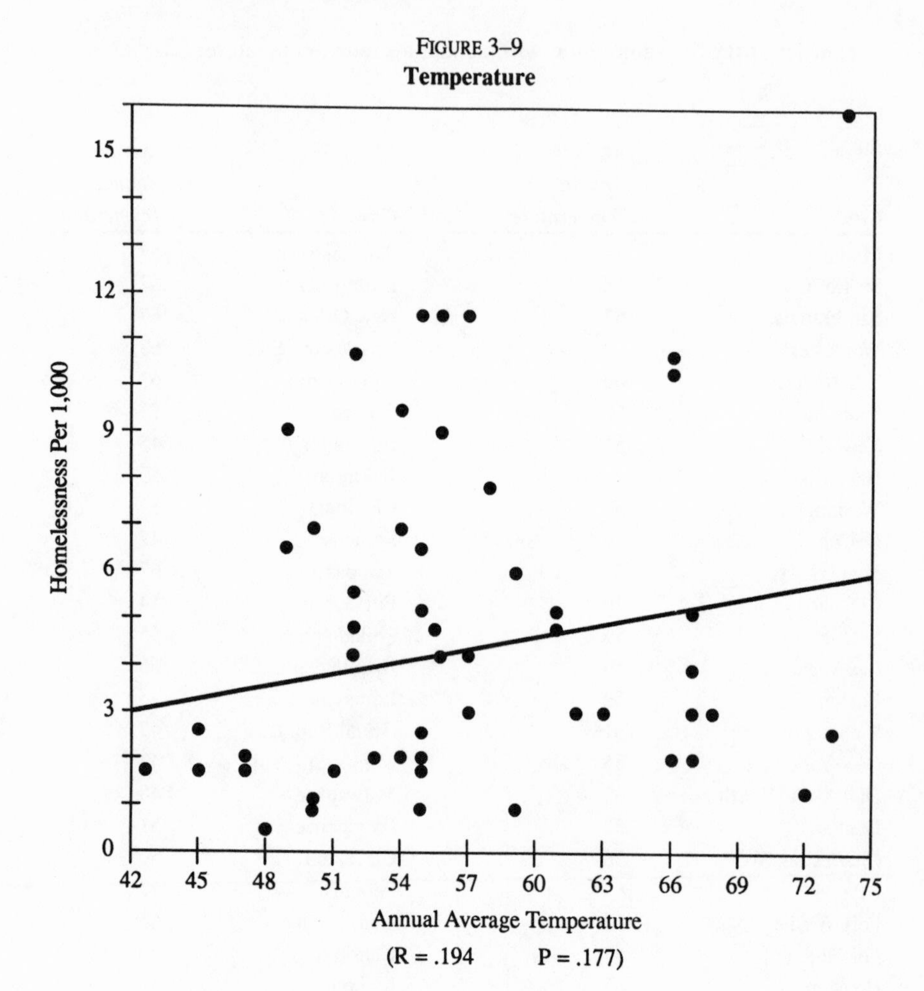

There is no significant correlation.

Let us now try a factor for which we have no immediate hypothesis, but which might prove significant—the percentage of minority population in the city. Many studies and reports have indicated a large percentage of minorities among the homeless—both single men and welfare mothers. A correlation here might mean one of two things. It might be connected with incomes, since minorities are generally poorer, or it might indicate that discrimination in housing has limited the opportunities of minorities.

We will look at the correlation two ways, blacks alone and blacks and Hispanics.

City	*Blacks percent*	*Hispanics percent*	*Blacks and Hispanics percent*
Miami	25	55	80
St. Louis	45	1	46
San Francisco	12	13	25
Worcester	5	7	12
Los Angeles	16	28	44
Santa Monica	4	13	17
Newark	58	18	76
Hartford	34	21	55
Washington	70	3	73
Detroit	62	2	64
Yonkers	11	9	20
Chicago	39	14	53
Seattle	9	3	12
Las Vegas	13	8	21
Boston	22	6	28
Richmond	51	1	52
New York	25	20	45
Dallas–Ft. W.	29	12	41
Denver	11	19	30
Charleston, W.V.	12	2	14
Atlanta	66	2	68
Ft. Wayne	15	2	17
Portland	7	2	9
Houston	27	18	45
San Diego	9	15	24
Salt Lake City	2	9	11
Little Rock	32	1	33
New Orleans	55	3	58
Charleston, S.C.	47	1	48
Albuquerque	2	34	36
Tucson	3	25	28
Burlington	2	0	2
Baltimore	54	1	55
Cincinnati	33	1	34
Syracuse	16	2	18
Tampa	23	13	36
Pittsburgh	24	0	24
Philadelphia	37	4	41
Birmingham	55	1	56

City	*Blacks percent*	*Hispanics percent*	*Blacks and Hispanics percent*
Louisville	28	0	28
Grand Rapids	16	3	19
Minn.–St. Paul	7	1	8
Milwaukee	23	4	27
Providence	12	6	18
Cleveland	43	3	46
Phoenix	4	15	19
Kansas City	27	3	30
Charlotte	31	1	32
Lincoln	2	2	4
Rochester	26	5	31

FIGURE 3–10
Percent Blacks

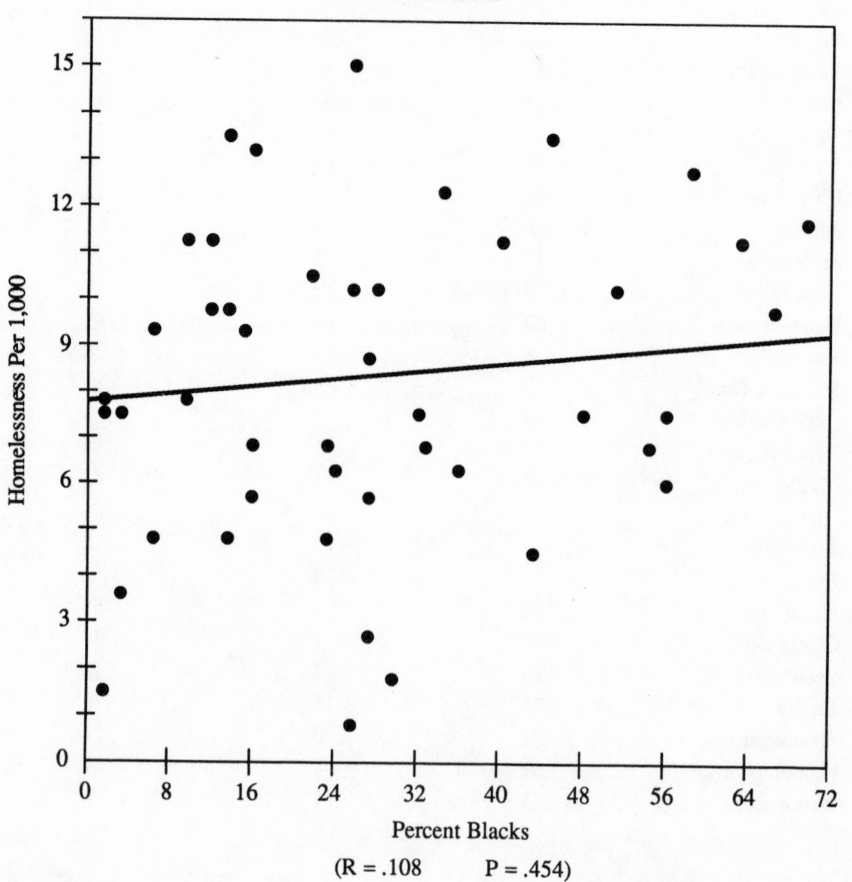

(R = .108 P = .454)

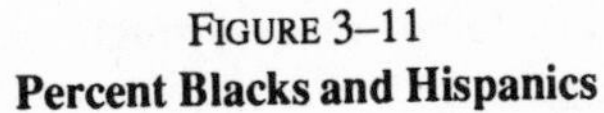

FIGURE 3–11
Percent Blacks and Hispanics

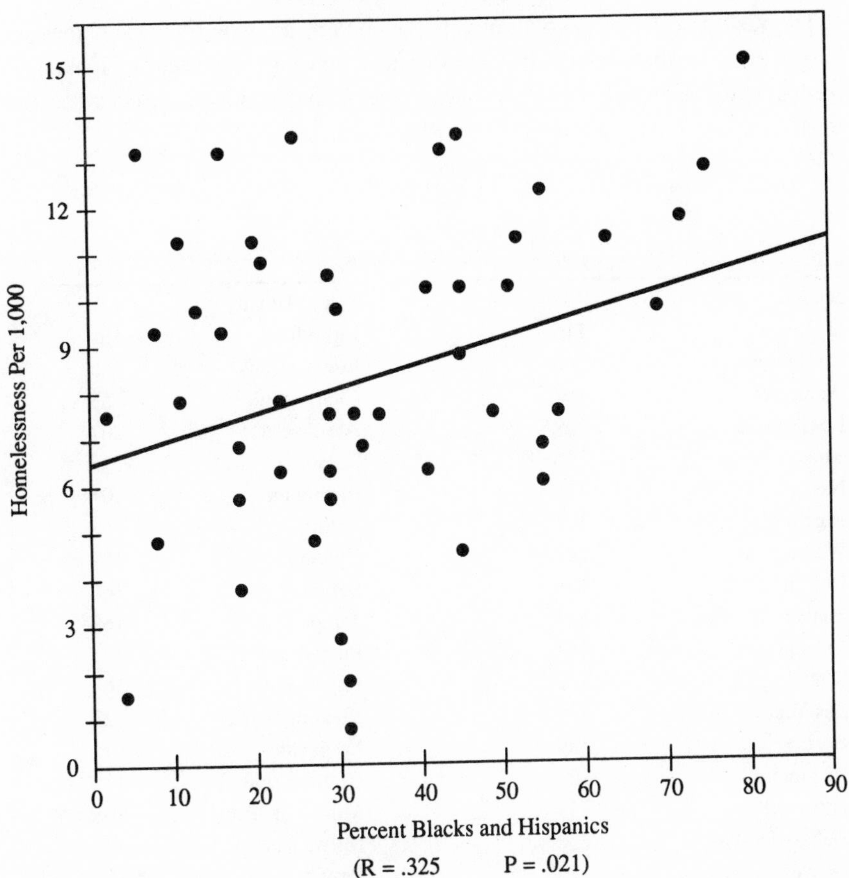

Neither the figure for blacks alone nor for Hispanics alone (not depicted) shows any correlation. However, the graph for blacks and Hispanics together gives us our first significant result. The R-factor is .325 and the P-factor is .021, indicating the results are quite reliable. Taking R-squared, we find that about 10 percent of the variation in homelessness between cities can be accounted for by comparing the population of racial minorities within each city.

Once again, this could mean two things. It could suggest that minorities are in an adverse economic position and therefore incapable of paying for their own housing, or it could mean that these groups find fewer housing opportunities because of racial and ethnic discrimination.

Now let us turn to the one factor that we might expect to be paramount in homelessness—housing itself.

The vast majority of the poor around the country are renters. Since homelessness is often attributed to the lack of affordable housing, let us start by looking at median rents. Although the census bureau does some updating in select cities, the most complete figures are those in the 1980 census.

City	*Median Rent (1980)*	*City*	*Median Rent (1980)*
Miami	187	Salt Lake City	178
St. Louis	115	Little Rock	184
San Francisco	266	New Orleans	153
Worcester	152	Charleston, S.C.	155
Los Angeles	229	Albuquerque	207
Santa Monica	296	Tucson	213
Newark	178	Burlington	201
Hartford	174	Baltimore	161
Washington	207	Cincinnati	159
Detroit	154	Syracuse	168
Yonkers	254	Tampa	162
Chicago	188	Pittsburgh	171
Seattle	232	Philadelphia	168
Las Vegas	235	Birmingham	122
Boston	189	Louisville	140
Richmond	177	Grand Rapids	172
New York	214	Minn.–St. Paul	208
Dallas–Ft. Worth	230	Milwaukee	184
Denver	213	Providence	139
Charleston, W.V.	173	Cleveland	127
Atlanta	148	Phoenix	246
Fort Wayne	178	Kansas City	165
Portland	105	Charlotte	180
Houston	255	Lincoln	192
San Diego	249	Rochester	178

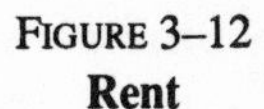

FIGURE 3–12
Rent

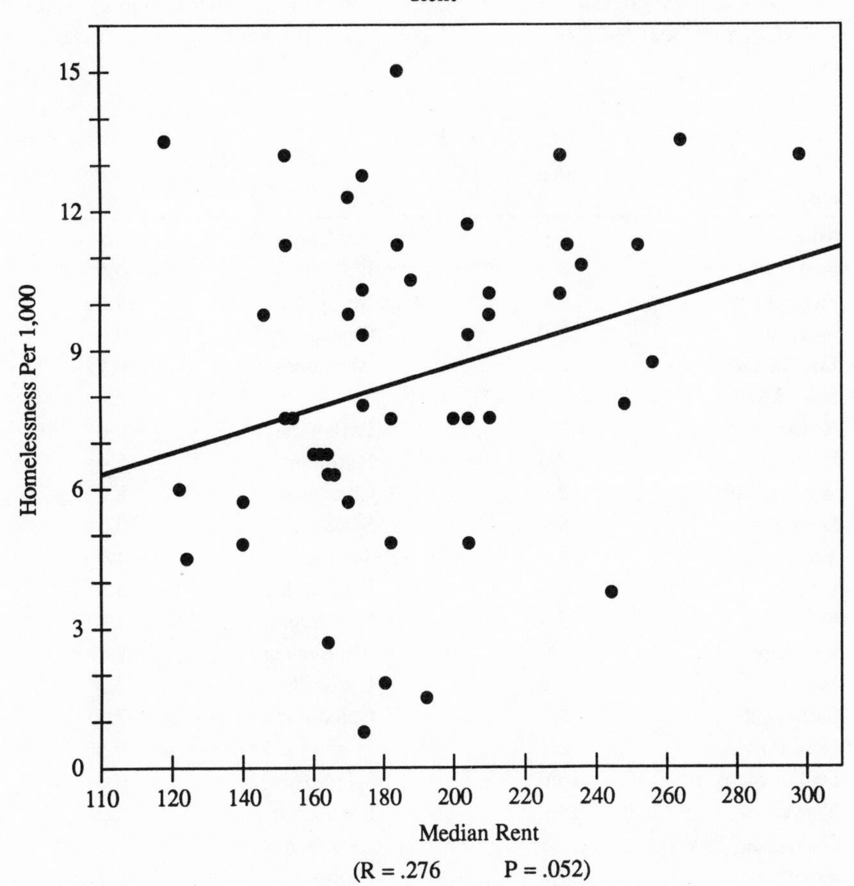

(R = .276 P = .052)

The R-factor is significant and the P-factor is strong, although neither is as good as what we got with the percentage of minorities. About 7 percent of the variation in homelessness can be associated with higher rents.

Let us look at another factor—housing vacancies. The vacancy rates in single-family homes are rarely more than about 1 or 2 percent and vary little from city to city. Rental vacancies vary widely, however, from more than 15 percent in Dallas, Houston, and New Orleans to less than 3 percent in San Francisco, New York, and Washington. A 6 percent vacancy rate is considered normal. In 1989, the national vacancy rate was 7.8 percent, an unusually high figure.

The following vacancy figures were assembled from a variety of sources—census data, local government reports, private surveys, academic studies, and the knowledge of local realtors:

City	*Average Rental Vacancy Rate (1983–6)*	*City*	*Average Rental Vacancy Rate (1983–6)*
Miami	7.0	Salt Lake City	14.5
St. Louis	8.5	Little Rock	6.5
San Francisco	1.6	New Orleans	18.0
Worcester	3.0	Charleston, S.C.	9.0
Los Angeles	2.2	Albuquerque	9.7
Santa Monica	1.8	Tucson	12.0
Newark	2.3	Burlington	6.0
Hartford	2.6	Baltimore	5.4
Washington	2.0	Cincinnati	8.6
Detroit	5.4	Syracuse	9.5
Yonkers	2.1	Tampa	14.7
Chicago	6.0	Pittsburgh	5.8
Seattle	5.5	Philadelphia	4.0
Las Vegas	9.0	Birmingham	7.1
Boston	2.6	Louisville	7.3
Richmond	5.5	Grand Rapids	7.5
New York	2.2	Minn.–St. Paul	6.1
Dallas–Ft. Worth	16.0	Milwaukee	6.0
Denver	14.0	Providence	5.0
Charleston, W.V.	5.9	Cleveland	6.5
Atlanta	9.0	Phoenix	12.2
Fort Wayne	9.2	Kansas City	7.2
Portland	5.5	Charlotte	8.8
Houston	17.0	Lincoln	6.5
San Diego	5.3	Rochester	9.0

FIGURE 3–13
Vacancy

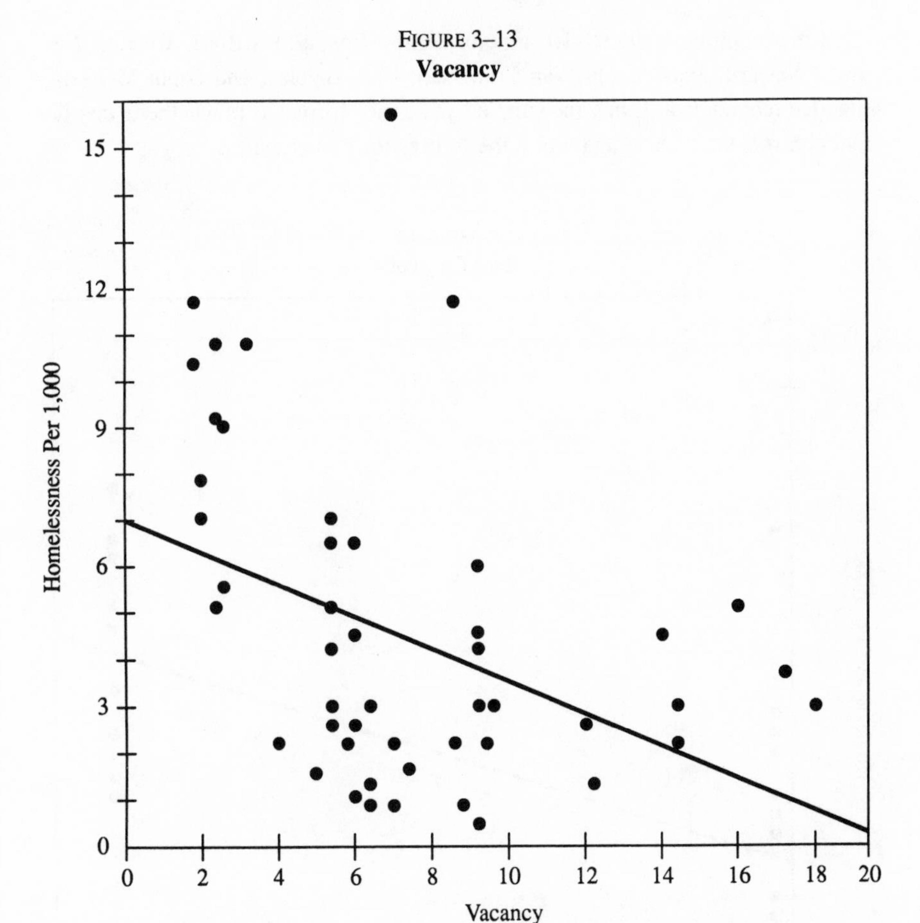

(R = .387 P = .005)

The correlation is again significant. Cities with lower vacancy rates have higher homelessness. The vacancy factor can account for about 15 percent of the variation between cities. Put another way, a one percent decline in the rental vacancy rate is associated with a 10 percent increase in homelessness.

Now let us consider another factor, the presence or absence of rent control. Many cities, in trying to deal with their housing problems, have resorted to rent control, wherein the price of apartments is regulated by the city government. Economists are highly critical of rent control, arguing that it causes housing shortages. Thus, we might expect some correlation with homelessness.

Of the 50 cities in the model, nine of them—Boston, Hartford, Yonkers, New York, Newark, Washington, San Francisco, Los Angeles, and Santa Monica—practice rent control. Using the simple "yes or no" format as to whether a city has rent control, let us once again plot the figures for homelessness:

FIGURE 3–14
Rent Control

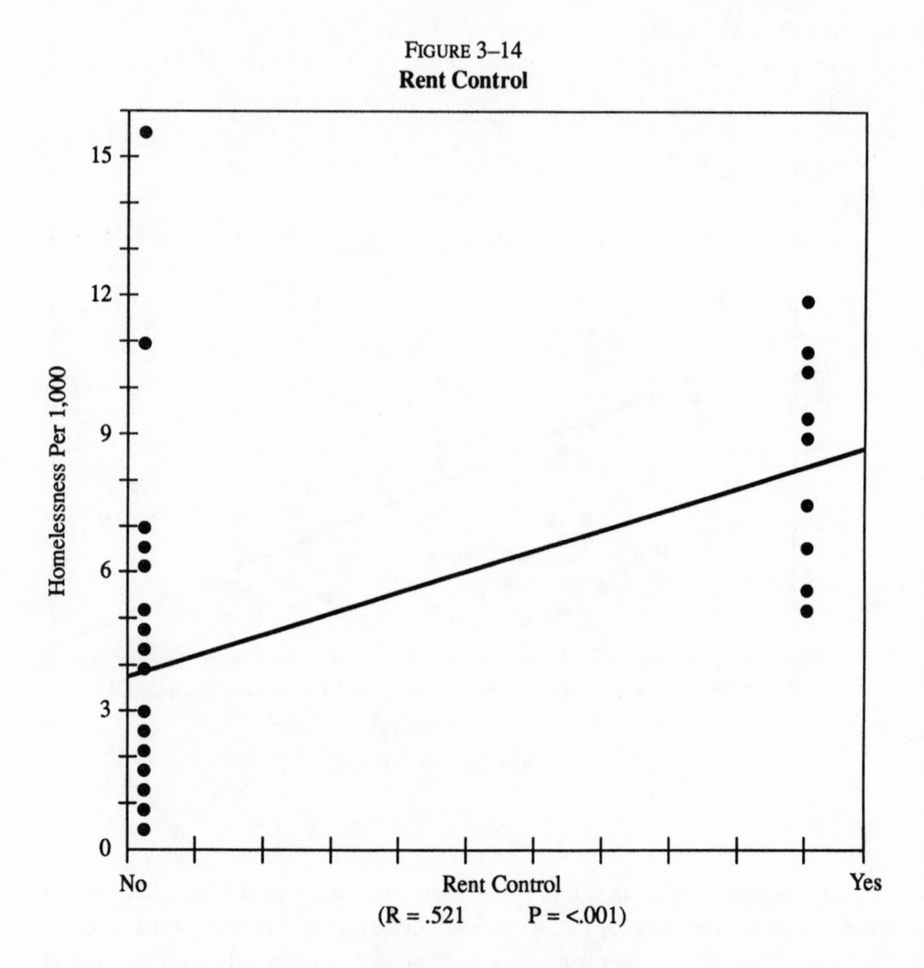

The simple presence or absence of rent control gives the strongest correlation so far. The R-factor of .521 means that 27 percent of the variation among cities is associated with the presence or absence of rent control. The presence of rent control is associated with a *250 percent* increase in homelessness. The P-factor of less than .001 has a statistical significance of almost complete certainty.

We now have three distinctly strong correlations. Discrimination gives us a 10 percent correlation, vacancy rates 15 percent, and rent control 27 percent. However, we cannot simply add these figures together. Some may turn out to have less significance while others have more when different factors are screened from the picture. The next step should be to measure the factors together and see if there is any duplication.

When we do this, the rent-control and discrimination factors remain, but the vacancy factor disappears. All the variation measured by vacancy rates is also measured by the rent-control factor (but not vice versa).

When we look at the figures on vacancy rates, the explanation quickly becomes plain. *The nine rent-controlled cities have the nine lowest vacancy rates in the country.* No city with rent control has a vacancy rate *over* 3 percent and no non-rent-controlled city, except Worcester, has a vacancy rate *under* 4 percent. The variation in vacancy rates among all other cities—from 4 percent in Philadelphia to 18 percent in New Orleans—does not have any effect on homelessness.

What this suggests is that vacancies above 4 percent represent normal fluctuations in the market. Only when vacancy rates descend below 4 percent do pathological consequences appear. At this point the correlation with homelessness emerges..

Now let us try one final correlation—home prices themselves. Since the majority of people now often live outside the city limits in suburban areas, let us extend our reach at this point and look at median home prices for the entire Standard Metropolitan Statistical Area (SMSA). The figures are from the Census Bureau's regular updates of the 1980 figures. (Not all the cities have SMSAs and some SMSA figures have not yet been updated.)

City	*Median Home Price SMSA (1984) ($1,000)*	City	*Median Home Price SMSA (1984) ($1,000)*
Miami	86	Salt Lake City	66
St. Louis	62	Little Rock	na
San Francisco	130	New Orleans	73
Worcester	100	Charleston, S.C.	na
Los Angeles	115	Albuquerque	73
Santa Monica	115	Tucson	na
Newark	105	Burlington	na
Hartford	87	Baltimore	66
Washington	93	Cincinnati	60
Detroit	48	Syracuse	51
Yonkers	105	Tampa	58
Chicago	79	Pittsburgh	na
Seattle	76	Philadelphia	65
Las Vegas	76	Birmingham	65
Boston	100	Louisville	50
Richmond	na	Grand Rapids	43
New York	105	Minn.–St. Paul	74
Dallas–Ft. Worth	82	Milwaukee	68
Denver	82	Providence	60
Charleston, W.V.	na	Cleveland	63
Atlanta	na	Phoenix	75
Fort Wayne	na	Kansas City	59
Portland	63	Charlotte	na
Houston	78	Lincoln	56
San Diego	100	Rochester	60

na = not available

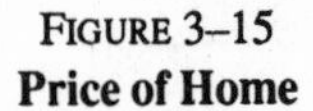

FIGURE 3–15
Price of Home

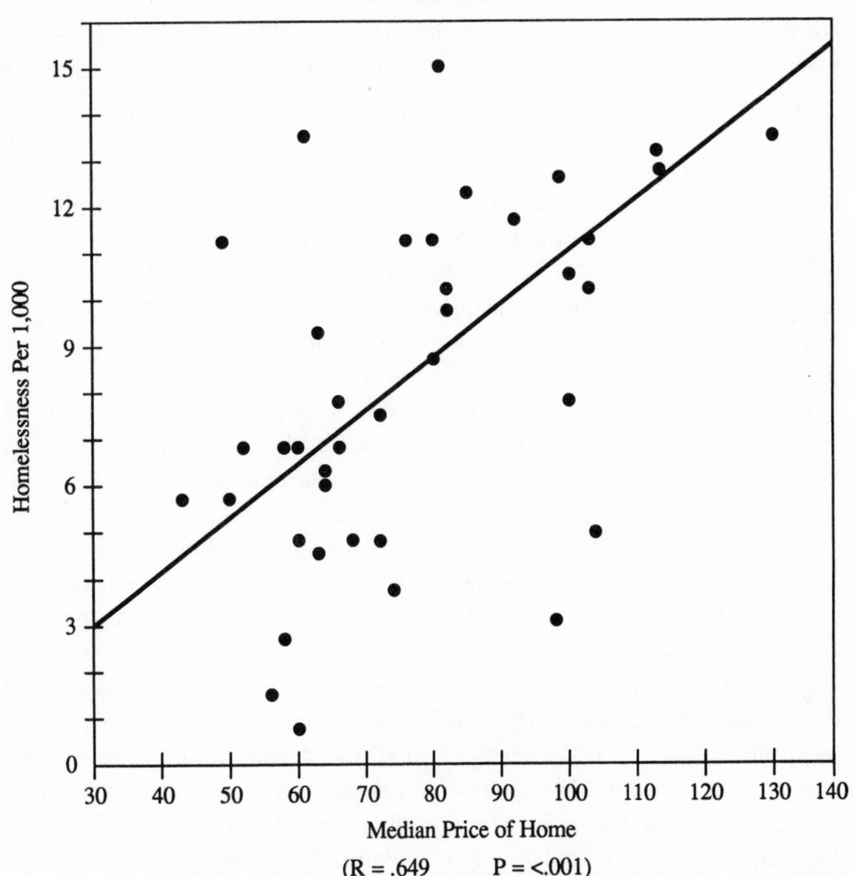

(R = .649 P = <.001)

Remarkably, the median price of homes in the metropolitan region turns out to be by far the single most significant factor for predicting homelessness. The R-factor is .649, meaning that 42 percent of the variation in homelessness can be accounted for by measuring median home prices. The P-factor is less than .001, making it all but statistically certain.

It is not immediately clear why home prices and homelessness should correlate. People on the edge of destitution are usually not in the market for buying homes. In trying to account for homelessness, people often talk about the "affordability" of housing, yet this is usually associated with the price of low-income housing. If anything, we would expect to see median rents correlate more strongly. Yet we have already seen that it is the *availability* of rentals, and not their median price, that has more significance. People living in the suburbs are likely to feel that, if home prices are high, that is their problem and does not connect with homelessness, which is regarded as an urban issue. Yet the data suggest that this may not be the case.

Once all these factors have been measured, we can once again combine them to find out which duplicate each other and which add together.

The best model turns out to be a combination of median home price and the percent of blacks and Hispanics in the city. Together these two factors account for 51 percent of the variation in homelessness between cities. The significance factor is 0.0000 (as low as the computer can measure).

Just as the vacancy factor disappeared when we measured rent control, so the rent-control factor disappears when we measure median home prices. This does not necessarily mean rent control has lost its significance. It still has the second-highest individual correlation, behind home prices.

What is most interesting is that the two factors—rent control and home prices seem to be confounded. High home prices and rent control correlate better with each other than any of the other significant factors. Although they are obviously not the same thing, they do seem to be part of a common syndrome, as the following graph indicates. There are a few outlying cities (Miami, St. Louis, and Detroit) that have developed high homelessness without either high home prices or rent control. (The rate of homelessness in St. Louis, remember, may be exaggerated by its narrow city limits.) But the vast majority of cities cluster right around the trendline, with cities with high home prices and rent control concentrated at the upper end. In those cities not near the trendline, high minority populations may be a more important factor.

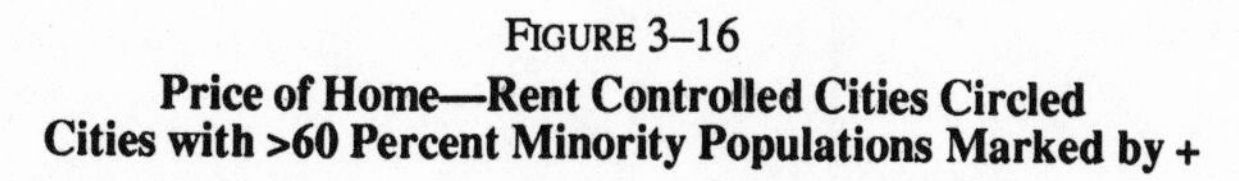

FIGURE 3–16

Price of Home—Rent Controlled Cities Circled
Cities with >60 Percent Minority Populations Marked by +

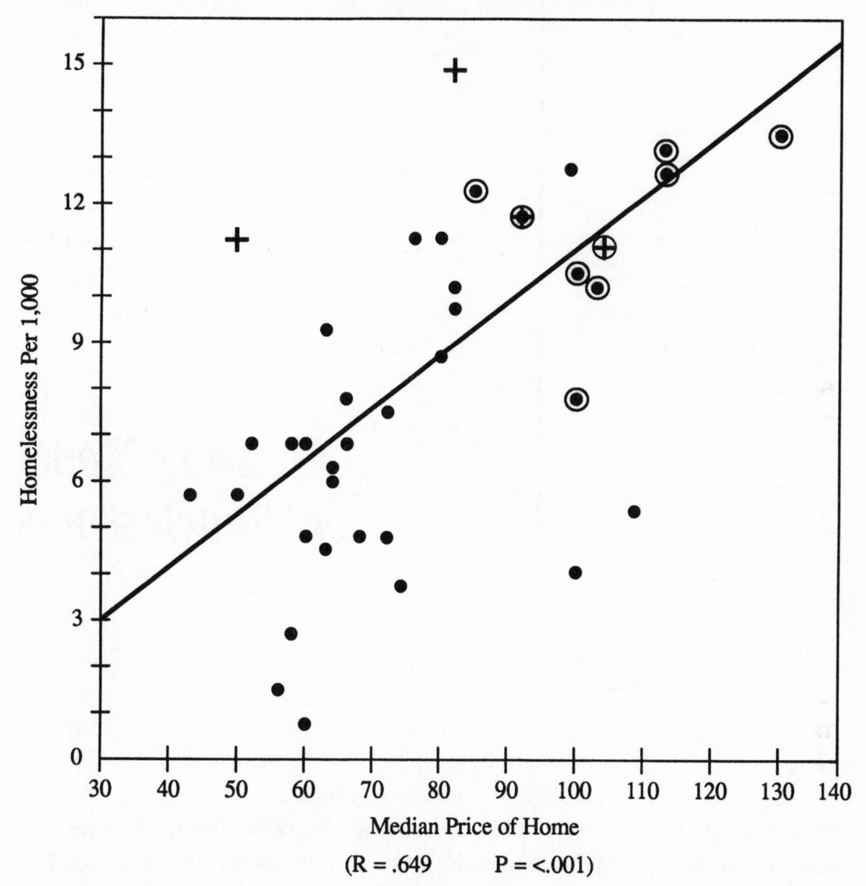

Once again, none of this explains cause and effect. We do not know exactly why cities with high minority populations have more homelessness. Nor do we know why high housing prices and the presence of rent control are closely correlated. What we do know is that the combination of high home prices and a large minority population produces the best predictive model for homelessness.

That these factors can account for only about half the variation also reminds us of one more thing. Although the model suggests some important explanations, homelessness remains a complex social phenomenon.

Chapter 4

A Housing Model for Homelessness

Our regression analysis has revealed several things: 1) the median price of homes is the best predictor of homelessness, 2) rent control is the second-best indicator and vacancies the third, 3) the three seem to be part of a single complex, 4) the size of the minority population has an effect that is smaller and distinct from the housing factors. Finally, it is good to remember in constructing any model that all these factors combined account for only about half the variations in homelessness from city to city.

Taking these four points, let us try to construct a basic model for homelessness.

At the core of every city's homeless population, there seems to be a group of homeless—released mental patients, drug addicts, and alcoholics—whose problems are unrelated to housing. These are people disturbed and isolated enough from friends and family as to be unable to maintain their own dwelling. Many welfare mothers (often substance abusers themselves) fall into this category.

As Ellen Bassuck wrote after working with homeless women at eight Boston shelters:

> Although not psychotic, two-thirds of the women suffer from personality disorders. They are unable to form and maintain stable relationships, have poor or nonexistent work histories, [and] have been unsuccessful in establishing stable homes *even when housing is available*. . . . [Emphasis added.][1]

Using HUD's 1984 statistics, we can estimate the hard-core homeless population affected by mental problems to be about 400,000—1.6 per 1000. Given the recent rise in drug abuse associated with "crack," the growth of the pathologies population has probably equaled the growth of the other "economic" homeless since 1984. If both have risen 50 percent, each would now stand at 600,000, giving the nation a total homeless population 1.2 million—not an unrealistic figure.

What can be done about the 30 to 35 percent of the homeless population who are victims of mental illness? The choice seems to be between reinstituting the old state mental hospitals, or perhaps revitalizing the community mental-health concept (which has not yet been shown to work), and allowing these people to continue to live on the street.

Beyond treating the insane, the old "mental asylums" undoubtedly took care of many marginal people who are among today's homeless. One of the first things observers always noticed in the old state mental hospitals was how un-crazy many inmates seemed. Instead of being lunatics, they were just old men and women, alcoholics, vaguely retarded individuals, and people who were perhaps not quite sharp enough to make it on the outside. Like the jails that served as drunk tanks, the old mental institutions offered "asylum," often voluntary, to people who cling to the margins of life. (Recall, for example, the shock of Randle Patrick McMurphy, the hero of Ken Kesey's *One Flew Over the Cuckoo's Nest,* when he discovers that the fellow patients, whom he has been trying to liberate from the state hospital, are all *voluntary* inmates.)

It was this lack of notable pathologies, of course, that made reformers want to open the doors to the hospitals and set everyone free. Yet the judgment (often a self-judgment) that these people could not make it on the outside proved largely justified. To solve the problem of mentally ill street people, we are going to have to revive some form of mental asylum.

Substance abusers are an even more difficult problem. Many advocates are just now beginning to admit that drug and alcohol abuse are, as one observer put it, "the nasty little secret of the homeless."

"Our initial premise was that if you provide food, shelter and hygiene, then [the homeless] will be able to help themselves," said the Rev. Jack Pfannenstiel, a Franciscan priest who runs six shelters in Washington. "We were naive about the drug and alcohol problem."[2]

Whether the drug problem is best dealt with by law enforcement, supply interdiction, education, drug treatment, or some other method is an issue that is still under debate and that in some ways goes beyond the scope of this book.

For the remaining 50 percent of the homeless population, however, housing is the most important issue. Nor can we completely discard the possibility that even people with serious personal problems can somehow be helped by better housing opportunities. Kim Hopper and Jill Hamberg, of the Community Service Society of New York, probably stated it best:

> [T]he problem is not primarily one of personal inadequacies . . . [D]einstitutionalization as an alternative to hospitalization ran into problems early on. But the faltering program crashed once the linchpin of affordable housing—however indecent it may have been—was pulled. The decisive factor that transformed the wretchedly quartered deinstitutionalized into the wandering deranged was—and remains—the depletion of the low-income housing stock. . . .
>
> Again, our argument is not that homelessness is a housing problem simply. Rather, it is that in the absence of housing, living circumstances that had been tenable—if but marginally so—become frankly desperate. The causes of contemporary homelessness, as we have shown, are multiple. But the determining factor that gives this form of impoverishment its distinctive imprint is the inability to secure housing.[3]

The best way to help the majority of the homeless, then, is to make housing more affordable and accessible. But what makes housing affordable? Housing activists argue that adequate housing can only be provided by the government. (The term "housing activist," in fact, will be used to refer to someone who believes the answer to housing problems lies in having the government provide housing.) Yet we have already seen that the amount of public housing in a community makes little or no difference to the rates of homelessness. On the other hand, the price of suburban homes makes an enormous difference—*even though these homes are far beyond the reach of homeless people.*

Thus, we have arrived at a key insight. Government action—at least in terms of public housing construction—does not seem to have much impact on the availability and affordability of housing. *Private* construction does. Now the question can be posed, what is it that has made private housing affordable in some cities and unaffordable in others and why does the pattern vary from city to city?

As a way of trying to get at this question, let us begin by looking at the first factor we discovered—the relationship between vacancy rates and rent control. As we saw, every city in the country with rent control has a vacancy rate below 3 percent while no city without rent control, except Worcester, has vacancies under 4 percent. Obviously, low vacancies and rent control go together. But which came first, the chicken or the egg?

The common response from advocates of rent control has been that rent control has been imposed in more than 200 cities since 1970 as a *response* to low vacancies. Writing in *The Progressive,* John Atlas and Peter Drier proclaim:

> By some twisted logic, [people who oppose rent control have] concluded that rent control causes homelessness.
>
> In fact, the reverse is true. When there is a severe housing shortage and low vacancy rates, rents begin to escalate. Low-income tenants get pushed into the streets and shelters. Those tenants who can hold on start to push for rent control.
>
> Arguing that rent control causes homelessness is like arguing that the sun comes up because the rooster crows.[4]

Yet arguing that low vacancies caused rent control is putting the cart before the horse. Without exception, all 200 cities that have adopted rent control imposed it as a result of *inflation,* not low vacancy rates. As Anthony Downs put it:

> [People] cannot retaliate against distant farmers or Arab oil sheiks who raise prices, but they can against their landlords. Immobile rental properties are easily made hostages of a local government sensitive to the desires of renting constituents.[5]

Every city that imposed rent control in the 1970s had a normal vacancy rate in the 1970 census. Ten years later, even though they had recently imposed rent control, many *still* had normal vacancies. Boston had a 7.5 rate, Newark 6.5, and Washington 5.9, while San Francisco had slipped to a still acceptable 4.1. Only Santa Monica (2.3 percent) and Berkeley (2.4 percent), which adopted rent control in 1979, already had abnormally low vacancies by 1980. This was because, as we shall see, both cities adopted particularly draconian ordinances that were part of an overall effort to prohibit new apartment construction.

In every city where rent control has been adopted, the regulatory action has *preceded* low vacancy rates. (Even New York City, which has had rent controls since 1943, had a 10 percent vacancy rate in 1940.) Nor were rents rising. As we have already seen, rents remained fairly level between 1967 and 1980 and only began climbing after 1981. Rent controls have been the *cause* of low vacancy rates, not the other way around.

The important lesson to learn is that *government regulations do not always do what they are intended to do*. Rent controls are adopted to "halt skyrocketing rents" and "make housing more affordable." Yet, as we shall explore at length in chapter 10, the invariable result is a housing "shortage" that drives prices up (usually through some loophole in the market) and makes housing unaffordable and unattainable for a growing segment of the population.

If the connection between rent control, vacancy rates, and homelessness seems fairly clear, what about the association between high home prices and homelessness? Once again, the response is that housing has become unaffordable because the government does not provide people with sufficient aid. Congress's response to the problem of affordable housing, for example, has been to explore further subsidies to help middle-class buyers purchase new homes. Yet no one has sufficiently explained why housing that was so affordable in the 1950s and 1960s suddenly became unaffordable in the 1980s.

One argument has been that prices have risen because in particularly desirable areas home builders have been unable to keep pace with the demand and therefore government intervention on behalf of new housing construction is required.

The cities that seem to be involved in this upward spiral are, once again, Boston, Hartford, New York, Washington, Los Angeles, and San Francisco. First, it must be admitted that, on the whole, these are all very desirable cities. San Francisco, because of its beauty and climate, is often considered the most livable city in the country. Boston is a hub of culture and education, while New York, despite the beating it takes in the press, is still the cultural center of the nation. Washington, of course, is attractive to anyone with political or policymaking ambitions, and Los Angeles, with its glamor and sunshine, is being touted as the "doorway to Asia" and the "city of the 21st century." It is easy to understand why demand for housing in these cities should be so high.

Yet that is not the whole story. After all, other cities that are equally desirable have not had the same housing problems. Philadelphia, America's fifth largest city, is a center of history and culture with a thriving job market. Chicago, America's third largest city and the hub of the Midwest, was recently dubbed as "America's Greatest City" by *The New Republic* magazine.[6] Houston, the fourth largest city, is the center of the oil industry and over the last two decades has been the fastest growing city in the nation. San Diego, the seventh largest city, has grown faster than Los Angeles, has better air, and has been the focal point of illegal Mexican immigration, which could be expected to contribute to homelessness.

The truth is that, despite the cultural attractions of San Francisco and Boston (the 12th and 19th largest cities in the nation), more people choose to live in Philadelphia, Chicago, Houston, and San Diego. Thus, it is not entirely apparent why, from demand alone, housing should be so much more expensive in Boston,

New York, and San Francisco, or for that matter in Hartford, Newark, and Berkeley, which have the same problems.

Let us try to unlock this puzzle by taking a good look at the metropolitan area that has become the most expensive and inaccessible housing market in the country—the San Francisco Bay and its surrounding counties.

In the early 1970s, housing prices in San Francisco were not out of line with the rest of California, which was itself not much out of line with the rest of the country. In 1972, the median price of a home nationwide was $31,900, while the median price in California was $32,400.[7] California had already experienced explosive growth over the 1960s, its population climbing 27 percent during the decade. Yet housing was still quite affordable.

In the early 1970s, however, a change in public attitudes developed. Instead of welcoming new development—as the state had done for decades—people began to resist it. Whereas suburban subdivisions spreading across the landscape were once viewed as proliferating symbols of the good life, now they became "little boxes on the hillside, little boxes made of ticky-tacky," (the words of a 1965 folk song).

Perhaps the best place to follow the evolution of these attitudes is in the once sleepy rural area of Marin County, right across the Golden Gate Bridge from San Francisco. Before the 1970s, Marin County was a picturesque region of rolling countryside with a few small towns strung along Route 101, which runs up the Bay shoreline. The inland area was sprinkled with dairy farms, while 50 miles of rugged cliffs and towering redwood groves overlooked the Pacific shoreline.

From 1960 to 1970, the population of Marin County grew only modestly, by California standards, from 149,000 to 210,000. By 1970, only 7 percent of the county's land area had been developed, while 50 percent was in agricultural use and 26 percent was in public ownership.[8]

Beginning in the late 1960s, however, the residents of Marin County began a campaign to prevent further suburban development. First, they persuaded the Federal government to purchase a large portion of the Pacific seashore for Point Reyes National Seashore and the Golden Gate National Recreational Area. Using Federal dollars, this protected large portions of the country from all future development.

A short time later, however, when the Federal and state governments started making plans to open these lands for recreational uses, Marin County residents decided they didn't want *that* kind of park in their area. When the state announced plans for a freeway connecting Route 101 with Point Reyes Park, residents blocked it on the grounds that its exits would become focal points of development. Five years later, when the Federal government proposed a limited-access highway with no exits, Marin residents blocked it again on the grounds that it would upset the local ecological balance. In the end, the two parks remained largely accessible only to Marin County residents via local roads.

Next came an effort to preserve the county's farmlands. As late as 1971, zoning laws still permitted farmers to sell off parcels in two-acre lots—a little larger than the traditional suburban home. In 1972, the law was changed to require *60-acre* lots. Farmers protested, arguing that they were being robbed of the use of their land. (As every real-estate agent will tell you, farmers are often the best land speculators around.) Yet, despite their protests, the law remained in place.

The concerns of Marin County preservationists for saving farmland, however, had its limits. Casting around for other ways to stop development, the activists discovered the Marin Municipal Water District, an obscure elected board traditionally dominated by farmers. In 1973, suburban residents won control of the board. The new majority immediately set about blocking new water sources on the grounds that it was the best way to prevent new development.[9]

Two years later, when California experienced a statewide drought, Marin County farmers found themselves trucking in water at enormous expense. Yet the drought was perfect for no-growth advocates. The water board declared a complete moratorium on new residential hook-ups, making new housing construction impossible. Enthusiasm for no-growth became so widespread that during the 1976 Bicentennial, citizens in the coastal town of Bolinas set up roadblocks, telling vacationers to please turn back because their presence was threatening the parched local ecology.[10]

As a result of all these strategies, Marin County has been almost completely successful in staving off new suburban growth, even though it lies within easy commuting distance of San Francisco. Municipalities now routinely require 20-acre lots for new homes.

Not incidentally, the few homes that have been built have become enormously expensive. Whereas in 1970, the median home in Marin County cost $33,000, by 1980 it had climbed to $151,000, a 500 percent increase that ran far ahead of the inflation rate. Today, the median home costs $224,000, the highest in the country. Through a combination of zoning restrictions, blocked highway construction, weakened municipal services, and other strategies, Marin County has turned itself into perhaps the most exclusive suburban residential area in the nation.

But notice that none of this has done much harm to the people who already lived in Marin County in 1970, or who have been wealthy enough to move there since then. Controlled growth and exclusionary zoning only work against outsiders and *future* residents. For people already established in the environment, no-growth is a powerful strategy for *raising the prices of their homes.* The only fly in the ointment is local property taxes, and, as we shall see, this has pretty much been taken care of by California's Proposition 13 property tax reform. Meanwhile, suburban development has been forced to leapfrog into nearby Sonoma County.

This process of improving one's property values by blocking new development has certainly not been limited to Marin County. Indeed, the whole San Francisco area has been overflowing with no-growth sentiment since the early 1970s. One of the leading practitioners has been the City of San Francisco itself, which first limited apartment construction, then tried to undo the damage by imposing rent control. Neighboring Oakland, San Jose, and Berkeley have done the same thing.

As a result, builders put up only 2,000 new housing units in San Francisco in 1986, while Dallas, which already had a surplus of housing, got 10,000. Rental vacancies have descended to a miniscule 1.8 percent, the lowest in the nation. New luxury apartments have four-year waiting lists before they are even completed. San Francisco has also imposed severe limits on office construction, allowing the equivalent of only one new office building to be built each year. In 1988, *The Wall Street Journal* told the story of a house-hunting San Francisco couple who ended up looking at a $200,000 converted boxcar. "It wasn't even cute," said the dismayed young bride.[11]

The worsening housing shortage and the accompanying rise in homelessness in San Francisco raises an almost daily cry for the government to supply "affordable housing." Yet herein lies a paradox. While everybody wants affordable housing, nobody particularly wants it in their neighborhood. In fact, they don't want *any* new housing if it is going to be near them. Plans may be considered to house the homeless in converted lighthouses, abandoned army bases, perhaps even in portable wooden homes that are now selling on the streets of San Francisco for $20 apiece. Yet when it comes to laying bricks or nailing boards together on small plots of urban or suburban land, everyone objects that new housing will "ruin the quality of life in our neighborhood."

Thus, the San Francisco area has become the most expensive housing market in the country. In 1984, median home prices were $129,000—the second-highest in the country. Three years later they had climbed another *75 percent,* to $206,000, easily outdistancing second-place New York at $186,000.

Government management of the housing economy has been practiced more intensely in San Francisco than anywhere else in the United States. In fact, while all this was going on, urban planners, housing activists, and growth-control enthusiasts were holding up San Francisco as a model for the rest of the nation. Yet all this government intervention had only made the city and region the hardest place in the country to find a place to live—as its large homeless populations affirm.

What has happened in the San Francisco area on a large scale has been happening on a more modest scale everywhere else as well. The truth is that housing has become one of the most highly regulated industries in the nation. This regulation tends to escape notice because it is administered at the county and municipal level, rather than the state or Federal level. But the results have been just the same. If General Motors had to negotiate separately with every little planning and zoning board around the country before it sold cars, we would have an "auto shortage" as well.

On a single Sunday in May 1989, *The New York Times* real-estate page carried two stories about new opposition to development. The first told how the Natural Resources Defense Council, the Municipal Art Society, the Astor Foundation, and other blue-blooded groups, were organizing to block new construction almost everywhere in New York City. "Neighborhoods are going to the barricades," said Philip Howard, a board member of the Municipal Art Society.[12] (A month later, the same groups proposed a plan for major zoning and planning restrictions in New York based on the model of San Francisco!)[13]

The second story told how environmental groups in Suffolk County, at the eastern end of Long Island, were girding to prevent a development of 307 single-family homes in a remote wooded area. The development would cut into "not just the heart, but the right aorta of the pine barrens," said Steven Englebright, of the Suffolk County Legislature.[14]

The very next week, another story told of how residents in Queens were upset because older single-family homes were being torn down to make room for small apartment houses. "We are seeing neighborhoods that are more suburban in character turning more urban," complained Sandy Hornick, zoning director for the New York Department of City Planning. "As you move away from mass transit you become more dependent on the automobile, so you have to spread the housing out more to accommodate cars."[15]

So if new housing is inappropriate among the skyscrapers of Manhattan, the pine barrens of Long Island, and the suburban neighborhoods of Queens, where then can it be built?

Perhaps the best way to get some perspective on the situation is to look back for a moment at the nation's housing situation in the late 1960s, before the ethos of opposing new development took hold. Although it is hard to remember, the major national problem in 1968 was a *surplus* of housing. It went under the general term of "urban blight."

At the time, the major cities had essentially been emptied of most of their long-time residents. The middle class had moved to the suburbs, leaving most older urban housing in the hands of small ethnic communities and blacks who had migrated recently from the South. Much of this housing was still sound stock. Yet through a combination of poor maintenance and neglect, it was in danger of being lost well before its useful life was completed.

Urban experts from all over the country were summoned to Washington to study the problem. Almost without exception, they came to the same conclusion—there was *too much housing* available in urban neighborhoods. Because vacancy rates were so high and urban rental markets so soft, building owners could not charge enough rents to keep up their properties.

In 1965, George Sternlieb, who was then emerging as perhaps the country's leading housing expert, was commissioned by the Federal Urban Renewal Administration to study Newark's slums with an eye toward stemming urban blight. Sternlieb emerged from the task somewhat pessimistic. "Vacancy rates in the hard-core slums are increasing sharply, with larger scale landlords being hardest hit," he wrote in *The Tenement Landlord.*[16] In some neighborhoods, vacancies were as high as 18 percent. (These figures were gathered *before* the 1967 Newark riots, which depopulated much of the city.)

With such high vacancies, Sternlieb said, landlords were unable to charge high enough rents to justify rehabilitating their properties. In addition, the high vacancies made tenants far more casual about falling behind in the rent or damaging property, since they knew they could always find another place to live. At one point Sternlieb even speculated that the pending large-scale demolition of one neighborhood for highway construction might improve the situation by reducing the overabundance of cheap housing.

In his 1973 book, *Opening Up the Suburbs,* Anthony Downs came to essentially the same conclusions. Slums would be difficult to contain, he said, because there was too much housing available:

> [E]very net increase in a metropolitan area's housing supply relative to its housing demand tends to "loosen" its entire housing market—not just where new construction is occurring. In addition, available vacancies eventually become concentrated in the oldest and worst housing. The owners of better quality units keep adjusting their rents and prices [downward] to attract occupants. It is true that ethnic segregation impedes unrestricted movement of many economically capable households upward through the existing inventory. Yet large net housing supply increases in predominantly white areas soon affect conditions in nearby mainly nonwhite areas too. Thus the spreading of crisis ghetto [Downs' term for urban blight] in older inner-city areas is made possible—even encouraged—whenever there is enough *net* new housing

> construction within the metropolitan area to increase area-wide vacancy significantly. [Emphasis in original.][17]

Thus, the most notable feature of the cities in the late 1960s and early 1970s was the oversupply of housing available to the poor. This housing was not always in the best condition and decay was certainly a problem. But *homelessness and housing shortages were the furthest thing from anyone's mind.* It was the overabundance of cheap housing that made the spread of urban blight appear inevitable.

The tide of urban blight was soon stemmed by something called "gentrification." During the 1970s, a trickle of middle-class people began moving back into the city, buying up abandoned buildings and rehabilitating them with their own money and effort. Gentrification has been a kind of private urban renewal, accomplished without the powers of condemnation that made the Federal urban renewal so widely resented in the 1950s and 1960s. Gentrifiers are often called "urban pioneers," a term *The New York Times* once noted was not entirely inappropriate for young couples who often slept for months in vacant, unheated buildings in order to make sure the new plumbing and wiring they had installed was not stolen at night. Since the 1970s, gentrification has mushroomed into a broad-scale revival that has rescued many old residential areas.[18]

It is somewhat ironic that this small, unsubsidized effort to stem urban blight is frequently blamed for causing homelessness. As George Sternlieb and James Hughes point out, gentrification "certainly has affected parts of some cities, but the statistics show that it is a miniscule trend compared with the other forces affecting cities."[19] Its main economic base has been the surplus of sound housing that seemed doomed to abandonment in many city neighborhoods.

Far overshadowing this downtown revival has been the general resistance to new housing in other areas of most metropolitan markets. As Anthony Downs noted in 1973, new housing anywhere will soon provide vacancies in the worst slum neighborhood. By the same token, choking off new construction will tighten the market for everyone, pushing up prices and making housing unavailable for the poor.

James W. Rouse, the noted Baltimore developer and chairman of the National Task Force on Housing, described the predicament this way in his 1988 testimony before Congress:

> The people who might be moving into [new] housing for sale or moving into rental housing left behind [by new buyers] are pushing down into housing that would be occupied by lower income families. And those people are . . . being pushed out to become the homeless.[20]

What has produced this choking off of new housing supplies? Higher interest rates have obviously pushed new housing starts off their all-time peak in 1971–72. Shrinking supplies of available land have also had some effect. Equally problematic has been the quasi-monopoly of building trade unions, which put up barriers to cost-cutting methods and new technologies that would lower housing prices. Cheaper plastic pipes, for example, have long been blocked by the plumbing industry. But the biggest impediment to new construction has been the growing determination of municipalities to make it as difficult and expensive as possible to put up new housing within their borders.

In a nine-part study of housing costs undertaken in 1989 by *The Newark Star-Ledger,* the newspaper concluded that "it is not the value of labor and building materials that are pushing the average price of homes beyond many, but rather the uncontrolled growth of a massive and costly system of regulation and bureaucracy, much of which has been found to be wasteful."[21] *The Star-Ledger* estimated that as much as 35 percent of the cost of a new house in New Jersey is now due to regulation.

East Coast developer Ara K. Hovnanian, a builder of low-cost suburban housing, told *The Star-Ledger* he can build a four-bedroom house in any major North Carolina market for $95,000, getting through regulatory approval in three months. In New Jersey, the same house will cost $230,000 and take three years of regulatory review—with much greater risk that it will never be approved at all. It is not surprising that housing prices are low and homelessness less common in areas where regulation is restrained, while prices are high and homelessness much more serious in regions where the regulation of housing has been much more intense.

The situation is illustrated even more clearly in California, where growth controls and regulatory requirements have now been supplemented by "impact fees," which attempt to shift the costs of general community services onto new residents. A side-effect of Proposition 13 (which, as we shall see, did much more than just lower property taxes), impact fees have become one more way in which established residents shift their costs onto outsiders and newcomers, with the result that housing becomes more expensive for people trying to get into the market.

As a good example of how affordable housing is affected by restrictive building and zoning regulations, take the case of prefabricated housing and mobile homes.

Ever since World War I, housing analysts have been predicting that home-building would be put on the assembly line, with factory-made parts stamped out for assembly on building sites. During the Nixon administration, HUD Secretary George Romney, an enthusiast of mass-production, spearheaded "Operation

Breakthrough," a national effort to get the prefabricated-housing industry off the ground.

It failed miserably. Building and zoning departments in local municipalities, as well as trade unions, were able to block it. For the unions, it meant losing jobs to factory workers. For the local municipalities, it meant allowing "little boxes made of ticky-tacky" to be built within their borders. Prefabricated homes, after all, are "low-income housing," with all the negative implications.

Mobile homes have suffered much the same fate. These factory built units, which now average 950 square feet, have long been recognized as the most accessible form of home-ownership for low-income people. In 1988 a standard mobile home sold for $18,400, compared to $78,000 for a free-standing home. Almost 60 percent of all mobile-home owners earn under $20,000.

Although few people realize it, 25 percent of the new homes sold each year are mobile homes. They are particularly popular in the South and the West, where 80 percent of the units are placed. During the early 1980s, the number of mobile-home placements in the South exceeded the number of housing starts in the entire Northeast.[22]

Yet once again, the trend has been toward excluding this type of housing. The low availability of mobile homes in the Northeast is entirely the result of zoning restrictions. "There's an historic image of a trailer home as an undesirable, low-income phenomenon," said Welford Sanders, associate director of research at the American Planning Association. "In many communities, mobile homes are restricted to industrial zones—if they are allowed at all."

In James Rouse's *Report of the National Housing Task Force* on affordable housing, mobile homes were completely ignored. Complained Jeffrey Hire, of Owens Corning Fiberglass, which services mobile homes, "As people talk about solutions to the low-income housing problem, nowhere can you find any mention of manufactured housing—I mean nowhere."[23]

Thus, it is in no way fair or accurate to say that the housing industry cannot produce low-income housing. The industry is strong and versatile enough to produce just about anything people want.[24] The problem is where to *put* the housing. The bottleneck is at the municipal level, where communities have decided they don't want new housing, particularly housing of a low-income cast. These exclusionary practices now essentially determine what happens in the housing market.

So the high home prices and the low vacancy rates in certain important cities can be directly attributed to local government intervention in the housing market. But what about the association with minority populations that shows up in the regression analysis? How does that relate to homelessness?

Racial discrimination and exclusionary zoning, of course, are no strangers. Many housing experts have long argued that keeping low-income minorities out of suburban communities has been the primary aim of exclusionary zoning. All this attracted quite a bit of attention from scholars during the early 1970s. Academic critics like Anthony Downs and Michael Danielson, professor of government at Princeton University, argued that suburban zoning restrictions aimed at low-income minorities could end up causing a general housing shortage.[25] Yet now that those shortages have materialized, much of this earlier criticism has been forgotten.

The correlation between minority populations and homelessness might suggest that racial discrimination has forced minorities to look for housing in certain limited areas. As housing markets have tightened during the 1980s, this has produced high prices and homelessness.

But there is another possible explanation as well. It could be that many communities have become *more* resistant to new housing precisely because they fear that any new housing—particularly low-income housing—will be occupied by blacks and minorities.

The anticipation that any cheap housing will soon be occupied by blacks and minorities never seems far from the minds of suburban municipal officials. As we shall see, this fear has often been greatly exaggerated. Yet this constant anxiety obviously plays a large part in suburban zoning policies. Its results can be seen in the recent wave of "affordable-housing" programs, in which suburban jurisdictions abstemiously dole out tiny numbers of subsidized housing units to people who are usually well established—and frequently well-connected—in the community and could often afford the housing without help. These programs have been one of the more ludicrous outcomes of government management of the housing economy.

It should be emphasized, however, that fear of low-income blacks and other minorities is not the only thing that has motivated exclusionary programs. The unfortunate truth is that residents of any community can improve the value of their homes and turn their community into an exclusive enclave by practicing exclusionary zoning. It is this use of the political system to gain unearned advantages that lies at the heart of the housing problem.

Chapter 5

How the Housing Market Works

People visiting Harlem for the first time are always stunned by the beauty of the buildings. Expecting to find a slum, they are instead confronted with street after street of magnificent old brownstones with solid foundations, sturdy facades, and exquisite details. Granted, the windows of many of these buildings are now sealed with cinder blocks, the ominous message, "Property of the City of New York, Department of Housing Preservation and Development," stenciled on their walls. But as far as potential is concerned, the houses of Harlem are among the most beautiful ever built in America.

A similar surprise awaits people who visit Watts, the Los Angeles neighborhood that was the site of the 1966 riots. Once again, a neighborhood that is supposed to be a crowded ghetto turns out to be—from all appearances, at least—a placid middle-class suburb. The houses are relatively spacious, with wide lawns, neatly carved driveways, and an abundance of two-car garages.

These observations raise an obvious question. Were Harlem and Watts originally built as slums? Were they built for the poor at all? The answer, of course, is, no. They were actually built for more affluent people—Harlem for the Victorian gentry, Watts for the middle class of the 1940s. Only through a series of historical transformations did these buildings end up serving the poor—serving them quite well for a long time.

The lesson is a crucial one. In most urban areas, *housing occupied by the poor today was not originally built to be poor people's housing*. It was often built as middle-class or luxury housing. Only after a long series of demographic changes did it end up in the hands of poor people. This process is generally called "filtering."

The filtering system in the housing market is often compared to the workings of the automobile market. Ask yourself for a moment, what is a poor man's car? Is it a Ford or Chevrolet, the cars at the bottom of the price line? That might seem sensible, until you remember that the price of the cheapest Ford or Chevrolet in 1989 was $5,500. Even the spartan Yugo (before the company filed for bankruptcy in 1989) sold for $4,400. Moreover, these are all tiny compact models. The cheapest family car—a two-door Chevrolet Celebrity—sold for $10,600.

Nor is it likely that even families with the median income can afford brand new cars. According to *Newsweek's Annual Buyers of New Cars,* buyers of new cars in 1989 had a median household income of $41,000, significantly above the national median income of $30,000.[1]

So why doesn't somebody build a nice cheap car that the poor, or at least the lower-middle class, can afford? This has actually been tried several times. In 1945, Powell Crosley, the Cincinnati radio manufacturer, introduced the Crosley, a small, cramped car that could get 50 miles to the gallon and sold for $850. The Crosley ran on an engine not much bigger than a lawnmower and could barely accelerate to 50 miles an hour. Still, it was practical transportation.

It also failed miserably. Low-income people weren't interested, because they had a very attractive alternative—the used-car market. People preferred a solid, well-built second-hand car to a new car built to minimal standards.

The average car sold today has a life expectancy of 10.9 years. Yet the average first owner keeps a car for only 5.3 years. When a car is sold to its second owner it still has more than half its life ahead of it. The price, meanwhile, has been cut in half. The average car goes through four owners before it reaches the junkyard. Each owner is progressively poorer and pays progressively less.

Cheaper new cars do not necessarily serve lower-income people. Volkswagens, for example, rarely made it to the bottom of the heap because their frugal owners kept them so long. (Buyers of imported cars have slightly higher incomes and keep their cars slightly longer.) The better a car is built, the longer it will last. The longer it lasts, the more likely it will eventually serve the poor. That is why the well-built Cadillac is often called a "poor man's car."

What is true in the auto market, where the average product lasts eleven years, is even more true in the housing market, where the average home can be expected to last 75 years.

In 1988, the median price for a new home was $112,000. In order to buy that home (at 10 percent interest rates), a family needed an income of $50,000. The median "used" home, however, went for $89,000, requiring an income of $40,000.

Once again, it is obvious that poor people cannot buy new homes. Nor are they able to rent newly constructed apartments. But the average American moves every six years. After 60 years the average housing unit will have had ten occupants. The older a building becomes, the less affluent its owners are likely to be.

Another dimension to this filtering process is that large houses, originally built as single households, are often eventually cut up into apartments, offering low-income people cheaper housing on a rental basis. The process is one of the most common in our urban history. It has often been condemned by reformers who decried the creation of "tenements." Yet this recycling of housing serves an obvious purpose, as does the next step in the process, the "rooming" or "boarding house." It provides poor people with cheap housing.

Critics of the housing market often fail to appreciate this process. They argue that developers "only build for the rich and not for the poor." Yet that is not the point. The important thing is that when developers put up new homes, affluent people leave older housing behind. This housing, in turn, is occupied by the less affluent. Moreover, the better new housing is built, the more likely it will eventually filter down to people with low incomes. The best strategy for improving the overall housing stock is to build new housing and let it circulate.

Although the filtration process was long posited as a standard principle of the housing market, its actual workings were not observed closely until 1966, when a small study was undertaken by John Lansing, C. Clifton, and J. Morgan, at the University of Michigan's Institute for Social Research. Their slim, 70-page volume, *New Homes and Poor People,* has become a small classic in the field of economics.[2]

Lansing, Clifton, and Morgan began by randomly identifying 1,000 homes built during late 1965 and early 1966 in 17 major metropolitan areas around the country, including New York, Chicago, Los Angeles, Baltimore, St. Louis, Trenton, Atlanta, and San Diego. The authors sent out a team of researchers to interview the first occupants of these new homes. After recording the occupants' incomes and other social characteristics, the researchers asked for the addresses of their former residences. The researchers then went back and interviewed the people who had just moved into those recently vacated houses. As if reconstructing a row of fallen dominoes, the researchers traced back each individual chain of moves until they arrived at an end point.

The results of this painstaking research proved fascinating. For the 1,000 new homes constructed, the authors found, a grand total of 3,545 vacancies were eventually created. On average, each new unit produced a chain of 3.5 more vacant units. More than 10 percent of the chains extended for seven or more moves and one chain went on for 19 moves.

The results also showed that, while people buying or renting the new homes or apartments clearly had incomes well above the median, the chain quickly spread down to people with considerably lower incomes. The mean price of all new freestanding homes in the study was $25,900, while the mean rent for newly constructed apartments was $135. Yet by the time a chain had reached the fourth position, the mean price of the home was $17,300—below the mean price of $17,900 for the 17 metropolitan areas. The mean rent in the fourth position was $95, just above the mean rent of $75 in all 17 metropolitan areas.

Most interesting was that out of the 3,545 vacancies created (1,000 in new homes plus 2,545 in older units), nine percent—333 units—were filled by people *below* the poverty line. From position 3 onward, poor people were slightly *overrepresented,* claiming 14 percent of the vacancies while making up only 13 percent of the national population. For every three units of new construction, one vacancy opened up for someone below the poverty line.

The authors concluded that the filtering process does work:

> The working of the market for housing is such that the poor will benefit from any actions which increase the supply in the total market. There is a natural tendency for someone who is concerned with the provision of housing for the poor to take a direct approach. To provide housing for people, hand them the key to the door of a home! The evidence in this research is that the direct approach is not the only approach which will be effective. The housing market . . . operates as a single market. Any policy which shifts either the demand curve or the supply curve in the market will affect the price in the total market.[3]

Investigating further, the authors tried to determine exactly what kind of new housing worked best in providing vacant units for the poor. Again, the results proved fascinating.

The authors divided the newly constructed units into four categories, expensive single-family homes (priced over $25,000), cheaper single-family homes (under

$25,000), expensive apartments (over $150 a month rent), and cheaper apartments (under $150). They found that, for both homes and apartments, the most expensive housing produced the longest chains:[4]

Characteristic	*Length of chain in moves*
Homes over $25,000	4.50
Homes under $25,000	3.83
Apartment over $150	3.90
Apartments under $150	2.40

The figures might be taken to indicate that free-standing homes produce the longest chains. But apartments also start further down the income scale. So the authors also compared the four different categories to see how many vacancies each opened for people below the poverty line:

Characteristic	*Number of vacancies for poor people per 1,000 new units*
Homes over $25,000	323
Homes under $25,000	366
Apartment over $150	252
Apartments under $150	270

New *houses* in both categories did much better than *apartments* in both categories, with cheaper homes doing the best. This advantage may be somewhat offset, however, in that apartments can be built to greater densities.

At the same time, the authors admitted, the pattern they were observing in 1966 might not be universal. In particular, they noted that, while Americans were presumed to be having a love affair with the single-family home, fully 55 percent of the building permits selected at random in the 17 metropolitan areas were for rental apartments.

What they were observing, the authors concluded, was a process that might be called "decongestion":

> The explanation must be sought . . . in such factors as the changing proportion of the population at different stages in the family life cycle and the effect of rising incomes on people's ability to maintain separate dwellings. . . .
>
> We suggest that the time of the survey was a period of rising demand for separate dwellings for people who earlier had not been able to maintain homes of their own.

> There was an increase in what is sometimes called the "headship rate," i.e., in the proportion of adults who are heads of their own units. . . . We would expect that, when the headship rate stabilizes, as it must eventually, the sequences initiated by new apartments will become longer.[5]

This phenomenon, which received almost no attention at the time, is instructive in showing how the housing market tends to go about its business meeting people's needs without any centralized direction. There was no talk during the Great Society era about the need for increasing headship rates by building new apartments. Yet builders did it anyway, because that's what people wanted. As a result, George Sternlieb and James Hughes could write fifteen years later:

> [A] concurrent phenomenon [from the past decade] has been the vast reduction in overcrowding. . . . The number of units occupied by seven or more persons, for example, was reduced by 45 percent in a brief seven-year period [from 1970 to 1977]; units occupied by six-person groups was reduced by 28.6 percent; and those units with five or more persons by 17.4 percent. . . . In sum . . . the age old vision of overcrowding, while still leaving a remnant, has largely been overcome.[6]

There was one flaw in the market, however, relating to race. At almost every stage in the process, blacks were significantly underrepresented. "Negroes actually occupy something less than .61 of the new homes that one would expect them to occupy on the basis of their income," wrote the authors. Blacks also made up only 70 percent of the expected number in the chain of subsequent moves.

Only 33 percent of the blacks in the survey purchased homes, compared to 52 percent of the whites. Inversely, blacks rented more apartments—57 percent to 42 percent. Blacks were also more frequent purchasers of two- and three-family homes—10 percent versus six percent for whites. Purchasing a multi-family home in which the rental income helps pay the mortgage is, as we shall see, a common strategy for achieving homeownership among lower-income buyers.

The authors attributed this underrepresentation of blacks to "discrimination in the housing market and Negroes' low average assets." Discrimination, although obviously present, was difficult to quantify. In terms of finances, blacks had incomes only 60 percent that of whites. An even more devastating disadvantage lay in their lack of assets. Blacks' net worth averaged only *one-fifth* that of whites ($15,900 vs. $2,900). "It is obvious that a Negro couple seeking to buy a new home is likely to have difficulty raising a large down payment. They themselves may not have the needed capital, and they may not be able to obtain it by such expedients as borrowing from their parents."[8]

The authors also found that chains of moves that involved blacks tended to be shorter. They took this to indicate that many blacks were moving out of housing that was already overcrowded or deteriorating. Often, units left by blacks remained vacant, indicating it was deteriorating housing.

Overall, the conclusion of *New Homes and Poor People* was that, except for the problems of racial discrimination, there is a single housing market.

> We should not conclude from this analysis that the poor are well-provided (or ill-provided) with housing. Nor should we conclude that the price of housing is or is not reasonable. We *can* conclude that the poor are indirectly affected by the construction of new housing even if they do not occupy the new dwellings.[9]

The chains of vacancies created by new units is not the only important cycle in the housing market. Another is the way people's individual needs change as they age.

When young people first leave home and form an independent household, either alone or by marrying, they almost always begin by renting. They will probably move to a city or metropolitan area to be closer to social life and the job market.

Most young people do not start thinking about homeownership until they marry. At that point, the old adages about "two can live as cheaply as one" and "you won't end up with just a bunch of rent slips" begin to make sense. Their first purchase is likely to be a "starter home"—a condominium or a small, lower-priced single-family home.

A lower-income family is likely to start with a two- or three-family house in one of the older "streetcar suburbs." Multi-family houses were built more commonly in the earlier part of the century and probably remain one of the most overlooked resources in the housing market. They are particularly beneficial in that they are usually built to higher densities, offer homeownership to working-class families, and provide rental housing as well. Unfortunately, they have been largely curbed by more recent zoning efforts.

In two- or three-family homes, close relatives will often occupy adjoining apartments—parents downstairs and married children upstairs, or sometimes brothers or sisters in co-ownership. Ownership of a multi-family home also commonly serves as retirement security for older people.

For the more affluent middle class, however, homeownership is more likely to mean a detached home in the suburbs. After children arrive, a community with good schools becomes particularly important. As the couple improves their income, they may make several moves to bigger homes or to more child-oriented communities. By the time they are in their 40s and 50s, an upper-middle-class couple will probably own a relatively large home in the suburbs with plenty of room for teenage children.

Then the cycle starts to wind down. The children leave home. The couple grows older and their income levels off. They may find themselves presiding over an empty nest (unless their children move back in, which is becoming more common as housing becomes less affordable). The house will become too big for them. Raking leaves will be an onerous chore. Their high property taxes will pay for schools their children no longer attend. At this point, the aging couple may consider something more practical—a retirement village, a smaller home in the Sunbelt, even a condominium back in the city.

The housing market is always accommodating changes in people's life cycles, as well as their climb up the economic ladder. The average person moves every six years, while life expectancy is now 75 years of age. As a result, the average person can expect to occupy more than 12 homes in a lifetime.

The two key factors to a healthy housing market are a steadily expanding supply of new housing and the continued circulation of this housing. This constant mobility of Americans has often led to criticism that we do not put down roots and have become a "nation of strangers." Yet changing homes does not mean changing neighborhoods. If a community can tolerate all kinds of housing—starter homes and condominiums for young couples, smaller apartments for retired people—then it should not be necessary for people to leave the community as their housing needs change.

Of course, filtration is a long-range strategy for building up the country's housing stock. It cannot work as well in newer areas where there is less older housing available. For this reason, there have always been efforts to build poor-people's housing as well.

During the 19th century, the greatest effort was made by private companies constructing company housing. In Bethlehem, Pennsylvania, for example, Bethlehem Steel constructed several large housing complexes for its steelworkers in the early part of this century. The housing was in functional brick buildings. Workers generally received low rent as part of their salary. The Marvine and Pembroke complexes—which included several hundred apartments—were eventually taken over by the Bethlehem Public Housing Authority, as was another temporary project, South Terrace, put up for steelworkers by the Federal government during World War II. All these units were eventually torn down.

Other Pennsylvania coal and steel towns also had large company-housing complexes, as did other planned industrial communities like Lowell, Lawrence, and Holyoke, Massachusetts. Some of this housing still survives today.

Since 1937, most housing specifically built for low-income people has been sponsored by the Federal government. Besides the construction of new units by the public housing authorities, there have been various shallow-subsidy programs like the 235 and 236 programs of the late 1960s and the section-8 new construction program that was tied to housing certificates. (This program was virtually eliminated during the Reagan administration.)

The difficulty with building housing for the poor is that it often ends up being poor housing. Built with cheaper materials to minimal standards, it is often not expected to last a long time. Most company housing was of notoriously poor quality and the episode is generally remembered as one of squalor in American housing history. The same limitations apply to mobile homes, which have a life expectancy of only 20 years. It is precisely because their long-term value is limited that they sell relatively cheaply.

So it is as well with other forms of utilitarian housing. In his 1972 book, *Opening Up the Suburbs,* Anthony Downs proposed that apartments of 550 square feet, the size of a four-family unit in Moscow, could be built in the suburbs at a price that would be accessible to low-income groups.[10] (The Federal Housing Administration requires 850 square feet for two bedrooms.) Reforming such housing laws, he argued, would allow central-city residents to be dispersed. (Downs' book is a proposal to break up the ghettoes by scattering their population into middle-class neighborhoods.)

Yet once again, such an extreme solution may not really be necessary. In a perfectly free housing market, the countryside would not become covered with mobile-home parks. Nor would utilitarian, Soviet-style apartment complexes (which often make American public housing look good) march across the landscape. In effect, company housing and mobile homes serve as a transitional stage, before sufficient good housing becomes available. In a perfectly free market, the housing industry would probably produce just what most Americans want—large apartments and single-family homes big enough for the average family.

Public housing was also conceived as transitional, temporary housing when it was first adopted in 1937. Since then, however, it has become a more permanent part of the landscape.

Public housing's problems have been the same as those of company housing: poor construction materials, low building standards, and lack of durability.

In Chicago's Robert Taylor Homes, for example, the world's largest housing project, construction costs were reduced by putting the hallways on the *outside* of the buildings, only half-enclosed by a steel mesh. (Residents have named them "the galleries," after similar pedestrian tiers in prisons.) People must endure freezing temperatures when walking between apartments during the winter. In addition, parents are always scrambling to prevent toddlers from climbing the mesh and toppling a dozen stories to the ground. The galleries have also become convenient launching pads for bottles, television sets, even refrigerators.[11] While public housing has absorbed a large number of families who would otherwise have difficulty finding housing in the private market, it has not always constituted a long-lasting addition to the nation's housing stock—as the current wave of abandonments and demolitions indicates.

Where public housing can sometimes be justified—and criticized as well—is where it has become "black people's housing," the only real accommodations available to lower-class blacks. In a recent twelve-part series entitled, "The Chicago Wall," *The Chicago Tribune* documented how the administration of Mayor Richard Daley effectively segregated Chicago by building a "wall" of expressways separating white neighborhoods (including Mayor Daley's own) and a vast, four-mile stretch of public-housing complexes that is occupied almost entirely by blacks.

> The wall stretches north and south through the heart of the city, roughly parallel to the lakefront. It includes the nation's largest concentration of public housing, some of its busiest expressways, the Chicago River, railroad yards and the "L." [It is] a physical barrier of brick and steel and concrete that separates black from white, rich from poor, hope from despair.[12]

In one sense, the city government had shown some concern by spending hundreds of millions of dollars to build and maintain housing that was expected to be occupied almost entirely by blacks. On the other hand, this money was probably spent in the specific hope that blacks would not crowd into white neighborhoods.

The relationship between racial discrimination and housing has been a complex one. Several studies have found that, while blacks are usually restricted to certain "ghetto" areas, they often pay relatively low rents within these areas, since they are insulated from competition with whites.

After the Washington Park area of Boston underwent urban renewal in 1964, a team of researchers from Brandeis University tried to figure out why middle-class black families had refused to leave the neighborhood, even when the Boston Urban Renewal Administration offered to find them homes in the suburbs. The research team discovered that rents and home prices in the neighborhood were remarkably low, absorbing only 12 percent of the median family's income.[13]

Sociologist Herbert Gans found the same situation in 1963 when he studied

Boston's West End, an Italian enclave about to undergo urban renewal. Because the neighborhood was essentially closed to outsiders and because it contained plenty of older housing, rents were far below the citywide median of $75.

> [P]eople were so used to paying low rents that their whole mode of life was adjusted to them. Any apartment that rented for more than $50 for five or six rooms was thought to be outrageously expensive. Thus, when people had to start looking for new dwellings, they had difficulty in realigning their expenditures to the rent levels outside the West End.[14]

It seems possible that the adverse effects of gentrification have not been an actual loss of housing, but a breakdown of these informal barriers, which has forced low-income people to compete with more affluent people for housing.

In his 1967 study of Newark, George Sternlieb noted that discrimination against blacks usually took place in marginal areas where blacks and whites competed for the same housing. Both black and white landlords preferred white tenants, he found, judging them more reliable in paying rent and less likely to damage apartments. Consequently, landlords tended to give rent breaks to white tenants in the hope of retaining them. Sternlieb found whites often paid 25 percent less than blacks for virtually identical apartments.[15]

An additional problem was that whites were not usually disposed toward sharing apartment buildings with blacks. "If you're going to turn a building, you might as well turn it all at once because you're not going to keep the white people," one experienced landlord told Sternlieb. Landlords often reached a point where, instead of trying to hang onto white tenants, they quickly "turned" a building over to black tenants, trading reliability for higher rents.

The same dynamic applied to homeownership. Discrimination, Sternlieb found, did not always involve real-estate brokers "steering" black buyers into black neighborhoods. Instead, realtors would often show blacks and whites the same home but subtly raise the price to black buyers. This was regarded as a premium against the expectation that, once a certain number of black families moved onto a street, "white flight" would occur and housing prices would fall.

This frequently led to a phenomenon called "blockbusting." Although generally remembered as a disreputable real-estate tactic, blockbusting—it should be recalled—was essentially a way of opening up new housing opportunities for blacks.

A "blockbusting" real-estate agent would frighten white homeowners into selling at bargain prices by warning them that blacks were moving into the neighborhood. The realtor would hope to profit by reselling the homes to blacks at market prices. Another common technique was for realtors to buy single-family homes at "scare" prices and then subdivide the buildings into apartments, renting them to blacks.

This process, of course, has been one of the most common means by which housing filters down the economic scale. Although it may have created racial animosities, or been built on those animosities, it also made economic sense. It is revealing that techniques for preventing blockbusting usually involved deliberate plans to "sell to whites only" or otherwise retain a neighborhood's "racial balance."

In the end, the issue of racial discrimination goes beyond the issue of housing. It might be easy enough to make a few pompous pronouncements about how ending bias and discrimination would solve a good portion of the housing problem and leave us all living in a better world. In the abstract, this is undoubtedly true. Yet time and again, what has been called "racial bias" and "discrimination" has proved to be the simple and unbiased objections of middle-class people to the often violent and criminal behavior of the lower class.

In *The Making of a Slum,* written in 1972, Michael Dorman, a New York journalist and author, recounted the rapid deterioration of his old Bronx neighborhood, Hunt's Point, in which his family had lived for three generations.[16]

During the 1940s and 1950s, Dorman wrote, Hunt's Point had been "a garden spot of pleasant middle-class homes with verdant back yards—a pastoral setting where people of many national origins and religions lived together in tranquility."[17] Germans, Italians, Irish, Jews, middle-class blacks—all lived side-by-side in bewildering variety. "Nobody ever locked their doors," he recalled. One of the few regular disturbances was caused by the local boy scout troop practicing its emergency-service drills that trained the scouts "to carry out rescue missions . . . and to help policemen and firemen at disaster scenes."[18]

Ten years later, after low-income Puerto Ricans and blacks had taken over the neighborhood, one in four adult males was a heroin addict. A survey of one area showed that residents had only one chance in twenty of dying a natural death.

A favorite neighborhood activity was for a gunman to stand on a roof opposite a bank and shoot customers as they emerged after making withdrawals. An accomplice on the ground would run out and steal the victim's wallet while he lay bleeding.

> [V]iolence is so commonplace in Hunts Point that children scarcely pause in their street games while gun battles rage about them. Adults gaze calmly from the grimy windows of their tenements while robberies, stabbings, and shootings occur on the streets below. Often they don't even bother to call the police. St. Athanasius Catholic

> Church, which serves Hunts Point, has had to abandon using a poor box. The box was stolen so many times that the priests finally gave up.[19]

Dorman blamed the transition on "unscrupulous real-estate speculators known as 'blockbusters.' "

> Blockbusters are leeches who prey on the fears of white home-owners in changing neighborhoods. . . . In many cases, residents whose families had lived in Hunts Point for generations succumbed to panic-oriented appeals and sold out to the blockbusters. Most of them got only rock-bottom prices. The blockbusters then turned around and sold the homes at inflated prices to Negro and Latin-American families, or maintained ownership and converted the buildings into crowded apartment units.[20]

Such recollections have often been dismissed as romanticizations of the past and remembrances of a world that never really existed. Yet people are now beginning to realize that such things do happen and that they do affect the housing market.

Chapter 6

The Housing Market In Action

Kansas City is an American city that does not have a serious homeless problem. The 1984 HUD figures show a homeless population of only about 400 in a city of 443,000, the lowest rate for a city of over 400,000 in the entire country. Although the Conference of Mayors reported in 1987 that homelessness had increased in Kansas City by 20 percent, one of the largest increases in the country, this was building on a very low base.

"The city put in a homeless hotline—the first one in the country," said Julie Rohlfing, director of communications at the City Union Mission, founded in 1924. "We got about 6,500 calls last year." There are 653 shelter beds in the city. Rohlfing, whose father, the Rev. Maurice Vandenberg, runs the Union Mission, estimates Kansas City's permanent homeless population at about 550—although there have been other estimates as high as 20,000. "It's a very different population than we used to get," she said. "Twenty years ago, the homeless men were all very polite and grateful for what we did for them. Today there's a much greater sense of entitlement and consequently they seem much more violent. If we don't have enough desserts to go around at dinner time there's likely to be a fight."

Rohlfing, who grew up at the mission, says that although the homeless population is increasing about 30 percent a year, the shelters are not always full and almost no one sleeps in the streets. "If I rode around town at midnight I doubt if I'd find more than one or two people outdoors and they'd probably be dead drunk."

When we look at the housing market in Kansas City, it is easy to see why homelessness is so low. Kansas City and its suburbs are bursting with housing. New apartments and condominiums are being built everywhere. In 1988, rental vacancies stood at 8.0 percent, slightly above the national average. The price of the average single-family home was $70,800, 23 percent below the national average. Moreover, the price *declined* 2.7 percent from 1987 to 1988, while the national average was rising 4.1 percent.[1] Young couples who buy condominiums often find their prices have declined after five years. Realtors say that people moving from the East or West Coasts often buy two homes—a country place and a town house—with the money they make from selling their former home.

Kansas City's abundance of affordable housing could be attributed to geographical factors. Beyond its 30-mile radius, the city and suburbs are still surrounded by rolling farmlands easily converted to residential use. Yet other cities have started with the same natural advantages and still manage to create a housing problem. The key factor in Kansas City's robust housing market is the laissez-faire attitudes of the people—their general respect for free enterprise and lack of passion for zoning and exclusionary tactics.

Kansas City lies at the confluence of the Missouri and Kansas Rivers, right where the Missouri turns east to join the Mississippi at St. Louis. From the earliest days, this junction was regarded as a jumping off point for the Far West. Lewis and Clark camped atop a rise on the southern shore of the Missouri, overlooking the two rivers. Today their campsite is "Quality Hill," one of the city's oldest residential districts.

In 1810, Lewis and Clark returned to establish Fort Osage, also on the southern shoreline in what is now the city's northeast quadrant. In 1825, Samuel Becknell, an itinerant merchant, took the Kansas River south, pushing on until he reached New Mexico. His route became the Santa Fe Trail. Soon, merchants had set up shop just east in Independence (later the home of Harry Truman), outfitting the pioneering Santa Fe traffic.

In 1835, an entrepreneur named John J. McCoy decided to intercept returning Santa Fe traffic by establishing a trading post on the bluffs above the Kansas River, about two miles south of what is now downtown. McCoy cut a road down to the riverbank and called his settlement "Westport." It soon became the Trail's eastern terminal.

Central Kansas City was finally settled for farming in 1838. When the California Gold Rush began in 1849, a system of docks was established on the southern shore, where the city's railroad yards are today. Within a year, Kansas City was servicing 1,000 wagons a month. Buildings went up, a street grid was laid out, and by 1859 Kansas City had two opera houses.

During the Civil War, intense rivalries divided Kansas City. Many Missourians had strong southern sympathies but the Union Army controlled the city. After years of guerrilla warfare, General Thomas Ewing issued the famous "army order number eleven," telling residents in two-and-a-half counties that they must prove their loyalty to the union or leave the area. The resulting warfare leveled much of Kansas City and Independence. The area's strong Democratic sympathies still stem from this incident.

After the war, Kansas City received the first railroad bridge built across the Missouri. Lines through Kansas City connected most of the southwest with Chicago. By 1875, Kansas City was the country's third-largest railroad terminal.

In the early ranching days, Texas and Oklahoma cowboys drove their cattle to the stockyards of Kansas City and St. Louis. But when barbed wire was invented and the cross-country cattle routes were threatened, a group of Kansas City businessmen went to Abilene and established a new rail terminal that led directly to Kansas City. As a result the city's stockyards were saved.

The first fashionable neighborhood in Kansas City was Quality Hill, at the west end of town, overlooking both rivers. During the late 19th century, the entire grid from 10th to 14th Street and Jefferson to Washington Streets was lined with stately Victorian mansions. People with less money lived in the downtown and eastern sections, while Independence gradually became a suburb.

These outlying residential areas were soon tied to downtown by the first horse-drawn streetcars. A cable system was added and soon the cars were climbing the famous "Ninth Street incline" up Quality Hill. On the inaugural trip down the incline, half the politicians in Kansas City jumped off in panic as the car picked up speed, an incident still remembered with fond humor today.

Penned in by the rivers on the north and west, the city eventually pushed south. By the 1880s, electrified streetcars were climbing the hills and residential development soon followed. Westport was quickly engulfed and became "Old Westport."

As the gently rolling countryside to the south was opened for development, the city's leadership began to formulate a large-scale municipal plan. William Rockhill Nelson, founder of *The Kansas City Star,* proposed that the area be laid out in a boulevard-and-park network that would retain some of its natural beauty in an increasingly urban surrounding. A fountain motif was adopted for the parks and plazas and Kansas City became "The City of Fountains," making it one of the most beautiful cities in the world, according to French philosopher Andre

Maurois. At his death, Nelson dedicated his own 46th Street mansion, Oak Hall, to the park system. It became the site of the Nelson Art Gallery.

With the park-and-boulevard system in place, the surrounding residential neighborhoods, developed during the 1920s, became one of the most elegant suburban communities in the nation. As downtown was abandoned by people of fashion, the buildings on Quality Hill were divided into apartments. Irish and Italian immigrants arrived, pushing into the Northeast End in large numbers, where they became the backbone for the 1930s political machine of Mayor Tom "Boss" Pendergast and his brother-manager "Big Jim," originally a popular saloon keeper.

During Prohibition, the Pendergast administration turned Kansas City into a center of illegal gambling and nightclubs. The wide-open nightlife gave birth to the "Jazz Era," when Kansas City became the home of budding musicians like Count Basie and Charlie Parker. A sizable black population, migrating from adjacent Southern states, settled in an older downtown residential district with its hub at 12th Street and Vine (later memorialized in the popular song, "Goin' to Kansas City").

With downtown in the hands of the Pendergast machine, suburban Kansas City countered with the Country Club Plaza, the nation's first suburban shopping center. This extraordinarily elegant commercial project—a kind of Midwestern Rockefeller Center—was constructed in the teeth of the Depression by the J. C. Nichols Company. It still anchors the older suburban "Plaza District." In recent years, a commercial revival has spread back into Old Westport, where gentrifiers have been restoring 19th century buildings.

Yet the suburban development of the 1920s and 1930s was still only the beginning. During the 1950s and 1960s, new highway construction once again sent the suburbs hurtling outward. Interstate Routes 70 and 35, which intersect at Kansas City, spanned both rivers and sent development sprawling north of the Missouri River and westward into Kansas, where commuters go to escape city and state income taxes. College Boulevard, a five-mile stretch of corporate office space in Overland Park, Kansas, has become a new focal point of suburban development. Corporate Woods, a 15-acre private park with public access, has continued the boulevard-and-park motif.

So where do the poor live in Kansas City? Most are in the old downtown section. Central Kansas City is still dotted with small frame houses and occasional three- and four-story apartments. "Most of the housing we have in Kansas City was originally built to be good housing," said Lynnis Jameson, director of the city's neighborhood development department. Public housing projects are chiefly inhabited by blacks, who now make up 30 percent of the population. The northeast section is occupied by Irish and Italian families. There are no real luxury apartments downtown, because everyone with money lives in the suburbs.

Yet one neighborhood has undergone gentrification—Quality Hill. Two decades ago, as one historian wrote, "Quality Hill's once-stately . . . tree-lined avenues and prosperous nineteenth-century houses had long before declined to a shabby backwater of heartbreak hotels and derelict houses." Divided into apartments and rooming houses, the former mansions housed a parade of "laboring, service, or clerical employees for expensive downtown hotels, restaurants, and stores" or "catered to permanent alcoholics . . . off-duty prostitutes and pimps."[2]

In the 1960s, a far-sighted real-estate speculator named Arnold Garfinkel started buying up abandoned properties on Quality Hill at a time when everyone else was moving to the suburbs. "I fell for the history of the place," said Garfinkel. "Some of the houses go back as far as 1856."[3] In the 1970s, Garfinkel started renovating some old buildings. He eventually constructed new apartments, carefully molding them to the 19th century atmosphere. In the 1980s, Quality Hill became a prestige address for young urban couples.

At the same time, Kansas City continues to lose some of its old housing stock. The construction of the Crown Center and several new hospitals near Union Station took older housing. In 1985, 5,000 units of public housing were demolished when the Wayne Minor Houses, a drug-infested high-rise complex—was dynamited in what was billed as "the largest controlled explosion in history."

Yet altogether, Kansas City does not seem to lack affordable housing. Many old buildings on Quality Hill are still rented to transients or boarded up completely. The Old Westport revival is still in its early stages. Although the area now has chic restaurants, it also contains a large collection of second-hand stores.

The main reason why housing remains abundant is that suburban development has never stopped. At the same time that Quality Hill was being rediscovered, the Hall Family Farm, the estate of the founders of Hallmark Cards, was being subdivided for homes—nearly ten miles to the south of downtown.

So far, Kansas City has experienced none of the growth control, exclusionary pressures, or tenant-landlord warfare that has led to homelessness in other cities. People of different incomes and classes seem content to live in reasonably close proximity without using the political system to drive each other away.

Granted, Kansas City is still largely a city of single-family homes. Granted, there is not a large renting population in which to cultivate tenant-landlord frictions. Granted, there are municipal enclaves like Oakwood Manor, Platt Woods, and Raytown, that have resisted incorporation into Greater Kansas City because they do not want to share the tax burden. And granted, *de facto* residential segregation was so distinct that a Federal judge eventually ordered consolidation of the urban and suburban school districts and ordered the state legislature to raise taxes to pay the expenses. (This decision is being appealed to the U.S. Supreme Court.)

Yet on the whole, it seems fairly easy for almost anyone to find housing in Kansas City. Even given the city's geographic advantages, it has been the willingness of Kansas City residents to live with development that has led to the city's affordable housing market and low rate of homelessness.

A city with fewer natural advantages and a few more housing problems is Cincinnati.

Cincinnati was founded at a bend in the Ohio River, between the Little and Greater Miami Rivers. Chosen as a convenient landing dock for flatboats, Cincinnati dominated the early Ohio and Mississippi River trade and for decades was regarded as the gateway to the West.

When steamboats were introduced, the city also became a manufacturing center, building more steam engines than any other city in the country. The rise of the railroad gradually raised the fortunes of Chicago and St. Louis at Cincinnati's expense. Yet the city's skilled workforce and enterprising spirit continued to make Cincinnati a center of innovation, the home of several major corporations, including Procter and Gamble and Merrill, Dow.[4]

For the first 100 years, almost all Cincinnati's residential development was limited to "The Basin," a 3.6-square-mile alluvial plain surrounded by steep hills. As was customary in 19th century cities, the most fashionable areas were downtown, while the poor tended to live on the outskirts. Fourth Street, right near the river, was for decades the city's most elegant neighborhood, while immigrant tenements grew up on the West and East Sides. When runaway slaves from the Underground Railroad crossed the Ohio, they settled in a pocket between Sixth and Seventh Streets, known as "Little Africa."

The most famous residential district, however, was the German settlement in the northeast corner, separated from the rest of the city by the Miami-Erie Canal. Early German settlers looked at the muddy canal ditch and, with a healthy dose of sarcasm, called it "The Rhine." Their northeast corner of the city soon became "Over-the-Rhine," a name that remains today.

The Over-the-Rhine district was a densely packed German settlement in a city that was long dominated by its German immigrants. Street signs were in German, several German-language newspapers flourished, and German was taught in the elementary schools. Only when the city was struck by a frenzy of anti-German sentiment at the outbreak of World War I did this overt German culture disappear.

By 1850, Cincinnati had a population of 80,000 people and was the sixth largest city in America. Yet nearly all residential development remained within The Basin, penned in by the surrounding hills. With 30,000 people per square mile, The Basin was one of the most densely packed urban areas in the nation.

Only the wealthy were able to escape to wooded retreats overlooking the city. There they built magnificent homes atop Mt. Auburn, Clifton, and Walnut Hills. *Lippincott's* magazine celebrated "the incomparable mountain suburbs" of Cincinnati, where mountaintop mansions "inspired those looking out and awed those looking up."

With the arrival of the street railways in the 1870s, these mountain suburbs suddenly became accessible to the middle classes. At first, the cars were horse-drawn and remained within The Basin. By 1875, the lower area was crisscrossed with 14 lines and 45 miles of track, manned by 550 employees and 1,000 horses.

Still, the horses could not climb the hillsides. Then, in 1872, a steam-driven cable was installed to pull the cars up Mt. Auburn. Soon four more hills were conquered. Once on top, the lines linked with the inter-urban railway system that was rapidly tying together the eastern United States. (In 1890, it was possible to travel from New York to Milwaukee by streetcar.)

Finally, in 1888, the whole system was electrified. It was now possible to travel from downtown to a mountaintop suburb in 15 minutes. At almost the same time, John A. Roebling completed a suspension bridge across the Ohio between Cincinnati and Covington, Kentucky—which soon became the prototype for the Brooklyn Bridge. The Basin was now completely linked to the surrounding countryside.

In only a few years, nearly all of middle-class Cincinnati left for the suburbs. By 1890, there were 100,000 people living *outside* The Basin in the hill communities. Within these suburbs, a certain self-separation along class and ethnic lines took place. Pleasant Ridge became a German suburb, Avondale a largely Jewish community. Millcreek Valley and the "Norwood Trough," which lay between the mountains, became industrial suburbs, populated mainly by factory workers.

Meanwhile, Cincinnati's black population expanded into the West End and other fashionable downtown areas that had been abandoned. Except for the remaining German population in Over-the-Rhine, blacks became the predominant ethnic group in The Basin.

Having fled downtown, many people in the new suburbs wanted to remain politically independent of the city. But Ohio's Lillard Law of 1893 made this difficult. The city was given power to annex suburbs by majority vote of *both* the city and the smaller suburban community. The city's huge majorities usually predominated and by 1910 Cincinnati encompassed 45 square miles of neighboring communities. Only Norwood, with its large industrial tax base, escaped annexation by incorporating as a city itself.

Filled with older housing that was not entirely occupied, The Basin began to undergo redevelopment. Older homes were razed and banks, offices, and department stores grew up in their place. Union Station became the terminus for the region's rail lines. Through the 1940s, downtown remained the city's principal shopping district.

After World War II, city planners in Cincinnati drew up elaborate plans to reorganize the region into 22 mid-sized "communities," centered around local school districts. Neighborhoods would remain politically incorporated but would be given some autonomy. The aim was to reduce the scale of government and "recapture the advantages of the medium-sized city . . . at the same time mak[ing] available those institutions to be found only in a great metropolitan city."[5]

All these plans were quickly swept aside by the automobile. New highway construction pushed out the suburban rim from 10 to 25 miles. No longer limited to public-transportation corridors, tract homes sprang up everywhere.

Once again, the middle-class moved into these new homes. And once again, less affluent people moved into the homes they left behind. In Mt. Auburn, the city's first exclusive suburb, blacks went from 2 percent of the population in 1950 to 70 percent in 1970. Avondale, the old Jewish suburb, underwent the same transformation. Where the newcomers could not afford to maintain single-family homes, the old Victorian structures were divided into apartments. Eventually, Walnut Hills, Corryville, and Millvale—all the old hilltop suburbs—absorbed large black populations. When racial rioting broke out in 1967, it began in the still surprisingly fashionable suburb of Avondale.

By the 1970s, urban planners finally stopped resisting "suburban sprawl" and the "decline of downtown"—and with good reason. Suburban shopping malls had ravaged the old Fourth Street shopping district. Even office parks sprouted in the suburbs and it appeared that all but the poorest would leave The Basin. Cincinnati lost 1,600 housing units to abandonment in the 1970s, and by 1980, 25 percent of the homes in Over-the-Rhine—now almost entirely black—stood vacant.

Yet by the end of the 1970s the trend reversed itself again. Court Street, long regarded as a slum, was rediscovered by preservationists, who noted it contained one of the largest collections of Italianate buildings in the country. In 1978, it was declared a national historic district and redevelopment began, largely with private capital. An ambitious downtown renewal project created new office space, while the completion of the new Riverfront Stadium anchored a revived waterfront.

Suddenly, some of the old hotels became fashionable again. A few were emptied and rehabilitated. Not until small homeless populations started to appear in the 1980s did city officials realize that many displaced residents who had been living in single-room-occupancy hotels—"SROs"—had nowhere left to go.

As a result, efforts were made to preserve low-income housing. The YMCA was refurbished as a cheap residential hotel. In 1986, the Robert Woods Johnson Foundation, of Princeton, N.J., gave Cincinnati a $10 million grant to enable community groups to build new SRO housing for former mental patients. Yet officials have discovered that changes made in the political system to put power in the hands of neighborhoods have made the creation of low-income housing a formidable task.

In order to reduce the scale of city government, the neighborhood plan of the post-war era was revived in the 1970s. A series of locally elected "neighborhood councils" were created. Although they have no budgetary or zoning powers, the 48 councils have served as the focus of neighborhood sentiment—which turns out to be mainly opposition to new development.

As a result, efforts to maintain cheap housing have run into trouble. Community opposition has forestalled a zoning classification that would allow the construction of SRO hotels. Almost three years after receiving the $10 million Robert Woods Johnson grant, the city has been unable to build a single unit of housing under the program.

"Frankly, I am getting pretty fed up with the activities of the neighborhood councils," said Charlotte Birdsall, who has studied SRO housing for the city planning department. "Our homeless problem may not have the dimensions of the warmer climates or the Eastern seaboard, but it is definitely growing. There are very few neighborhoods in this city that will accept housing without a fight anymore. Everyone sees the opportunity to upgrade their own neighborhood and wants someone else to pick up the remainders. There's simply no place left for those people who are at the margins of society."

The relative abundance of housing in Cincinnati proves that filtering does work. Rental vacancies remain high and homes relatively cheap. So far the homeless population has been relatively manageable. Yet the noose is tightening. Efforts by the neighborhood councils to block SROs and exclude cheap housing have already had a perceptible effect. Although Cincinnati's homeless population remains small, the exclusionary syndrome that leads to homelessness may be taking shape.

Boston is a city that started with an excellent harbor but very little land. Located at the mouth of the Charles, Mystic, and Newport Rivers, and sheltered by outer islands, Boston was originally nothing more than a narrow neck of hilly land, the Shawmut Peninsula. Since its founding in 1630, Boston residents have often found it literally necessary to create the ground under their feet.

Yet the city broke out of its confines through several magnificent engineering feats in the 19th century. Its hinterland, although not as broad as Kansas City's, is certainly less confining than Cincinnati's. All that has differentiated Boston and its large homeless population is its recent housing policies.

Boston was first settled by a company of English Puritans, headed by John Winthrop. The aim, Winthrop later wrote, was to create a shining "city on the hill."

Winthrop's words could be taken quite literally. At its founding, Boston was nothing more than the rocky Shawmut peninsula, dominated by three hills—Pemberton, Beacon, and Mt. Vernon—and connected to the distant mainland by a narrow neck just wide enough for a road. The Puritan divines pitched their first homes on a cove facing the south harbor. Later, an inlet on the north side of the peninsula was dammed to form Mill Pond.

Boston prospered on fishing and sea trade and by the time Benjamin Franklin was born in 1706, the settlement had spread across the entire peninsula. Beacon Hill was covered with large colonial homes surrounded by spacious gardens. On the north side of the southernmost hill, Mt. Vernon, was a small community of black freemen. On the south side was a raucous, lower-class neighborhood nicknamed "Mt. Whoredom."

By 1743, Boston was the largest town in North America, with a population of 16,000. Yet over the next three decades, the city stagnated and was surpassed in population and importance by both Philadelphia and New York. Although prominent for its overseas trade and anti-British activity during the Revolution, Boston in many ways remained a quiet, comfortable New England seaport. Visiting Boston for the first time in 1794, Mrs. Josiah Quincy said that Boston was, "compared with New York, a small town." In the same year, Thomas Pemberton, in his *Topographical and Historical Description of Boston,* commented that "the town is capable of great increase, as many large spaces of land still remain vacant."[6]

Only after 1799, when land companies began to level the hills for building lots, did Boston begin to grow again. The first to be flattened was Mt. Vernon, shorn down 60 feet. The surplus earth was carried down to Charles Street by the nation's first rail line, powered only by gravity and horses. There it was used to fill the harbor, creating the West End.

In 1810, John Hancock's heirs took the top off Beacon Hill, excavating right to the door of the new State House, only recently designed and constructed by Charles Bulfinch (who also served a term as mayor). In the process, the Hancocks undercut Bulfinch's Revolutionary War Memorial Column, which was not rebuilt until 1865. They also cut within two feet of the mansion of one William Thurston, leaving it precariously hanging over a gravelly abyss. The elegant home eventually had to be torn down, too—after a celebrated lawsuit. The earth was used to fill in the old Mill Pond, which became the North End.

In 1821, Boston entrepreneurs set their sights on an even larger body of water—the marshy adjoining backwater of the Charles River called the Back Bay. In 1814, Uriah Cotting received a charter to construct a weir fifty feet wide by a mile-and-a-half long, where Beacon Street runs today. By enclosing the entire Back Bay, Cotting hoped to set up a series of tidal ponds that would power a series of water-driven mills on the far shore of Gravelly Point, near the village of Roxbury.

Cotting's complicated scheme never got very far. More farsighted investors were already moving out to the rapids of the Merrimack River, where they founded the industrial towns of Lowell and Lawrence. When the first railroads were built twelve years later, they were also constructed on weirs crossing the bay (messing up Cotting's tidal flows even more in the process). Soon it was decided to fill the whole Back Bay.

Boston was rapidly outgrowing the Shawmut peninsula. In 1825, the population was still only 58,000. But Irish immigration had begun and swelled to a tidal wave when the Potato Famine struck in 1845. In 1840 the population of Boston was 93,000 and rose to 137,000 by 1850. By 1855, the Irish population alone was 50,000—almost the size of the entire city 30 years earlier.

The history of Boston over the next half-century offers an interesting case study of the filtering hypothesis. There are actually two theories as to how filtering works. The first says that fashionable people are lured into new housing, leaving older housing behind them for the poor. The second says that upper-class people are actually *pushed* out of their older housing by waves of immigration. It is often hard to tell the difference.

In Boston, either theory could be applied. As the Irish immigration of the 1840s and 1850s swelled into the North End and Fort Hill, at the southern end of the peninsula, the South End was opened up as the new center of fashion. Oscar Handlin wrote in *Boston's Immigrants: 1790–1880*:

> In this transition originated the Boston slums—precisely the housing the Irish needed. Near the wharves and cheap in rent, these localities became the first home of such immigrants in Boston. . . . As a result, there were few natives in the North End and Fort Hill and even fewer non-Irish aliens, for these groups fled, sacrificing other interests in order to avoid the decline in social status that resulted from remaining.[7]

Yet even the South End did not last long. In *The Late George Apley,* John P.

Marquand describes an early instance of "blockbusting" when Apley recounts to his son how his own father had bought a "fine bow-front house" in the South End in the 1870s, at a time when:

> nearly everyone was under the impression that this district would be one of the most solid residential sections of Boston instead of becoming, as it is to-day, a region of rooming houses and worse. You may have seen those houses in the South End, fine mansions with dark walnut doors and beautiful woodwork.

One day, Apley says, his father looked across the street at a line of new row houses and saw a man in shirtsleeves.

> "Thunderation," Father said, "there is a man in his shirt sleeves on those steps." The next day he sold his house for what he had paid for it and we moved to Beacon Street. Your grandfather had sensed the approach of change; a man in his shirt sleeves had told him that the days of the South End were numbered.[8]

Thus, the Back Bay and Beacon Street were filled just in time to offer the Boston gentry a new refuge from the forces of immigration. Within a few decades, the beautiful new homes of the South End were in the hands of tenants and immigrants. By 1906, the area was the subject of a study by a Harvard professor, called *The Lodging Housing Problem of Boston.*[9]

From 1865 to 1880, the Back Bay was filled, piece by piece. Having exhausted the surplus dirt from Shawmut, excavators ran railroad lines into the hills of distant Needham. At the height of the landfill operation, a trainload of earth was unloaded every 45 minutes, round the clock, for more than two years. About two building lots were created each day.

Unlike Beacon Hill, where the streets were all a jumble, the broad avenues of the Back Bay were laid out straight and true, with magnificent Commonwealth Avenue its centerpiece. Handsome four- and five-story brownstone buildings lined the streets, evoking frequent comparisons with Parisian elegance. As Walter Muir Whitehill reports:

> As Summer Street, Pemberton Square and the West End ceased to be pleasant residential districts, and as it became clear that the South End was never likely to live up to its rather pleasing appearance, the attraction of the Back Bay increased. Conservative persons comfortably settled upon Beacon Hill tended to remain there. There is, indeed, a tale of a gentleman, who . . . firmly told a prospective son-in-law, who proposed to build a house in the Back Bay, that he could not consider having his daughter live on "made land." . . . Such compunctions were not, however, general,

> and . . . the normal means by which comfortably situated Bostonians sheltered themselves down to World War I was by buying or building houses in the Back Bay.[10]

Beyond this growing urban community lay the isolated villages of Dorchester, Roxbury, and Brookline. Until the 1850s, they remained rolling farmland, interrupted only by an occasional country estate. In the 18th century, Governor Francis Bernard and John Hancock established country homes at Jamaica Plain, the first piece of scenic high ground on the road south from the city. Later, many successful businessmen and civic leaders followed suit. The journey was a long one on horseback over muddy roads. Brook Farm, founded in 1841 in West Roxbury, only eight miles from Beacon Hill, was considered a distant, bucolic setting.

In 1852, the first horse-drawn rail lines were laid, connecting downtown with Dorchester and Roxbury. Soon lines criss-crossed the entire southwest area, skirting the Back Bay, which was still under construction. Isolated country villages—Rosindale, Forest Hills, Upham's Corner—became the focus of suburban development. When the horse-drawn lines were electrified in the 1880s, the entire southern suburban area was tied together in one large rail network. Bridges across the Charles River also spread suburban development into Cambridge, Chelsea, and Somerville.

The question soon arose, would these new communities be incorporated into municipal Boston or would they remain separate? Many old-timer country residents resisted incorporation, but the newcomers prevailed. The self-confident middle class wanted to remain a part of Boston, feeling it could provide effective leadership and avoid domination of the city's politics by immigrant-based political machines. After fiercely debated referenda, Dorchester, Roxbury, West Roxbury, and Brighton all voted to join Boston. The tide turned in 1873, however, when suburban Brookline, a much more affluent community, rejected incorporation. Fear of immigrants and a desire to separate from the city's problems had finally gained the upper hand. No other suburb considered annexation after that.

The new homes of the "streetcar suburbs" were built without zoning restrictions. As Sam Bass Warner, Jr., notes in *Streetcar Suburbs:*

> Some of these builders were carpenters, some real estate men, but most were not professionals at all. The vast majority were either men building houses for their own occupancy or small investors who built a house nearby their own residence in order to profit from rents of one to three tenants. . . .
>
> No legislation save the laws of nuisance and a few primitive safety codes prevented these 9,000 landowners from doing anything they wanted with their property.[11]

The results were spectacularly practical and efficient. From 1850 to 1900, Boston tripled in population, yet the vast majority of people were much better housed. Enthusiasts preached the benefits of the suburbs to health and family life. Henry M. Whitney, owner of the West End Street Railway, which consolidated most of the lines, told audiences that the suburbs would help America avoid the social problems of Europe's festering cities.[12] To ease this integration of city and suburbs, Whitney kept the "five cent fare" for many decades. As Warner reports:

> Tenement slums were the scandal of the age. Street railway managers, real estate men, politicians, philanthropists, health officers, school teachers, and the middle class generally all shared the attitude that open country surroundings and the small community were beneficent settings for family life. This widespread sympathy for the rural idea provided additional impetus for the expansion of public services over the entire metropolitan region.[13]

Different ethnic groups mixed freely in these new suburbs. Yet as Warner points out, there was a certain voluntary separation by *income.*

> Early twentieth century observers called the inner suburbs the "zone of emergence." Here, first and second generation immigrant families moved from their original ethnic centers and began to take their place in the general life of the American middle class. . . . The steady flow of new ethnic groupings to the suburbs demonstrated the continued openness of the metropolitan society and its ability to provide a middle class competence to a big proportion of its immigrants' children.[14]

Thus, the streetcar suburbs incorporated the English, German, French Canadian, Jewish, and Irish residents of the entire city. When Italians arrived in large numbers at the turn of the century, they followed the same pattern—establishing an ethnic enclave in the West End, but then scattering indiscriminately into the suburbs.

Segregation by income, on the other hand, occurred without any overarching design.[15] Some early builders copied the town houses of the Back Bay, but most soon shifted to detached, single-family homes. In the remote suburbs, they built imitation Newport mansions. Closer in, they built Colonial-style shingle houses. Manufacturers also moved to the suburbs (the trend is by no means recent) and built factory housing: "not the packed slums of Boston's North End or New York City, but rather a small drab section of little two- and three-story wooden houses and barracks such as could be found in any New England mill town."[16]

But the structure that came to symbolize Boston's streetcar suburbs was the "triple-decker"—a three-story wooden-frame house in which each floor was a separate apartment. With its rental income and possibilities for joint family ownership, the triple-decker became the signature of independent homeownership for large portions of the working class.

So the first ring of suburban development expanded. Yet the pattern did not remain for long. During the 1920s and 1930s, the automobile pushed the suburbs out to a new fringe. Towns like Newton, Braintree, and Woburn, were drawn into the ring of Greater Boston. When Interstate 128 was completed in the 1950s, ringing the entire metropolitan area, it too became a new focus of development. Downtown offices and high-tech industries that had sprouted around Harvard and MIT were lured to the suburban rim. Jobs and housing followed. For a long time, it appeared downtown Boston would be bled to death.

Meanwhile, in the old streetcar suburbs, wave after wave of immigration left neighborhoods progressively poorer. By the 1960s, Dorchester was filled with the aging sons and daughters of Irish and Italian immigrants. Roxbury had become the city's black neighborhood. The area depopulated so quickly that by the early 1960s many of the old suburban mansions sat boarded up. In the Back Bay, according to Walter Muir Whitehill (who is a bit of a snob):

> Only a fraction of the largest private houses are now occupied in the fashion for which they were built. Some have become apartments, others doctors' and dentists' offices; here and there one even sees the ill-lettered pest signal ROOMS in a ground floor window.[17]

Nobody, it seemed, wanted to live in the city anymore.

Then things turned around again. The leveling of the West End's Italian enclave for commercial redevelopment raised such an outcry that other Federal urban renewal projects were cancelled. Redevelopment began to concentrate on reviving older neighborhoods. Gentrifiers rediscovered Beacon Hill. The Back Bay underwent a revival. Older homes in Roxbury and Dorchester were rehabilitated.

State Street was redeveloped to house the financial industry. The waterfront redevelopment was crowned by James Rouse's revival of Faneuil Hall as an urban shopping arcade. The old Shawmut peninsula once again became a thriving nerve-center of Boston, with 200-year-old buildings sitting comfortably next to gleaming skyscrapers.

So what has gone wrong with Boston housing and why are there so many homeless? The answer once again lies with zoning, rent control and general overregulation.

By the 1930s, the impulse to zone out apartments and multi-family housing culminated with the outlawing of the three-decker. The reform effort was led by the head of the Boston-based Immigration Restriction League.[18] The suburban mentality triumphed over working-class homeownership, which is necessarily based on landlord-tenant relations.

Zoning has followed the same pattern: Most outer suburbs exclude apartments and even two- and three-family homes. Even single-family construction is resisted with growing regularity. Because these exclusionary communities form a tight ring around Boston, the type of suburban expansion that creates new housing opportunities in the city has been strangled. When Worcester—30 miles to the west—started experiencing an influx of Boston commuters in search of housing in the early 1980s, city officials immediately slapped a moratorium on new apartment construction and started talking about rent control.

In the entire Boston area, rent control was the wave of the 1970s. Cambridge led the way in 1969, egged on by student groups from Harvard and MIT. It was the first of many instances around the country where a large university population would impose rent control on the "townies" who provide them with housing during the school year.

Across the river, Brookline followed suit. The first suburb to resist incorporation, Brookline had become an affluent bedroom community of doctors, lawyers, and professionals from Boston's many hospitals and academic institutions. Despite this affluent tenantry—or perhaps because of it—the city imposed rent control on the small owners that made up the city's landlord population.

To clear up questions of jurisdiction, the state legislature adopted enabling legislation, allowing municipalities to impose rent control on their own. When President Nixon imposed temporary price controls in 1971, several other cities—including Boston—made rent controls permanent. Within five years, over 70 percent of the apartments in the Boston metropolitan area were under regulation. Only Somerville and Lynn, two blue-collar communities north of Cambridge, eventually dropped rent control.

The results were predictable. Vacancy rates in Boston—still at a normal 6 percent in 1980—have descended to below 3 percent. In Cambridge and Brookline, available apartments have all but vanished. Donald Solomon, director of Brookline Rent Control, estimates the city's vacancy level at one-half of one percent.

As a result of all this, Boston has become one of the tightest housing markets in the country. Few apartments are available anywhere. Even poor people with Federal section-8 housing vouchers find they cannot spend them and one-third of the vouchers are being returned unused. Along with this has gone Boston's high level of homelessness—fifteenth in the country in the 1984 HUD report.

After more than doubling Boston's land area, filling the Back Bay, building the streetcar suburbs, and accommodating wave after wave of immigration for more than a century, Boston in the 1980s suddenly found itself unable to provide housing for all its citizens. A few short years of regulation had changed things entirely.

Chapter 7

Exclusionary Zoning

In 1924, Ambler Realty proposed developing a 620-acre parcel in Euclid, Ohio, a suburban town of about 10,000 people right outside Cleveland. Adjoining tracts on both sides of the property had already been developed as single-family homes. Ambler wanted to build apartment houses and an industrial park on its property.

Two years earlier, the village council had adopted a new system of laws called "municipal zoning." According to the new rules, about half the property could only be developed as two-family homes, one-quarter as apartments, and the remainder as industry. Ambler went to court, arguing that its Constitutional right to use its property under the 14th Amendment had been violated.

The concept of zoning had been invented ten years earlier in New York City. According to legend, it was originally conceived by the residents of elegant Fifth Avenue in order to keep the hoi polloi from moving uptown.[1] The theoretical concept of separating residential and industrial areas proved to be widely popular and by 1923 the U.S. Department of Commerce had published a Standard State Zoning Enabling Act, showing municipalities how to adopt zoning.

The concept of zoning is actually based on *nuisance* laws. A municipality is allowed to employ its "police powers" to protect members of the community from health and safety hazards. Thus, zoning is justified, according to the Commerce Department's model ordinance:

> to lessen congestion in the street; to secure safety from fire, panic, and other dangers, to promote health and the general welfare; to provide adequate light and air; to prevent the overcrowding of land; to avoid undue concentration of population; to facilitate the adequate provision of transportation, water, sewage, schools, parks, and other public requirements. Such regulations shall be made with reasonable consideration, among other things, to the character of the district and its peculiar suitability for particular uses, and with a view to conserving the value of buildings and encouraging the most appropriate use of land throughout such municipality.[2]

The concept of "police power" has played a formidable role in our Constitutional history. It is generally set in opposition to those portions of the Constitution that protect property rights. As written and amended, the Constitution contains several clauses pertaining to private property and legal and commercial transactions. Most notable are the "contracts clause" of Article I, which forbids the states to pass "laws impairing the obligations of contract" and the "takings" clause of the Fifth Amendment, which says that "private property [shall not] be taken for public use without just compensation."

Under the Chief Justiceship of John Marshall (1801–1835) these Constitutional rights to private property were given broad interpretation. Under the leadership of his successor, Chief Justice Roger Taney (1836–1864), the countervailing concept of "police power" was considerably expanded. "Police power" actually has nothing to do with the police. It refers to the legislature's power to protect the health and safety of its citizens. Most government regulations are now justified under this concept. Needless to say, the distinction as to when a regulation constitutes a legitimate exercise of the police power and when it constitutes an unconstitutional "taking" of private property is one that is always being argued in the courts.

As the Commerce Department's model ordinance suggested, the aims of municipal zoning were already beginning to creep well beyond the realm of health, safety, and welfare and into areas like preserving "the value of buildings" and "the character of a district." Thus, even at the beginning, the Commerce Department seemed to invite communities to use their zoning powers to keep undesired development—and perhaps even undesirable people—out of the jurisdiction.

The Supreme Court of the 1920s was a conservative institution, thoroughly grounded in the rights of private property. Nevertheless, in *Ambler Realty Com-*

pany vs. Euclid the Court come down resoundingly on the side of government regulation. Writing for the majority, Justice George Sutherland wrote:

> Until recent years, urban life was comparatively simple; but with the great increase and concentration of population, problems have developed and constantly are developing, which require, and will continue to require, additional restriction in respect of the use and occupation of private lands in urban communities. . . . Such regulations are sustained, under the complex conditions of our day, for reasons analogous to those which justify traffic regulations, which, before the advent of automobiles and rapid transit street railways, would have been condemned as totally arbitrary and unreasonable.[3]

The Court recognized, even at that point, that the main purpose of zoning had become to insulate and isolate residential districts, particularly those containing single-family homes:

> The serious question in the case . . . involves the validity of what is really the crux of the more recent zoning legislation, namely the creation and maintenance of residential districts from which business and trade of every sort, including hotels and apartment houses, are excluded.[4]

Yet the Court said these distinctions were legitimate because business and industrial development—including the construction of apartments—could create nuisances that might endanger children, promote heavy traffic, or pose fire hazards.

> A nuisance may be merely a right thing in the wrong place,—like a pig in the parlor instead of the barnyard. If the validity of the legislative classification for zoning purposes be fairly debatable, the legislative judgment must be allowed to control. . . . Under the circumstances, apartment houses, which in a different environment would be not only entirely unobjectionable but highly desirable, come very near to being nuisances.[5]

Three justices saw a different issue at stake. Writing in dissent, Justice Willis Van Devanter wrote:

> The plain truth is that the true object of the ordinance in question is to place all property in a strait-jacket. The purpose to be accomplished is really to regulate the mode of living of persons who may hereafter inhabit [the community]. In the last analysis, the result to be accomplished is to classify the population and segregate them according to their income or situation in life.[6]

Thus, at the very outset, the lines were clearly drawn. To some, zoning is a means of preserving and protecting residential areas—notably those containing single-family homes. To others, it was an invidious practice by which the affluent could practice economic segregation. In effect, the majority of a community—acting through its legislature—could choose its own neighbors. Over the last 60 years, the terms of the debate have changed very little.

Anyone who has spent more than a month observing suburban or small-town politics knows that the vast majority of today's municipal controversies revolve around issues of zoning and planning.

Go to a town meeting anywhere in the United States and you are likely to find a local majority, struggling to protect environmental amenities and "quality of life," pitted against a "greedy developer" whose sole joy in life seems to be the raping and pillaging of landscapes. As the meeting progresses, a long procession of homeowners will step to the microphone, voices quavering with emotion, to charge that the new development—whatever it may be—will "only bring in more traffic, create pollution, ruin the quality of our lives, and turn this town into another (the name of the nearest large city)."

Public-opinion surveys regularly purport to show that Americans are most concerned about global issues like the Federal deficit and relations with the Soviet Union. Yet I would bet that if a category were included entitled "preserving the quality of life in my neighborhood," it would rank at or near the top as well.

As Richard Babcock, a Chicago zoning attorney, wrote in *The Zoning Game* (1966):

> No one is enthusiastic about zoning except the people. . . . The judges find zoning a monumental bore, most lawyers consider it a nuisance, and the planners treat it as a cretinous member of the planning family about whom the less said the better. Yet thousands of local officials regard zoning as the greatest municipal achievement since the perfection of public sanitary systems. . . . To the dweller on the urban fringe the usefulness of zoning as an exclusionary technique both present and potential must seem unlimited. . . . By the test of acceptance in the market place, zoning has been a smashing success.[7]

Briefly, here is the way zoning works. A community draws up a map in which each parcel of land is designated for a specific use—residential, commercial, industrial, and so forth. In principle, a town is supposed to be willing to entertain any of these uses, but is only anxious to keep them in their proper place. Commercial development should go along major highways and industrial development should adjoin a freeway interchange or railroad track. Apartments will be clustered near population centers, while single-family homes will spread through the network of residential streets.

In practice, however, what politicians and municipal planners soon discover is that there are some land-uses nobody wants to have anywhere. Noisome industries are never popular. A few local stores may be tolerated but large regional shopping centers are viewed warily. In addition, no suburban community wants any trace of "cheap housing"—apartments, multi-family homes, mobile homes, or anything involving rentals or tenants.

Whenever a developer comes forth with such a proposal, no matter how rational or legal it may be, local officials are put under enormous pressure to prevent it from being built. If the developer needs a zoning change, municipal officials will be urged to reject it. If the use is permitted by the ordinance, officials will be encouraged to "upzone" the property or find some loophole to prevent the development. Another favorite municipal strategy is to zone properties for "light industry," "laboratories," or some other high-sounding but unlikely facility. In this way, the community can reject any proposal on the grounds that it is waiting for some "higher" use.

All this has come to have an enormous impact on housing itself. "Zoning is now the most critical factor in the entire equation of home building," said Shirley McVey Wiseman, 1989 President of the National Association of Homebuilders. "What gets built, where it gets built, how much it's going to cost—all this is now basically determined by the regulatory apparatus at the local level. As these regulations have become more burdensome, housing has become more scarce and expensive."

To take a typical case, let us look at a property in Brookhaven, Long Island, a 349-square-mile township that is the largest in New York State. In 1980, the Suffolk County Interreligious Council on Housing proposed 160 garden apartments on 30 acres of land in the village of East Patchogue. The Council's express intent was to provide housing for low- and moderate-income people who were otherwise not able to find housing in the area, which is almost two hours driving distance from New York City. The parcel was already zoned for a nursing home. Nobody had ever proposed building a nursing home on the site, but the zoning classification at least made it sound as though the town were not opposed to any and all uses.

The town planning board, an appointive body with only advisory powers, approved the zone change. But the town council, which has final authority and is under far more political pressure, rejected the project. In response, the Interreligious Council came up with another proposal to put 60 units on a 12-acre site in nearby Setauket, along heavily travelled State Highway 25A.

As word of the second proposal got around the township, opposition mounted. By the time the town council got around to voting in 1983, there were enormous public pressures against it. Although the planning board also recommended the second project, the council once again voted it down. No housing would be allowed.

"We don't like low-cost housing because it brings in low-class people," one neighborhood resident told *The New York Times.* "I don't want those people coming in and degrading my property. I've got my life savings invested here. There's plenty of land elsewhere."[8]

Another area where zoning has had an enormous impact is in the rental of small rooms and apartments in single-family homes. Census data now indicate that more than half the homes in the country with five or more rooms are being occupied by people over age 65. This suggests that many people are "overhoused," meaning they have far more room than they need.[9] Property taxes and the difficulty in maintaining such a home often persuade elderly people to move to smaller units (although, as we shall see, property-tax "reform" has been working to undo these incentives). Another alternative for them is to rent out spare bedrooms or create small apartments in their homes.

Zoning laws generally forbid this. Suburban residents in single-family districts are extremely sensitive to the idea of living in rental districts. Complaints often center around density or parking space, but the objections obviously have to do with class distinctions as well. This prohibition against rentals is probably the major reason that the suburbs have never been able to provide the variety of housing that city neighborhoods do.

To see what a difference such regulation can make, consider the case of Takoma Park, Maryland, a suburb of Washington right on the District of Columbia border.

Takoma Park represents a perfect confrontation of the old streetcar suburbs and the new suburban ethos based on property values and single-family homes. First incorporated in 1883, Takoma Park was originally connected to Washington by a network of rail lines. Though it became a streetcar suburb, it also had small pockets of black freemen, who settled in the area right after the Civil War.

Most of the original housing was two- and three-family homes, with both owner-occupancy and rentals. During the 1920s and 1930s, a number of larger apartment houses were built as well. After World War II, the single-family home became predominant. Today the streets of Takoma are a hodgepodge of all kinds of housing: single-family homes, apartment houses, duplexes, and triplexes—many of them "non-conforming uses" that violate the zoning law but are allowed to remain in place.

Despite the growing number of single-family homeowners in the population of 16,000, rentals have continued to play a large role in the community. When thousands of army and government personnel came to Washington during World War II, homeowners in Takoma Park rented them apartments. When veterans used their GI benefits to attend neighboring Columbia Union College, they also became tenants. The demand was so high that many homeowners divided their homes into apartments or rented rooms.

In 1973, however, the more affluent single-family homeowners decided to crack down. Researching the zoning law, they discovered a 60-year-old Montgomery County statute forbidding rentals in a single-family zone. The homeowners petitioned the county (which controls zoning in Maryland) to enforce the law.

In 1978, the city council adopted a compromise, saying that anyone who had been renting before 1954 could continue for another ten years. The ten years expired in 1988, however, and evictions began. An estimated 1,000 tenants, many of them families with children, are expected to be forced out of their homes.[10]

What is the overall result of these zoning practices? Obviously, housing becomes more expensive and harder to find. In June 1988, for example, *The Wall Street Journal* reported:

> M. Ali Issari, a retired university professor, parked his car in front of a new-home sales office near Los Angeles one recent Saturday and stuck this sign behind the windshield: "The line for purchasing Deeridge homes starts from here."
>
> One week later, when selling started, the line had grown to 150 cars, and Mr. Issari bought the first Deeridge home to a round of applause from a mob of house hunters. "This is completely strange to me," he says. "But if this is what it takes to buy a house in California, then you have to play the game."[11]

In the New York area, only a year earlier, *The New York Times* had reported:

> They began arriving 10 days ago, dozens of people on the condominium trail. In warm sun and then cold rain, they lived in a community of cars, campers and trucks, assuring themselves a chance to pay $175,000 and up for one of the 100 town houses that will become Society Hill.[12]

The condominiums—in Mahopac, New York, 90 minutes commuting distance from Manhattan—were still five months from completion. But most buyers said they couldn't find any other housing in the New York metropolitan area. Residents of Mahopac, who for a while had mistaken the temporary campsite for an invasion of homeless people, were not as enthusiastic. "Earlier this week," noted *The Times,* "over 700 residents signed a petition asking town officials to impose a moratorium on all building permits. Those officials are already considering a plan that will reduce development densities and limit the rate of growth."[13]

For people who have already bought homes and are established in the community, the effort to exclude others and raise the price of homes is a cost-free good. In fact, it actually has a positive advantage.

The key factor to recognize is that, in addition to providing themselves with a place to live, homeowners are also investors, speculating in real-estate prices. Particularly in an inflation-prone economy, people now buy a home as a way of saving and investing money. Nor do they do badly. As George Gilder wrote in reviewing the inflationary 1970s:

> While 24 million investors in the stock market were being buffeted by inflation and taxes, 46 million homeowners were leveraging their houses with mortgages, deducting the interest payments on their taxes, and earning higher real returns on their down payment equity than speculators in gold or foreign currencies. . . . America's middle class was doing better in the housing market than all of the shrewdest investors in the capital and financial markets of the world. By 1979 the value of individually owned dwellings had reached 1.3 trillion dollars, twice the worth of individually owned corporate stock.[14]

Once they have their life savings invested in a home—and they often do—homeowners want to do everything possible to protect their investment. That means preventing cheap or undesirable development near them.

Of course, there are few investors anywhere who do not want to have the power of the government brought to bear to protect their investments. Farmers want agricultural support prices, manufacturers want protection from imports, savers want the Federal government to insure their bank accounts. The difference with homeowners is that, within any given political jurisdiction, they are likely to be the majority. The voice of each homeowner protecting his or her investment is immediately echoed by the voice of every other homeowner protecting his or her investment. In such a situation, it is only a matter of time before the majority convinces itself it is doing the Lord's work.

Thus, the concerns about affordable housing, when expressed by homeowners, have a certain disingenuous air. The fact is that, for people who already own a home, it does not matter how much home prices may rise. They are already on the escalator. If prices go up, theirs will go up along with everybody else's.

Their ability to trade for a better home is not compromised. It is only people who have not yet gotten their foot on the ladder who see homeownership continually receding over the horizon. Yet because these people are generally an unorganized minority and not usually represented in municipal decisions, their influence is not often felt.

"People always cite the National Association of Realtors affordability index, which says that in California, for example, only about 15 percent of the state's households can afford the median-priced home," said William Fulton, editor of *California Planning and Development Report.* "What that doesn't tell you is that half the households in California already own a home. They won't benefit if home prices come down. In fact, they'd be just as happy to see prices go up."[15]

As long as this majority is able to control where and how new housing will be built, the situation is unlikely to change. Carl Dahlman, professor of economics at the University of Wisconsin, puts it this way:

> The only theory of zoning that is consistent with available knowledge of zoning practices is that zoning is a means for keeping people out, and for sending them away to other communities for the residents there to cope with. Zoning in America today is done not to specifically control land, but primarily to control the migration of people.[16]

To see how things could be different, it is only necessary to look at Houston, America's fourth largest city. Because of the city's wild-west atmosphere and anti-government attitudes, zoning has never been adopted in Houston. City officials rejected zoning several times during the 1920s and 30s. It was also voted down in two non-binding public referenda in 1948 and 1962. Although people on the East and West Coasts often find it hard to believe, property owners in Houston can do anything they please with their property.

Well, perhaps it isn't all that easy. In fact, as Bernard Siegan discovered in his landmark study of Houston's no-zoning policies in 1972, property owners are often severely constricted, not by public ordinances, but by private covenants and deed restrictions.[17] Typically, the developer of a suburban subdivision will write deed restrictions saying the property cannot be used for anything but single-family residences for 30 to 50 years. (In fact, banks won't even lend money for such developments unless the restrictions are in the agreement.) As a result, Houston has its own exclusive residential enclaves like River Oaks and Sharpston. What is different is that people in these ritzy developments cannot prevent someone else from putting up cheap housing on the other side of town.

Thus, while Houston's exclusive subdivisions compare for snob appeal with any other enclave in the country, the city is bursting at the seams with every other kind of housing as well. In 1982, in the teeth of the recession, the Houston area built 60,000 new homes—one of every 15 new units in the country. Despite enormous population growth, rental vacancies have remained above 15 percent for more than a decade. Condominiums and starter homes still sell for $30,000 (that's the asking price, not the down payment), and homelessness has been extremely low, although not non-existent.[18] In fact, one of the major housing problems in Houston has been vacant suburban homes, which have led people to worry about the spread of "suburban slums."[19]

One other interesting observation is that, whenever there has been a groundswell in Houston for imposing zoning, it has always come out of the most affluent neighborhoods. In the 1962 referendum, 75 percent of the black population voted against zoning, while its only support came from exclusive suburbs.[20]

Another city that has at least relaxed its zoning effort and seen a payoff in housing is San Diego. The nation's seventh largest city, San Diego has experienced tremendous growth over the last two decades, mushrooming from 334,000 inhabitants in 1950 to 960,000 today. Almost 15 percent of the population is Hispanic, due largely to its location right across the border from Tijuana—with one million people of its own—which makes San Diego a center for illegal immigration.

During the recession of the early 1980s, building slowed and rental vacancies dropped to 4 percent. In 1985, there was a referendum campaign to adopt rent control, as more than a dozen other California cities had already done. San Diego voters rejected it by a two-to-one margin, and builders responded in 1986 by putting up 20,000 new apartments, most of them in the luxury category. The results were quickly felt in the lowest income groups:[21]

Vacancies in under-$250 category since 1982
1982–3.3 percent
1983–3.2 percent
1984–2.2 percent
1985–1.8 percent
1986–3.6 percent
1987–3.3 percent

The filtration process worked extremely rapidly.

Still, the gentrification of the old Gaslight District downtown threatened to create a wave of homelessness. "Several SRO hotels were lost and the charitable organizations serving the indigent were really getting kicked around down there," recalled Frank Landerville, director of the Regional Task Force on the Homeless.

At first, the city responded with a law that required builders who razed one SRO to replace it with another. This expired after three years, however, and served only as a stopgap. By that time, city officials decided that the real problem was zoning.

"We realized our zoning law had created a gap in the kind of housing builders could provide," said Judy Lenthal, senior planner for the city government. "An SRO unit is too small for permanent accommodations, while a studio apartment is more than many people can afford.

"So we changed the zoning ordinance to allow a new 'living unit'—an apartment that contains either a kitchen or a bathroom, but not both. You have to share one or the other in a common area. But it's a real home—something both landlords and tenants can afford."

As a result, San Diego has experienced what Lenthal called "the only mini-boom of new SRO construction in the country." In one year, private developers built four new hotels and rehabilitated fifteen old ones, creating 565 new units. Plans for 1,500 more units were on the drawing boards. San Diego legislators also sponsored a state law to enable other California cities to do the same thing.[22]

"Altogether, I'd say the most important thing we've done in providing housing for the poor is not alienate the development community," said Landerville, of the Regional Task Force on the Homeless. "Builders are still enthusiastic about San Diego and that helps provide housing at all levels." Perhaps not coincidentally, San Diego has one of the lowest rates of homelessness among the nation's 20 largest cities.

In most other parts of the country, however, the trend has been in the opposite direction—toward greater restriction of the housing market through tighter zoning.

In 1974, the U.S. Supreme Court reaffirmed zoning powers in the first comprehensive zoning decision since 1926. The village of Belle Terre, Long Island, had passed an ordinance forbidding three or more unrelated people from renting detached homes. The ordinance was aimed at students from the nearby State University at Stony Brook, who had pooled their resources to rent homes in the area. A group of students challenged the ordinance.

In a decision that united liberal Justice William O. Douglass and conservative Chief Justice Warren Burger, Justice Douglass wrote:

> A quiet place where yards are wide, people few, and motor vehicles restricted are legitimate guidelines in a land use project addressed to family needs. . . . The police power is not confined to elimination of filth, stench, and unhealthy places. It is ample to lay out zones where family values, youth values, and the blessings of quiet seclusion and clean air make the area a sanctuary for people.[23]

As Carl Dahlman, of the University of Wisconsin, put it: "[The courts] have . . . wrapped many residential neighborhoods consisting of single-family homes in a protective blanket that effectively has eliminated much or perhaps all of the pecuniary risks associated with the ownership of a home."[24]

Since 1975, however, there has been one successful challenge to exclusionary zoning, in the New Jersey courts, that has served as a model for other states.

The case involved Mt. Laurel, a 22-square-mile suburb of Camden, lying about 15 minutes outside of Philadelphia. Still largely rural, the town does not yet have a main street or a supermarket. Its first post office was constructed in 1983. In 1965, the township contained only 8,000 people. Interstate 295 opened up suburban development, however, and the population grew to 17,000 by 1980. More than 3,000 new housing units—all single-family homes—were built in that 15-year period. In addition, the town sited 50 acres of new offices and industrial parks on 50 acres of land adjacent to the intersection of Interstate 295 and the New Jersey Turnpike.

Mt. Laurel also has a small black settlement that traces its origins to the Civil War. For decades the blacks worked as tenant farmers. As suburban development ate up farmland, they retreated to a small community of summer cottages in the Springville section. By 1969, only 120 people remained. The town refused to extend sewer, water, or paved roads into the area. The houses were labelled non-conforming uses, meaning they could not be remodeled, replaced, or repaired in any significant way. Occasionally, the town would condemn a building. Springville residents saw quite clearly that they were being driven out of town.

In 1969, a group of Springville residents formed the Springville Action Committee. Securing a state grant, they proposed building 100 apartments on a three-acre parcel in Springville to house most of the black population. The town turned down the proposal on the grounds that it violated the zoning ordinance, which only allowed single-family homes on half-acre lots. The Burlington County NAACP sued the town in state court.

In 1975, the New Jersey Supreme Court overturned Mt. Laurel's ordinance and ordered the town to zone some of its land for apartments. Moreover, the court extended its decision to cover all "developing" communities in the state and said that they would have to make similar provisions for low-income housing as well.

Mt. Laurel's response was typical of municipalities in similar positions. It rezoned three small parcels for apartments, *but not the property of the successful litigant.* One of the parcels was already being subdivided for homes. The other two were swampy and inaccessible. All three owners said they had no interest in building apartments or cheap housing.

Meanwhile, other towns around the state began resisting the Mt. Laurel decision by arguing that they were not "developing" communities, but were either already developed or had never even considered development. As a result, eight years after the first Mt. Laurel decision, no new housing had been built.

Once again, Springville Action went back into court. In 1983, after two years of deliberation, the New Jersey Supreme Court handed down "Mt. Laurel II," a case that has been called "the most significant zoning decision since *Euclid vs. Ambler Realty.*"[25] The court wrote:

> The constitutional power to zone, delegated to the municipalities, subject to legislation, is but one portion of the police power and, as such, must be exercised for the general welfare.
>
> When the exercise of this power by a municipality affects something as fundamental as housing, the general welfare includes more than the welfare of that municipality and its citizens: it also includes the general welfare—in this case the housing needs—of those residing outside of the municipality but within the region that contributes to the housing demand within the municipality.[26]

The court conjured up an image of what the state would eventually look like if exclusionary practices were allowed to go unchecked:

> poor people forever zoned out of substantial areas of the state, not because housing could not be built for them but because they are not wanted; poor people forced to live in urban slums forever not because suburbia, developing rural areas, fully developed residential sections, seashore resorts, and other attractive locations could not accommodate them, but simply because they are not wanted.

Yet at the same time, the court was not about to turn the state over to housing developers:

> We reassure all concerned that Mt. Laurel is not designed to sweep away all land-use restrictions or leave our open spaces and natural resources prey to speculators. . . . No forests or small towns need to be paved over and covered with high-rise apartments. . . .

Instead, the court decided that the state government would be the ultimate authority on zoning.

> The state controls the use of land, *all* of the land. In exercising that control, it cannot favor the rich over the poor. It cannot legislatively set aside dilapidated housing in urban ghettos for the poor and decent housing elsewhere for everyone else. The government that controls this land represents everyone. While the state may not have the ability to eliminate poverty, it cannot use that condition as the basis for imposing further disadvantages. [Emphasis in original.][27]

As specific remedies, the court stated that municipalities must follow one of three strategies: 1) encourage or require the use of available Federal and state housing subsidies for the construction of low-income housing; 2) provide incentives or require developers to set aside a portion of their developments for low-income housing; or 3) zone areas for mobile homes or extremely small units that can be sold to low-income people.

In 1985, the New Jersey State Legislature responded to all this prodding by adopting the Fair Housing Act. The law set up the New Jersey Council on Affordable Housing, which requested all 567 municipalities to send in proposals on how they planned to comply with Mt. Laurel II.

Thus, the Mt. Laurel decision, although it addressed some of the effects of zoning, was not really a frontal attack on the whole concept. There was no inclination to allow housing transactions between willing buyers and willing sellers without municipal interference, as Houston has done. Instead, a deliberately cumbersome local process used to resist new housing construction was replaced with an even more cumbersome state process that might create some low-income housing (although it should be remembered that, even at the state level, the poor are a distinct minority).

Progress has been painfully slow. As of 1989, only 161 of the state's 567 municipalities had even submitted plans to conform with the state law. The Council does not have any real powers of enforcement and the prospects for widespread cooperation are not encouraging. Overall, about 2,000 new units have been built in 14 communities since the 1983 decision.

The favored technique for conforming with Mt. Laurel II has been something called "inclusionary zoning." The process was invented in California and has since been adopted by many cities and smaller municipalities. It is particularly popular with jurisdictions that are practicing exclusionary zoning but don't want to give the impression that they are trying to wall out the poor.

With inclusionary zoning, a builder is given a density bonus (usually 20 percent more units) in exchange for a promise that the additional units will be sold at "low-income" prices. The municipality then sets up a selection process (often including a lottery) whereby a few local applicants get to buy or rent the new units.

Much to the consternation of housing advocates (and the quiet relief of suburban officials), these units have not fallen into the hands of the urban poor. Instead, they have attracted what might be called "subsidy hunters"—young couples, divorced single mothers, the elderly, and other middle-class people who are knowledgeable enough to take advantage of the system. In 1988, *The New York Times* reported:

> [T]he first trickle of affordable homes built [under Mt. Laurel] has not gone to the inner-city poor, even though the court held in 1975 . . . that the poor in cities were entitled under the State constitution to the same housing opportunities in the suburbs as other economic classes. . . . With their meager incomes and weak credit ratings, [the poor] either cannot qualify for or afford a down-payment or closing costs, experts on the Mt. Laurel doctrine say.
>
> Instead, the homes, generally priced between $30,000 and $70,000, have been snapped up by others who qualify as low- and moderate-income buyers, most notably young professional families and divorced, single, and retired people.[28]

One town official called the new residents "junior yuppies, young professionals in entry-level positions [who only] qualify by the numbers."

This outcome should not surprise anyone. One problem has been that the situation upon which the whole case is built—Mt. Laurel itself—was somewhat atypical in that the poor people involved were *already* living in the community. Given the *information* required to take advantage of Mt. Laurel housing, the urban poor are not likely to be participants. As Anthony Downs noted in 1974:

> In reality, blacks will probably be much less aggressive about taking advantage of such new opportunities than whites. Not many blacks have moved to the suburbs up to now—even among those who could afford it. In fact, I am convinced that the belief of many whites that opening up the suburbs will cause an immediate large-scale influx of black households is completely false. . . . Nevertheless, if even 10 percent [of new residents] were black, that would create at least some integration of black households throughout the suburbs.[29]

Mt. Laurel is not going to produce the "diaspora of the urban poor" that some observers anticipated.[30] Nor are the benefits of the Court's decision likely to filter down to the poor very quickly. In reality, it makes absolutely no difference whether the few prizewinners of subsidized units are "low-income," "middle-income," or even "upper-income." Housing is housing and the only way to have it is to build more of it. The only likely benefits of Mt. Laurel will come from the density bonuses, which will allow more housing units to be built.

Yet even this advantage is likely to be offset because the new housing will not circulate. The new owners, after all, are subsidized and cannot move without giving up their subsidy. They are usually not even allowed to sell their unit without giving up a significant portion of the capital appreciation, either to the municipality or the next owner. Thus, they will stay in their units long after the units have ceased to suit them and long after they have ceased to be "low-income." By attaching subsidies to housing units, rather than the people who live in them, governments effectively take these units off the market.

The only truly promising feature of Mt. Laurel and the Fair Housing Act has been the provision that, if a town does not wish to accept its "fair share" of housing, it can still meet its quota by *paying to have apartments built in towns willing to accept them*. Because this housing will undoubtedly end up in the hands of deserving people, it will do far more good than the housing snapped up by subsidy hunters.

The great attraction of exclusionary zoning has always been that it is a free good. A town could zone out whatever housing it didn't want without having to pay a price. Indeed, it rewarded itself by raising property values and avoiding social spending. Under Mt. Laurel, towns will finally be held financially accountable for their exclusionary practices by having to pay for housing built elsewhere. That, at least, is an accomplishment.

Chapter 8

Who Pays the Piper?

Some say it all began with the "case of the crooked assessor."

In 1966, San Francisco county tax assessor Russell L. Wolden was caught with his hand in the till. A popular public figure who had held his elective office since 1938, Wolden—like assessors everywhere—had the responsibility of determining the value of every property in the county so that it could be billed for property taxes.[1]

Although the recipient of only a modest civil-servant's salary, Wolden somehow managed to own an expensive co-op apartment in San Francisco and a magnificent country estate. When an eccentric subordinate started going through his files in 1965, it soon became clear why. Wolden had long carried on a simple scheme of demanding bribes from businesses in return for lowering their property assessments.

The story hit the papers in 1966 and soon Wolden was in jail. For a whole summer, San Francisco residents read about the "huge tax breaks" that businesses had been getting. The wave of public indignation set off a cry for statewide assessment reform.

As with most states, the California constitution requires that properties be assessed at "full value" for the purpose of setting their property taxes. Because of the enormous difficulty of keeping tens of thousands of assessments up to date, however, nearly all communities practiced "fractional assessment"—a confusing system wherein properties are listed at outdated figures that are supposed to represent a uniform fraction of their real value.

Spurred on by the Wolden scandal—and cheered on by municipal reformers all over the country—the California legislature adopted the Reform Act of 1966. All communities would now be required to maintain all their assessments at 100 percent of real value. Reassessments would be required every three years. The state assessor's office would contribute money and computers to do the job. Good-government reformers everywhere celebrated the passing of "gaslight government." At last, the antiquated property-tax system would be made fair, reasonable, and equitable.

Then a funny thing happened. When the first new assessments started appearing in 1967, homeowners found themselves facing big tax *increases.* "How could this be?" they asked. "We thought it was businesses that were getting all the tax breaks."

In fact, what tax reform had uncovered was one of the oldest, best-kept secrets of municipal government. For decades, Wolden and assessors like him around the nation had been practicing a very peculiar brand of corruption. Whether elected or appointed, assessors knew which side their bread was buttered on. The best way to keep the majority of voters happy was to keep their assessments low. And the majority of knowledgeable voters—those who confronted property taxes most directly—were homeowners.

Assessors, it turned out, had been following a universal practice of *over*assessing industrial and commercial properties and *under*assessing private homes. Although there was no uniform rule, private homes were usually assessed at no more than 70 to 90 percent of their real value, apartment houses at 90 to 120 percent, commercial and industrial properties at 95 to 140 percent, and railroad and utility companies at 120 to 150 percent.[2]

The logic was simple. While homeowners voted in large numbers, tenants were generally unaware of their property taxes and so their buildings could be assessed higher. Industrial and commercial properties had no votes and could be squeezed—although not too hard, because they might leave town. Utilities companies were the most vulnerable. The gas and electric companies couldn't move to another county, the railroads couldn't pull up their tracks. As regulated industries, they could also pass on their tax bill to their customers. As a result, utilities companies often became informal tax collectors for municipal governments.

Thus, those few commercial and industrial property-owners who had bribed Wolden were not really getting "tax breaks"—at least nothing compared to what homeowners were getting. Instead, they were just having their inflated assessments brought a little more into line with reality. With the new assessments, homeowners were now being asked to pay their fair share.

And so, it wasn't surprising when, shortly after tax reform went into effect, bumper stickers started appearing around California reading, "Bring Back the Crooked Assessor."

Some say that when he finally did reappear, his name was Howard Jarvis.

The property tax is probably the oldest form of general taxation. The Romans practiced it, the Chinese empire was built upon it. Never limited to "real property" (land and buildings), the property tax was usually levied on *personal* property as well. Roman assessors included horses and wagons. Chinese bureaucrats counted pots and pans. In Colonial America, plows and bushels of corn were considered taxable property. Even in California in 1965, assessments included an estimate of a homeowner's furniture. (Wolden delighted everyone by assessing them at a uniformly low $50.)

The reason the property tax has always been so popular with government officials is that it is easy to administer and hard to avoid. "We feel it's the most efficient way of raising revenue at the local level," said Cathie Eitelberg, assistant director of the Government Finance Officers' Association, in Washington. "The other forms are much more dependent on self-declarations." The Internal Revenue Service estimates that 20 percent of American income is "off the books." Sales taxes can also be dodged by dealing in unrecorded cash transactions. Property, on the other hand, is visible, tangible, and eminently assessable. Talk long enough to a passionate opponent of the property tax and he will probably end up giving you a crooked little smile and admitting, "Besides, you can cheat on your income tax but you can't cheat on your property tax."

In the United States, property taxes have always been the principal means of raising local revenues. Until the advent of income, sales, and corporate taxes, it was also the principal source of state revenues. The Federal government—although few remember it—was completely dependent upon the tariff until the income-tax amendment was adopted in 1913. As late as 1934, the revenues raised from local property taxes still exceeded the entire tax levy of the Federal government.

At that time, property taxes paid for 90 percent of local schools and municipal government. The figure declined somewhat as cities turned to income and sales taxes, but by 1970 it was still 83 percent. Today, property taxes still account for 33 percent of state and local revenues and 20 percent of all taxes raised in the nation.

In cities, the property tax has been relatively painless to homeowners—even without rigged assessments—because the large number of commercial and industrial properties picks up most of the tab. One of the most common "mixed uses" in old urban areas is the three- or four-story building with a commercial space on the ground floor and several apartments upstairs. Since the commercial tenant pays the bulk of the rent, these structures can be taxed at full without weighing too heavily on residential tenants. Municipal officials call these buildings "taxpayers."

When the streetcar suburbs opened, the tradition of mixed uses and commercial and industrial districts went along with them. Shopping streets often extended along trolley lines. Industries also followed (recall the Norwood district outside Cincinnati). This mix of industrial, commercial and residential properties kept taxes low.

The situation began to change, however, with the emergence of bedroom communities in the 1950s and 1960s. In the "auto suburbs," major stores and shopping centers did not have to be within walking distance. Some towns developed commercial strips, but others rejected them altogether. Factories and industrial plants were not always welcome, either. Property taxes began to shift onto residences themselves, becoming for the first time a significant burden on the homeowner.

Faced with this dilemma, municipal assessors began looking for new ways to alter the property tax. One way was to assess the few industrial and commercial properties even higher. But even this had its limits. And so another practice began of subtly shifting the tax burden among residences themselves. This became so common that assessors gave it the sardonic title: "Welcome, stranger!"

Welcome-stranger assessments work as follows. Because of the difficulty in keeping assessments up to date (most assessors work only part-time), the practice developed of revaluing homes only when they were sold. This made the new assessment indisputable, since it was based on the sale price. But it also had another subtle effect. Assessing on sale gradually shifted the tax burden from established residents to newcomers in the community.

Say that Mrs. Oldtimer and her husband originally bought their home in 1965 for $50,000. The market value probably went up to $100,000 by 1978 and stands at $200,000 today. The current tax rate is $2 per $1,000 of assessed value. (A range of $1.50 to $2.50 is common). Thus, Mrs. Oldtimer pays $1,000, whereas she should be paying $4,000. Her husband passed away in 1980, however, and she only has a pension. As her many friends in the community point out, making her pay at the current value of her property would literally put her out of her home.

Besides, they add, forcing her to move would probably mean her house would be occupied by a large family with children, which would further burden the school system. Why not leave well enough alone?

Meanwhile, Mr. and Mrs. Newcomer moved into town five years ago. They bought their house for $150,000. It was the first home they ever owned and for a while they didn't even realize they were paying property taxes. When they finally took the trouble to look at their assessment, they found that their property was valued at $150,000—just what they paid for it. Their tax bill came to $3,000. All seemed fair enough.

Only after a few years did Mr. and Mrs. Newcomer start hearing the stories that many houses around town are assessed at far below their present value. Right down the street, the Widow Oldtimer lives in a house that is much bigger than theirs but supposedly pays only about $1,000. They are tempted to complain about it, except for one thing—the system is now starting to work in their favor as well. Right across the street another new family just paid $175,000 for a house that is virtually identical to theirs. They are assessed at $175,000 and are paying $3,500 in taxes. The Newcomers have decided that, as long as things don't get any worse, maybe they'll just leave well enough alone.

In 1989, *The New York Times* carried a whimsical story of how welcome-stranger assessments had completely divided the small Catskill town of Delhi, New York:

> People here have started thinking of each other as assessments. "It's making it difficult to have friendly relations with neighbors," said [Marion] Ragsdale, [a newcomer, whose tax bill was double that of oldtimers with similar homes]. "I had dinner with my neighbor—an old assessment. We had to avoid the issue. I sense it at the bank, from longtime residents. . . .
>
> The new assessments have formed a tax protest group, led by Avi Golub, owner of . . . a lovely bed-and-breakfast place, with one of the most up-to-date assessments in town ($100,000). They've complained to Delhi village and town board members (8 of 9, old assessments). Next month, on tax grievance day, they plan to protest to [town assessor Frank] Bovee ($39,000, old).[3]

In January 1989, the U.S. Supreme Court ruled that welcome-stranger assessment policies are unconstitutional. As with the Mt. Laurel decision, however, implementation will be at the local level and therefore probably slow. Although computers have made full-value, up-to-date assessments eminently feasible, the real resistance is likely to be at the political level.

* * *

Given a limited ability to redistribute the property tax among homeowners, there is only one real way that suburban municipalities can lower the tax burden for the owners of single-family homes. That is to attract "good ratables"—tax-paying stores, businesses, industry.

Sometimes this effort has been spectacularly successful. In 1959, for example, the town of Mahwah, New Jersey, 15 miles northwest of Manhattan, sited a gigantic Ford assembly plant that was leaving an outmoded facility along the Hudson River, in Edgewater, N.J. Mahwah, which lies adjacent to the New York State border, put the plant right on the state line. Traffic was funneled onto an interchange of the New York State Thruway only a few hundred yards from the plant. Mahwah itself felt little impact.

For over 20 years, 5,000 auto workers trooped to Mahwah every day to work on the assembly line. (The plant closed in 1978.) Yet few of the workers ever lived in Mahwah or even close to the town. The town never allowed more than a few apartments to be built. It also put restrictions on rented rooms. Auto workers—about 30 percent of them black—regularly commuted from as far away as Newark and Philadelphia. Meanwhile, Mahwah residents paid one of the lowest property taxes in the state.

For the vast majority of suburban communities, however, such huge tax ratables are neither feasible nor desirable. Instead, they must search for that elusive entity that often takes on almost mythical properties in the suburbs—the "good, clean ratable."

The search for good, clean ratables is the holy grail of urban and suburban planning. Everyone's ideal is "light industry"—meaning a clean, non-polluting industry that is staffed by white-collar workers, does not generate much traffic, and demands little in municipal services. Office parks, corporate headquarters, laboratories, insurance companies—all are eagerly sought by suburban governments.

Commercial development is regarded with slightly less enthusiasm because it produces a lot of traffic. A few local mini-malls will be tolerated, but large shopping centers are viewed warily. Generally, towns will try to confine heavy commercial development to one or two major highways—although even this "strip zoning" and "honky-tonk development" comes under criticism from suburban residents.

Apartment houses have always occupied an ambiguous position on this battlefield. Apartments usually contain a mixed population—elderly people and young couples, rather than just families with children—and do not place such a burden on the school system. They are often easier on municipal services as well. Because they are usually located near population centers, apartments do not require extending fire and police protection into remote areas.

On the other hand, apartments can add to municipal expenditures. They may require a new hook-and-ladder truck or foul up downtown traffic patterns. If the town already has a sewer system, apartments will be easier to service than spread-out single-family homes. But if there is no sewer system, a cluster of apartments may make it a requirement—an enormous municipal undertaking. Towns have often rejected apartments until they got their sewers in place, then become more receptive.

In the 1950s and 1960s, the suburbs generally resisted apartments because of the prevailing ethos of ownership and single-family homes. Then in 1964, George Sternlieb published a carefully calibrated study showing that studio or one-bedroom apartments would pay their own way in property taxes, apartments with two bedrooms would break even, and apartments with three or more bedrooms would consume more than they returned in municipal services—because they would be occupied by families with two or more children.[4] As a result, suburban communities became much more receptive to apartments—but only after putting strict zoning limitations on the number of bedrooms.[5]

The other question about apartments is whether they attract low-income families. The simple solution has been to *make the apartments as expensive as possible.* As Michael Davidson noted in *The Politics of Exclusion:*

> A common goal of suburban governments [in approving apartments] is "to bid up the price or cost . . . in order to limit the number of people who can come in at lower cost." For one suburban planner, "the thing to focus on" in negotiations with apartment developers was "the rent schedule. If the rent schedule is high enough . . . I don't think you have to be apprehensive about being flooded by a slew of school children."[6]

Thus, apartments are acceptable if they don't contain too many low-income school children. Industry may be attractive if it doesn't require worker housing. Commercial development is good, except that it generates too much traffic.

Still, the central paradox of the suburbs boils down to this. The one type of development that everyone has usually been willing to accept—detached single-family homes—is precisely the kind of development that is a net consumer of municipal tax revenues. Single-family homes are expensive to service. An extensive road network must be maintained, police and fire services must be extended, enormously expensive sewer interceptors must eventually be built. Most important, single-family homes generally produce a lot of school children. A family with two children living in a detached home on half-an-acre may consume $10,000 in school services alone, while paying a total tax bill of only $5,000 to $6,000. Yet if suburban residents remain resistant to apartments and industrial and commercial ratables, who is going to make up the difference?

In *1400 Governments* (1964), Robert C. Wood, professor of political science at MIT, chronicled the evolutionary growth of this pattern in the New York Metropolitan Area.[7] Comparing the distribution of land uses in 34 small New Jersey municipalities, Wood found two distinct trends: 1) the assessed value in the older streetcar suburbs lay mostly in business properties, while the value in the newer bedroom communities had become concentrated in single-family homes; and 2) the average value of residential property in bedroom communities exceeded the *combined* average values of business and residential properties in the older suburbs.[8]

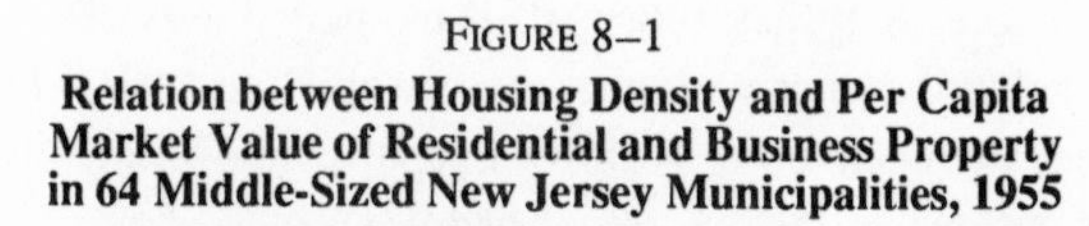
FIGURE 8–1
Relation between Housing Density and Per Capita Market Value of Residential and Business Property in 64 Middle-Sized New Jersey Municipalities, 1955

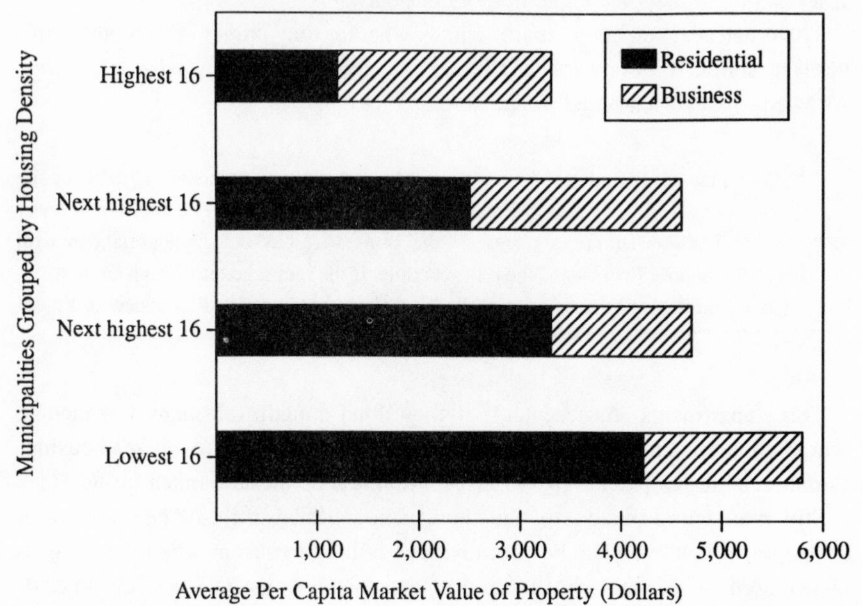

Using regression analysis, Wood also discovered that, whereas the older, streetcar suburbs spent more money on municipal services like police and welfare, the newer suburbs spent more on schools. "High industrialization" and "high density"

were the best predictor of high spending for municipal and social services, whereas "high residential affluence" was the best indicator for high spending on schools.[9]

It was clear that the bedroom suburbs were painting themselves into a corner. Still dependent upon local property tax for their revenues, they were building expensive school systems while undercutting the property-tax base by excluding industries, businesses, apartments, and "all the things we came here to get away from."

It wasn't at all surprising that by the early 1970s, the idea began to take hold in the suburbs that the property tax itself was "unfair" and needed to be replaced as the main source of funding for local schools and municipal services.

In 1971, John Serrano, father of John, Jr., a student in Baldwin Park, a suburb of Los Angeles, filed suit against the state commissioner of education, arguing that his child was not getting a proper education because of the property-tax system. The case was joined by several anti-poverty groups and became a class action on behalf of all poor children in the state.

The argument, which was to become the standard tack in dozens of similar suits, went as follows:

A child's education depends on local finances, which in turn depend on the amount of tax ratables available in the school district. This is inherently unfair, since children in poor districts can't get as good an education, while children in rich districts got a superior education. Therefore, the local property tax discriminated against the poor. The only way to remedy the situation was to switch to a statewide property, sales, or income tax, or even universal school funding on the Federal level.

The plaintiffs in *Serrano* went for a ruling before the California Supreme Court even before the trial. In 1971, the court startled the nation by ruling that the constitutionality of the property tax was indeed subject to question. Similar suits were filed in Texas and New Jersey, and in 1971, the Texas Supreme Court ruled in a San Antonio case that the property tax was indeed unconstitutional.

Soon, this "highly visible, much-hated levy"[10] was under attack everywhere. In 1972, President Richard Nixon himself charged the Advisory Commission on Intergovernmental Relations to study whether the funding of local education should be switched from property taxes to a federal value-added tax.

Although the legal arguments centered on the poor, much of the debate outside the courtroom simply reflected the complaints of suburban homeowners. "The property tax is regressive," went the common argument. "It was designed to tax large estates, not little people's homes. Homeownership isn't a sign of wealth, it's only a sign of your ability to get into debt. I don't own this home, the bank does. Why should I pay taxes on something I don't own? Taxes should be placed on real wealth—stocks and bonds—not the place where you live."

Bergen County, New Jersey, was an ideal vantage point to view the property-tax rebellion of the early 1970s. Stretching north and west from the George Washington Bridge, Bergen County encompasses almost the entire spectrum of suburban development. At the southern end, clustered around the Hackensack Meadowlands, are older suburbs like Lodi, Carlstadt, and Moonachie—lower-middle-class communities built near the turn of the century where people live cheek-by-jowl with heavy industry. The scenery is grim, trucks rumble through the streets day and night, and the air is filled with fly ash and indescribable industrial odors.

At the northern end of the county are pleasant residential communities, nestled in rolling countryside. The towns have bucolic names like Alpine, Northvale, and Upper Saddle River. Often the only sign of commercial activity is a grocery store sitting beneath the town's only traffic light.

The people in the southern factory suburbs had elected to live with industry for two obvious reasons. First, it offered jobs. Second, it paid the property taxes. Living in two- and three-family homes, usually down the street from a chemical plant or a regional shipping depot, the blue-collar residents of these towns accepted industry for one simple reason—it allowed them to own their own homes.

The people in the northern suburbs, on the other hand, had firmly rejected industrial and commercial development. Why? Because it detracted from the quality of life and threatened the environment. Some towns had deftly landed a few large, clean ratables—corporate headquarters or office parks—to ease the tax burden. But for the most part, anything except single-family homes on large lots was fiercely resisted.

When agitation for property-tax reform started in the early 1970s, *all* of it came from the northern bedroom communities. The pattern was so clear that reporters applying for jobs at *The Bergen Record* took a test in which they were asked to write up a hypothetical meeting in a northern suburb where, at one point, a local reformer requested the town council "condemn the Vietnam War, fund a local ecology club, and pass a resolution urging the state government to switch school financing from the property tax to a statewide income tax."

Despite the patina of anti-poverty rhetoric that always surrounded the subject, the move to "reform" the property tax in the 1970s was largely an effort by suburban communities to undo the effects of exclusionary zoning. Having closed their doors to industry, apartments, and shopping districts, the suburbs now tried to change the rules of the game, shifting the tax burden elsewhere and perhaps even laying claim to some of those good ratables that had been piled up in other communities.

"The big problem with property-tax reform was that the numbers never bore out the basic premise," said Michael Kirst, of the Stanford School of Education, who studied the problem extensively. "Just because a community has low incomes doesn't mean it's poor in tax ratables. In fact, most cities have a pretty good property-tax base. The districts with problems are the bedroom communities. When the state finally got around to implementing its new equalization formulas, money moved out of Oakland and San Francisco and into the suburbs."

Despite this obvious illogic, property-tax reform gained enormous momentum in the early 1970s. Only after the initial enthusiasm wore off did a few people start considering the situation more rationally. One study in California revealed that more than half the state's poor children were *already* living in "rich" school districts. In 1973, the Advisory Commission on Intergovernmental Relations reported to President Nixon that the property tax was a fair and equitable system and recommended against switching to a Federal financing system. In the same year, the U.S. Supreme Court overruled the *San Antonio* decision and decided the property tax does not violate the Constitution.

In 1975, Henry Aaron, of the Brookings Institute, published *Who Pays the Property Tax?*, a brief but influential analysis which concluded that the property tax is actually "one of the more progressive elements in the national tax system rather than one of the most regressive."[11] The tax closely parallels people's long-run ability to pay, Aaron argued, since homeownership, more than any other factor, reflects long-term income achievement. The tax, he found, is progressive among homeowners since people spend progressively more on housing as their incomes rise. It is slightly regressive for renters, but only because higher-income tenants tend to shift their consumption to other items, rather than paying progressively higher rents.

While the property tax could be better administered by keeping assessments up-to-date, the principle of property taxation was sound. "Advocates of greater progressivity in the [tax] system should recognize that the property tax advances rather than obstructs achievement of egalitarian objectives," concluded Aaron.[12]

Despite these caveats, many states made significant changes in educational funding. New Jersey imposed a state income tax and lowered the local share of the education burden from 60 percent to 25 percent. Other states made similar changes. Nationally, the property-tax portion of the school bill declined from more than 60 percent to less than 50 percent.

Nine states and the District of Columbia also legalized fractional assessments in order to protect homeowners. In Massachusetts, for example, homes are now assessed at only half the rate of commercial property. Minnesota, which adopted differential assessments in 1913, now has 34 different classifications, ranging from 5 percent of value for homesteads to 50 percent for unmined iron ore.[13]

Another new tactic was the "circuit-breaker"—a limit on property taxes for specific people. Some circuit-breakers put ceilings on the tax to low-income households (sometimes including tenants), but most were aimed at homeowning senior citizens. Although based on favoritism toward long-time residents, these senior-citizen exemptions were also advertised to the community as a way of keeping large homes from being occupied by families with school children.

Altogether, then, the net effect of all these property-tax reforms was to insulate homeowners from the disadvantages of refusing to live with better tax ratables. By shifting the tax burden away from local sources, municipalities freed themselves to pursue more exclusionary practices.

Yet the main event in property-tax reform was still to come. Even as the effort to abolish the property tax was losing momentum, a new movement was taking shape to shift the tax base and make welcome-stranger assessments a permanent institution. This was, of course, California's Proposition 13.

Although widely regarded as a conservative-led "tax revolt"—one of the first rumblings of the Reagan Revolution—Proposition 13 has not always been recognized for its other important aspect—a culmination of suburban efforts to get rid of the adverse effects of exclusionary zoning.

The story of Proposition 13 is well known.[14] Howard Jarvis, a former prizefighter and successful businessman, had long been trying to use California's referendum route to lower property taxes. He had helped put similar measures on the ballot in 1968 and 1972, only to be defeated both times.

In 1978, he finally found a sympathetic audience. Inflation was causing mayhem in the entire economy. Particularly hard-hit were California homeowners. As already chronicled, the wave of environmental concerns and exclusionary zoning in the 1970s had driven California home prices far above the national average. These price increases were quickly reflected in California's reformed assessment system. Particularly hard-hit were older owners who had bought properties earlier and then saw them appreciate rapidly. By 1976, homeowners around Los Angeles making only $15,000 a year found themselves paying $6,000 a year in property taxes.

Although these taxes were paid to local municipalities, the policies of the state government also aroused resentment. Governor Jerry Brown, in an effort to prove his managerial abilities, had piled up a $10 million surplus in the state treasury and was talking about launching a communications satellite as part of a California space program. Taxpayers decided they had had enough of such entrepreneurial government. By a 2-to-1 majority, they responded to Jarvis by voting to put legal limits on the property tax.

Proposition 13 stipulated that henceforth property could be taxed at no more than one percent of its actual value—an unusually low rate. Nor could any new taxes be raised by state or local governments, except by a two-thirds vote of the electorate. This shifted the tax burden to the state level.

In addition, Jarvis added a "grandfather clause" that effectively institutionalized welcome-stranger assessments. For *present* homeowners, assessments were rolled back to their 1975–76 level and could rise only 2 percent annually. For everyone who bought a new home after 1978, however, assessments would be set at market value.

Thus, in addition to reducing taxes, Proposition 13 was a blatant effort to shift the tax burden to new homeowners. Because the vast majority qualified for the benefits, the grandfather clause was readily accepted. The long-term effects, once again, have been to clog the circulation of housing, subsidize people in large homes, and generally aggravate the "housing shortage."

Yet that was not the end of it. As it turned out, Proposition 13 provided communities with still another tool for resisting new development. With local revenues vastly reduced, communities now had a ready-made excuse for not providing essential services to new residents. Eventually, municipalities hit on a new tack of charging "impact fees," which have made new housing even more expensive.

The result of Proposition 13—whether inadvertent or not—has been to reinforce the pattern that was already taking shape, whereby people who are already established in the community make it harder and harder for new people to get through the door. In both California and the rest of the country, all this was beginning to converge under the new municipal rallying cry: "no-growth."

Chapter 9

Controlling Growth

In 1978, Professor Bernard Frieden, an urban expert from the Massachusetts Institute of Technology, went to the San Francisco area to study housing policies. Like many academic liberals of the period, Frieden was concerned that suburban communities were excluding racial minorities. He had completed a long study of exclusionary practices in the Boston area and wanted to extend his studies to the West Coast.

After a year of observing municipal governments in action, Frieden decided he had been mistaken.

> Suburban interests formerly managed to defeat legal challenges to their exclusionary zoning and to block federal politics that aimed at opening the suburbs to subsidized housing. Now a new alliance combining environmentalists with the old protectors of the suburban status quo has come up with techniques for keeping out not only the poor but even the middle class.[1]

Far from worrying about racial minorities, suburban exclusionists had decided to exclude *everybody.* For them, the best development was no development at all.

Contra Costa County tried to stop one housing development because "it's a possibility that [endangered bald eagles] fly over the project area."[2] Santa Barbara prevented development by refusing to build a new drinking reservoir. Santa Cruz demanded that houses in one area must be built on stilts in order to avoid disrupting the migrations of a local salamander that came out of the hills once a year to mate at a nearby pond.[3]

In the hands of these enthusiasts, said Frieden, legitimate concerns about environmentalism had been turned into "a ready rationale for the defense of privilege."

> Resistance to growth began as a very reasonable political shift, concentrating on saving such priceless assets as San Francisco Bay and Napa Valley wine country. But as it gathered power, and as *people discovered they could stop growth at little cost to themselves,* the movement became a good deal less reasonable. Soon it turned into general hostility towards homebuilding for the average family, using the rhetoric of environmental protection in order to look after the narrow interests of people who got to the suburbs first. [Emphasis added.][4]

What Frieden noted in California was the first stirrings of a movement that would soon sweep across the nation. Over the next 15 years, "stopping growth" became the concern of communities everywhere. From one end of the country to the other, just about every little town and hamlet decided that "things have gone too far" and it was "time to call a halt to our senseless, unrestricted growth."

In Vermont, for example, Governor Madeline Kunin announced in 1987 that growth was out of control and proposed the state government take over planning and zoning responsibilities. She proposed a new state planning agency, funded by a special property tax on new, non-residential development.[5]

In Fauquier County, Virginia, 60 miles from Washington, D.C., county supervisors increased the minimum lot size for new homes from five acres to ten acres in order to slow development. While realtors complained "we're drastically short of apartments and homes for the first-time home-buyer," the county government imposed a two-year moratorium on all new construction. "Right now, you could get an overwhelming vote to keep the county just the way it is," said Richard McNear, director of the county's planning and zoning department.[6]

From Gwinnett County, Georgia, ("We don't want to be another Atlanta") to Eugene, Oregon, ("We don't want to be another Portland") every city, small town, and suburb was scurrying to draw up plans for a building moratorium or a zoning master-plan, all designed to "control our explosive, unplanned growth." The common theme of all these plans, of course, was that the people already living in the community wanted to prevent anybody else from moving in after them. As Arthur Kondrup, assistant commissioner of the New Jersey Department of Environmental Protection, put it: "Everybody who ever moved out here from New York City always wanted to close the door behind them."

The granddaddy of all growth-control states has been California. For many years the fastest-growing state in the union, California has now slowed down somewhat and Arizona and Florida are growing faster. Still, in absolute numbers, California continues to expand at an astonishing rate. Over 4,000 people move into the state every *day* and one-quarter of the nation's population growth still occurs in California.

California can hardly be accused of turning people away at the border (even at the Mexican border, where the Immigration and Naturalization Service has been fighting a largely futile battle to stem the flow). The question is, where would these people live once they arrived? Overwhelmingly, local communities have been answering, "Not in this town."

During the 1987 elections, voters in Southern California passed eight out of ten "no-growth" measures and defeated 12 of 14 "pro-growth" measures. The momentum slowed a bit when no-growth advocates tried to go countywide in 1988. Measures in both Riverside and San Diego Counties failed narrowly. But Southern California no-growth activists linked up with Northern California environmental veterans to form the "Save California" coalition and take the battle statewide in 1990.[7]

Moreover, Californians, with their usual enthusiasm for popular democracy, have been moving toward public micromanagement of land. In 1988, the City of Poway, in San Diego County, adopted a law requiring popular approval of all major residential projects. In Chula Vista, the city council is required to prepare quality-of-life reviews for each new development project. A 1986 law adopted by referendum in San Mateo County required farmers to seek voter approval before clearing fallen trees off their land or stacking wood on their property.[8] Politicians and planning officials call it "ballot-box zoning."

A typical community shaken by growth issues has been Oceanside, a sleepy resort town 20 miles north of San Diego. As late as the 1970s, Oceanside's main street was a dilapidated "Cannery Row," sprinkled with porn shops and tattoo parlors. "People wouldn't even admit they lived here," recalled Mayor Larry Bagley, a 28-year resident. Then a city-led effort to renovate the beachfront area was successful. Tourist traffic grew and visitors began to inquire about year-round homes. Soon the building department was flooded with applications. Apartment complexes sprouted on the beachfront and subdivisions spread into the neighboring chaparrals. In 1987 alone, 3,000 new housing units were begun.

The town's rapid development soon caused a split. Old-timers, remembering Oceanside's seedy past, were not terribly upset. But newcomers formed a vociferous opposition, arguing that the town's 96,000 population had already grown too large. Having found their secluded beachfront hideaway, they didn't want anybody else moving in. A petition drive, organized by civic associations in the new developments, put forth "Proposition A," legally reducing building permits by more than two-thirds, to 800 a year. The city administration countered with "Proposition B," which cited no numbers but promised not to develop parcels until schools, roads, and water hook-ups were in place. In April 1987, Proposition A won with 57 percent of the vote.[9]

By 1988, a statewide straw poll indicated that more than half the population favored a proposal to stop all new construction until Federal clean-air standards were met—a goal that probably will not be achieved in this century. "There's a new political power base out in suburbia that's hard to put your finger on," said Mark Baldassare, professor of urban studies at the University of California at Irvine. "It's not really liberal and it's not really conservative. But whatever it is, the seeds are being planted that may sweep the country."[10]

Of course, all these people had their point. Having escaped to the suburbs and small outlying towns, most people expected to find quiet residential streets, grass and trees—"your basic Ozzie-and-Harriet life," as Baldassare put it. Instead, they found themselves in a denuded landscape, sprinkled with office parks and shopping centers, and trapped in traffic jams that often made city streets seem relatively uncongested. "Traffic is usually the major problem," said Baldassare. "But the real difficulty is that people come to these areas expecting a small-town environment and find themselves in a community that is not really city or rural."[11]

Traffic, for example, has increased 60 percent on American roads since 1970, while the mileage of roads has grown only 5 percent. Even the smallest rural town often finds itself choked in rush-hour traffic. In Fairfax County, Virginia, a suburb of Washington, D.C., whose 600,000 population now exceeds the 450,000 population of its urban core—traffic has completely overwhelmed antiquated rural roads. In California, a survey in Rancho Penasquitos, south of Los Angeles, found it took residents 40 minutes to drive two miles to a nearby freeway entrance. Once on those freeways, California drivers spent 10 percent of their time standing still or travelling at less than five miles an hour.

Yet while there were obvious problems, there were good indications that no-growth policies were not going to be the solution. While opponents of growth fretted about "suburban sprawl," they showed little interest in more compact development. When residents of San Gabriel decided to control growth, they overlooked single-family homes and voted a one-year ban on apartments. Alhambra, Monterey Park, Sierra Madre—all suburbs of Los Angeles—clamped down on attached housing, rather than single-family homes, as well.[12]

As William Fulton, editor of *California Planning and Development Report,* put it, "Everybody that comes to California wants a single-family home with a two-car garage just ten minutes from the expressway. Then they wonder why they can't get out of their driveway in the morning."

A decade earlier, Bernard Frieden noted the same pattern of unprincipled obstruction to all development. While opponents of development usually pretended to have some overall strategy, he said, in practice they tried to block everything.

> Sierra Club chapters . . . have opposed some suburban housing on the grounds that it would generate unnecessary long-distance commuting; . . . other housing near suburban jobs centers on the grounds that it should be located closer to the central cities; and . . . new housing near the central cities on the grounds that it would use up scarce open space. Another California environmental group, People for Open Space, has objected to housing in the valleys near San Francisco because the soil is better suited to farming, and . . . construction on the hillsides because it claims hill development will increase landslides, floods, and fires.[13]

Most communities claimed they were "not opposed to progress" but "only want to channel it in the right direction." Yet when the master plan for development of the community was finally revealed, it usually added up to as little new development as possible. "Channeling things in the right direction" usually meant moving it right out of town.

Is it pure selfishness that lies behind these exclusionary efforts? The answer is probably, "yes." Yet it may be an enlightened selfishness, rather than an unenlightened one.

The peculiar thing about opposition to growth is that it is usually the newest people in town who are the most rabid opponents. Said Arthur Kondrup, of the New Jersey DEP, who once served as mayor of Freehold: "The last guy to move into a town often wants to be just that—the last guy. Two months in town and he's already attending the planning board meetings trying to stop anyone else."[14]

On the other hand, "old-timers," for some odd reason, are often not as concerned about growth. They have seen the town change before and realize that it will probably change again. "I can remember when the whole town knew each other by name," they will reminisce. Yet strangely, it is the people in subdivisions or condominium complexes not six months old who are usually the most organized opponents of further growth.

As a cub reporter for the Rockland County *Journal News* in the early 1970s, I used to cover meetings in a little town called Suffern (famous in my youth as a place where New Jersey teenagers could buy beer). The mayor was a crusty old badger named Jim Rice, who seemed to have been in office since shortly after the Iroquois left the area. In the preceding years, Suffern had rezoned several properties to allow sizable condominium complexes, which were quickly filled by commuters from New York City. Before long, these eager young lawyers and stockbrokers (not yet called "yuppies") had organized their civic associations and were clamoring before Rice that the town was being overrun by uncontrolled growth.

Mayor Rice used to sit up on his elevated perch on the village board and scowl down at them. "Uncontrolled growth?" he would snort. "Is that what you called it when we let *you* move into this town?"

Interestingly enough, economic studies have shown there may be some rationality to all this. There is indeed good reason why old-timers should welcome new development. And there is also good reason why people will eventually decide that development has "gone too far." The whole thing has to do with the economic concept of "average" and "marginal" costs.

To the taxpayer, the bill for municipal services equals the total cost of the services provided, divided by the number of residents sharing the tax burden. The quotient of this division is the "average cost" to the taxpayer.

The "marginal cost," on the other hand, measures how much things change each time a new person moves into town. This is determined by the cost of the services that each new resident adds, divided by the taxes he will pay at today's rates.

Marginal costs can be either higher or lower than average costs. If they are lower, then average costs will come *down* as each new taxpayer is added to the rolls, thus reducing everyone's taxes. If marginal costs are *higher* than average costs, however, each new taxpayer will increase the average costs and push everyone's taxes up.

Economists have even worked out a general model for how the system works. It looks like this:[15]

FIGURE 9–1
Average and Marginal Costs

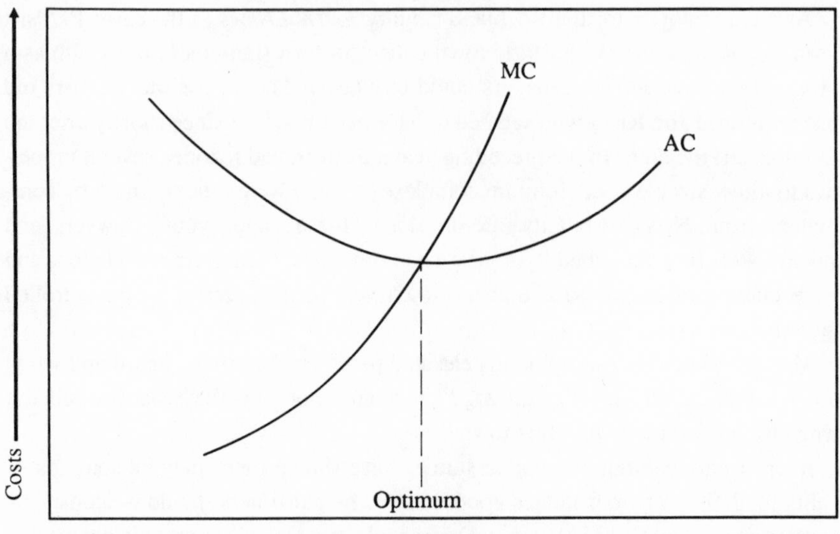

Generally, the pattern seems to be that, while a town is still small, the marginal costs of new taxpayers remain below average costs. As new residents are added, the average tax bill goes down. At a certain point in population growth, however, marginal costs surpass average costs and everybody's tax bill starts to go up. Each new resident will raise everyone's taxes.

Robert C. Wood noted this phenomenon in the 1950s in *1400 Governments.* "Significantly, the communities of rapid population growth, embroiled in the get-going costs of creating a municipal establishment, fall to the bottom [in per-capita operating expenses] as they begin the process of transformation from rural to urban status," he observed.[16] Only as they reached "high density" did per-capita costs begin to rise again.

Later studies have actually pinpointed where this change occurs. The turning point seems to come around a population of 80,000—a city about the size of Lynn, Massachusetts, Lafayette, Louisiana, or (wouldn't you know it?) Oceanside, California. Below 80,000, each new resident adds more in taxes than he consumes in municipal services. Beyond that point, new residents consume more than they add. Thus, a town can minimize its tax burden by optimizing growth at around 80,000 people.

Why do things work this way? Take fire prevention as an example. In a small town, the fire department will probably consist of a firehouse, one or two engines, and a part-time chief who is the foreman at a local factory. Everyone else is a volunteer. When the siren sounds, barbers, realtors, and drugstore clerks go rushing down the street to fight the fire.

With such a system in place, a small town can actually save money by increasing its population. Fires still occur only rarely and new homes can be serviced without adding much new equipment. A growing population will increase the pool of volunteers. With more people to share the fixed costs, there will be lower taxes for everyone.

At some point, however, the trend starts to reverse itself. The informal system will become strained. Fires occur more frequently and volunteers will have to be available around the clock. At some point, someone is going to stand up at a town meeting and say, "Here we are a city of 15,000 people and we're still relying on a volunteer fire department. Are we going to have to have a disaster before we wake up and realize we need a paid fire department?" The insurance companies will agree, promising lower insurance rates. The firefighters' union from a neighboring town will second the motion.

The town will eventually end up with a paid fire department, which will raise everybody's taxes. But once again, with the system in place, the *average* costs can be lowered by increasing the number of people who are served and augmenting the pool of taxpayers. And so the cycle goes on.

Just what all this means for a Constitutional republic like ours, of course, is anyone's guess. Should communities be able to optimize their growth and start closing the doors at the 80,000 mark? Is it an unconstitutional "taking of private property" to require existing residents to increase their tax bills by admitting people who will cost more in services than they pay in taxes? Or are towns involved in the business of interstate commerce, like lunch counters or movie theaters, and therefore obliged to take on all customers? Few courts have been willing to confront these issues and municipalities have generally gone their own way.

What municipalities are now trying to do is shift the *marginal* costs of growth onto new residents. This means making developers pay large "impact fees." First imposed in California as a result of Proposition 13, impact fees have since spread rapidly across the country.

For decades, towns and cities have been requiring builders to install roads, sidewalks, sewer laterals, and other infrastructure items that will be used directly by the new residents. These facilities are then "dedicated" to the town. As land grows more scarce and municipalities find themselves in a better bargaining position, however, they have raised their demands. They are now asking for parks, land for a new school, even the school itself. "We used to just ask for land to put the fire station," said Gaddi Vasquez, of the Orange County Board of Supervisors. "Now we ask for everything but the dalmatians."

Many towns are now demanding improvements and facilities that are only peripherally related to the marginal costs created by new housing. Developers are required to build day-care centers, senior-citizens' clubs, or parking facilities at a local beach. New Jersey towns now require that developers pay the engineering costs incurred when the town engineer reviews their plan. One New Jersey developer tells of being forced to dedicate a $100,000 trunk line to the local private water company—and then being told he would have to pay $28,000 in utility taxes on the new line as well.[17]

Impact fees are now adding an estimated $20,000 to new homes around Los Angeles, $4,500 in Orlando, Florida, and $2,000 in Northern Virginia. As impact fees have risen, developers have tried to absorb these costs by building fewer, more expensive homes. As *The New York Times* pointed out, "[A]n additional $5,000 or $10,000 is less important to the buyer of a $300,000 home than to the buyer of a $100,000 home."[18]

Yet, as you will recall from *New Homes and Poor People,* more expensive suburban homes have shorter tails. They are not as likely to filter vacancies down to the poor. After studying impact fees, the San Francisco Bay Area Council concluded that they "contribute to a shortage of entry-level housing and an oversupply of housing at the upper end of the market and tend to constrict local development."[19] Once again, the result is limited opportunities for the poor.

Growth control has been a kind of super-zoning, enabling communities to practice exclusion even beyond the supposed limits of what-goes-where. At the same time, many suburban communities profess to have a social conscience about the poor and homeless. Caught between their environmental rhetoric and their professed social concerns, many have gone to great lengths to try to reconcile the problem through inclusionary zoning.

The pioneering effort was made during the 1960s in the upstate suburban town of Ramapo, New York. Faced with an explosion of suburban growth opened by the New York Thruway, Ramapo—like so many towns on the urban fringe—found its farmland being chewed up into suburban housing tracts. Like so many other towns, Ramapo responded by slapping down a building moratorium and promising a master zoning plan.

The town was run by a liberal Democratic administration a bit more sophisticated than most. Deciding to go beyond ordinary zoning, Ramapo came up with a point system designed to slow down new development until it could be provided with municipal services. Parcels of land were awarded points on the basis of their proximity to sewer interceptors, elementary schools, and public parks. When a parcel accumulated enough points, it could be developed. One of the aims of the plan was to avoid "leap-frog" development, whereby builders moved to the cheapest land on the suburban perimeter and forced the town to extend services to meet it.

Then Ramapo did something that was both enlightened and clever. The town voluntarily accepted 200 units of Federal public housing—at a time when building low-income housing in the suburbs was considered tantamount to opening the doors to the urban masses. Ramapo Supervisor John McAlevey, who originated the program, confidently proclaimed: "I'd be willing to absorb 500 units to make the point that public housing isn't the horrible thing that most of the recent expatriates from New York City think it is."[20]

McAlevey turned out to be correct—as Anthony Downs predicted. Subsidized housing (in this instance 30 miles north of New York City) did not immediately fill up with urban migrants. The town reserved 150 units for the elderly and filled the remainder with carefully selected town residents. For this willingness to accept "all kinds of housing," the Ramapo plan passed muster before the U.S. Supreme Court in 1971.

Yet by this show of accepting 200 units of public housing, Ramapo was able to reduce building permits by *300 units each year.* Moreover, developers, finding it much more expensive to operate under the point system, abandoned tract housing and started building "estate homes" aimed at the very top of the market. As a result, Ramapo became an exclusive community. In neighboring Clarkstown, which practiced only old-fashioned zoning, housing prices were almost identical in 1970, but fell to 70 percent of prices in Ramapo by 1980. By pursuing growth-control, with appropriate genuflections to public housing, the suburban-liberal administration was able to achieve exclusion that would be the envy of any conservative administration.

In addition to serving as the model for many similar "point" systems around the country, the Ramapo program has also become the prototype for what later became "inclusionary zoning."

With inclusionary zoning, municipalities impose strict zoning restrictions or growth controls, then try to prove they are not prejudiced against anyone by accepting token amounts of subsidized housing. More often than not, the subsidy must be provided by the builder, who is usually awarded a density bonus, then required to sell or rent the additional units below market. As a result, towns don't even have to pick up the costs of building or maintaining the housing.

As with the Mt. Laurel program, most of the benefits have ended up in the hands of middle-class people. Eligibility requirements are always carefully hedged to include "low- and *moderate*-income" people and often extend to people above the median income. In the early stages, a town will keep quiet about the program, awarding units to people "in the know" on a first-come, first-served basis. But as application lists grow long, specially favored categories are often created.

In one of the first inclusionary programs in Palo Alto, California, the first inclusionary unit was awarded to a 22-year-old dental assistant. In Wilton, Connecticut, the first of six affordable condominium units was raffled off among town employees. The first winner was the 27-year-old assistant to the superintendent of schools.[21]

In 1989, a HUD audit revealed that the Village of Island Park, Long Island, had steered almost all of 44 HUD-subsidized, low-income single-family homes to friends and relatives of village officials—including the cousin of Senator Al D'Amato, a long-time resident of Island Park. More than one-third of the single-family homes—subsidized by HUD to cost only $44,000—were supposed to be specifically steered to blacks. But dozens of people were tipped off and got their applications into the village clerk's office before the homes were first advertised in the newspaper.

As a result, homes subsidized to less than half their price were awarded to a niece of the village clerk, a niece of a village trustee, two village public works supervisors, and a lawyer who soon became village attorney. The son of another village trustee also won a home, even though he didn't file until much later. Twelve winners subsequently sold their houses at prices up to $270,000. Meanwhile, Richard Rodriguez, a 35-year-old airline worker who occupies a one-bedroom apartment with his wife and two children in Island Park, sued the village, saying he had tried for eight years to apply for the first-come, first-served program without success.[22]

While rewarding a few spectacular winners, who usually have good information or inside connections, inclusionary zoning does almost nothing for the broad range of housing consumers. In fact, it probably makes things worse. By allowing communities to go on restricting housing while performing the proper rituals of affordability, it actually shrinks the housing supply.

Suburban zoning and growth controls have created an ever-tightening ring around the cities. Yet that in itself should still not create a housing shortage. Even if the cheaper, open land of the suburbs is closed off to development, the citie[s] themselves should be able to pick up most of the slack. It is in the cities, after all, where the poor usually live anyway.

Unfortunately, the cities have been playing their own games of restricting the housing market to the advantage of already established residents. The most common and effective tactic is something called "rent control."

er 10

151

Municipal Rent Control

Berkeley, California, just across the bay from San Francisco, is in many ways the ultimate college community. The city of 100,000 has long been dominated by the second-largest campus of the University of California, which enrolls 32,000 students. Each year the university provides dorm space for only 6,000 students, leaving the remainder to find accommodations in the community.

Berkeley has traditionally been divided into two sections. The "hill" behind the university, filled with winding roads and large single-family homes, has traditionally been occupied by professionals and people connected with the university community. The "flatlands," spreading westward from the university toward neighboring Oakland, has been the home of the city's blue-collar class, including many factory workers from Oakland and Richmond.

The typical flatlands home is a "working-man's bungalow"—a two-, three-, or four-unit structure where the owner-occupant rents out one or more apartments. Over 20 percent of these small landlords are black. It is among these working-men's bungalows of the flatlands that University of California students have traditionally found off-campus housing.

During the 1960s, Berkeley—formerly just a university town—became the mecca for counterculturalists across the county. Migrants from near and far began crowding into the city's small precincts. Although hippies and college students were often willing to live with 5 to 10 people in an apartment, housing became very tight. In the 1970 census, Berkeley's vacancy rate was an unusually low 2.8 percent—although the median rent was still only $128.

Builders responded by putting up apartment houses. With few vacant lots left, this often meant buying and razing an older structure. No one was forced to sell, but with land values climbing rapidly, many an owner of a working-man's bungalow received a handsome price for his property.

At almost the same time, the student/hippie population was moving toward political power. In 1967, yippie leader Jerry Rubin ran for mayor in what was widely regarded as a comic protest candidacy. By 1971, however, the 26th Amendment had lowered the voting age to 18 and the U.S. Supreme Court had ruled that college students could vote in the community where they were receiving their education. Suddenly, the University's 32,000 students became Berkeley's largest voting bloc. Like upper-middle-class people everywhere (be they suburbanites, college students, or "drop-outs"), this majority didn't want any more new housing and economic growth.

In 1973, an emerging student/radical faction, called Berkeley Citizens' Action (BCA), placed the Neighborhood Preservation Ordinance on the ballot for public referendum. The bill required that developers file a variety of environmental- and economic-impact statements before they could put up new housing. The measure passed easily and slowed new housing construction to a trickle.

While opposing new development, the BCA also acknowledged that this would worsen the housing situation. To this they had another simple solution—rent control. First adopted by referendum in 1971, rent control was delayed in court for five years and finally overturned on a technicality by the California Supreme Court in 1976. In 1978, the BCA came back with another rent-control referendum, which was adopted by a wide margin. The Berkeley statute is now considered the strictest ordinance in the nation.

At the other end of California, on the western border of Los Angeles, right on the Pacific, lies Santa Monica. For decades a sleepy resort town, Santa Monica was inhabited mostly by retirees and blue-collar workers from nearby Douglas Aircraft. Then, in 1965, the state constructed the Santa Monica Freeway. Suddenly, the sleepy seaside community was within twenty minutes of downtown Los Angeles.

Santa Monica quickly attracted an influx of upper-middle-class Los Angeles professionals, many of them with East Coast backgrounds. For a decade, the city boomed with new construction, most of it in luxury apartments. Over 40 percent of the city's housing stock was built between 1965 and 1975. The concentration in luxury apartments gave Santa Monica the state's highest proportion of tenants—75 percent, as opposed to 60 percent in San Francisco, 50 percent in Berkeley, and 40 percent in Los Angeles.

By the mid-1970s, however, Santa Monica's affluent new commuter population decided things had gone far enough. When a developer proposed two new high-rise apartment buildings near the waterfront, the city government—now dominated by the new professionals—slapped on a building moratorium. In order to protect tenants from inevitably rising rents, the city also imposed rent controls.

Nor did it stop there. Tom Hayden and Jane Fonda, who had led the movement in Santa Monica, started touring the state under Hayden's Movement for Economic Democracy, urging municipalities up and down the coast to adopt rent control.

At the time, there was widespread resentment against landlords as a result of Proposition 13. Howard Jarvis, in an effort to enlist tenant support, had blandly promised tenants that they would receive large rent reductions if Proposition 13 passed. When California's tight housing market prevented any reductions from being passed through, angry tenants took retribution. Within one year, Los Angeles, San Francisco, Oakland, San Jose, Beverly Hills, Palm Springs, and four other smaller cities had rent regulations. By 1980, more than half the state's population was under rent control.

A similar campaign had taken place in New Jersey, Long Island, Westchester County, Hartford, Boston, and other cities of the northeast during the early 1970s. Spurred by general inflation, more than 180 East Coast municipalities adopted various forms of rent regulation. By 1980, more than 200 cities—containing one-fifth of the nation's apartments—were under rent regulations. Rent control—long a phenomenon associated only with New York City—had suddenly become one of the principal factors of the nation's housing market.

So what is rent control and how does it influence housing and homelessness?

To economists, the answer is a straightforward one. Rents, like all prices, are determined by the laws of supply and demand. Any attempt to manipulate prices can have only one of two consequences. It can produce surpluses or shortages. If the government holds prices *above* market level, the result will be a surplus. If prices are held *below* market level, the result will be a shortage.

This basic law of supply and demand is usually illustrated with the following graphs:

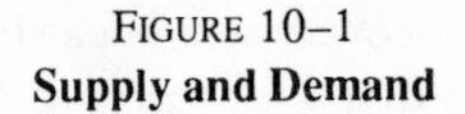
FIGURE 10–1
Supply and Demand

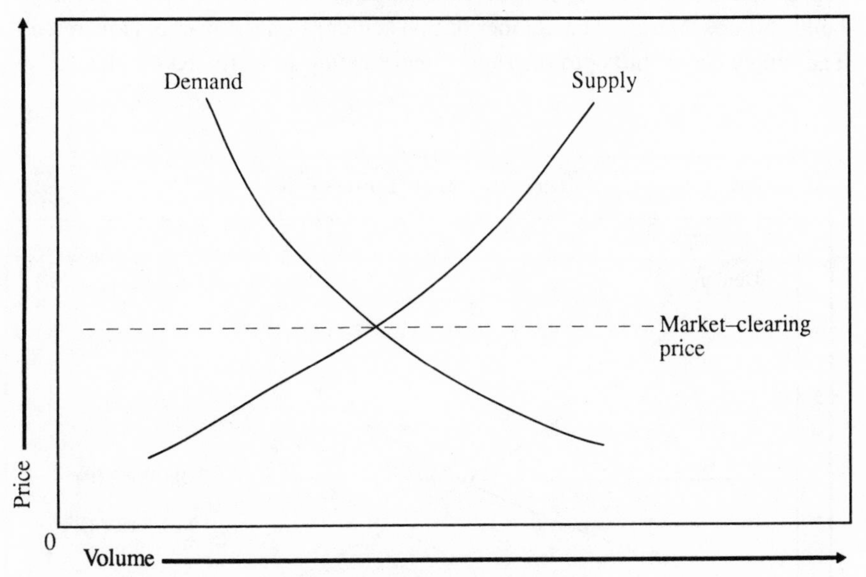

The vertical axis represents the price at which a commodity sells and the horizontal axis represents the number of commodities transacted ("volume"). The line sloping downward from the left—usually called the "demand curve"—represents the amount that consumers will be willing to buy at every price level. The line sloping up to the right—"supply"—represents the number of commodities sellers will be willing to sell at each price.

As can be seen, the interests of buyers and sellers are working in opposite directions. Sellers will offer more for sale at higher prices, while consumers will want to buy less. As prices come down, the opposite occurs—consumers will want to buy more, while sellers will sell less. (Although the slope of the curves may differ, their general shape always remains the same.)

At one point, however, the lines will intersect. This point is called the "market-clearing price," or simply the "market price." At this point—and this point only—the desires of buyers and sellers coincide. Every willing buyer will find a willing seller. This does not mean that every consumer will get the price of his or her dreams, nor does every seller get the highest price he or she can possibly imagine. But the opposing desires of buyers and sellers will be reconciled.

Most of the general principles of economics can be illustrated through the law of supply and demand. Let us look at what happens, for example, when a developer builds 50 new houses. The number of housing units on the market is increased. The supply curve shifts "to the right," representing an increased supply:

FIGURE 10–2
Increased Supply Lowers Price

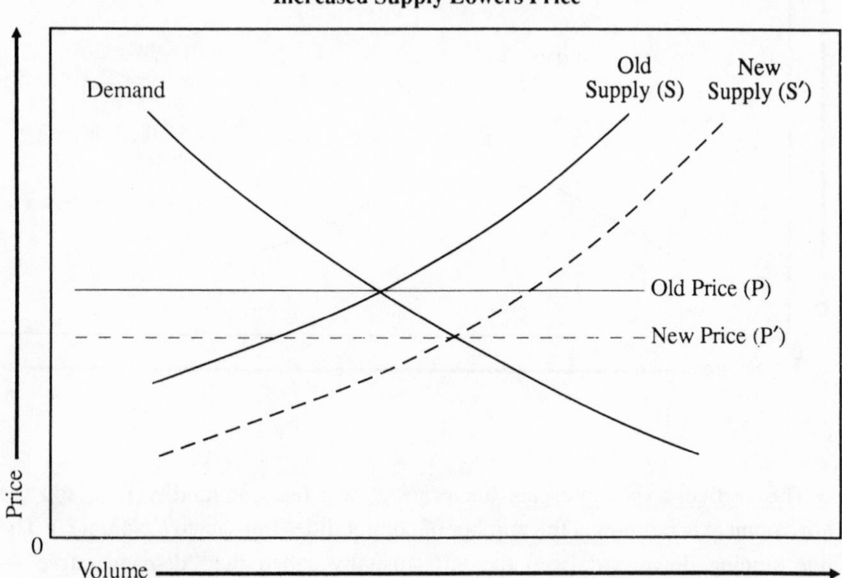

The interesting result is that the point of intersection moves *downward* on the demand curve. In other words, housing prices fall. Thus, the construction of new housing not only makes more housing available, it also *lowers the price of existing housing,* since each consumer now has more options and is in a better position to bargain.

Now let us see what happens if 50 newcomers move into a city's housing market. The number of potential buyers is now greater. There is more "demand" and the demand curve shifts to the right. Unless more supplies are provided to meet the demand, prices will go up:

FIGURE 10–3
Increased Demand Raises Price

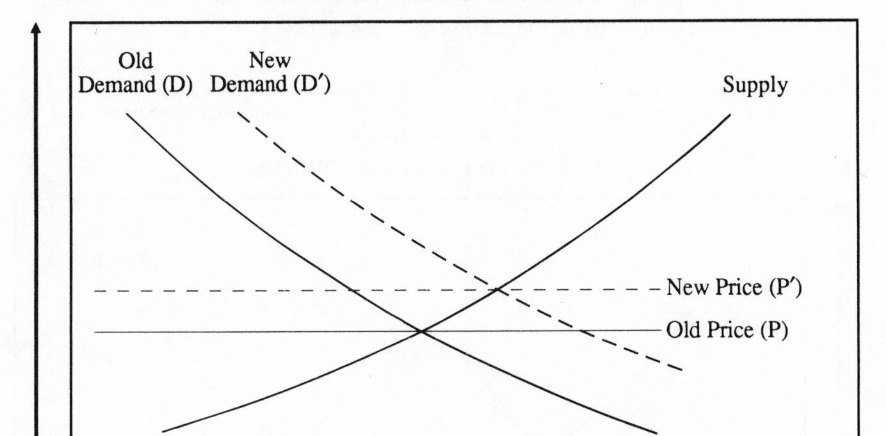

The important thing to realize about a free-market economy is that *neither buyers nor sellers can set prices all by themselves.* Prices are not "dictated" by anyone, but set by negotiations between buyers and sellers. They are the result of the great mass of private transactions, on which each individual transaction has only very little impact. This may make each individual buyer and seller feel powerless, but this is only because there are so many other buyers and sellers in the market.

Unfortunately, throughout history, the majority of people have labored under the illusion that if prices can be fixed at some favorable level by the government, an unlimited amount of the desired commodities will be available at that price. This is not true. *Prices cannot be forcefully moved away from market levels without throwing supply and demand out of alignment.* The real affect is to foul up the *flow of information* between producers and consumers. If buyers and sellers cannot communicate through prices, neither can tell what the other wants to do. The result will be a surplus or a shortage.

Let us look at a more unusual case—"price supports." In some rare circumstances, producers are able to persuade the government to guarantee them an above-market price for their commodities. This has been the case in American agriculture for the last 50 years. Farmers, because of their strong legislative voice and general sympathy from the public, have been given guaranteed prices that are above market. Let us look at the results on the graphs:

FIGURE 10–4
Price "Supports" Create a Surplus

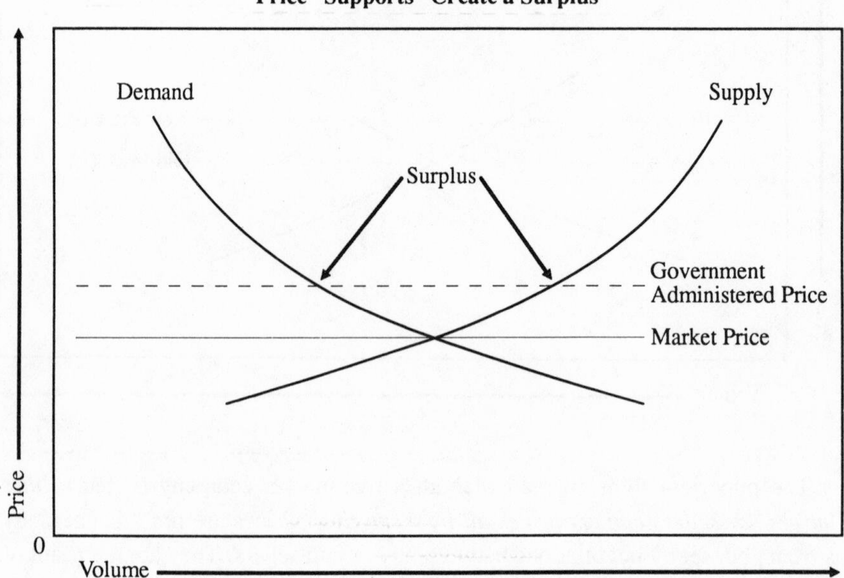

With price supports, two things happen. First, suppliers bring more to market because they are attracted by the higher price. Second, consumers buy *less* because they are discouraged by the higher price. An opening occurs between supply and demand. This gap is called a "surplus"—as in "farm surplus." Our chronic agricultural surpluses over the last 50 years have been the result of farm price supports.

The far more common case, however, are price controls imposed at the behest of consumers, who are always the majority. Let us see what happens in this case:

FIGURE 10–5
Price "Controls" Create a Shortage

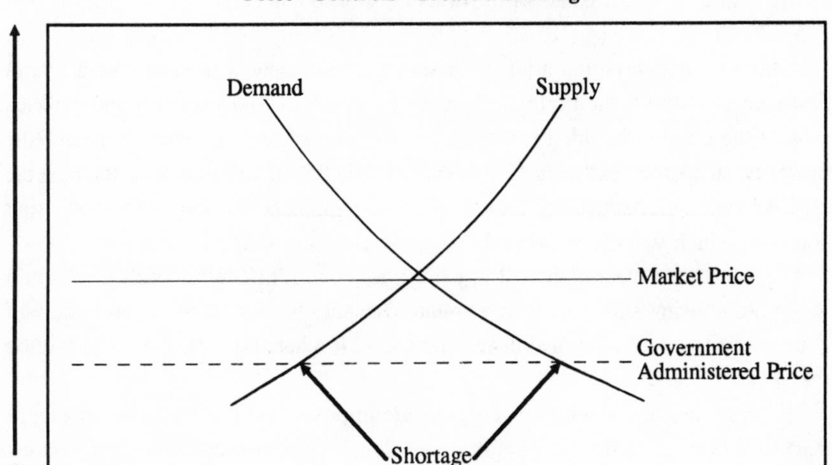

Once again, a gap opens up between supply and demand, but this time in the opposite direction. Consumers try to *increase* their consumption because they see a low price, while sellers cut back because they see the same low price. The result is a shortage—as in "oil shortage" or "housing shortage."

The oil shortage of the 1970s, for example, was entirely the result of oil price controls. The controls were first imposed in 1971 as part of President Nixon's general price freeze and not lifted until 1981, at which point the oil crisis magically disappeared. Throughout that era, the majority of the public was obsessed with the idea that oil companies were "gouging prices" and could "charge anything they wanted." Yet it was actually the public that was undercutting the market by imposing price controls. The result was the inevitable shortage.

Rent control produces an identical housing shortage. The most obvious evidence is the remarkably low vacancy rate in every city with rent control. Officials in these cities always tend to blame some other factor. New York City officials argue that "land is too expensive," or "we're an island and don't have much room." Los Angeles officials say, "We've got so many people moving here all the time we don't have any place to put them." In San Francisco, they say, "We've got so many hills." Yet the cause of the housing shortage in each of these cities is rent control.

After seeing a perpetual housing crisis emerge in New York after World War II rent controls were turned into a permanent institution, most other municipalities around the country avoided rent controls for several decades. During the 1970s, however, academic enthusiasts of rent-control began arguing that its adverse effects could be avoided by adopting "moderate" or "second-generation" rent controls, which would not press down so severely on rents.

The words are meaningless. Imposing moderate rent controls will give you a moderate housing shortage. Impose second-generation rent controls and you will get a second-generation housing shortage. Call it what you will, the result will be the same.

At the same time, when price controls are imposed and the inevitable shortages start to appear, governments—either consciously or unconsciously—start to look for a "hole in the market" through which the shortages can be alleviated. This is usually some small, unregulated sector where extra supplies can be brought forth—although inevitably at higher prices.

A good example was our shift to foreign oil during the oil price controls of the 1970s. Congress, after all, only had the power to set prices on *domestic* oil. When the shortages appeared, we made up for it by *importing more foreign oil.* Imports rose from 30 percent in 1971 to over 50 percent in 1979, then fell back to 33 percent when price controls were removed.

With rent control, there are several possible holes in the market. One is new housing. Realizing that developers do not want to build in a rent-controlled market, cities will often exempt new buildings from the controls (unless, of course, they don't *want* new construction, which is why Berkeley and Santa Monica have not allowed this exemption). Sometimes smaller buildings are also left unregulated. Often these holes in the market develop spontaneously—as when Berkeley homeowners started renting out spare bedrooms to students desperately seeking housing.

To people who are forced to shop in these holes in the market, prices will be *higher* than they would be in a free market. This is because the excess demand spilling over from the regulated sector is chasing after the limited supplies in the hole-in-the-market sector. Often this unregulated sector will a "black market," where a premium must be paid for underground dealings. In any case, people forced outside the regulated sector by shortages will end up paying more than they would at market prices.

When averaged, the results of price controls are often neutral:

FIGURE 10–6
Black-Market, or Unregulated Price

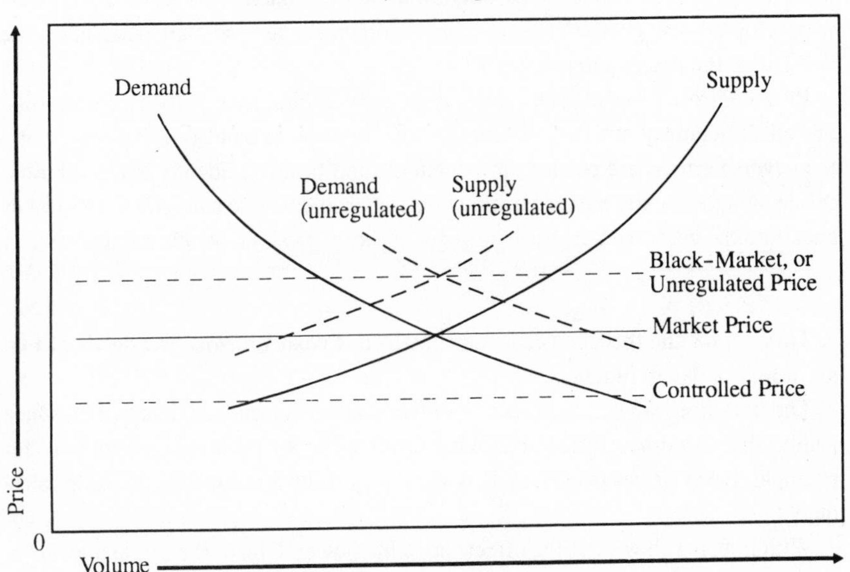

With oil, for example, our domestic prices were artificially low, but our resultant demand on foreign oil pushed those prices up (and left us open to embargoes as well). When the two prices were blended, consumers actually ended up paying a price that was *higher* than market value. This is why oil prices tumbled so dramatically once price controls were removed.

Unfortunately, there is one crucial difference between oil and rental apartments—one that gives rent control its peculiarly maddening effects.

With oil, everyone consumed a tank of gas and then had to go back into the market next week for another. When oil was short, everyone waited in the same gas lines. When prices were pushed above market, everyone paid the same high price. There was a certain democracy to the whole fiasco.

With housing, however, each tenant consumes an apartment discretely. Rents cannot be "blended" the way oil prices were. A person whose apartment was rent-controlled in 1979 can still be in the apartment today paying a below-market price and may be there in 1999, paying an even further below-market price. But other people will not be so fortunate. They will find themselves shopping in a market where either *nothing* is available or rents are considerably *above* what they would be without rent controls.

Rent control tends to split the housing market in two. *Some people end up with great deals while others face higher prices and housing shortages.* Almost inevitably, it is the people who were *already established in the market* when the controls were adopted who get the benefits. Those who must enter the market at a later date will suffer the disadvantages.

Rent control is very much like exclusionary zoning and growth control. The present residents of any community can vote themselves handsome benefits, while the adverse effects are pushed onto outsiders and future residents. In the suburbs, this technique usually means pushing housing problems into a neighboring town or back into the cities. In the cities, however, it means pushing people into the streets.

This is what the theory of rent control tells us to expect. Now let us go back and see how it looks in practice.

The first thing we would expect from rent control is a cutback in supplies. Once again, the dynamics differ somewhat from other commodities. With oil, for example, lower prices caused drillers to shut in wells and supplies dried up fairly quickly.

With housing, however, the effects are a bit slower. One of the initial appeals of rent control is that landlords are in certain ways captives of the municipality. They cannot move their buildings into the next town to avoid the regulations.

What usually happens is that developers stop building new apartments. In both Berkeley and Santa Monica, that has been the exact result. In Santa Monica, there were 697 building permits issued in 1978 and 555 in 1979, the year rent control was adopted. By 1983, only 43 new units were built and in 1984 the figure fell to 19.[1] Moreover, of 2,296 building permits issued from 1978 to 1984, only 1,776 units were ever constructed.

Another way of escaping the regulations is to build condominiums rather than rentals. The figures for completion of apartments and condominiums in Santa Monica since 1978 demonstrate a clear shift to this higher-priced housing:[2]

Year	*Rental Units*	*Condominiums*
1978	141	104
1979	15	161
1980	6	424
1981	70	249
1982	0	201
1983	91	195
1984	36	83

In addition, landlords have tried all sorts of measures to withdraw apartments from the market. Buildings have been converted to owner-occupancy, landlords rent only to friends and relatives, and some have even knocked their buildings down. About 3,600 units have been lost since 1979 and the Santa Monica Rent Board now estimates the figures have risen to 100 units a month.[3] For all these reasons, rental vacancies have declined to a microscopic 1.8 percent.

The same thing has happened in Berkeley. The city had already slowed construction considerably through the Neighborhood Preservation Ordinance, so new construction was not difficult to stop. Between 1978 and 1983, Berkeley added only 120 new private housing units—almost all of them expensive, single-family homes in the hill section. The private construction of rental housing in Berkeley has essentially come to an end.

Like Santa Monica, Berkeley has also experienced a growing wave of withdrawals from the market. Since the majority of Berkeley apartments are in small units, some landlords stopped renting altogether while others turned to family and friends. Condominium conversions were also rampant—until the city made them illegal. Another strategy has been for the parents of several university students to buy a house for their children to share during their college years. The shares are then sold to incoming undergraduates. This solves the housing shortage for those students whose parents can afford it, but it also removes rentals from the market.

The figures on the actual loss of apartments in Berkeley have been very much in dispute. The 1980 census showed 28,000 rental units in the city. In 1988, the Berkeley Rent Board had 19,000 apartments registered for rent control. The Berkeley Property Owners' Association said that this proved 9,000 apartments had been withdrawn from the market. Joe Brooks, director of the Rent Control Board, disputed this conclusion, arguing that most of the "missing apartments were illegally unregistered or exempt from the regulations."[4]

In October 1988, however, the university campus planning office issued a report on housing that concluded: "Between 1979 and 1984, university studies document the fact that the number of private dwelling units in Berkeley occupied by University of California students declined from 9,700 units (apartments and houses) to 6,700 units—a 3,000 unit or 31 percent decline in five years. Thus, if the trend continues, there has been a decline in the past nine years of about 40 percent of the private housing supply that was formerly available to students."[5]

As a result, finding an apartment in either Berkeley or Santa Monica has become almost impossible. In Berkeley, signs litter telephone poles and bulletin boards offering rewards and finders' fees of up to $600 for apartments. Students report that it takes at least until one's sophomore or junior year to find an apartment.

Many have found it necessary to live in Oakland and other adjoining communities. Having a car has become an essential part of living off campus.[6]

In Santa Monica, "Jack," a single professional, was described in a newspaper article as feeling "lucky as a lottery winner" because he found an apartment after only two months. A 42-year-old with "a good job and excellent credit references," Jack "talked to everybody [he] could and came to the conclusion that unless you know someone, you don't have a chance." After leafletting several neighborhoods and taking out a newspaper ad offering a $1,500 finder's fee, Jack finally hit paydirt when a tenant *sublet* him his apartment—while demanding only half the finder's fee.[7]

On the other hand, Tish Schwinn, a 30-year-old nurse who spent two years looking for an apartment in Santa Monica, finally gave up after learning a friend had landed an apartment by paying a $3,000 bribe. "I'm kind of sick of Santa Monica," she told *The Los Angeles Times.* "It's convenient and a nice place to live, but there is so much dishonesty."[8]

In his otherwise flattering book, *Middle Class Radicalism in Santa Monica,* Mark Kann, of *The Los Angeles Herald Examiner,* was forced to admit, "I know one professional woman who tried to get a Santa Monica apartment for more than a year without success, but she broke into the city, finally, by marrying someone who already had an apartment there."[9]

Economists have long noted that prices are a rationing system whereby scarce resources are allocated according to people's ability to buy. When prices are prevented from functioning, another system of allocation must take their place. In wartime, for example, ration cards are usually used to ration goods in conjunction with price controls. In socialist countries, a first-come, first-served system is substituted—often called "waiting in line." Today's restricted suburban municipalities are allocating affordable-housing units by lottery.

Without any of these systems, however, rationing is likely to take place through inside information, good connections, informal agreements, bribes, or other under-the-table arrangements (often called the "black market"). In a rent-controlled community, favoritism, friendships, and insider connections usually become the principal means of distribution. People with networks of family or friends can usually find housing. Those without connections cannot.

The gap between supply and demand created by rent controls is usually called a "housing shortage." Another name for it would be an "excluded population." Here is the way it would look for a city like Santa Monica:

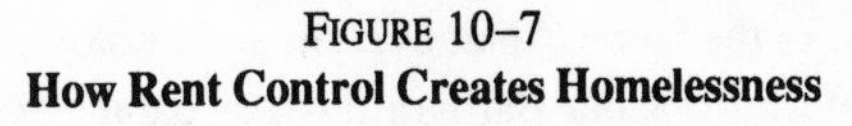

FIGURE 10–7
How Rent Control Creates Homelessness

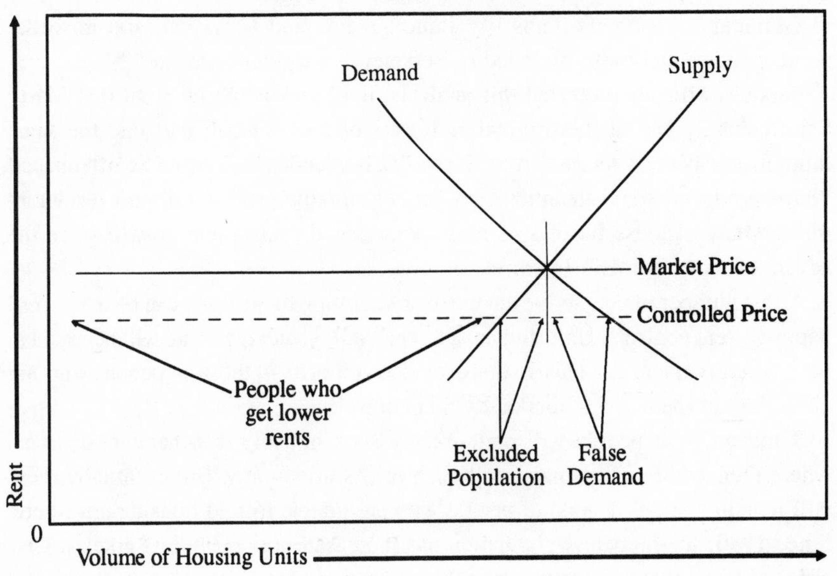

The gap represents people who cannot find a place to live because of rent control. This entire segment, however, cannot really be called "excluded." Some of it reflects what can be called "false demand." This means that the artificially low rents created by rent control will attract a few people who would not ordinarily consider the Santa Monica market. The segment to the right of the perpendicular line represents false demand.

The gap to the left is a truly excluded population. These people would ordinarily be able to find housing in Santa Monica, but under rent control are unable to do so.

And herein lies the horrifying aspect of rent control. As can be clearly seen, rent control will make the vast majority of tenants very happy. Both in Berkeley and Santa Monica, the majority are probably paying about 30 to 50 percent less rent than they would in a normal housing market, leaving them with much discretionary income to spend on other things.

In *Who Benefits from Rent Control?* (1985), for example, Richard J. Devine, of the Center for Community Change, a low-income advocacy group in Oakland, found that Santa Monica residents now spend twice the state average in shoe stores and restaurants and three times the state average in television and music stores. In

Berkeley, the pattern is the same. "Not even in such notorious centers of wealth such as Orange County or Santa Barbara did per capita expenditures for truly discretionary consumers items like liquor, radios and television, and miscellaneous goods equal those recorded in Berkeley!" concluded Devine.[10]

Berkeley officials protested this analysis, until Devine pointed out that Marty Schiffenbauer, one of the original architects of rent control, had said the same thing in *The Wall Street Journal:* "Berkeley's rent controls," wrote Schiffenbauer, "have produced some unanticipated benefits for the city's retail and restaurant trade. Many of these businesses have experienced remarkable growth since the advent of rent controls."[11]

A vast number of people—even the overwhelming majority—can be made very happy by rent controls. Unfortunately, a *very small group of people* will be asked to pay the consequences. This is the excluded minority—the few people who are closed out of the housing market by rent controls.

Some of these people will undoubtedly seek housing in other jurisdictions, where their additional demand will push prices up slightly. But eventually there will remain a small residue of people who are unable to find housing anywhere. Since 1980, the homeless population has increased noticeably in Berkeley. City officials argue that it is the result of the attractions of the city, plus the municipal government's general tolerance for street people. Housing policies, they say, have nothing to do with the problem.

Yet the situation is getting worse. At a city council meeting in 1986, attended by large numbers of homeless people, anger ran so high that Mayor Loni Hancock eventually gavelled for quiet, shouting, "Look, if we can't have order here, we'll just end the meeting and go home"—to which a homeless man shouted, "How can we do that? We don't have a home!"[12]

Meanwhile, in Santa Monica, a whole new population has emerged over the last decade—the "beach people." City officials argue that they are attracted by the pleasant seaside environment and the city's tolerant attitude toward the homeless. The city's housing policies, they say, have nothing to do with the problem.

Nevertheless, the beach people have now grown to number more than 1,000, one of the highest per capita rates in the country.[13] They have given Santa Monica the informal title, "The Homeless Capital of the West Coast."

Chapter 11

Housing Reform (I)

Rent control does not really stand by itself. In actuality, it is usually only one part of an entire approach to housing problems, called "housing reform."

The basic principles of housing reform are as follows:

1) the free, private market cannot provide everyone, particularly the poor, with decent housing. Therefore it is necessary for the government to intervene in the housing economy.

2) the filtering method is both unfair and inefficient and should not be relied upon. Particularly bad is the trend toward dividing up older housing to create "tenements." The poor should be served by new housing.

3) rent control is important because landlords are often able to set rents on a monopolistic basis, enabling them to make unfair profits. Rent control can help stabilize the housing market.

4) the long-term solution to the housing problem lies in "taking the profits out of housing. The business of providing rental housing should be turned over to non-profit groups, charitable organizations, or, ultimately, the government.

Almost all housing activists subscribe to one or more of these principles. Usually they form a kind of four-fold path to housing reform.

The spiritual heritage of this movement usually traces itself to Jacob Riis (although Riis himself represented the continuation of an earlier tradition). A Danish immigrant who spent several years in New York living in poverty, Riis ended up a newspaper reporter, tramping the streets of the Lower East Side night after night—often in the company of Police Commissioner Theodore Roosevelt—eventually coming to know every nook and corner of the slums. Riis finally pulled together his observations in *How the Other Half Lives* (1890), a classic of American reform.[1] Riis remains interesting and relevant today, not only because many of the problems he chronicled still exist, but because he embodies many of the attitudes that still characterize today's reform movements. He deplored the slums without necessarily understanding or sympathizing with the people in them. He tended to direct all his wrath toward neutral objects—mostly the buildings themselves. He lacked the tragic sense of life—the realization that, however bad things may be, it may be very difficult to make them much better. Instead, he had the utopian's confidence that if something bad can be destroyed, something good will necessarily spring up in its place.

Here, for example, is Riis's description of "Mulberry Bend," a busy commercial sector of the Lower East Side that Riis saw as the embodiment of all that was repulsive about the slums and their "swarming . . . unwholesome crowds."

> [T]he moment [an observer] turns the corner he finds spread out what might better be the marketplace in some town in Southern Italy than a street in New York. . . . When the sun shines the entire population seeks the street, carrying on its household work, its bargaining, its love-making on the street or sidewalk, or idling there when it has nothing better to do, with the reverse of the impulse that makes the Polish Jew coop himself up in his den with the thermometer at stewing heat. Along the curb women sit in rows, young and old alike with the odd head-covering, pad or turban, that is their badge of servitude—hers to bear the burden as long as she lives—haggling over baskets of frowsy weeds, some sort of salad probably, stale tomatoes, and oranges not above suspicion. . . . The women do all the carrying, all the work one sees going on in "the Bend." The men sit or stand in the streets, on trucks, or in the open doors of the saloons smoking black clay pipes, talking and gesticulating as if forever on the point of coming to blows. . . . Those who are not in the street are hanging half way out of the windows, shouting at some one below. All "the Bend" must be, if not altogether, at least half out of doors when the sun shines.[2]

All this might seem innocent enough. Yet Riis found the Bend "not fit places for Christian men and women, let alone innocent children, to live in."[3] Through his crusading efforts, Mulberry Bend was completely leveled shortly after the publication of *How the Other Half Lives.* Defending the action in *The Review of Reviews,* in 1895, Riis wrote:

> Are we better off for scattering the poison and the poverty of the Bend? Yes. It is not scattered. The great and by far the worst part of it is destroyed with the slum. Such a slum as this is itself the poison. It taints whatever it touches. . . . Its poverty is hopeless, its vice bestiality, its crime desperation. . . . There *is* a connection between the rottenness of the house and that of the tenant that is patent and positive. There will never be another Mulberry Bend. . . . In its place will come trees and grass and flowers; for its dark hovels light and sunshine and air.[4]

As one housing commentator has noted, "From Mulberry Bend to urban renewal is only a short distance."[5]

To Riis, as to so many reformers after him, the primal sin of housing was the tenement house—either newly constructed or divided up from a large, older dwelling:

> The first tenement New York knew bore the mark of Cain. . . . It was the "rear house," infamous ever after in our city's history. There had been tenant-houses before, but they were not built for the purpose. Nothing would probably have shocked their original owners more than the idea of their harboring a promiscuous crowd; for they were the decorous homes of the old Knickerbockers, the proud aristocracy of Manhattan in the early days.[6]

Quoting an 1857 report to the New York State Legislature, which was itself a criticism of tenements, Riis noted:

> [I]n its beginning, the tenant-house became a real blessing to that class of industrious poor whose small earnings limited their expenses, and whose employment in work-shops, stores, or about the warehouses and thoroughfares, render a near residence of much importance.[7]

But gradually:

> Their "*large* rooms were partitioned into *several smaller ones,* without regard to light or ventilation, the rate of rent being lower in proportion to space or height from the street; and they soon became filled from cellar to garret with a class of tenantry living from hand to mouth, loose in morals, improvident in habits, degraded, and squalid as beggary itself." [Emphasis in original.][8]

Riis wrote searing, heart-rending accounts of the poverty and misery, disease and filth, that pervaded life in these tenements. But like so many reformers after him, his simple solution remained: "tear them down." In describing one effort to enforce housing codes in Lower Manhattan in 1885, Riis wrote:

> [O]bstacles were thrown in the way of the officials on the one side by the owners of the tenements, who saw in every order to repair or clean up only an item of added expense to diminish their income from the rent; on the other side by the tenants themselves, who had sunk, after a generation of unavailing protest to the level of their surroundings, and were at last content to remain there. . . .
>
> It took long years of weary labor to make good the claim of the sunlight to such corners of the dens as it could reach at all. Not until five years after did the [building] department succeed at last in ousting the "cave-dwellers" and the closing of some five hundred and fifty cellars south of Houston Street, many of them below tidewater, that had been used as living apartments. In many instances the police had to drag the tenants out by force.[9]

The problem that has bedeviled housing reformers throughout the whole modern era has been that, however bad conditions may be for some people, there is no guarantee that anything better is immediately available. And if that something could be made available, there was no guarantee that the poor will be able to afford it.

Almost every city in the country, for example, now has an elaborate building code that assures decent, secure, sanitary housing for everyone. Yet time and again, cities have found it very difficult to enforce these codes. As Anthony Downs explained in 1973:

> [I]n very low-income areas, where many households live in extremely deteriorated units that clearly violate the law, housing codes are almost totally unenforced. This is not a conspiracy between evil landlords and local authorities. Rather it is an economic necessity resulting mainly from the poverty of the residents. They cannot afford enough rent to allow property owners to maintain their housing at legal quality levels and still obtain a reasonable return on their investment. . . .
>
> Under these circumstances, rigorous enforcement of housing codes would require local authorities to evict thousands of households from illegally substandard units. But where would they go? . . . These households would have to leave the area or live in the streets, as in Calcutta.[10]

In fact, some of the greatest resistance to upgrading housing has often come from tenants themselves, who fear that as soon as the landlord starts fixing things up, they will be asked to pay higher rents—or to leave entirely.

One of the earliest reform efforts that attempted to remedy this situation was the "model tenement" movement. Tracing its beginnings to the early 19th century, model tenements were based on the principle that middle-class reformers could, through charitable efforts, provide decent housing, while at the same time using the opportunity to train the poor in middle-class behavior. (Model tenements in some ways paralleled the settlement-house movement, which began in the 1870s.)

A typical example was the Octavia Hill Association, which began renting model tenements in Philadelphia in 1896. Founded on the teachings of Octavia Hill, an English reformer who was funded by John Ruskin, the association taught that housing should be used as an opportunity for the "spiritual elevation of the poor." The association collected rents regularly, while teaching lessons in fiscal responsibility and good housekeeping.

Octavia Hill proved successful. The association still runs 217 apartments to the working-class families in Philadelphia at a median rent of $270 a month. Because Philadelphia does not have an intense housing shortage, vacancy rates, even in this low-rent housing, were at 7.2 percent. Although Octavia Hill ran an operating loss of $94,000 in both 1986 and 1987, it made a net profit by selling several older buildings.[11]

Unfortunately, in historic terms, Octavia Hill has been a rare exception. As Lawrence Friedman, author of *The Government and Slum Housing*, points out, "The model tenement movement has provided housing history with more than its share of black irony."[12]

Jacob Riis found the remains of another early effort—Gotham Court—amid the worst slums of the Lower East Side.

> It is curious to find that this notorious block, whose name was so long synonymous with all that was desperately bad, was originally built (in 1851) by a benevolent Quaker for the express purpose of rescuing the poor people from the dreadful rookeries they were then living in.[13]

Another famous project, The Big Flat, built in 1855 by the New York Society for Improving the Condition of the Poor, became a haven for prostitutes and drunks. Riis was on hand to celebrate its demolition in 1885.

The difficulty with model tenements was that they depended on a steady stream of financial benevolence or volunteer effort. Once the charitable spirit flagged, rules tended to be ignored and routine eventually abandoned. Since rents were cheap, all kinds of irresponsible slum types were always ready to take up roost. If discipline was not maintained, the situation quickly degenerated. On the other hand, those model tenements that were successful often ended up as middle-class refuges for clerical or professional people.[14]

As early as the 1860s, housing reformers turned to another strategy—building codes. Tenements had often been built without running water or with common sinks and toilet facilities. Interior rooms had no windows and lacked ventilation and light. These conditions were associated with the spread of disease. Another problem upsetting reformers was the lack of privacy. Bedrooms were often accessible only through other bedrooms, exposing children to adult sexuality.

In 1867, spurred by a cholera epidemic, New York City adopted its first tenement law. Dealing only with the basics, the law required only small air shafts in the middle of the building for some interior light. For a long time, the standard design became the "railroad flat"—a long, narrow layout where each bedroom was connected to a front-to-back hallway. In an architectural contest in 1880, James Ware proposed the "dumbbell" design, with small, four-room apartments in front and back.

In 1887, a much tougher tenement law was adopted. Eventually called the "Old Law," the 1887 statute required a window in every room. Air shafts were enlarged considerably and every apartment was required to have running water.

By the time of Riis's efforts, however, reformers had already come to regard the "Old Law" as inadequate—even a betrayal of their efforts. Air shafts had become fire hazards, conduits for noise and stench, and receptacles for garbage. Toilets were still not required for each apartment. And so, the reform administration of Mayor Seth Low adopted the New Tenement Law of 1901. Builders were required to shorten their lot coverage, leaving small back yards. Air shafts were again enlarged. All this, it should be noted, was done at a considerable cost of *interior* space.

Builders protested, arguing that the requirements were too expensive. Yet they were missing the rising tide of affluence. The New Law apartments were well received by tenants and proved profitable as well. By 1916, 500,000 people—one-third of New York's population—was living in New Law buildings. By 1931, the figure had risen to three million.[15]

The New York law was quickly imitated in New Jersey, Connecticut, Indiana, and Wisconsin. By 1920, more than twenty cities—including St. Paul, Cleveland, Portland, Duluth, and Berkeley—had housing codes requiring similar improvements. Thirty-five years later, reformer James Ford called the New Law "the most significant regulatory act in America's history of housing."[16]

Riding the success of these reforms, Lawrence Veiller, a leading housing advocate and director of New York's Tenement Housing Department, helped found the National Housing Association in 1914. The Association published *Housing Betterment* and held an annual National Housing Conference, which published its own journal, *Housing Problems in America*.

One main objective of the reform movement was to stop the spread of multi-family housing—both subdivided tenements and new forms like the three-decker that were invading the suburbs. As early as 1912, Massachusetts had adopted the "town tenement act," enabling municipalities to ban any "wooden tenement house" in which "any cooking shall be done above the second floor."[17]

At the National Housing Association's annual conference in 1916, Prescott Hall, a housing reformer from Brookline, Massachusetts, presented a paper, "The Menace of the Three Decker," in which he argued against "vertical as compared with horizontal housing of people."[18] Hall—who was also head of the Immigration Restriction League—blamed three-deckers on "jerry builders" who "with the help of the working man's capital is really putting in his pocket . . . an extortionate reward for his work."[19]

In the place of tenements and three-deckers, housing reformers dreamed of new communities of single-family homes. The National Housing Association published a pamphlet called, "One Million People in Small Houses." It also supported government subsidization of "wholesome homes for low-paid workers"—meaning public housing. As Howard Husock, of the Kennedy School of Government, points out, the reformers' agenda consisted of "public and subsidized housing in the cities [and] single-family homes in the suburbs, with precious little in between."[20]

What the reform movement disliked more than anything was small landlords, rentals, and anything that smacked of tenements. Lawrence Veiller, who served as secretary of the Association, resigned from the tenement house committee of the Charity Organization Society—a major philanthropic organization—rather than support a New York law that allowed single-family homes to be converted into three-family dwellings without being regulated as tenements.[21]

When the Federal government imposed rent controls and built some housing during World War I, reformers urged that both policies be continued into peacetime. Edith Elmer Wood, in *Housing for the Low-Income Wage Earner* (1919) admitted that trying to improve housing through building codes was only forcing people into the streets. She argued that municipal governments should build and maintain housing for the poor.[22]

Over the next decade, several new communities were actually completed. In Cincinnati, Mary Emery, widow of wealthy industrialist Thomas Emery, funded Mariemont, a planned community designed to integrate all classes into the setting of an English country village. Schools, shopping centers, theaters, libraries, and churches were all incorporated into a pleasant neighborhood of Tudor townhouses. Unfortunately, when Mariemont opened in 1926, the rents turned out to be so high and the buildings so appealing that it was occupied almost entirely by the middle class. Nevertheless, Mariemont was widely praised as an exemplar of housing reform.[23]

As the prosperity of the 1920s gave way to the Depression of the 1930s, the crusade for reforming the slums returned. Although few people remember, the 1930s was actually a decade of high housing vacancies. New construction had come to a standstill and people had trouble paying rent. Many mortgagees foreclosed. As a result, young people stayed at home and postponed marriage, while older people doubled up with friends and relatives.

The high vacancy rates were seen by reformers as an opportunity to at last tear down the slums. Mayor Fiorello La Guardia, of New York, elected in 1934, was the leading advocate of this policy. Particularly galling to him were the 67,000 Old Law tenements that still stood in New York, housing almost a million people. La Guardia promised to tear every one down, "taking the profit out of the slums" in the process. When Langdon W. Post, chairman of the new Municipal Housing Authority, pointed out that the city government itself was now the largest owner of Old Law tenements, through tax foreclosures, La Guardia didn't flinch. "We'll tear them down," he persisted. "Every last one of them!"[24]

In La Guardia's first year in office, nearly 1,500 older buildings were vacated. "If there's one thing I hope to do before my time is up it is give the people of my city, in place of their tenements, decent, modern, cheerful housing with a window in every room and a bit of sunshine in every window," declared La Guardia.[25] The difficulty was that, while vacancies were up around 10 percent, few buildings stood completely empty. Thus, tearing down 1,500 buildings meant dislocating tens of thousands of people.

To deal with this problem, La Guardia sent Nathan Straus, special housing commissioner, to Europe to study plans for a municipal housing program. Straus came back with plans to clear the slums and build government housing for 1.5 million people. The program would cost $1.5 billion—all to be paid by the Federal government. "Piecemeal slum clearance, without a comprehensive plan or purpose, can never constitute a housing program," Straus reported.[26]

In the meantime, evictions proceeded. In 1936, a group of savings banks—fearing criminal prosecution for conditions in buildings they held in foreclosure—announced plans to shut down 2,000 Old Law tenements in the dead of winter, turning tens of thousands into the streets. La Guardia was beginning to have misgivings and offered the banks a six-month exemption from prosecution. Even so, 500 buildings were eventually vacated. Chastened, La Guardia admitted on his Sunday radio program:

> I must confess to you we have some 30,000 tenement buildings that are inhabited today that are in violation of law, that disregard every provision of the Multiple Dwelling Law as to safety and health, air and ventilation. And yet, I dare not vacate those houses. I cannot order them demolished. Why? Because there's no place that the people living in these houses can move to.[27]

Today, Old Law tenements are being renovated as middle-class housing.[28]

In Washington, meanwhile, the New Deal was bringing all the ideas of the reformers into the mainstream. Various utopian and philanthropic schemes that had limped along for decades on volunteer effort and charitable donations suddenly became the recipients of Federal funds.

One of the first New Deal experiments was the Resettlement Administration, which proposed a series of "greenbelt" communities around urban centers. New towns were planned outside Baltimore-Washington, Milwaukee, and Cincinnati. Only one was completed—Greenhills, in suburban Cincinnati, containing apartments, row houses, duplexes, and single-family homes for the lower and middle class.

Bitterly opposed by the real-estate industry, which feared competition, Greenhills eventually foundered on the question of whether blacks would be admitted. Local opposition finally restricted admission to whites. By the time Greenhills was finished, construction costs had risen and few working-class people could afford it. Eventually sold to its residents in 1949, Greenhills has remained a modest, middle-class suburb.[29]

The main New Deal effort, however, was public housing. The Federal government had been edging toward construction of low-income housing since 1933, when the National Industrial Recovery Act authorized the Public Works Administration to construct new housing as a means of relieving unemployment.

The effort hit a snag in Louisville when property owners whose land was being condemned for Federal housing challenged the proceeding on the grounds that taking land to build housing in which only a few people would live was not a "public use." A Federal court accepted their argument, putting the whole program on hold. In New York, however, a state court had already upheld the condemnation of land for housing by local governments. Public-housing advocates clamored for Congress to clear the legal thicket and fund a national program.[30]

In 1937, Senator Robert Wagner, of New York, introduced a new housing act. Having already suffered several setbacks in his second administration, President Franklin Roosevelt was reluctant to undertake a new effort, but was eventually persuaded. The Housing Act of 1937 was very much a New York bill. Reformers, led by Mayor La Guardia, flocked into Washington to testify. When the bill passed and funds became available, New York was first in line. The Jacob Riis Homes, the nation's first public housing project, opened in 1938 on the Lower East Side.

As numerous commentators have pointed out, public housing was not originally intended to be *poor* people's housing. "There are some people we cannot reach; I mean those who have no means to pay the rent," Senator Wagner told Congress during the debate, adding that "people of ill repute would not be permitted to occupy the premises."[31] Rather, the target was the "submerged middle class"—people with middle-class habits who had been temporarily impoverished by the Depression. The first tenants were often called "the aristocrats of the slums."

The subsidies were not expected to be great. In the original conception, the Federal government would pay for construction, while tenants' rents would cover operating and maintenance costs. Tenants had to meet *minimum* as well as maximum income standards. Many early public housing managers competed with each other for 100 percent rent collection. Others took pride in "graduating" their tenants into homeownership.

Public housing was in many ways patterned after the old model tenements. Until 1949, welfare payments could not be counted as income, largely excluding welfare recipients from the projects. This ban was lifted by the Housing Act of 1949, but then reimposed by Congress in 1961, although it finally proved unenforceable. Drug addiction, unwed motherhood, having a family breadwinner in prison—all were regarded as cause for eviction. As late as 1965, Chicago public housing tenants were subject to annual reviews of their housekeeping practices.

Edie Bishop, a long-time resident of the Robert Taylor Homes, told *The Chicago Tribune* how the housing authority checked her background when she applied in 1960:

> "They wanted good people in public housing then," Bishop remembers. "I had to have references, and they really checked me out. How much money did I make, did I take good care of my kids, and was I telling the truth about how many I had? I got calls from Memphis, which is where we had come from, and they said, 'Edie, the housing authority called us and they wanted to know about your attitude, if you take off from work, if you drink.' "[32]

As the submerged middle class graduated and moved on to the Levittowns, however, all that remained in the cities were problem poor families and middle-class blacks blocked by discrimination. By 1965, 83 percent of the public-housing tenantry in St. Louis was black, as was 94 percent in Chicago. When the explosion of single motherhood hit the ghettoes in the 1960s, the tide became irresistible. Over 90 percent of today's public-housing tenants in St. Louis and Chicago are single-parent welfare families.

All this was magnified in the 1950s and 1960s by the decision of the public housing authorities—for sound economic reasons—to build high-rise apartment houses. Whether it was the pathologies that created the environment or the environment that created the pathologies has long been debated. As early as 1958, however, Harrison Salisbury, of *The New York Times*, was arguing that the new high-rises had "institutionalized the slums," leaving them devoid of the "interwoven relationship of stores and neighbors" that characterize normal communities.[33] In *The Life and Death of Great American Cities,* Jane Jacobs argued brilliantly that it was precisely the elimination of the old "taxpayers"—the small buildings with street-level stores—that had ruined street life and created the barren open spaces that would eventually become battlegrounds for crime and drug wars.[34]

In any case, few judged public housing a success. In 1959, a broad panel of housing experts in *Architectural Forum* expressed dismay that the dreams of garden cities and model tenements had been betrayed by the reality of the projects. Public housing had "failed to achieve even a temporary solution to the housing problems of the low-income group, let along a lasting solution," said Robert K. Brown. He proposed that housing construction be replaced by a voucher system, which would allow the poor to find shelter in existing housing. Charles Abrams, one of the country's leading experts on housing, suggested selling existing projects to their occupants as cooperatives.[35] Both of these suggestions would finally be implemented by the Reagan administration 30 years later.

Thus, by the 1950s, public housing was already in trouble. Yet the drive to clear old neighborhoods was just beginning. The old reformers' dream had finally become a reality in a new program called "urban renewal."

Chapter 12

Housing Reform (II)

In 1945, Robert Moses, who already headed several public agencies in New York City and would go on to control many more, wrote an article for *The Atlantic Monthly* defining the problem of the slums. In terms eerily reminiscent of Jacob Riis, Moses wrote:

> The general pattern of the development of the slums is always the same. They begin with the overcrowding of existing buildings and the addition of tenements built by conscienceless speculators to a considerable height on little land, without reference to light, air, sanitation, and other standards of decent living and safety. The place of a single family in a reasonably comfortable house is taken by a number of families, and in the tenements people are packed in like chickens in a coop. Wave after wave of newcomers inhabit these rookeries. As soon as one generation achieves enough prosperity to get out, it moves on and another with lower standards and income takes its place.
>
> By the time civic and social workers succeed in impressing upon the old-line politicians the enormity of this process, the neighborhood has degenerated to such an extent that it becomes a question whether anything short of complete clearance is worth attempting.[1]

"Slum clearance," although always a part of the reform agenda and given acknowledgement in the 1937 legislation, did not become official Federal policy until Title I of the Housing Act of 1949.

The principle obstacle to slum clearance had always been that *neither the owners nor the tenants in such properties wanted to give them up.* In the planners' jargon, ownership in the slums was too "fragmented." What this meant in reality was that the poor, despite their poverty, still had enough buying power to make it difficult to dislodge them. Title I dealt with this by encouraging the municipalities to use their powers of eminent domain, while promising to reimburse them for two-thirds of the buy-out costs with Federal funds.

The rhetoric of urban renewal was that it would allow cities to "diversify" their populations. In practice, this meant condemning areas occupied by poor people and converting them into "mixed-income" neighborhoods—which meant putting up middle-class housing. Defenders of the program argued that the poor would be compensated by the on-going public housing effort.[2] Yet there were no guarantees for replacement housing, which often took years to build.

To many cities, urban renewal was the Federal fulfillment of the long-sought dream to "bring the middle class back into the city."[3] In 1950, the New York Citizens' Housing and Planning Council urged the leveling of 171 square blocks of East Harlem by asking rhetorically:

> What will East Harlem be like in 1975? Will it be an area with wide thoroughfares, parks, adequate schools, health and community services, and housing for various income groups and for people of different races? [Or will] it be an uncoordinated collection of community facilities and of public housing projects tenanted by low-income Negroes and Puerto Ricans?[4]

As late as 1966, Roger Starr, former head of the Council and a member of *The New York Times* editorial board, wrote that the purpose of urban renewal was to "provide models for interracial living patterns," even if it meant "moving poor people to make room for wealthier ones."[5]

The renewal area was inevitably a poor neighborhood. Nashville demolished a whole black neighborhood on the grounds that it was an "eyesore." St. Louis and Detroit leveled black residential districts that eventually stood vacant for ten years. Boston's West End was demolished shortly after Herbert Gans' study of that tightly-knit, low-income Italian neighborhood. It was these widespread practices that led urban renewal—quite accurately—to be called "Negro removal." "Diversifying the population" meant moving aside poor people to make room for affluent ones.

In 1964, Martin Anderson, then a graduate student at MIT (and later President Reagan's chief domestic policy adviser), published a devastating analysis of urban renewal entitled *The Federal Bulldozer.*[6]

Anderson noted that, despite popular impressions to the contrary, urban renewal was doing nothing to improve housing conditions for the poor. Until 1964, he noted, 215,000 housing units had been demolished, 110,000 of them "substandard" and nearly all of them occupied by poor people. Over two-thirds of those displaced were blacks, Puerto Ricans, and other minorities. To replace their former housing, only 25,000 units of private housing and 3,000 units of public housing had been built. The rents for demolished units had averaged only about $40 a month, while the rents on private replacement units averaged $200 a month. "Of course, there are some publicly subsidized units available," he noted, "but 3,000 units or so do not go very far among several hundred thousand people."[7]

Moreover, as the program accelerated over the 1960s, he noted, *four million people* were scheduled to be displaced. And although some of them might *eventually* find accommodations in public housing, the overwhelming majority would have to find new homes among the current stock. "Buying, moving, and destroying has proved much easier to accomplish than building," noted Anderson.[8]

Just how these people were supposed to find housing, he said, had not been much of a concern for urban renewal officials.

> If standard housing is available at rents they can afford in convenient locations, why haven't they moved long ago? Perhaps they were not aware of it. If this is the case wouldn't it be far simpler and much cheaper to advise people of these attractive bargains without going to all the trouble of tearing their homes down?[9]

Planners and housing officials reacted to these criticisms with howls of protest, but the critics eventually prevailed. Under a steady barrage of intellectual criticism and growing community resistance, large-scale projects were drastically curtailed. When Congress attached realistic reallocation costs to the program in 1967, it died of its own weight. By 1987, *Time* magazine could pronounce the following epitaph:

> The redevelopment binge of the '50s and '60s came disastrously close to indulging the American antiurban instinct to the point of no return. . . . Urban renewal, a well-intentioned and wrongheaded federal mission . . . meant tearing down quirky, densely interwoven neighborhoods of 19th and early 20th century low-rise buildings and putting up expensive, charmless, clots of high-rises. Or, even worse, leaving empty tracts. (The resistance of Charleston, S.C., and Savannah to Great Society efforts to clear their slums accounts for those cities' remarkably intact historic

> districts today.) . . . Not only in Viet Nam was the U.S. Government proposing to destroy the town in order to save it.[10]

At this point, the question might legitimately be asked, if urban renewal was destroying so much housing during the 1950s and 1960s, why didn't homelessness appear at that point?

The answer seems to be, once again, that what was happening in the suburbs was more important. The great suburban expansion of the 1950s and 1960s was still in full swing. This created enough housing so that the overkill of urban renewal did not prove immediately disastrous. It was only when suburban expansion stalled in the 1970s that back-pressures began to be felt in the cities.

All this does not mean that we must keep expanding the suburbs forever. Building new housing in the cities or inner suburbs will serve just as well. Rising energy prices created plenty of reasons for slowing suburban growth and reclaiming the cities. Nor does any of this mean that old urban neighborhoods shouldn't be cleared or dilapidated housing abandoned. Rampant preservationism in the cities can be just as disastrous to housing as rampant environmentalism in the suburbs. The important thing is to follow the economic incentives and build where the market indicates housing is needed.

While urban renewal was giving way to scholarly dissent and public protest, the criticisms of public housing were also being heard. In 1968, Congress banned the construction of any new public housing over six stories, except in a few cities like New York.

But what would take the place of high-rises and urban renewal? In 1968, the Johnson administration—shaken by the urban riots—persuaded Congress to adopt what was probably the most ambitious Federal housing program in American history. The Kaiser Commission Report—a Federal study of housing problems—had estimated that six million homes in the country were substandard. In one sweep, Johnson proposed replacing all these homes in ten years—600,000 subsidized units a year, more than *ten* times the average of 40,000 units over the previous twenty years. With justifiable hyperbole, Johnson called the program the "Magna Carta to liberate our cities."[11]

The centerpieces were sections 235 and 236 of the Housing Act of 1968, the first aimed at creating new homeowners, the second at subsidizing tenants. With section 235, slum dwellers could buy modest homes on the private market for as little as $200 down payment. Their mortgages would then be subsidized so that they would pay as little as 20 percent of their income in monthly payments.

Section 236 encouraged non-profit groups to build rental housing by offering government mortgage subsidies that lowered their interest rate to one percent. These savings would be passed on as lower rents. In 1969, Congress expanded the program by offering a ten-year accelerated depreciation program for profit-making investors, turning subsidized housing into a tax shelter.

Although the Johnson administration was displaced shortly after, the Nixon administration surprised many people by energetically implementing the new policies. After three years, the program was nearly on schedule, creating 1.3 million subsidized units—more than all previous Federal construction put together. By 1972, the Department of Housing and Urban Development was assisting 398,000 homeowners and 593,000 tenants in the two programs.

Then the 235 program collapsed in scandal. Fast-buck artists had bought deteriorating ghetto homes, slapped on a few improvements, and then sold them at inflated prices to low-income residents. Inspectors for the Federal Housing Administration were in on the deal, giving approval for FHA mortgages in exchange for bribes. Once the new homeowners' repair bills started mounting, they walked away, leaving the FHA to pay off the banks. The biggest housing program in history had turned into the biggest housing scandal in history, with more than 500 people eventually convicted.[12]

The 236 program fared only a little better. Non-profit sponsors usually sold shares to private investors, whose main interest was the tax deductions from accelerated depreciation. But this time scale gave the investors a very short-term interest in the project. A HUD audit in 1972 projected that, because of the inexperience of non-profit sponsors and short-term interest of investors, 20 percent of the 236 projects were already projected to go bankrupt within ten years.[13]

Even more objectionably, the benefits of the programs were once again drifting up into the middle class. Of the homeowners subsidized under section 235, only 13 percent were actually poor. Of tenants subsidized under 236, only 43 percent were poor. People lucky enough to get these subsidies often received benefits of almost $1,000 a month, while most of those eligible were left out in the cold.

In the face of the growing scandal, President Nixon suspended funding for both programs in 1973, and told Congress to come up with something more manageable. This was one impoundment of funds that held up in the courts. As Allen Matusow, a chronicler of the era, writes: "It had by now begun to dawn on housing officials that the real housing problem of the poor was not the physical condition of their dwellings but lack of money to afford better."[14]

Right in the midst of Watergate, Congress and the Nixon administration hammered out the Housing and Community Development Act of 1974, section 8 of which set up something entirely new—a housing certificate. Not a real "rent stamp," certificates constitute a 15-year commitment by the government to pay the difference between a tenant's rent and 30 percent of his income. The payment is made to the landlord, not the tenant. Because the 15-year life span entails such a commitment, HUD must be very careful how the money is spent. Recipients must go through a lengthy applications procedure in which the government must approve their housing situation.

The Ford and Carter administrations set up three programs. One large bloc of section-8 certificates was concentrated in the "new construction" program. Similar to section 236, the new construction program encouraged builders to put up low-income housing by awarding them whole blocs of section-8 certificates—enough to fill their entire buildings. This assured the financial success of the project for at least fifteen years. A similar bloc was set aside for tenants in existing housing. A smaller program went for the "substantial and moderate rehabilitation" of existing housing. The overall breakdown looked like this:[15]

FIGURE 12–1
Subsidized Housing Production 1969–1984

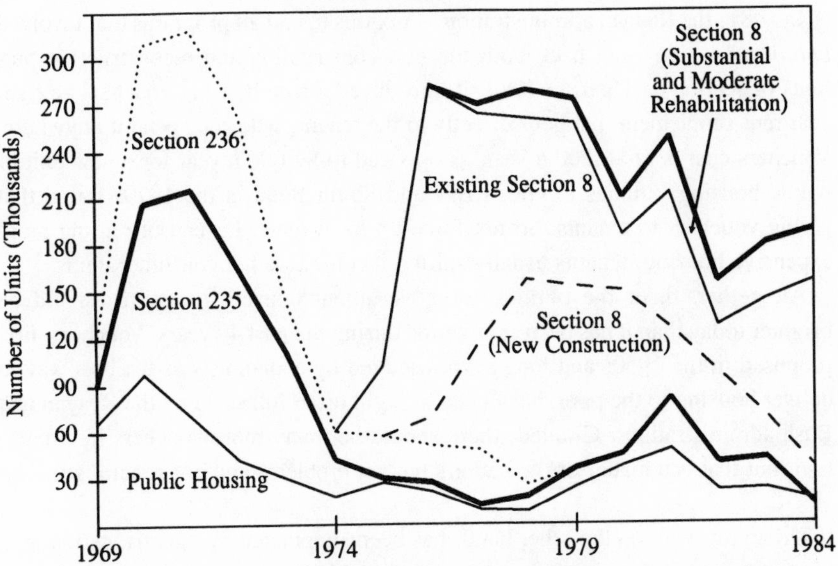

SOURCE: Pre–1975 data from HUD, 1979 Yearbook; Post–1975 data compiled by National Low Income Housing Coalition from HUD sources.

Needless to say, the manner in which these blocs of certificates were distributed became extremely political. Cities like New York and Chicago gave them to favored political organizations and non-profit groups. On a national scale, they went to builders with good connections. Thus, it was not surprising when in 1988 the section-8 program also broke out in scandal.

Influential former officials from the Reagan administration, it emerged, had been paid huge "consulting fees" for shepherding applications for section-8 certificates through the HUD bureaucracy. James Watt, former head of the Environmental Protection Agency, had received $300,000 for lobbying with former HUD Secretary Samuel Pierce for one award. The late John Mitchell, attorney general during the Nixon administration, received $75,000 for a similar effort. Pierce's executive assistant, Deborah Gore Dean (whose mother was living with Mitchell at the time), had spearheaded an effort that awarded many blocs of section-8 certificates to well-connected Republicans. As the scandal mushroomed, HUD Secretary Jack Kemp discontinued the program in 1989.[16]

Section-8 certificates, like so many other Federal housing programs, have proved susceptible to fraud precisely because they give money directly to housing developers, rather than to the poor themselves. With large sums of money being handed out to developers in bloc grants, well-connected entrepreneurs inevitably emerge to try to win grants for their clients.

In 1981, the Reagan administration—anxious to end all programs that involved *building* housing—cut back both the new-construction and reconstruction portions of section 8. Then, in 1984, it introduced a true housing voucher—a five-year rent supplement that goes directly to the tenant, who can spend it anywhere. Vouchers cost only $4,500 a year, as opposed to $9,000 a year for a new unit of public housing. Studies in Green Bay and South Bend in the 1970s found that giving vouchers to tenants did not force up local rents. Instead of renting more expensive housing, tenants usually shifted income to other consumer items.

Altogether, then, the outlook for government housing programs should be brighter today than it has been at any time during the past 40 years. Vouchers, first proposed in the 1950s and long acknowledged by economists as the best way to deliver housing to the poor, have been brought up to full scale by the Reagan and Bush administrations. Granted, there should be many more vouchers in circulation, but that is a matter of the nation's budget problems and not general strategy.

Urban renewal, on the other hand, has been supplanted by "gentrification"—a kind of house-by-house urban renewal done without either government funds or powers of condemnation.

As already mentioned, gentrification has been censured in some quarters as causing homelessness. The restoration of old city buildings, it is argued—however well-intentioned—has produced a "reverse filtering," whereby housing that had finally fallen into the hands of the poor is wrested back by the middle class. Michael Carliner, vice president for housing policies at the National Association of Homebuilders, points out that while most cities were stable or losing population from 1960 to 1980, the trend has now reversed. Of the ten largest cities, only Detroit has continued to lose population into the 1980s. "[This] net migration into metropolitan areas probably displaced many poor people and contributed to homelessness," he concluded.[17]

There is undoubtedly some truth to this argument. Gentrifiers were originally attracted into older neighborhoods by the bargain prices on many dilapidated, but architecturally appealing buildings. This new demand has put upward pressure on housing prices—in some cases breaking through the safety zone that had allowed low-income people to live in ethnically isolated neighborhoods at very low rents.

Yet to argue that homelessness can be solved by stopping gentrification is to take a very short-term view of the housing economy. With no-growth, exclusionary zoning, and rent control exerting exclusionary pressures, gentrification has hurt—if at all—only because it is the last straw. If other pressures can be relieved, there is no reason why old buildings and downtown districts cannot be renovated without aggravating homelessness.

What the critics of gentrification overlook is the tremendous financial improvement that private investment has made for the urban economy. In 1983, for example, Michael Lang, professor of urban studies at Rutgers University, studied the effects of gentrification in four neighborhoods in Philadelphia.

"We compared Queen Village and Fairmont, which were gentrifying, with Kensington and Francisville, which were not," said Lang. "We found that with rising property values and improved tax collection, Queen Village and Fairmont produced $12 million in tax revenues, while the two non-gentrifying areas produced only $4 million. At the same time, the City of Philadelphia spent $12 million in new capital expenditures in Kensington, while Queen Village—the gentrifying area—got only $1 million. The result was a huge tax surplus from the gentrifying areas—money that could obviously be used to improve the lot of poorer areas. The myth that gentrification is not helping the poor seems to be just that—a myth."[18]

Lang and his colleagues also discovered that, by and large, the poor themselves have welcomed gentrification. "We did a survey in Camden, New Jersey, one of the most depressed urban areas in the country," he said. (Camden is 15 miles west of Mt. Laurel.) "We found that 57 percent of the population supported gentrification, even though 80 percent of these people made less than $20,000 a year and 47 percent made less than $10,000. Camden residents were desperate for someone to come in and try to improve their city. They realize that the cities can no longer regenerate themselves out of tax revenues. They see private investment as the only hope."[19]

What will be the fate of public housing? When the housing now in the pipeline is completed, there probably will be no new units in the foreseeable future. This is not necessarily bad since—as we have seen—public housing is the most expensive way to deliver housing subsidies. Its popularity among politicians, to a large degree, has been based on its usefulness in concentrating large blocs of voters in readily identifiable precincts. Often a large housing complex will form a single voting district. Election booths are often located right in the lobby, making it extremely easy to monitor and deliver votes.

The big problem in public housing will be maintaining what we already have now. Granted, the Reagan administration's attitude toward public housing has often mirrored the old reformers' attitudes toward private housing—the best thing to do would be to tear it down. Jack Kemp, Secretary of HUD, has been moving toward a program that would allow tenants to take over existing units as tenant-run cooperatives. Although the results have been spotty so far, the program seems to have promise. In addition, HUD has been giving housing authorities greater leeway to evict drug dealers—promising to restore at least some of the civility that was lost during the 1960s.

Housing reformers have learned the lesson of urban renewal and there is now little support anywhere for clearing the slums. Yet the other attitude—that housing must be provided by non-profit groups and that "taking the profit out of housing" is the key to success—still persists.

Mayor Raymond L. Flynn, of Boston, and Congressman Joseph P. Kennedy III, argue that "decent, affordable housing for all" can be provided by "churches, unions, community development corporations and tenant cooperatives," all of which are "not averse to measures that limit rent increases and resale prices." All they need is that "the Federal Government . . . provide matching funds, in a three-to-one ratio, to locally based nonprofit housing groups" since "only the Federal Government has those kinds of resources."[20]

In *Rethinking Rental Housing,* John Gilderbloom and Richard Appelbaum sum up the case as follows:

> In our view, the principal reason our society is unable to provide adequate, affordable housing for everyone is that housing—a necessity of life—is treated not as a community good, but as a commodity. Housing in our society is produced, owned, operated, and sold in ways designed to maximize profits, rather than to provide

> needed shelter. The consequence is waste and inefficiency in production and allocation; a highly volatile housing economy; chronic shortages, particularly among low-income households; and a growing gap between income and housing cost.[21]

The authors support rent control and a European model for extensive government intervention in the housing market.

Perhaps the most blunt statement of purpose came from the Community Ownership Organization Project, which outlined the purposes of Berkeley's housing reform in *The Cities' Wealth,* published in 1976:

> In a community like Berkeley, where two-thirds of the residents are tenants, rent control could provide important protection from the effects of the city's chronic housing shortage. It would protect the individual tenants from skyrocketing rents and protect the community from severe population restructuring as poorer residents are forced out entirely. . . .
>
> By enacting rent control and thereby restricting increases in future rents, a city may actually reduce the present value of a property. This is essentially community expropriation in favor of tenants. . . . Since other private owners would be unlikely to buy the property in such an unfavorable climate, the city could purchase the property at below market prices or aid tenants in converting the property to cooperative ownership. If rent control were part of a coordinated program that includes a shift away from property taxes, this policy would not cut city tax revenues.[22]

Such policies have been deliberately put into effect in Berkeley over the last decade—and have been implemented in New York and other cities on a more informal basis.

What all housing reformers have had in common, since the time of Jacob Riis, has been their distaste for private landlords. Landlords, it is believed, are too greedy, too unscrupulous, too lacking in moral character to be trusted with the task of providing housing.

Even such a sophisticated and neutral observer as William C. Apgar, director of Harvard's Joint Center for Housing Studies and co-author of *State of the Nation's Housing, 1988,* seems to share this view. When asked by *The New York Times* why HUD's low-income housing programs have been subject to recurring scandal, Apgar responded that, "unlike defense procurement fraud, which usually requires a detailed knowledge of the workings of the Pentagon and the weapons industry, and securities fraud, which often demands a sophistication in the ways of Wall Street and an ability to raise large amounts of money, housing fraud does not require a lot of skill or investment.

" 'In housing, a lot of people start off with a hammer and a truck,' Mr. Apgar said. 'You don't have to be a rocket scientist to do this.' "[23]

To housing reformers, the ultimate problem has always been that the wrong people are in the housing business. If housing could be limited to people of good character—instead of those in search of profits—the problems would solve themselves. This is why church groups, labor unions, and non-profit organizations are always being enlisted to the task.

Yet as the recurring failure of Federal housing programs has shown, good intentions do not always make good housing.

Chapter 13

Landlords

What we have learned so far is that the key to homelessness and low-income housing seems to lie in the vulnerable region of private rentals. Poor people cannot buy new homes—although the construction of new homes certainly affects what is available to them. Public housing can fill a small hole near the bottom of the income scale, but it tends to concentrate poor people and exaggerate their pathologies. "Affordable housing" is basically a boondoggle—a system whereby middle-class people award cheap housing to their friends and relations on the grounds that they are helping the poor.

The place where the hopes of the poor will live and die is in the private rental sector. This is the best and only housing available to them. With Federal housing subsidies beginning to concentrate entirely on rent vouchers for low-income people, the private rental sector is becoming ever more important to the nation's housing supply.

But what is the private rental sector? Who owns it? Who operates it? What is it that leads housing reformers to regard private owners as the problem? And why is it that landlords end up as the object of such scorn and vilification—particularly where housing reform measures have been adopted?

Perhaps the best way to understand this perplexing situation is to begin with the question, "Who are landlords?"

The common view is that all landlords are rich. Names like Donald Trump inevitably pop up when landlords come to mind. Almost every tenant believes his or her landlord is rich because the landlord owns the building and the tenant doesn't. Buildings are always expensive—the most expensive kind of property the average person ever buys. Because buildings are judged as liquid assets (and the money owed on them usually forgotten), it would seem on paper that every landlord is rich.

The truth is somewhat different. There are indeed very, very rich landlords. Most of them, however, are concentrated in *commercial* real estate. They own shopping complexes, city skyscrapers, large industrial parks, or an occasional luxury apartment house.

Rental housing, on the other hand, has a remarkably diversified ownership—and is, in fact, probably the most decentralized business in the country. There are all kinds of landlords. Some are very rich, some are distinctly upper-middle-class. There is a broad swathe of lower-middle-class landlords and there are some distinctly poor landlords.

There are few completely reliable statistics, but the conclusion of most experts has been that the ownership of rental housing is generally distributed across the entire population. If anything, it may be weighted toward the lower end of the economic spectrum, for reasons that will soon become clear.

Where landlords obviously seem to differ from the general population is in their level of education. In a survey of 700 New York landlords, the Arthur D. Little Corporation, found that 49 percent had only a high school education. This pattern seems to hold true throughout the country. One thing that strikes every observer is the number of immigrants in the landlord trade. Another is the number of people who "started off with a hammer and a truck"—the carpenters, plumbers, and other craftsmen in the business. In fact, the description "carpenters and immigrants" roughly categorizes a large portion of the landlord population.

A little consideration indicates why this might be true. The skills of a landlord are, after all, basically janitorial. Many people enter the profession precisely because they believe they can save money by "being their own janitor." This is why so many people from the construction trades become landlords. Carpenters, plumbers, electricians, handymen (and handywomen) enter the field precisely because they see their ability to care for a building *physically* as their main entree into the job.

On the other hand, the number of professional owners who "speculate" in rental housing is actually rather small—and even those who speculate do not do it in the way most people suppose. The common view is that landlords speculate on properties by buying them cheap and waiting until the price goes up. But unless a buyer has inside information (usually involving some municipal improvement) or is unusually gifted about anticipating future values, it is difficult to make property values rise simply by sitting on a property. The most common way to speculate in rental housing is to *make improvements* on a property and then try to sell it with a higher rent roll.

Here is the way an old-time New York landlord described the process in the 1920s:

> We bought strictly for speculation, for resale. We thought we'd build up the rents in 311 [East 100th Street] and then sell it. . . .
>
> The neighborhood was poor, the rents were cheap—fourteen dollars an apartment—there was no steam, no electric, no gas ranges and walls were papered an ugly green in most of the buildings. . . .
>
> We put heat in many of the houses, we pulled out the coal stoves and put in gas ranges. Before that they had to work with the black iron sink and the old washtubs, but we replaced them with nice enamel sinks and we scraped the old paper off the walls. . . .
>
> I remember we painted each apartment for four dollars a room, but just before the Jewish holidays we did it for nothing—for good will. They expected it after a while and we were glad to do it. . . .
>
> We bought number 311 to make money. We improved it. Then we resold it. . . . People were paying six times the rent roll in those days.[1]

Besides being miscast as uniformly rich, landlords are often characterized as having monopoly powers over the rental-housing market. Sometimes the term is used with sheer sloppiness. "All landlords" are said to have a monopoly on "all rental housing." In this kind of snapshot term, all professions are a "monopoly." All oboe players have a monopoly on being oboe players. All heart surgeons have a monopoly on being heart surgeons. The important questions are: 1) how broadly diversified is proprietorship within the field; and 2) how easy is it for new proprietors to enter the field?

Because landlords are the object of such peculiar resentments, there has been a great deal of work done among housing activists to prove that landlords hold monopoly powers over rental housing. Gilderbloom and Appelbaum, authors of *Rethinking Rental Housing*, for example, even find it vaguely sinister that there are fewer landlords than tenants:

> The relationship between buyers and sellers of rental housing is asymmetrical. Tenants, typically, are numerous; consume single units of housing; and, depending on local conditions, may be in strong competition with one another for the units they consume. These conditions need not obtain for the sellers of rental housing, however.

> While rental housing market structure is a largely neglected topic of study, those few studies that examine market share concur that the ownership of rental housing tends to be concentrated in a relatively small number of hands.[2]

What Appelbaum and Gilderbloom are describing is simply the division of labor. Any field will contain more consumers than producers. There are more clients than lawyers, more patients than doctors, more college students than college professors. This is what the division of labor is all about. Yet no one suggests that any of these fields must be the subject of special government intervention in order to protect consumers from monopoly prices.

Moreover, although ownership of rental housing may be concentrated in a "relatively small number of hands," the question is, "relative to what?" It is certainly small compared to the number of tenants. But when compared to the concentration in any other profession, we find that the proportion of market share for each individual owner is miniscule. Rental housing is, quite simply, the most fractured and diversified field of enterprise in the country.

In Santa Monica, among 26,000 rentals, the largest landlord owns 530 units—two percent of the market. In New York, the largest private owner—until he quit the field—was Harry Helmsley, with three percent. (The City of New York is the largest owner of all, with nine percent.) In California, there are four million rental units and 340,000 owner households. The median landlord owns only eight units.

Of course, these numbers can always be twisted and turned to try to make ownership seem concentrated. In pursuing the idea of a landlord monopoly, Gilderbloom and Appelbaum write:

> Mollenkopf and Pynoos, for example, found that in the early 1970s a small proportion of the population owned the rental housing stock in Cambridge, Massachusetts. They estimated that 60 percent of the rental housing units were owned by just 6 percent of the city's population. Mollenkopf and Pynoos further estimated that 90 percent of the city's apartment owners belonged to the local property owners' association (a political action group of 700 members). Within this association, 20 members owned 40 percent of the rental housing.[3]

Yet 6 percent of the population of Cambridge (100,000) is 6,000 people, owning the most concentrated 60 percent of the housing stock. The total number of owners is closer to 15,000. Just how 90 percent of these owners have crammed themselves into an organization of only 700 members is something that Gilderbloom and Appelbaum do not bother to explore. Even accepting these obviously faulty numbers, however, 40 percent of 90 percent would mean that the 20 largest members own 36 percent of the city's apartments. On average, that would give each large landlord 1.5 percent of market share. Even with an unequal distribution, it is unlikely that any individual landlord owns more than four to five percent of the rental market. (The owners association, by the way, became a "political action group" only when rent control was imposed in 1969.)

Given the difficulty of wrestling these numbers into a monopolistic profile, Appelbaum and Gilderbloom try several other tacks.

> If the local apartment owners' association is unfamiliar with some local conditions or rates, it may refer inquiries to large-scale owners of real estate or to members of the local board of realtors to get an idea of "how much the market will bear." "Pulling up" rents that are "below market" is a recurrent concern in both organization and informal network contacts; for example, the landlords' association will, upon request, suggest an annual minimum rent increase to its members. Informal pressure may also be brought to bear through conversation among landlords in which rents are compared and "acceptable" increases identified. . . . Robert Bruss, writing in his nationally syndicated real estate column, recommends to landlords: "To find out what rent to charge, shop comparable rentals through newspaper want ads for house rentals."[4]

In other words, landlords talk and read the newspapers. Yet this constitutes neither "collusion" nor "market control." As Adam Smith said, "People of the same trade seldom meet together . . . but the conversation ends in a conspiracy against the public, or in some contrivance to raise prices." But as Smith also pointed out, it was impossible to gain control over the market unless they persuaded the government to *exclude competitors* by offering monopoly charters or other trade restrictions. As Gilderbloom and Appelbaum admit, the only significant entry barriers to rental housing are "zoning ordinances, health and safety regulations, and land-use planning." If we ever see landlords supporting exclusionary zoning on the basis that there is "too much rental housing on the market," then we should begin to worry.

Finally, Gilderbloom and Appelbaum argue that rental housing has become "professionalized" in recent years, particularly by the collective management of properties by management agencies.

> If management companies control a large portion of the rental stock, their role in determining rents can be crucial. Since these companies have closer contact with daily operations than the owners, company opinions concerning [rent] increases are often decisive. The companies are thus in a position to effect uniform rent changes that, in turn, affect numerous owners, this constituting a major force for reducing

> competition. Management companies have a large stake in increasing rents, since their fees are directly tied to gross revenues.
>
> A number of studies have found that rents are higher when properties are operated by management companies rather than by individual owners. A study of Isla Vista, California, [performed by Appelbaum and Gilderbloom, with one other author] found that only five management companies controlled three-quarters of all apartment buildings of ten units or more. In another study of the same rental market, Gray estimated that managed units charged an annual average of $168 more than non-managed units.[5]

But because management companies "control" large numbers of landlords does not mean that they control either tenants or prices. It simply means they have a large number of clients. Nor should it be surprising that management companies try to raise rents—any more than it would be surprising to learn that tenants hunt bargains. What is important is that management companies must still compete with each other, and with other non-managed landlords. If a management firm tries to raise rents above market values, it will have higher vacancies, which will give it a bad reputation among landlords, which will cause it to lose clients. Large management firms cannot control rents any more than small, independent landlords can.

In addition, the numbers once again belie the theory. Five large firms in Isla Vista may manage three-quarters of all buildings *of ten units or more.* But on a national average, such large buildings constitute only 30 percent of the rental market. Everything else is in smaller buildings. Thus, the five firms divide 22.5 percent of the market (75 percent of 30 percent), which gives them each 4.5 percent. Considering that each of these firms probably handles dozens of landlords, we see once again how completely atomized the ownership of rental property really is. (Isla Vista, moreover, is not even a municipality, but only a small neighborhood of about 3,000 people where students at the University of California at Santa Barbara find housing. If rental ownership is so decentralized in this small area, we can only imagine what it is like in a large municipality.)

Nevertheless, the basic point is probably true. Large apartment complexes owned by "professional" landlords (Gilderbloom and Appelbaum's term) and operated by management agencies do seem to collect generally higher rents, even if the buildings are no more desirable than non-managed units. But this is not necessarily the result of collusion or monopoly power. Gilderbloom and Appelbaum are much closer to the truth when they attribute this to the management firms' "opinions concerning [rent] increases." The far more likely explanation is that *the vast majority of small, amateur landlords are highly unsophisticated and do not always charge market rents.*

This phenomenon has been well-observed among housing experts. As George Sternlieb and James Hughes point out, the bulk of rental housing is in extremely small units owned by a bewildering variety of people. As of 1980, there were 26.9 million rental units in the country, providing housing for 80 million people. Of these units, 30 percent—8.3 million units—were in *one-family* structures. Another 27 percent—7.4 million units—were in two-, three-, or four-family structures. A total of 70 percent was in buildings smaller than 10 units, while 9 percent—2.5 million units—was in buildings with over 50 units. "The supply of rental housing is far more heterogeneous than is sometimes understood," concluded Sternlieb and Hughes.[6]

Anthony Downs offers a similar analysis:

> Reliable data on who owns the nation's rental housing are not available, but my impression is that ownership is scattered among many small-scale landlords. This impression is based on the high percentage of rental housing containing fewer than five units, and on my experience in talking to realtors and investors across the nation over the past fifteen years. Many large-scale real estate investors avoid residential properties, primarily because the high tenant turnover . . . raises management costs . . . compared with other rental real estate. But small-scale investors who manage their own properties rarely take full account of the cost of their time. So they have lower management costs . . . than large-scale operators who employ professional management and maintenance personnel. That often leads small-scale operators to charge lower rents than those needed by large-scale operators to earn yields competitive with alternative investments.[7]

In fact, Downs concludes, it was precisely *because* the vast majority of landlords are small, unsophisticated operators that rents have long lagged behind other consumer items:

> If a hundred units are operated by a hundred different owners, every vacancy represents a 100 percent loss of rental income. . . . Such owners try to avoid that outcome by raising rents cautiously. . . . This situation makes most small-scale landlords *turnover minimizers* rather than *rent maximizers.*
>
> One way to minimize turnover is to find good tenants who will stay a long while, pay on time, and not damage the property. Most small owners give such tenants an incentive to remain by keeping their rents relatively low. As a result, long-term tenants typically have lower rents than short-term ones. . . . When a market is dominated by small-scale operators, most of whom restrain rent increases to avoid turnover, even large-scale operators may not realize they could charge more than the prevailing rents, based on the actual balance of supply and demand.[8] [Emphasis in original.]

What Gilderbloom and Appelbaum are probably measuring, then, is the small percentage of large-scale owners who have recently discovered that the market will bear higher rents. They argue that professional landlordism has increased during the 1980s. This is probably correct—although the tight housing market created by growth controls in many communities has certainly made a difference as well.

Yet even if professional landlordism is responsible for the entire rise in rents since the 1980s, *this does not mean that either landlords or rent-management agencies have coercive power over the market.* It simply means that they are moving away from the long-time practice of *undercharging,* as set by the vast majority of smaller landlords. (It should also be noted that because professional landlords are paying large fees to these managing agencies, their profits from higher rents may not be that much greater.)

Unfortunately, the movement for housing reform has never been willing to settle for this reality. Instead, it constantly casts the landlord as a powerfully wealthy individual—much the way small children imagine that the owner of the corner candy store must be the richest man in the world. Landlords were indeed once the "lords of the land," owning not only vast manors and estates but even owning many of the people through various forms of vassalage and serfdom. Even in American folklore, the landlord is Snidely Whiplash, about to throw Little Nell out of her cottage because she can't pay the rent.

What has happened, though, is that democracy and capitalism have brought about a vast decentralization of property ownership. A landlord today is far more likely to be a person climbing the economic ladder, than the inheritor of generations of opulence. Landlords no longer control the productive resources they did in the Middle Ages, when the term originated. Still, the historic image persists.

It is important to keep these historical ironies in mind. As we have already seen, becoming a landlord is often the *first step* in upward mobility for members of the lower-middle-class. People do not always become owners of property because they have more money than everyone else. Often it is because they have *less.* Affluent professional people with good incomes become the owners of single-family houses. People with a little money buy duplexes, triplexes, and sometimes small apartment houses. They become landlords.

Once again, Jacob Riis offers a starting point for understanding how housing reformers have approached the problem. At the beginning of *How the Other Half Lives,* Riis casually claims that landlords seek at least a 15 percent profit on their investment and often get 30 percent. He quotes Senate testimony claiming 40 percent was an average return and that profits often ran at 100 percent.[9] These figures are frankly preposterous. Industrial profits at the time averaged about 12 percent and bank deposits paid about 3 percent. If slum landlords routinely made 30 to 100 percent profits, there would have been an avalanche of investment in the housing business.

There *was* a great deal of housing built during this era. More housing was built in New York in the 1920s, for example, than has ever been built before or since. This indicates that profits were good in the rental-housing business and probably remained that way until the vast new demand created by immigration was sated. But most of this new construction was aimed at the upper end of the market, where profits are likely to be greater. It is unlikely that slum ownership (or any other business, for that matter) could ever produce profits that were consistently double or triple that of other investments.

What always escapes the reformers' imagination is the risks of slum ownership. Just because a building is swarming with people doesn't mean they are all paying rent. As Riis himself acknowledged, at least half the people in any tenement were not tenants at all, but relatives, boarders, sub-tenants—even strangers who paid the prime tenant a few pennies for a bed at night. Commonly, tenants themselves took in boarders and sub-tenants to relieve their own rental burden.

For obvious reasons, Riis emphasized those instances where wealthy people owned slum properties:

> What if I were to tell you that this alley, and more tenement property in "the Bend," all of it notorious for years as the vilest and worst to be found anywhere, stood associated on the taxbooks all through the long struggle to make its owners responsible, which has at last resulted in a qualified victory for the law, with the name of an honored family, one of the "oldest and best," rich in possessions and in influence, and high in the councils of the city government? [The Astors.] It would be but the plain truth. Nor would it be the only instance by very many that stand recorded on the Health Department's books of a kind that has come near to making the name of landlord as odious in New York as it has become in Ireland.[10]

Trinity Church, one of the most respectable parishes in Manhattan, was also for many years the owner of several slum tenements.

Still, these examples were exceptions. Even to Riis, it was clear that tenement ownership was not an investment that appealed to the wealthy, but to ambitious slum-dwellers themselves:

> Within recent days, [Penitentiary Row] has become peopled wholly with Hebrews. . . . These thrifty people are not only crowding into the tenements of this once exclusive district—they are buying them. The Jew runs to real estate as soon as

> he can save up enough for a deposit to clinch the bargain. As fast as the old houses are torn down, towering structures go up in their place, and Hebrews are found to be the builders. Here is a whole alley nicknamed after the intruder, Jews' Alley. But abuse and ridicule are not weapons to fight the Israelite with. He pockets them quietly with the rent and bides his time. He knows from experience, both sweet and bitter, that all things come to those who wait, including the houses and lands of their persecutors.[11]

Although an enthusiastic supporter of public housing, Lawrence Friedman, author of *Government and Slum Housing,* spent a whole section of his book dispelling what he called the "myth of the slum landlord."

> What is known, though spotty and speculative, suggests that the lords of the land were not big business. Many small tenements were owned by men and women of the same ethnic background and originally of the same social class as their tenants. . . .
>
> In Washington, D.C., the characteristic slum house was the alley house, put up for Negroes in the period starting with the Civil War. The alley house had no sewers, no water mains, no indoor plumbing, "no pavement, no lights, no provisions for the removal of garbage." [Quote from Edith Elmer Wood.] It was bare shelter, little else. Life in these shanty-towns was grim and unyielding; but it was not a life dominated by baronial overlords. No class of big tenement house owners corresponded to the big businessmen, manufacturers, and bankers of the day. To a striking degree, the slum landlord was himself a product of the slums.[12]

Friedman cites many studies illustrating that housing has always been the province of small, unorganized entrepreneurs operating mainly in their own neighborhoods. A 1903 study in Jersey City found more than one-fifth of all landlords living in their own building. The study also noted that, "As a number of these landlords own two or more houses, while a number of other houses are owned by landlords in neighborhood streets, the actual number of houses managed by owners practically resident is considerably greater."[13]

A 1966 study of 300 properties in a Los Angeles slum found that one-third of the properties were owned by occupants and another third by people living in the same postal zone. A 1961 study in Milwaukee found similar results.

"Of course, most landlords were absentees," wrote Friedman. "Some people grew rich on the slums and moved elsewhere. Slums were owned by the Astors and by Trinity Church. But slum ownership, by and large, was and is more local, more decentralized, and more widely-spread than most other forms of enterprise."[14]

Friedman also catches the related theme that echoes through reform movements—it is precisely *because* landlords are people of such small means, so unorganized, and often of immigrant stock, that they have always been so easy to scapegoat:

> The tenement house movement helped fix (the small landlord) in his permanent position as an American devil and scapegoat. . . . Since reform laws imposed costs on landlords without reimbursing them in any way, and since no one expected or wanted rents to rise, it was really necessary to believe that rents were exorbitant and that costs could be absorbed without giving up a fair return. It was convenient, therefore, to assume that landlords were a class of evil men, overcharging ignorant tenants and callous to the point of criminality. The fact that tenement house owners were not respectable old-American businessmen, by and large, made it easier to adhere to this notion.[15]

These general conclusions were reaffirmed once again in the 1960s by what is perhaps the most thorough study ever performed on rental-housing ownership, George Sternlieb's *The Tenement Landlord.*

Working on a grant from the Department of Housing and Urban Development in connection with the Johnson administration's Model Cities program (an attempt at widespread code enforcement), Sternlieb conducted a survey of property ownership in most of central Newark, one of the worst slums in the nation. Randomly sampling every sixth property, the team of researchers interviewed more than 385 landlords. The statistics gave dramatic confirmation to the long-held impression of experts that rental housing is a thoroughly atomized business.

Of those surveyed, 42 percent owned only one building and 64 percent owned less than three. Only 16 percent (61 landlords) owned more than twelve buildings. Eighty-nine percent of all landlords owned all their properties in Newark and only two percent owned outside surrounding Essex County.

> More than half of the parcels are owned by people to whom real estate represents a trivial supplement to income. Only 19.5 percent are in the possession of people who think of themselves as securing three-quarters or more of their income from real estate holdings. To a considerable degree this reflects the comparatively amateur kind of holder who predominates in the market. . . . There are [however] a significant number of small holders who depend on rental income substantially. Not infrequently these are elderly, retired, or disabled individuals. . . .[16]

Breaking down the landlords by occupation, Sternlieb discovered the largest group to be "craftsmen"—both factory workers and household craftsmen—at 31 percent. The second largest group was "retired" (13 percent). Professional real-estate managers and real-estate brokers made up 12 and 10 percent respectively, with their holdings concentrated in larger buildings. "Lawyers, who are often thought of as major investors in slum real estate, are much less important than might have been anticipated," said Sternlieb. "Only twenty of the parcels [5 percent] were owned by this occupational category."[17] "Housewives" constituted four percent of ownership, while "big businessmen" were only one percent.

Another significant factor was the average age of landlords. More than half were over age 50 and one-quarter were over age 60. Sternlieb, like many others, attributed this to the common practice of buying rental housing as a security for retirement:

> The function of tenement realty as an annuity for old age was probably the most common response. For example, a sixty-six-year-old attorney pointed to the fact that he started buying properties some ten years before with the idea that ultimately, once he had paid off his mortgages, he would be able to subsist on the cash flow derived from the parcels in question. Another owner, a seventy-four-year-old retired bricklayer, owns twelve parcels. . . . He said:
>
> "I started out figuring on a small addition to my income while I was working, but now I have money and I am retired. I used to be a bricklayer. I saved my money. I invested in these properties. Now, besides my pension and my social security, I get a good income.[18]

Although about two-thirds of the population in the study area were black, only one-third of landlords were black. On the whole, however, this seemed to reflect a time lag in the transfer of properties. Many resident owners were elderly Italians, Poles, and Jews who had remained in the neighborhood precisely because they owned a building. At the same time, many absentee owners once lived in the neighborhood but had moved to the suburbs. Other owners were sons and daughters who had inherited the property from elderly parents.

Among blacks, on the other hand, owners were younger—average age 49, as opposed to 58 for whites. Most had bought their properties more recently. Black ownership was also concentrated in the smaller parcels. "As white resident owners die out," Sternlieb concluded, "they will in all probability be replaced, not by equivalent white single-parcel resident owners, but either by Negro residents or by white major real estate holders."[19]

When blacks were asked why they had become landlords, the most consistent answer, once again, was "for the purpose of a home."

> We couldn't find a nice place for the children. . . . We couldn't afford a one-family house. . . . We were raised in the neighborhood and we knew the people. . . . I bought the property because I wanted a comfortable place to live. . . . I thought it would be easier to pay off the mortgage if I could rent. . . . I tried to get into a white neighborhood but no one would sell to me. . . .

A forty-eight-year-old Negro iron molder said:

> I always wanted to own a home. . . . I got tired of paying rent, so I figured for a few more dollars I would own a home. I live right down the street . . . so when I found out that this home was for sale I got it. I couldn't afford to own a one-family home. Some day I will be able to build me a home out somewhere, but I will live here until it is built.[20]

Of course, *The Tenement Landlord* surveyed only the poorest rental housing in one of the poorest cities in the country. Therefore, the occupational and racial patterns are by no means typical. Yet the general pattern is clear. Overwhelmingly, landlords are *local* people who buy property either to help them buy a home, for supplementary income, or as security for retirement. Of those who plan to make their living solely from rental property, many plan to spend considerable portions of their time on the operation and maintenance of the building.

For the middle-class landlord, former presidential candidate Michael Dukakis would probably serve as a typical example. As a young attorney in Brookline, he once bought an apartment house in which he and his family were living. As the son of an immigrant, he probably fit the major categories.

The general case, then, can probably be stated as follows: *Landlords are generally of the same social class as their tenants.* Rich tenants usually tend to have rich landlords, middle-class tenants have middle-class landlords, poor tenants have poor landlords. If anything, this argues that landlords may be generally less affluent than the average American, since rentals are concentrated at the bottom of the economic scale.

Landlords are also much less affluent than large developers. Instead, they are kind of hand-me-down developers who buy buildings away from their original owners as they become second- and third-hand. Yet it is this very hand-me-down process that eventually makes formerly expensive housing available to people with low incomes. It is through the hand-me-down efforts of landlords that housing eventually becomes available to the poor.

All this remains a little-noticed fact of American life. Despite popular impressions, the historical "lord of the land" is far more likely to be a carpenter or an immigrant who has invested his or her life's savings in a building.

All this becomes terrifyingly clear only when a community imposes rent control. Then the governing faction—almost always an educated elite puffed up with left-wing rhetoric—suddenly has to confront the question, "Who in heaven's name are these people?" Landlords are supposed to be greedy, rich, powerful businessmen. Yet the people who are dragged before the rent board are always so elderly, so poor, so pathetic.

Cheryl Rhoden, former Santa Monica City Councilwoman and an exponent of rent control, "says she feels sorry for small landlords making their first appearance before the rent board. It was obvious that they weren't used to dealing with governmental authorities. Their voices quavered and their hands shook. 'They were so scared,' says Rhoden. And the irony of it all was that they 'were upset over things that weren't true—they thought their savings and property were going to be confiscated.' "[21]

The irony here works both ways. The only purpose of rent control, after all, *is* to confiscate the property of landlords on behalf of tenants. The difficulty is that, much to everyone's surprise, landlords turn out to be far less affluent and sophisticated than everyone expected. As former Berkeley City Council member William Segesta put it: "During the public hearings over rent control, it became obvious that if Berkeley did have a working class, it was the landlords themselves."[22]

Chapter 14

The War Between Tenants and Landlords

Ingrid Pfeiffer is a 52-year-old divorcée who has worked for 17 years as a librarian at the University of California at Berkeley. After owning her own home for many years, she decided in 1984 to buy another small bungalow down the street for her two grown sons. "I wanted to give them a little stability and also give myself a little retirement security," she said.

After renovating the home, however, she found that neither son wanted to move in. One had a very cheap rent-controlled apartment in Berkeley and the other had just lost his driver's license and had to remain near his job in Oakland. So in June 1985, Pfeiffer rented the bungalow to two Berkeley law students for $250 apiece. She asked the two women to find a third roommate, who would pay $225 to live in the dining room.

The first two tenants stayed only until September, then moved to San Francisco. The third tenant, Romano Ratliff, stayed and moved in three more tenants without telling Pfeiffer, keeping their rents for herself. In January 1986, Pfeiffer's youngest son had decided to move into the bungalow and she asked Ratliff to leave. Ratliff refused. Instead, she filed a complaint against Pfeiffer with the Berkeley Rent Board.

When Pfeiffer went to answer the complaint, the board told her the building was not registered. Pfeiffer said it was. She brought in her copy of the registration and a receipt for her annual $80 filing fee. Nevertheless, the board refused to accept her records because they couldn't find them in *their* files. The board told Ratliff she could stop paying rent because the apartment was unregistered.

By March 1986, Pfeiffer and Ratliff had a hearing before a rent-board examiner. The examiner finally accepted her registration but ruled that the dining room should not have been rented. Pfeiffer was ordered to pay back *all* the rent she had collected from Ratliff, plus 10 percent to the other two tenants for their "inconvenience." Moreover, Ratliff must now be given one of the bedrooms. Ratliff stayed but stopped paying rent.

Now Pfeiffer went to municipal court to pursue the eviction. After four more months and $3,000 in legal expenses, she finally won a jury trial for an eviction. Ratliff was ordered to pay $500 in unpaid rent. She agreed to move but refused to pay the back rent.

Two weeks later, when Pfeiffer arrived with the sheriff to reclaim the bungalow, she found it in a shambles. The tenant had strewn garbage throughout the entire downstairs. Inside the refrigerator was a dead seagull, its wings spread, the eviction papers clipped to its beak. Scrawled in blood was the message: "EAT THE LANDLORD."

In an ordinary city without rent control, tenant-landlord relations are usually invisible. "Believe it or not, I've seen tenants and landlords in Berkeley who were absolutely best of friends, until the rent board came in and destroyed their relationship," said Gregory McConnell, former director of Berkeley rent control.

To be sure, individual tenants have always had problems with individual landlords—just as individual landlords have problems with individual tenants. But landlords as a class are rarely singled out as in the following letter to a Berkeley newspaper:

> Mountains rise and fall. Strange new species up and walked the face of the earth, then vanish. The epochs of human activity supplant each other with ever increasing rapidity. Economic systems we thought were decreed by God now seem preposterous. As Karl Marx said, "The times, they are a-changin'."
>
> One day the landlord will no longer walk the earth. He will be as extinct as the feudal lord or the divine right of kings. People will react to the idea of being a landlord the way they now react to the idea of being a slave trader or a pimp.[1]

The landlord-tenant relation has often been called "the most difficult personal relationship outside of husband and wife." This is probably true. Yet it generally reflects the *propinquity* of the landlord, plus the amount of money at stake. Like marriage, the landlord-tenant relationship is never entirely cooperative and never entirely competitive. In theory, it should be no different than your relationship with the corner newsdealer. Landlords can indeed be almost paranoid in worrying about how tenants treat their apartments. But this is probably born out of experience, plus the size of their own investment.

In a normal market, landlords make money by offering reasonable housing at reasonable prices. Rents are set by supply and demand. If housing is scarce, landlords will be able to charge higher prices. If the market is glutted, they will worry about securing tenants.

One thing a landlord can do about attracting tenants is to keep his place attractive and clean. If a landlord lets his building run down, he risks losing tenants. Likewise, if tenants don't like an apartment, they can usually look for another one.

As Anthony Downs points out, landlords usually have only two basic requests of their tenants: 1) they should pay the rent on time, and 2) they should not damage the apartment or bother other tenants. When landlords get good tenants they try to hang onto them as long as possible. When tenants establish themselves as stable and reliable, they are usually given little breaks in the rent.

One recent study in Baltimore found that, even in the worst slums, there is generally a three-tier system of rents. Tenants who are well-behaved and pay on time pay below-market rents. Those who are average in their behavior pay market rents. Tenants who present behavioral problems generally pay rents that are above market. Setting a rent level is an important means of social control, and landlords serve as informal policemen, maintaining order in their buildings.[2]

Under rent control, however, all these things change. Landlord-tenant relations become *completely* adversarial. Landlords turn into greedy villians who seem to want to do nothing except let their buildings run down and get rid of tenants. Meanwhile, tenants are in a constant state of agitation, see themselves as helpless prisoners of a voracious landlord class. Only the heroic efforts of the rent-control authorities keep them from being eaten alive. As the author of the previous disquisition on landlords goes on to recount:

> Several years ago, our landlord was charging us over 100 percent more than legally allowed.
>
> When we petitioned, she waved the $80-a-month garbage bill in our faces and said she was losing money. When your landlord makes this claim, as they all do, you can

> point to the provision of Berkeley's ordinance which allows landlords to petition the board for a rent increase if they are not making a fair return on the property. The catch is that the landlords have to haul out their books and prove it. . . . Be prepared for this type of landlord to unleash some of the energy of their frustrated greed on you.[3]

What is it about rent control that sets off open warfare between tenants and landlords and seems to turn landlords into exactly the heartless monsters that tenant activists claim they are?

The key point to recognize is that rent control turns a voluntary exchange into a coerced transaction. Regardless of how much griping tenants or landlords may do in a free market, the fact remains that nobody is able to *force* anyone into a transaction they don't want to make. But rent control is purely and simply an attempt by tenants to use the power of the government to set prices. As we have already seen, this effort inevitably produces a shortage. But what it does for tenant-landlord relationships—and eventually for the entire civic order of the community—is an entirely separate story.

Forced to sell at a price below market, any merchant will do one of three things: 1) he will withdraw the product from the market; 2) he will try to circumvent the regulations; or, 3) he will let the product deteriorate to the point where its value matches the legal price.

The first and most obvious response to rent control is to get out of the business and invest in something else. This is easy enough if you are a *builder* of houses—you just stop building. This is why, sooner or later, all rent-controlled communities eventually see new construction all but disappear—even when they try to exempt new housing.

If you already own rental apartments, however, getting out of the business is not such an easy matter. This, in fact, is what makes rent control so initially attractive. As the authors of *The Cities' Wealth* put it: "Housing can be controlled far more easily than other forms of wealth which are movable and beyond the scope of legal regulation by the city." If Berkeley tried to set prices on food or stereo equipment, the stores would just relocate across the border in Oakland. But a landlord does not have that option.

What a landlord can do, though, is withdraw from the *rental* market and try to put the unit into some other market. Condominium conversion is always an option, and rent-controlled communities are soon forced to try to outlaw it. Another possibility is owner occupancy. In Berkeley, where small buildings predominate, this has become attractive. "I have about twenty people in my office every week," says Michael St. John, who runs a consulting service for landlords in Berkeley, "and all anybody wants to know is, 'How do I get out of this business?' For most, selling to an affluent person who can occupy the entire building is the best possibility."

In Santa Monica, one young man who had inherited a rent-controlled apartment building simply filed to tear the whole thing down. "I never wanted to be a landlord," Jerome Nash told the rent board. "All I want to do with the property is grow flowers." The rent board turned him down. Its decision was upheld by the California Supreme Court (then under Chief Justice Rose Bird), which ruled that it was within the "police power" of the municipality to *force* Nash to stay in the business in order to try to solve the "housing shortage."

In 1986, State Senator Jim Ellis, of San Diego, persuaded the state legislature to pass a bill reversing this decision and allowing landlords to go out of business. "Under the Constitution, a person is supposed to have certain basic protections," said Ellis. "One of them is not to work for others without reward."

The "Ellis Act" has given California landlords the right to go out of business. Rent-controlled cities have continued to make it as difficult as possible, however, requiring departing landlords to pay their tenants $4,000-and-up "relocation fees."

One of the first landlords to take advantage of the new law was John Rodriguez. A Santa Monica barber, Rodriguez owned a small motel where once, out of sympathy, he allowed 27 Mexican immigrants to stay in his cabins for a few weeks. He soon discovered that, under rent control, he couldn't evict them. Soon, his 14 units were being occupied by 93 people—none of them paying any rent. Rodriguez found that claims to his apartments were being bought and sold for hundreds of dollars. "I had to go down to one of their auctions and buy back my own apartments," he said. "But I got them back." He has since demolished the motel and is moving his barber shop to the site.

Al Markevicius, another Santa Monica landlord, has emptied most of his 18-unit building and is waiting for the appellate courts to decide whether he can tear it down and put up a commercial building. "At least with an empty building I have predictable expenses and no more hassles," said Markevicius, a Lithuanian immigrant. "In Lithuania, we always regarded real estate as the most stable investment you could make—at least until the Soviets took over."

John Jurenka, another Santa Monica immigrant landlord, has emptied his ten-unit apartment building and is living in it with members of his own family. "In Santa Monica, a single-family home is worth $1 million, while two blocks away an eight-room apartment house is worth only $800,000. If I'm ever going to sell, I'll do better offering it as a single-family home."

Still, closing up shop completely remains difficult for most landlords. What many landlords do instead is gradually replace their tenants with friends, relatives, or anyone with whom they can exchange some kind of favor. Barter replaces commerce. Apartments change hands through personal connections—"blat" as the Russians call it. A study of the Berkeley market commissioned by the Rent Stabilization Board itself found that two-thirds of all tenants were now finding apartments through "personal connections and word-of-mouth," rather than normal market procedures.[4]

For the large landlord, however, this option is less feasible. He can't very well rent 50 apartments to members of his own family. What he can do is start charging "fixture fees" or "key money" to in-coming tenants. Even if these payments are outlawed (which they will be), desperate apartment-seekers will often make them voluntarily. "I've got a pile of applications on my desk right now from well-heeled young tenants, all making absolutely unsolicited offers to completely renovate one of my apartments in exchange for a lease," said James Baker, a retired businessman who owns several buildings in Santa Monica. "I haven't had a vacancy in a long time, but if I get one, you can bet I'll choose one of these people."

When the landlord is forbidden from accepting "key money," the superintendent will start charging it instead. Or perhaps it will be the real-estate agent, or "professional" apartment-finders, or anyone else who can insert himself into the line of transaction. Signs in Berkeley regularly offer $2,000 rewards for finding apartments.

Eventually, tenants themselves will start selling their leases to in-coming tenants. Or else they will hang onto apartments after moving and become landlords themselves, charging market rents to their sub-tenants in under-the-table transactions. The desperate sub-tenants, of course, will be only too happy to pay.

When these options have been exhausted, however, the only other real possibility for a landlord is to let his building deteriorate. As long as mortgages and taxes have to be paid and operating costs aren't getting any cheaper, the only real way to cut expenses is to reduce maintenance. Paint jobs can be deferred, floors left uncleaned, broken fixtures unfixed. "The feeling is, as long as you're not going to pay market rents, I'm not going to give you market conditions," said Michael Sandel, president of the Berkeley Property Owners' Association.[5]

Many landlords are initially reluctant to pursue this strategy. Postponing repairs can mean even greater expenses down the road and a landlord still instinctively fears losing tenants. In a normal market, a building that gets a bad reputation can be thrown into a downward spiral of falling rents and deteriorating conditions that can lead to bankruptcy.

But almost imperceptibly, the situation has now changed. To his surprise, the landlord soon discovers that, even after he has cut back on maintenance, none of his tenants wants to leave. In fact, there are new people at the door every day trying to get in. The problem is that there is now a housing shortage in the city. Vacancy rates, once at six percent, have now dropped below three percent. Whereas it used to take about a day-and-a-half to find an apartment, now people hunt fruitlessly for months.

Moreover, there is now another factor that offsets the usual disadvantages of losing tenants. Normally, frequent vacancies in a building are a sign of trouble. But now rent control has changed the equation. Almost inevitably, cities end up offering "vacancy allowances" that allow the landlord to increase rents to new tenants. Los Angeles, San Francisco, and San Jose all have such allowances and Santa Monica is considering it. The purpose is to give landlords some fiscal relief while shifting the costs to newer tenants.

But vacancy allowances create a new incentive for the landlord. Before, he always looked for good, long-term tenants who would pay the rent on time and not damage the apartment. Now, with everybody paying artificially low rents, his long-term tenants are the biggest problem. Their rents sink far below market, while apartments that have "churned" a few times have much higher rents.

One day it hits the landlord square in the face. All his former instincts have been wrong. Before, he worried about keeping his place clean and attractive to tenants. Now he's got people who could pay higher *legal* rents beating on his door every day, yet he never gets any vacancies. He should be *getting rid of* tenants. And strangely, the best way to do this is to make tenants as unhappy as possible by letting the building fall apart.

Not all landlords, of course, are willing to pursue this strategy. Some will stay with the old ethic, right to the point of bankruptcy. Yet landlords who "churn" apartments and harass tenants into leaving can make money under rent control, while those who stick with the old rules may go bankrupt.

A kind of natural selection sets in, with bad landlords driving out the good. Landlords who make tenants unhappy will make money, while those who please their tenants are defeated by the system.

And so, tenants and politicians will soon respond by looking for ways to prevent tenants from being evicted and force landlords to maintain their own buildings. The result will be a "tenant protection act."

The first important measure will usually be strong eviction controls. Under a normal market, eviction is governed by leases, which give both tenant and landlord protection against sudden interruptions of the arrangement. Tenants want security that they will not be asked to leave on short notice, while landlords want assurance that their tenants will not leave unexpectedly. Leases both protect tenants from arbitrary eviction and also penalize them for leaving before a lease has expired.

Under rent control, however, everything is changed once again. The landlord is no longer worried about holding the tenant to a lease. He knows the tenant isn't going anywhere, both because the current apartment represents the "deal of a lifetime" and because there is nowhere else to go. The landlord's only concern is that a lease be short so he can have the periodic opportunity to change tenants.

The tenant, on the other hand, would like a perpetual lease. Since the landlord now has every reason for vacating the apartment, the tenant knows that the landlord is likely to use any little provision of the lease as an excuse for getting rid of him. Thus, the need for strong anti-eviction laws.

Once these safeguards are in place, however, tenants will soon realize they can be much more casual about paying the rent. They can also worry less about damaging the apartment. Even if the landlord has a good case against them, it may take more than a year to fight it through the eviction proceedings. During that time, the tenant will often not have to pay rent at all. Even if the tenant loses, he or she can skip out owing several months' rent. Landlords will soon realize this and try to minimize their losses by offering tenants large bribes to move out. The $4,500 "relocation fees" in Berkeley and Santa Monica essentially formalize this procedure.

Far more important, however, is that well-protected tenants now become much less worried about *bothering other tenants.* One of the chief functions of a landlord, remember, is to act as the building's policeman. People who make loud noises, throw wild parties, let their dogs bark, deal crack—all must be dealt with by the landlord. Under ordinary circumstances, the threat of eviction is the landlord's strongest weapon. But under rent control, loud and troublesome tenants no longer have much to worry about. Now the guy on the seventh floor can blast his stereo all day and night with the supreme assurance that nobody can do a thing about it.

Andy Raubeson, executive director of SRO Housing Corporation, in Los Angeles, says he doesn't know how landlords can operate without the power of eviction. "We evict people and brag about it," said Raubeson. (Since SRO Housing is non-profit and sponsored largely by city funds, it is exempt from most of Los Angeles' tenant-protection laws.) "We had one tenant here with a history of drug addiction. He behaved himself for a while, even got elected head of one of our tenants' committees, but then all of a sudden he was back on drugs. He brought some friends into the building and they started robbing people left and right. They would pose as pizza delivery people, get people to open their doors, and then push them in and beat them up.

"It took us eight weeks to evict him. During that eight weeks we had to hire Pinkerton security guards to patrol the building. The cost of the guards was more than our entire rent roll. If we had to keep that up for a year, we'd be out of business. People just don't realize how much trouble one bad tenant can cause. I don't see how anyone can run rental housing without the power to evict people quickly."[6]

That's one side of the results of the new tenant protection laws. The other side concerns what to do when the landlord stops making repairs in the hope that his tenants will decide to leave. Having created this new kind of landlord, the municipal government must now protect tenants from him.

The solution is always the same. Sooner or later, someone will come up with the bright idea, "Why don't we let tenants enforce the housing code by giving them power to withhold rent, or even receive permanent rent reductions, if the landlord doesn't maintain his building?" And so, procedures for rent reductions and rent strikes will be formalized.

What political leaders do not want to acknowledge is that, in both the short and long run, tenants are generally far more interested in not paying rent than in worrying about the overall condition of the building. Tenants will demand rent reductions for the most trivial complaints. Since the rent board is almost always loaded with tenant activists, the whole process soon becomes a kangaroo court. (When Berkeley landlords finally elected one property owner to the rent board, the board decided she was not allowed to *vote* because ownership was a "conflict of interest.")

In Santa Monica, the rent-control board has voted such awards as a $35-a-month rent reduction because a tenant's garbage disposal broke down on Friday night and the landlord didn't have it fixed until Monday morning. Another tenant was awarded an $81-a-month reduction because eight of the little rubber prongs on the dishwasher were broken. Still other tenants have gotten $25 rent reductions because the plastic covers on electrical outlets were cracked.

Finding building-code violations soon becomes a sport—one that rich and poor alike can play. The affluent will form committees and comb their buildings with righteous indignation. The poor may just continue to break things out of habit. Either way, the rent reductions mount up. When trivial violations can't be found, it is always possible to create a few. A broken window, a damaged mailbox, a missing smoke alarm—all may be worth sizable rent reductions in what becomes known as the "violations game."

Such rent reductions are usually supposed to be temporary—removable when the violation is corrected. But now comes the next level of play, known as the "access game." Having been awarded a $45-a-month rent reduction for a small crack in the bathroom wall, the tenant now says to himself, "Do I really want this crack fixed or would I rather keep the $45 a month?" The answer, of course, is obvious. So when the plasterers arrive two days later to patch the wall, the tenant *refuses to let them in*.

This scenario is repeated over and over again in rent-controlled cities. Landlords make appointments, tenants make sure they are not at home. Landlords catch them at home, tenants say they can't be disturbed. Landlords send registered letters setting up appointments, tenants send them back. "We've had to call the police several times where tenants were physically threatening workmen who were trying to make repairs in their apartments," said Al Markevicius, who manages several hundred apartments in Santa Monica.

The further their rents descend, the angrier tenants become. "The rents here are great," they will say, "but the landlord is a complete scum. He never fixes anything. You have to drag him into court just to get him to change a lightbulb." When confronted with the idea that their below-market rents might have something to do with all this, they will cry out, "Market rents? Are you kidding? This place isn't worth the money we're paying for it now!"

And so it goes, on and on, until it becomes one of the ugliest spectacles in America—landlords and tenants fighting in hand-to-hand combat over housing that is falling down around their ears.

Dan Walters, of *The Sacramento Bee,* describes the process in Berkeley:

> While neighborhoods around other state college and university campuses . . . have experienced an unprecedented level of private apartment construction in recent years, there is none in Berkeley. Landlords even refuse to paint or perform minor maintenance chores because they can't recover costs from the rent board. Berkeley now has a dingy, Third Worldish aura that coincides with its politics.[7]

The battle may go on for years, but in some areas it will finally pass the point of no return. If tenants are to drain the building dry by destroying things and refusing to pay rent, why shouldn't the landlord beat them to it? He will start "milking" the building—collecting rents while paying no mortgage, taxes, or other bills. In the two or three years it takes for the banks to foreclose or the city to take the building for back taxes, a landlord can pull $50,000 out of a lost investment. Collecting on fire insurance is another option. If a landlord cannot stomach all this, he may be forced to sell to a "slumlord" who can.

Once again, the government must intervene to protect tenants. Victims of landlord arson will be given special welfare grants to help them find new apartments, maybe even be put at the top of long waiting lists for public housing.

Yet this Rube Goldberg patchwork of incentives only produces more contrary results. Now *tenants themselves* have an incentive to burn down their own buildings. They will receive large cash grants from welfare or immediate placement in coveted public housing. Now tenants will start burning down their own buildings—often moving their television sets and other important belongings onto the sidewalk before the fire starts.

And so it goes, on and on, with the South Bronx as the result. Just as the rents have been reduced to near-zero, so the value of the building has been reduced to zero. The cycle of housing destruction is complete.

All this may seem like an exaggeration, but everything described here has already happened in one or another American city under rent control. And it will happen eventually in *every* city that adopts rent control. The economic logic is inexorable.

Yet throughout all this, there will still remain a sizable minority of tenants—perhaps even a majority—who continue to reap benefits from rent control. They are the tenants whose landlords are wealthy enough to withstand the economic pressure and can maintain their buildings despite constant losses. Naturally, these tenants will tend to be the most affluent.

And this is what causes such massive public consternation—almost a kind of mass insanity—that ultimately overcomes every city with rent control. Everyone can see the system working *somewhere.* Stories are forever circulating about somebody who has a great apartment at a ridiculously low rent. So why can't it work for everybody?

It must be the politicians haven't enforced the law strictly enough. Probably they have been bought off. The landlords—those sinister, ruthless malefactors—have turned out to be far more subtly powerful than anyone imagined. They can pull all the strings, manipulating things from behind the scenes. Perhaps it is time for sterner measures. Maybe the government should take over all housing. Perhaps a few landlords should be sent to jail. . . .

The truth, of course, is just the opposite. Like suburban zoning, "welcome-stranger" tax assessments, and controlled growth, rent control is a system where the majority tries to vote itself benefits while leaving a small—but growing—number of people to bear the consequences.

And so homelessness mounts. By blocking new housing and destroying old, rent control leaves swelling numbers of people without anyplace to live. The poorest will be the first left out in the cold.

Chapter 15

The Paperworking Class

All this describes the *normal* ways in which things go wrong under rent control. Yet there is something else at work as well. The almost unbelievable tyrannies that have begun to emerge in cities like Berkeley or Santa Monica demand further explanation.

James Baker head of ACTION, a landlords' group in Santa Monica, offers an insightful suggestion. "You have to have two things for rent control," he argues. "You have to have a very large tenant majority, but you also have to have an educated elite. Long Beach has 66 percent renters, but turned down rent control because it's a working-class town. But Beverly Hills, West Hollywood, Berkeley, and Santa Monica have all adopted it."

The real distinction is probably the one between the working class—people who actually deal with physical objects—and what might be called the "paperworking class"—people who are particularly skilled at manipulating the law. By virtue of its superior educational abilities, the paperworking class tries to gain control of the physical environment by *getting control of the people who provide goods and services* through its knowledge and facility with the law. Berkeley and Santa Monica, both with high concentrations of lawyers and education professionals, have been the places where this administrative tyranny is carried to an extreme.

Take a few examples of things that have occurred in Berkeley:

A young man and his elderly father, a retired plumber, occupied the upper unit of their own duplex. When the father had a stroke, the son decided to move him to the downstairs unit for better wheelchair access. He advertised for a person to live rent-free in the three-bedroom unit in exchange for caring for his father.

A woman graduate student accepted the offer. After a few weeks, however, she decided she did not want to care for the father. Instead, she asked to pay rent of $350. The woman paid sporadically for about six months, then stopped altogether, arguing that sharing the apartment with the father constituted care. The son went to court for an eviction. The woman pleaded for three extra months in order to find an apartment, then had the eviction voided on a technicality.

Meanwhile, the son was forced to go away for two weeks. Once again, the tenant agreed to offer temporary care. When he returned, however, the tenant would not let him in the apartment. He called the police. The father was found malnourished and so emaciated he had to be taken to the hospital. The son asked the tenant to leave. She refused, arguing that she was abiding by the original agreement.

Next, the tenant went to the rent board, asking that her apartment be placed under rent control. Owner-occupied duplexes are exempt, but the tenant claimed that a shed in the back yard where the father had stored his plumbing supplies was a third unit. During the hearings, one rent board member told the son, "Our policy is that if someone sleeps in an orange crate in the yard, it constitutes a unit." After two hearings on the matter, however, the board ruled in the owner's favor. Still, the tenant stayed.

Finally, after four years, she left voluntarily. During that time the son spent $5,000 in legal fees in trying to evict her. She lived rent-free the entire time.

Clare Morrison, another Berkeley resident, was 70 years old in 1980 when both her husband and brother died within nine months of each other. She suffered a nervous breakdown and was hospitalized for about a year. During that period, she signed papers making her sister-in-law, Patricia Ackerman, conservator of the property.

While Morrison was hospitalized, Ackerman rented the home for $300 a month to John Kojro, a graduate student at the University of California. He moved to Delaware, but sublet the apartment to Janet Shraer, a 26-year-old graduate student. She moved in two of her friends.

In 1981, Morrison recovered and decided to move back into her house. Shraer and her two roommates refused to leave. Morrison claimed she didn't remember signing the conservator papers and never wanted the property rented. A county judge removed Ackerman as conservator. Morrison refused to accept any rent checks. Shraer agreed to move only if Morrison agreed to refund the entire $4,000 in rent she had paid over the previous 14 months.

When Morrison went to the house to check on her antique furniture, the tenants refused to let her in. Morrison broke two windows in the front of the house out of frustration. The tenants complained Morrison was disturbing the "tranquility of their environment." "I believe in the rent control laws and I feel as a tenant my rights have been violated," Shraer told *The Berkeley Voice.*[1]

Soon pickets for both sides were marching in front of the house. Shraer told the newspapers that Morrison should register the property with the rent board and then try to evict her. "If she won, I'd move," she said.

Morrison, knowing such an eviction would take years and cost thousands of dollars, refused. "I've never been a landlord and don't want to be," she said. "All I want to do is move back into my father's house where I've lived since I was 11 years old." Meanwhile, she was forced to live in a hotel in nearby Pittsburg.

The case dragged on until June 1989, when Morrison's $50,000 law suit for damages to her house finally went to trial in Alameda County Court. In October 1989, the judge ordered the tenants out of the house. When Morrison finally regained entrance she found all her furniture had been stolen.

Ove and Eva Floystrup, Danish immigrants, refused to register their buildings in 1979 in protest of the rent-control law. Although they complied with the law in all other respects and did not raise rents above legally prescribed limits, they refused to comply with the basic registration on the grounds that it invaded their privacy.

In 1982, the City of Berkeley signed a court stipulation agreeing to accept the incomplete registration. Then, six years later, in 1988, the Rent Stabilization Board *unilaterally* reneged on the agreement and ruled that the Floystrups' rents had been illegal since 1979. The Floystrups were ordered to reimburse their tenants $71,000 in rent "overcharges." The Floystrups were forced to sell another building in order to meet the debt. They are now appealing in Federal Court.

After ten years of rent control, the entire city administration in Berkeley has become so rigged in favor of tenants that even State Senator Nicholas Petris, who represents Berkeley and originally supported rent control, calls it "no better than any totalitarian government."[2]

One remarkable catch-22 has been the "Measure I trap," which has made almost every rent in Berkeley "illegal." Whenever tenants become involved in a dispute with their landlord, they simply challenge the legality of the rent and end up receiving huge refunds.

The situation evolved as follows. When Measure I, the 1978 rent-control referendum, was adopted, it required landlords to reimburse their tenants 80 percent of all the property-tax savings from Proposition 13. It also allowed landlords to take a five percent increase on January 1, 1980. This popular referendum was widely publicized and understood.

In 1979, however, the Berkeley City Council passed ordinance 5212, which amended Measure I by requiring landlords to justify their five percent rent raise with extensive documentation of rising costs. The amendment—little publicized—became the "Measure I trap."

Today, whenever tenants face an eviction or a dispute over a rent increase, they challenge the legality of their rent by arguing that the landlord did not justify his Measure-I increase in 1980. A form letter routinely sent by the City of Berkeley to tenants facing eviction reads as follows:

> Even if you have not paid the rent, you may have defenses you do not know about. For example, the following defenses may be available in your case:
>
> 1) Your rental unit or any other rental unit on the property is not property registered with the Rent Stabilization Board.
>
> 2) The rent charged for your unit or any other rental unit on the property is in excess of the lawful rent permitted by the Rent Ordinance; or
>
> 3) Your rental unit or any other rental unit on the property is in substantial need of repair.
>
> IN ADDITION, YOU MAY HAVE OTHER DEFENSES NOT MENTIONED HERE. [Emphasis in original.]

Routinely, the rent board now rules that landlords did not sufficiently document their 1980 increases. The board then *rolls back* rents to their 1978 level and *requires that landlords refund all the "illegal overpayment" collected since then.* Michael St. John estimates that the amount of refunds paid by Berkeley landlords now exceeds $800,000. When the landlord cannot pay the refund, the board allows tenants to live rent-free until proper restitution is made.

In addition, the rent board has interpreted the phrase "not properly registered" in the most extreme manner. Typing errors and innocent mistakes on registration forms are routinely interpreted as "failure to register properly." Moreover, if *one* apartment is found to be out of compliance, *all* the rents in the building are deemed to be illegal and all tenants are eligible for rebates.

Gregory McConnell, the former director of the rent board, recalls one elderly woman being deemed "improperly registered" because she left blank an application question that asked, "Is parking included?" (It wasn't.) Another owner, after being sent only two applications for his three apartments, typed up his own form for the third, but forgot to include the line, "signed under penalty of perjury." Several years, later, on a tenant's challenge, the registration was ruled improper and thousands of dollars in refunds were ordered.

Senator Petris has tried to counter this procedural tyranny by passing several state bills compelling the city to accept "substantial compliance" with the law. But the Berkeley City Council simply ignores them or passes their own bills overriding the state legislature. As late as March 1989, the city council adopted an ordinance reaffirming that, in rental registrations, "fraud or misrepresentation means intentional, negligent, or *innocent.*" (Emphasis added.)

Hunting rental refunds has become a sport among Berkeley tenants. Cleveland Williams is a retired construction worker who built his own five-unit building on a vacant lot in 1961, doing most of the concrete work himself. In 1979 his rents were only $130 and $150. After doing extensive renovation to an apartment that a tenant had damaged, he raised the rent from $150 to $160. Five years later, his tenants protested the increase. The rent board ruled he had not justified the $10 increase and he was forced to refund his tenants $1,877.

In another case, a tenant installed her own bathtub in her apartment without telling the landlady. When the tenant later called the building inspector to look for housing-code violations, the inspector noted the makeshift hookup and said it was illegal. The tenant then filed for a rent reduction on the grounds that the apartment was worth less without the tub. The rent board ordered a refund of $534.

As word gets around Berkeley that landlords can be easily gouged for thousands of dollars in "overpayments," the pace of tenant petitions has accelerated. "I've had hundreds and hundreds of calls in this office over the last six months of 1988," said state senator Petris, himself a Berkeley landlord. "People are suffering personal and economic devastation for actions much less than criminal in nature."

Nor is it only small landlords who are adversely affected. In December 1985, James Guthrie and Don Anderson, chairman of the board and president of the Berkeley-Albany YMCA, petitioned the state legislature in the following letter:

> The rent control ordinance in Berkeley began to be applied to the YMCA in June 1982. The results have been disastrous. [The enclosed material] documents the tragic four year history endured by the YMCA and . . . the $207,000 lost to community programs as a result of the rent ordinance. Rent control has put the YMCA in financial ruin and we no longer have the right to determine who we serve. This is irrespective of how dangerous an individual might be to himself, other resident members, or children at the YMCA. Able bodied men have lived free at the

> YMCA for several years making a mockery of a well intentioned law, the YMCA, and the members of the community who support it.

Originally believing itself to be exempt from rent control, the "Y" made no effort to register until its rents were challenged by a transient resident in 1982. The rent board ruled the "Y" must register and disallowed all post-1979 rent increases. The "Y" was ordered to refund overcharges, placing ads in newspapers, if necessary, to hunt down its past tenants. Rents were rolled back 20 percent until all the refunds were made.

All this eventually caused Gregory McConnell, former director of the Berkeley Rent Stabilization Board, to quit his job in disgust and join the other side. McConnell, who is black, had been recruited to Berkeley in 1985 after heading the rent-control board in the District of Columbia.

"The only blacks I ever saw in my office were landlords," recalled McConnell. "The only Asians I ever saw were landlords. Then I'd go to the tenants' meetings and all I'd see were affluent yuppies, college students and what I'd call the 'perennial hippies.' "

The turning point for McConnell came when an elderly black came into his office, tears streaming from his eyes, and handed McConnell the deed to his property. "He said, 'I can't take this anymore. You're going to take this away from me anyway, so I just want to give it to you.' I finally said to myself, 'Am I really helping the right people in this job?' " McConnell has since formed a consulting firm that helps small landlords deal with Berkeley rent control.

In Santa Monica, the results have been the same. Barbara Thom, an elderly landlady, was forced to reduce a tenant's rent from $400 to $300 because she would not let the tenant use an abandoned laundry room to store antique furniture. Norma Williams, another elderly landlady, was forced to reduce 22 tenants' rent by $10 a month because she refused to rehabilitate an old sauna that tenants discovered in the building. In another case, a 300-pound tenant broke a chair by sitting in it and then won a $15 rent decrease for loss of the chair. When the landlord offered to replace it, the tenant opted for the rent reduction instead.

After winning a court battle in 1988 that had delayed rent reductions, rent board chairwoman Susan Packer Davis announced a new punitive policy toward landlords. As *The Outlook,* Santa Monica's daily newspaper, reported:

> Tenants can withhold up to $80 a month for leaks in the roof, windows or doors. The previous limit was $40. Stained and deteriorated drapes and window coverings can cost a landlord up to $80 a month, up from $40; while shabby carpeting and floor coverings can mean a $150 monthly rent cut.

> And in the past, a tenant had to prove there was a hole or rip in the carpeting. Now a decrease is granted if the carpeting is merely frayed. . . .
>
> Veteran board member Dolores Press says the board is being more protective toward tenants because of the on-going legal attacks by landlords over the constitutionality of rent control.[3]

In 1988, tenants won 97 percent of the rent-reduction appeals brought before the board.

Nor do the stakes remain small for long. John Feigel, a Czech immigrant who worked in ice cream stores all his life, eventually saved enough money to buy three small buildings of 4, 11, and 14 units. He had managed them without problems for ten years. When rent control was adopted, his tenants began seeking rent reductions for petty violations. Unlike many other landlords, Feigel fought them vigorously before the rent board. Hostilities escalated until Feigel's tenants finally had him thrown in jail when a sump pump failed in an underground garage. Feigel eventually lost all his buildings. At age 70, he is now a bankrupt and broken man.

What underlies all this, of course, is what de Tocqueville called "the tyranny of the majority." Tenants are a political majority in most rent-controlled communities and always outnumber landlords. Bending the system to their will, they rig things so that tenants always win and landlords always lose. Judges—often frightened by the majority themselves—acquiesce in the process.

"I once stood before a judge in one of my cases and said, 'Aren't you just giving in to mob rule? If a mob of people got together on a streetcorner and voted by majority rule to rob somebody, would that make it right?' " said Al Markevicius, of Santa Monica. "The judge threatened me with contempt of court for trying to defend myself."

Also at work is the ethic of the paperworking class—the educated elite who almost always spearhead rent control. Moving into an older, established community, these highly educated professionals often express open contempt for the carpenters and immigrants who provide them housing. What is most galling to them is that they must pay 25 percent of their income to uneducated people who don't seem to do anything but sweep the hallways and "speculate in housing." That these people usually have far less education than themselves only makes them more contemptuous.

As a result, the paperworking class devises a system that revolves around the thing in which they themselves excel—legal formalities. Landlording is soon forced away from its natural base of hammering nails and fixing plumbing and becomes an exercise in dealing with arcane rules and deliberately confusing procedures. As Berkeley landlord Timothy Kaarto put it, "I've had to put down my hammer and learn to type."

John C. Dvorak, a columnist with *The San Francisco Examiner*, caught this drift on one visit to Berkeley:

> A spokesperson at the [rent] board offices (who wished to remain anonymous) told me with disdain that the little landlords shouldn't be in business if they can't handle the paperwork requirements. "They'll have to get used to the fact that if you're in business you have to do paperwork," [she said.][4]

Ultimately, "community ownership of housing" becomes nothing more than the educated expropriating the uneducated. Yet, it is the latter who, in the end, provide the nation with most of its rental housing.

In 1984, T. Sumitomo was the owner of a small triplex at 2436–38 10th Street in West Berkeley. Sumitomo had three tenants, paying $250, $180, and $150. Upstairs in the six-room, $250 apartment, were Ann Arbogast, her female companion, Sebena Stark, and their child, Shaya Arbogast-Stark. Arbogast, a former city employee and long-time activist in Berkeley politics, served as coordinator for the Tenants Action Project and was one of the authors of the original 1979 rent law. Downstairs, in a one-bedroom apartment, was Arbogast's sister, Patricia. In the back, in another one-bedroom apartment, lived Rocky Jones, a construction worker, and his girlfriend.

In 1982, Sumitomo went to the rent control board asking for a rent increase on the grounds that his "absurdly low" rents did not even pay his expenses. Arbogast, a law student, argued the case for the tenants. Sumitomo became one of the first victims of the Measure I trap. Unable to document his 1979 expenses, Sumitomo had his rents *lowered* to $123, $73, and $115 and was ordered to pay a $6,637 refund. The tenants were told not to pay rent until the reimbursements were made.

Sumitomo quickly sold the building. In March 1985, it was bought with a $30,000 down payment by Joseph Levesque, a Navy carpenter from Oakland who had a wife and two children, and his brother, Roland. Originally from Boston, the Levesques were the first members of their family ever to own a home. "I'm a carpenter all day and then I wait on tables for six hours a night," Levesque later told the newspapers. "My wife says I'm going crazy from working, but it's the only way I know how. She just started a job at the minimum wage herself."[5]

The Levesque brothers knew about Sumitomo's troubles but bought the building on the presumption that they could take two apartments for joint owner occupancy—a move that had been ruled acceptable by the city attorney. Three months later, however, the Berkeley City Council, dissatisfied with the attorney's rulings, bought out her contract. Her replacement ruled the joint occupancy was a condominium conversion, illegal under a 1982 Berkeley law forbidding the conversion of rental units.

The new ruling was challenged in court by several other landlords. Meanwhile, Joseph Levesque went ahead with eviction proceedings against Ann Arbogast and her roommate on the grounds of his own individual owner-occupancy—still perfectly legal. Arbogast vowed to fight the eviction. "If someone can find me a place in Berkeley that's available at [the same] rent, I might reconsider it," she told the newspapers. "But I don't think it's possible. . . . [Levesque] needs to take a look at how he got into the situation and realize he made a serious mistake."[6]

Arbogast and her roommate went on a rent strike, claiming the building had code violations. Then they began playing the usual games, refusing to allow Levesque to make the repairs. "We'd go over there to do the work, ring the doorbell, and no one would answer," Levesque later told television reporters from his prison cell. "Then we'd start to leave, turn around, and see her peeking out from behind the curtains."[7]

After a year of unsuccessful court action, collecting no rents, and continuing to pay rent on their Oakland apartment, the Levesques went bankrupt. In June 1986, the Hamilton Savings Bank foreclosed on the mortgage. The Levesques lost their $30,000 life savings. Joseph Levesque suffered a nervous breakdown. Three months later, he broke into a motel and raped an anonymous young woman. He told prosecutors that he was taking revenge on Arbogast. In 1986, Levesque was sentenced to eight years in prison. He is now serving his sentence.

Title to the building was now held by the Hamilton Savings Bank. Having no desire to deal with the tenants, the bank announced it was turning off the utilities and providing no more services. Patricia Arbogast had moved out, turning her downstairs apartment over to another law student, Ramona Ratliff (Ingrid Pfeiffer's old tenant). Although paying no rent herself, Arbogast continued to collect rent from Ratliff for several months.

With the utilities shut off, Ann Arbogast, Stark, and their child finally left in June 1986. Arbogast assigned her lease over to David Linn, an attorney who does advocacy work for the homeless. She told Linn he should "maintain the apartment as affordable housing for low-income people."

In the back, Rocky Jones decided to stay. He persuaded Pacific Gas and Electric to put utilities in his name. All three apartments had a common meter and Jones—concerned that Ratliff and Linn would not pay their bill—cut off the wiring to their apartments. Fights broke out in the hallways. Ratliff finally moved out and sued Jones for $50,000 for assault and harassment.

Linn had originally planned to move in with his wife and daughter. As the war with Jones escalated, however, he decided to turn his apartment over to four homeless men. They invited in several of their friends, including Al Winslow and Bob Mills, two veteran Berkeley political activists. Winslow and Mills put up a sign on the front yard announcing the formation of "Headache"—the Homeless Direct Action Collective—and invited other homeless people to join them. Soon, about 15 people were living in the two apartments, plus a converted garage and laundry room.

"They would stay night long singing and banging on the ceiling," Jones later told the court in his deposition. "They would burn open fires in the back yard and many would sleep in the yard." When Jones complained, the homeless banged on his door at night and pushed his truck out of the driveway. Jones finally left, filing his own $25,000 cross-complaint against Ratliff and Lynn for harassment and emotional distress.

With Jones gone, the homeless population grew to about 35 people in three apartments. Among them were drug addicts, alcoholics, and people with assorted mental problems. Winslow had originally promised to accommodate homeless women and children, but found women too frightened to enter the increasingly lawless premises. Over the next eighteen months, the police responded to 42 complaints from neighbors, ranging from all-night parties and junked cars to battery, burglary, and grand theft. Speaking for the group, Oscar Gutierrez, one of the homeless, complained the charges were overblown. "In this house no one has killed anyone," he told the newspapers.[8]

As the population outgrew the house, residents built shacks in the back yard. Winslow went on television at one point, inviting the homeless to "bring your own plywood down to 10th Street" to build homes. A back-yard pit was dug to bury garbage. When the plumbing failed, the pit became a latrine. "The stench was so overpowering we couldn't even open our windows," said James Kelly, a next-door neighbor whose small duplex sits only three feet from the property line. When a series of rapes occurred, neighbors suspected someone at the Homeless Collective was responsible.

Hamilton Savings talked about making evictions, but backed off when assistant vice-president Ken Johnston received death threats. The bank announced that the property now belonged to the Federal Home Loan Mortgage Corporation (Freddie Mac), which had inherited the defaulted mortgage. City officials said they could do nothing because no one would admit ownership to the property. In spite of all this, the collective received sympathetic coverage in the Berkeley press.[9]

Eventually, even Winslow fled the house, leaving the situation to mend itself. "It basically broke down because of the numbers and because people weren't being properly socialized," he told *The Berkeley Express.*[10]

Finally, on the morning of January 24, 1988, Kelly, the 46-year-old neighbor, stepped onto his back porch and threw four molotov cocktails into the adjoining back yard, burning down three wooden shacks and setting a man's clothes on fire. "The next thing is going to be dead bodies," Kelly, who is black, told police in a written statement. "If the city cannot clean up this mess, I will." Alarmed by Kelly's remarks, a judge set bail at $10,000, keeping him in jail for four days. "We thought he was one of our best friends," complained one of homeless. Kelly eventually pled guilty to felony arson and was placed on three years' probation.

Neighbors expressed support for Kelly and petitioned the city council to close down the building. Finally, on March 8, 1988, Hamilton Savings re-entered the picture. At 6:30 A.M., bank officials arrived at the house—in the company of 25 Berkeley police officers—and routed the remaining 20 tenants for trespassing. The City of Berkeley, supporting the action, called it a "citizens' arrest."

The evictions raised great alarm among Berkeley's radical newspapers and tenant activists. "The city of Berkeley is supposed to uphold rent control," said Jim Chanin, a tenant attorney. "They ought to know what a tenancy is, and they ought to know that these people were, in fact, tenants."

David Linn, the attorney who had started the whole thing, noted the "interesting coincidence that the bank would use the firebombing as an excuse to evict tenants" and suggested that Kelly had been "hired" by the bank to commit the arson.[11]

Mayor Loni Hancock, although admitting she had "legal and philosophical problems" with the evictions, defended the action. "The real tragedy is that the neighborhood was prepared to bend over backwards to be hospitable and to make a place for them in the neighborhood," she said.[12]

In 1989, the house on 10th Street was finally bought by a new owner. After evicting one last homeless resident who was claiming occupancy—paying him a $4,500 "relocation fee" under the Ellis Act—the new owner converted the two front apartments into a single residence and is occupying it himself. The rear apartment is now vacant. Under the Ellis Act, it cannot be rented for another ten years.

Chapter 16

Landlords and Economic Rent

We can now better understand the role of the landlords. A landlord is someone who provides housing to people who can't otherwise afford it. By allowing a person to live on his or her property, a landlord saves the tenant the trouble of having to buy the property himself.

Few people realize what a bargain such an arrangement can be for a tenant. To make a comparison, we need only look at the automobile market again.

The most expensive Mercedes Benz sells for about $81,000. At the same time, the median home in this country sells for about $88,000. Yet if you want to rent the Mercedes, you will have to pay about $1,500 a month, whereas if you wanted to rent the home, you would only have to pay about $800 a month.

Why is this so? The answer, once again, lies in the longevity of real estate. The average Mercedes—a well-built car if there ever was one—has a life expectancy of only about 25 years. That is still less than one-third of the life expectancy of a new apartment building, which will probably last for 75 years. Therefore, the owner of the apartment building can amortize his purchase very slowly. He knows that 25 years from now it will still be standing and collecting rents. But the owner of the Mercedes knows that after 30 years the car will be ready for the scrap heap. Therefore, he is forced to pay for it more quickly, which forces him to charge a higher rent.

Profits in real estate are generally measured with different expectations than profits in other businesses. Real estate people can think in the long, long term. They are not prisoners of investors who demand a quick profit or rapid capital appreciation. The banks that lend them money are willing to accept long-term mortgages because they too know that the building will always be standing even if the owner eventually defaults.

One veteran Manhattan landlord put it this way: "When you're a landlord, you don't mind breaking even for a long, long time because you know that one day you're going to hit the jackpot." That day comes when the landlord pays off the mortgage. Until then, he or she may do no more than meet expenses while retiring the debt. Their only "income" may be the apartment they give to themselves. But once he or she owns the building free and clear, they are assured a sizable annuity.

This is why so many people buy rental buildings as retirement security. They may have to put a lot of work into the building while they are young. They may even carry it a while on their salary. But once the mortgage is paid off, they will have financial security for their old age. Traditionally, this is what has made rental housing such a bargain for tenants.

All this places special long-term responsibilities on landlords. It is often noted that landlords can be almost paranoid about what tenants do to their property. When we understand the economics of real estate—the long lifetime of the asset required to recapture the investment—it is clear why landlords are such fanatics about tenant behavior. Rental housing has to last a long, long time if it is going to pay off. Landlords worry about the long term while tenants do not.

Still, two questions remain unanswered. First, why is it that rents have been rising so rapidly since 1980? And second, what is it exactly that landlords do? How can they claim such a large portion of a tenant's income simply by *owning* something? And since the role of landlord seems so passive—if not parasitical—couldn't we make housing more affordable by eliminating the middleman and turning housing into community property?

Both questions are good ones. As it happens, all can be resolved by looking into an arcane but enlightening concept called "economic rent."

Economic rent is a subject with which economists have been wrestling since the 18th century.

The first person to define the subject was Adam Smith. In *The Wealth of Nations* (1776), Smith posited there are three basic ways in which people earned their living:

> The whole annual produce of the land and labour of every country . . . naturally divides itself . . . into three parts; the rent of land, the wages of labour and the profits of stock; and constitutes a revenue to three different orders of people; to those who live by rent, to those who live by wages, and to those who live by profit. These are the three great, original, and constituent orders of every civilized society, from whose revenue that of every other order is ultimately derived.[1]

Wages are earned by those who contribute their time and labor. Profits are earned by those who own and employ capital. Rent, on the other hand, is collected by those who own *natural resources* and provide them to others.

Even for Smith, the rents collected on natural resources were somewhat objectionable:

> As soon as the land of any country has all become private property, the landlords, like all other men, love to reap where they never sowed, and demand a rent even for its natural produce. The wood of the forest, the grass of the field, and all the natural fruits of the earth, which when land was in common, cost the labourer only the trouble of gathering them, come, even to him, to have an additional price fixed upon them. He must give up to the landlord a portion of what his labour either collects or produces. This portion . . . constitutes the rent of land.[2]

Despite these misgivings, Smith stuck by his main point—rent can be collected on natural resources *only because a product is scarce.* Where there is more land than anyone can use—as in early America—rents drop to zero. Smith also applied the concept to forests, mines, and other natural resources. Certain minerals were expensive, he noted, not simply because of the labor or capital employed to obtain them, but because of their natural scarcity. Economic rent was the portion of the product attributable to the scarcity itself.

The next economic philosopher to grapple with economic rent was David Ricardo. Writing 40 years after Adam Smith, Ricardo was heavily influenced by his friend and correspondent, Thomas Malthus.

With an eye to Malthus' concern over agricultural scarcity, Ricardo tried to limit the concept of economic rent to land.

> Rent is that portion of the produce of the earth, which is paid to the landlord for the use of the original and indestructible powers of the soil. It is often, however,

> confounded with the interest and profit of capital, and, in popular language, the term is applied to whatever is annually paid by a farmer to his landlord.[3]

Ricardo somewhat discounted Smith's application of rent to forests and mines. Yet in his own way, he made a better definition of the term by applying the concept to such natural amenities as air and water:

> On the common principles of supply and demand, no rent could be paid for [endlessly abundant] land, for the same reason stated why nothing is given for the use of air and water, or for any other of the gifts of nature which exist in boundless quantity. With . . . the assistance of the pressure of the atmosphere, and the elasticity of steam, engines may perform work, and abridge human labour to a very great extent; but no charge is made for the use of these natural aids, because they are inexhaustible, and at every man's disposal. In the same manner, the brewer, the distiller, the dyer, make incessant use of the air and water for the production of their commodities; but as the supply is boundless, they bear no price. If all land had the same properties, if it were unlimited in quantity, and uniform in quality, no charge could be made for its use. . . .[4]

Still, said Ricardo, rent was "merely . . . a transfer of value, advantageous only to the landlords, and proportionably injurious to the consumer."

> Rent, then, is a creation of value, but not a creation of wealth; it adds nothing to the resources of a country, it does not enable it to maintain fleets and armies; for the country would have a greater disposable fund if its land were of a better quality, and it could employ the same capital without generating a rent.[5]

Other economists also struggled to define the concept. One memorable effort was made by Nassau William Senior, an early 19th century economist. Using the example of a popular opera singer, Senior wrote:

> Most persons would be puzzled if they were told that when Madame Goldschmidt receives 200 pounds for a night's performance, 10 shillings of it are the wages of her labour, 30 shillings more the profit on her acquired capital of knowledge and skill, and the remaining 198 pounds is a rent derived from the extraordinary powers of which nature has given her a monopoly.[6]

Gradually freeing the idea from its moorings in land and natural resources, economists groped toward a concept of economic rent as representing the value of any natural quality that is scarce and irreplaceable.

A model who receives $30,000 for gracing the cover of a magazine, for example, is receiving economic rent. A movie star whose style and manner appeal to millions receives economic rent. In *Anarchy, State, and Utopia,* philosopher Robert Nozick used the example of Wilt Chamberlain to refute the possibility of a perfectly egalitarian society. Even with an initially equal income distribution, wrote Nozick, thousands of people would pay a few dollars to watch Wilt Chamberlain play basketball. This would eventually make Chamberlain a bit richer and everyone else comparatively poorer.[7] (The Russians have tried to avoid this by forbidding sports heroes to collect private rents, but compensate by giving them lush state subsidies, which amounts to the same thing.)

What emerges about housing, then, is that not all of what the landlord collects on the first of the month is economic rent. A portion covers someone's wages for maintaining the building. Another sizable portion covers the capital investment represented by the cost of the building itself. Only a small portion attached to the value of the *land*—the only truly irreplaceable commodity—represents pure economic rent. (In truth, though, buildings constitute a gray area. Their long life cycle makes them such a part of the landscape that they approach being a permanent resource.)

What does a landlord do to earn this income? First, he provides the labor for taking care of the building. If he doesn't do it himself, he pays someone else to do it. Second, his initial capital investment may earn a profit. (Although he probably didn't construct the building himself, these costs are reflected in the purchase price.) Finally, he collects economic rent, since his building and no other occupies that particular space.

An old proverb of real estate says there are three important factors about a piece of land—location, location, and location. This is the commodity for which people pay economic rent. Location is irreducible—as fundamental as the principle that no two objects can occupy the same space at the same time. Only so many people can have a view of Central Park. At the same time, millions more people would like to share that view. Anyone who secures an apartment with a view of the Park will pay a lot of economic rent—simply because so many others find it so desirable.

The same principle works everywhere on an attenuated scale. Cities with thriving job markets are desirable places to live precisely because they are good locations to make money. As a result, housing prices are likely to be higher. At the same time, many people like to live near the seashore. Space is naturally limited, so people must pay economic rent. In places like The Hamptons or Malibu, people pay higher housing costs, with prices usually determined by proximity to the ocean. Beachfront property is the most expensive.

In most respects, landlords earn their living pretty much like everyone else. In the national economy, labor usually takes home 80 percent of the gross national profit, capital investment earns about 12 percent, and rents represent the remaining 8 percent. For a building owner, capital investment usually represents about 50 percent of his total output, labor about 40 percent, and economic rents about 10 percent (if we consider only the location value of the land and not the durability of the building).

How has a landlord earned the right to collect this rent? The answer is simple—he paid for it. The value of the rent was reflected in the original price he paid for the building.

There are two ways of coming into possession of resources that produce economic rent. One is to be endowed with them, the other is to earn them. Singers with beautiful voices, basketball players who grow to be seven feet tall, beautiful movie actresses—although they all work hard—collect a great deal of economic rent on their natural endowments.

It is one of those strange twists of human nature that endowments bestowed by nature seem to generate less resentment than those that have been earned through drudgery. Few people resent a movie actress who collects millions for her beauty. Yet the same people will bridle at the economic rent collected by a person who has worked hard all his life to buy a small piece of property. (In the strangest twist of all, it is often the beautiful actresses who lead the campaign to deprive the small property owner of his tiny corner of the world's resources.)

Housing costs have risen rapidly over the past decade because there are more Americans with more buying power looking for more space in which to live. In the Midwest, where there is plenty of space still available, prices have not been rising as rapidly. On the East and West Coasts, where more people apparently want to live, they have skyrocketed.

But once again, this only covers the demand side of the supply-and-demand equation. "Location" is, after all, a very flexible concept. There may be some finite limit to the number of people who can live with a view of Central Park, but we have by no means approached that number. It would be perfectly possible today to double or triple the number of apartments overlooking the Park. The main impediment is zoning laws, which limit the height of buildings.

The same principle applies everywhere else. Given free rein, the housing industry could easily construct enough housing to give every American a decent home. The problem is not high interest rates or private ownership or a failure of Federal effort. (The "failure of Federal effort" is actually a big filing basket in which people throw their unresolved problems.) The only major impediment is that, when it comes right down to it, the vast majority of Americans do not want this housing built if it is going to be in their neighborhood.

Instead, a vast number of people, particularly on the East and West Coasts, have become "rent-seekers." By this term, economists mean people who try to raise the value of their own resources by making alternatives difficult for others to obtain. All over the country, people are raising the value of their own little portion of the real-estate market by using the *political* system to limit other people's access to what they already have.

Remarkably, the people who try to *provide* housing are cast as the villains in this process. Such a characterization would seem to defy all logic, yet it is the opinion of the majority and so it prevails.

If nothing else, the history of economic rent shows us that, while natural resources may be inherently scarce, their limitations can usually be overcome.

Both Ricardo and Malthus, for example, believed that humanity was headed for some state of permanent poverty because of the limited supply of farmland. Malthus worried that population would outrun production. Ricardo, thinking in more abstract terms, worried that economic rents on scarce farmland would eventually rise to a level where most of society's wealth was transferred to landlords. Both were subsequently proved wrong by improving agricultural technology.

A curiously similar scenario for economic catastrophe was drawn up by American philosopher-economist Henry George. Although not as well remembered, George forms an interesting counterpart to Malthus, Ricardo, and Europe's other prophet of economic apocalypse, Karl Marx.

In *Progress and Poverty* (1879), George formulated the idea that the economic rents collected by *urban* landlords were creating an insurmountable barrier to human progress.[8] Just as Ricardo identified the rents of rural landlords as the source of difficulty—and Marx identified the profits of capitalists as the illegitimate form of income—so George felt that rents on urban land would be society's limiting factor.

Surveying the boom-and-bust cycles of the 19th century economy, George noted that while everyone else worked for a living, landlords seemed to do nothing. Capitalists earned their profits by inventing and employing new machinery. Laborers earned their wages by the sweat of their brow. But landlords only bought property. Often they simply raised rents as the city grew up around them. These rents, argued George, were an illegitimate drain on the productive portions of the economy.

George's solution was the "single tax." The economy could be restored to its equilibrium, he said, if the government taxed away all the economic rents earned by owners of real estate. This would ease the burden on the more productive sectors, restoring both social justice and economic equilibrium.

George's system remains in many ways more relevant to contemporary thinking than that of Karl Marx. Few people today would be willing to accept Marx's thesis that entrepreneurs and capitalists are unproductive and that the workers could design, build, and operate factories all by themselves. Yet people accept this same argument with respect to housing. For people who seek general theories of history in which one class of people is held to be the source of all human misery, George's work probably has more contemporary relevance than does Marx's.

As with Malthus's and Ricardo's predictions, however, George was eventually overtaken by technology. Even as he wrote, elevators were creating the skyscraper, enormously increasing the productivity of urban land. Streetcars were opening up the suburbs for new housing. The bottleneck of urban land never materialized. Landlords did not end up accumulating all of society's wealth.

Still, the original question remains. Why should a person be allowed to collect rent on natural resources that he has done nothing to create himself?

In order to defend the providers of housing, it ultimately becomes necessary to justify economic rents. Yet who would be willing to do such a thing—especially when even such a tolerant philosopher as Adam Smith could not quite bring himself to do it? Interestingly enough, after 200 years of economic philosophy, a defense of landlords has emerged from an unlikely source—the American environmental movement.

In many ways, this is not altogether surprising. American history has been lived largely without landlords. We did not have the big feudal baronies that dominated European history and have never developed a landed aristocracy. For most of our history, huge portions of land have been either "free"—so abundant that it could not claim a price—or owned by the government.

The turning point came during the Conservation Era of the late 19th century. With the despoilation of Western lands seemingly imminent, Conservation leaders like Theodore Roosevelt and Gifford Pinchot resolved to save America's natural resources by setting up the government as the "steward" of natural resources—in other words, the landlord.

The various conservation agencies were instructed to manage resources wisely. The Bureau of Land Management would handle grazing lands. The Army Corps of Engineers would bring water to parched regions. The Forest Service, under Gifford Pinchot, held timber *off* the market in order to drive up the price of timber on privately owned land. By reducing the seemingly inexhaustible abundance of resources, the Federal government would *raise* prices, making people consume resources more carefully.

After a half-century, however, conservationists and environmentalists realized the system wasn't working. Cattle land leased by the Bureau of Land Management was consistently overgrazed. Timber in the National Forests was often being sold at *below* cost. Western water projects ran amok, with huge dams built for totally unjustifiable economic reasons. In short, the Federal government had made a very poor landlord.

And so, surprisingly, the theory began to emerge that it was precisely the *public* ownership of natural resources that led to their overconsumption and degradation. In a famous 1967 essay, "The Tragedy of the Commons," Garret Hardin, a prominent environmentalist, used the example of the overgrazed common pastures of the Middle Ages as an example of "[f]reedom in a commons bring[ing] ruin to all."

Carrying David Ricardo's arguments full circle, Hardin pointed out that such common resources as air and water were being degraded precisely because no one owns them (or everyone owns them) and therefore no one feels personally responsible for their long-range conservation. "The tragedy of the commons . . . is averted by private property, or something formally like it," Hardin concluded.[9]

An even more powerful argument on behalf of landlords was made by Herman Daly, of Louisiana State University, often called the leading economist of the environmental movement. Daly pointed out that long-range conservation had been undermined by government ownership of resources. The landlord's economic rent, he pointed out, is precisely the mechanism that preserves scarce resources for future use. As any resource becomes scarce, landlords raise rents, which causes people to use it more carefully, or substitute other, cheaper resources.

Economic rents are the mechanism that balances current consumption against future use. The consumer always wants a resource today at the cheapest possible price. Only the landlord—who owns the resource and is personally interested in preserving its long-term value—has the economic incentive to postpone current waste for future consumption.

The outcome of government ownership, Daly pointed out, has been to *eliminate* economic rent. By failing to charge rents, governments create the illusion that they are providing resources more cheaply. In fact, all they are doing is sacrificing future use for present consumption. Government price controls on natural resources—like natural gas—achieve the same effect. The vast majority of present consumers are made happy, but *resources themselves* are depleted. In effect, concluded Daly, government interference with the market has been the principle cause of the environmental crisis:

> Landlords were the most powerful social class in feudal times, but in modern capitalism they are the least powerful class, and whatever power they might exert toward raising resource prices is undercut by the government, which is the largest

> resource owner and which follows a policy of cheap resources in order to benefit and ease conflict between the two dominant classes, labor and capital. . . .
>
> Capital and labor . . . are in basic conflict but must live together. They minimize conflict by growth and by throwing the growth-induced burden of diminishing returns onto resource productivity. How do they get away with it? In earlier times it might not have worked; a strong landlord class would have had an interest in keeping resource prices from falling too low. But today we have no such class to exert countervailing upward pressure. . . .
>
> Should we, by a kind of reverse land reform, reinstate a landlord class? Landlord rent is unearned income, and we find income based on ownership of that which no one produced to be ethically distasteful. No one loves a landlord. Adam Smith tells us that landlords love to reap where they have never sown, and not many lament the historical demise of the landowning aristocracy. But not all the long-run consequences of this demise are favorable. Rent may be an illegitimate source of income, but it is a totally legitimate and necessary price, without which efficient allocation of scarce resources would be impossible.[10]

After two centuries of economic thought, someone has finally found something nice to say about landlords.

So how does all this apply to housing? It reaffirms what we have been saying all along. The owner of a long-lived capital resource—a building—is the only person who has a *permanent* stake in its long-term conservation. Landlords are really the sons-of-bitches everyone always thought they were. They may have a short-term interest in renting to tenants and a long-term interest in finding good tenants. But their ultimate loyalty is to their buildings.

All this may seem "inhumane," but only to those who think in the short term. Buildings, after all, are housing and housing is built for people. Without the preservation of present buildings, future tenants will not have anywhere to live. Somebody has to be concerned about the future as well as the present and that person is the landlord.

This also allows us to see why a city's housing stock quickly falls apart under rent control. Rent control simply *puts the short-term interest of tenants ahead of the long-term interests of landlords.* For a while, this seems like a dream come true. Landlords are finally brought under control and tenants are left free to spend their money on more ephemeral consumer items.

But this shortsighted policy quickly comes home to roost. Without the landlord's instincts for preserving future housing—or the developer's incentive to build new housing—the deadly game of musical-chairs-over-vanishing-apartments soon begins.

In ecological theory, all natural populations need checks and balances against *overconsumption* of their environment. Unless their natural appetite is curbed by outside forces or internal mechanisms, the natural voracity of any population will soon overwhelm the "carrying capacity" of its resource base.

Overriding the landlord's instinct for preserving housing has the same consequence. In ecological terms, a rent-controlled tenantry is a natural population in the process of destroying its own environment.

Finally, we find that the location factor that forms the core of economic rent also serves a crucial purpose. Increasing population density may force up land prices, but this is nothing more than a signal that more people want to use the land. If we are to provide for their needs, we must respond to these signals. Every builder who wants to tear down a single-family home and replace it with a six-family apartment house is only responding to the demands of people seeking housing. Every developer who wants to tear down a six-family apartment and put up a 50-unit high-rise is only responding to the needs of people seeking housing. And every "slumlord" who wants to convert a former luxury hotel into a cheap SRO where people will share a bathroom down the hall is only responding to the legitimate needs of real people.

Housing is housing. The only way to have enough of it is to build more of it and to protect and preserve what we already have.

PART II

NEW YORK: A MATURE REGULATED HOUSING MARKET

"Appearance is reality."

—comment by Anthony Gliedman, former Commissioner of the New York Department of Housing Preservation and Development, when the Department announced in 1984 that it would fill the windows of thousands of vacant, city-owned apartments with vinyl decals painted with pictures of flowerpots and curtains in order to make it appear that people were living in them.

Introduction to Part II

The second section of this book will deal exclusively with New York City and its housing problems. The elements will be familiar. Yet there is a quality to New York's housing problems that goes beyond what has already been presented.

Few cities have more homeless. No city has had a longer, on-going "housing crisis." In no city is more public rhetoric spent on the housing problem. In no city in North America does a municipal government do more to intervene in the housing market. In no city are there fewer positive results.

So far as public housing is concerned, New York has always led the nation. The first Federal housing projects under the Works Project Administration (WPA) were constructed on East 3rd Street in 1935. Three years later, the nation's first housing projects under the Housing Act of 1937 were built on the Lower East Side. Today, New York has more than five times the public housing of Chicago. Yet in Chicago, people can find an affordable apartment in one afternoon, while in New York the process can consume six months.

As a result, housing and homelessness in New York really transcends zoning and rent control—though they are essential elements of the problem. The real dilemma is that a whole generation of New Yorkers has grown up without ever experiencing a free housing market. People in New York honestly and sincerely believe that housing is not a commodity that is bought, sold, and rented like other commodities, but something that must be physically and legally wrestled out of the hands of their landlords.

I will begin in chapters 17 and 18 with a broad impression of New York housing and a history of rent regulations. Chapters 19 and 20 will deal with the inequities between those already established in the market and those trying to enter it. Chapter 21 will deal with the experiences of landlords and chapter 22 will describe city government's ever-growing role in the housing market.

The entire section will be presented in a more impressionistic and anecdotal fashion, since there is an exotic quality to New York housing that cannot really be captured in any other way. The problem in conveying all this is that nobody outside New York believes such things can be happening, while nobody in New York believes things can be any different. It is to both of these perspectives that the following section is addressed.

Chapter 17

Moscow on the Hudson

There are an estimated 50,000 homeless people in New York City. As a result of Robert Hayes' 1979 law suit, New York has an elaborate shelter system under which housing has been established as a right under the state constitution. Within these 100-or-so public and private shelters, the city government keeps an elaborate head-count of homeless people.

On an average night in 1988, the system sheltered 6,000 homeless men and 12,000 members of homeless families, almost all minority women and children. City officials make the reasonable assumption that for every person in a shelter there are two more on the street. Anyone who has seen the sleeping bodies packed side-by-side in Grand Central Station, the Port Authority Bus Terminal, and any one of a hundred other public places would not dispute this figure. With 18,000 people in the shelters, a figure of 40,000 to 50,000 for the whole city is not inappropriate. This means that about 1 out of every 140 New Yorkers is homeless.

But all this barely begins to describe the housing market in New York City. Few people outside New York realize that newly arrived transferees with major corporations like American Express and Paine Webber often spend their first few months in New York paying $400 a month to sleep on a stranger's couch. Few outsiders understand "key money," where sublets are auctioned off for prices of up to $20,000. Few non-New Yorkers can sense why, on the afternoon Joel Steinberg was arrested for beating his six-year-old illegally adopted daughter, Lisa, his landlord received dozens of phone calls inquiring whether, if the little girl died, the apartment would be available.

Apartment-hunting in New York is a full-time occupation that can drain the energies of any new arrival. Kathleen Larkin, a young actress, was once shown a $1,000-a-month apartment that turned out to have no shower, no bathtub, no heat, no kitchen, and no pipes for a kitchen. "They told me if I wanted to install my own, they'd knock $50 off the price."[1] John F. Kennedy, Jr., spent two months trying to find an apartment in Manhattan. Is there any wonder so many are homeless?

Yet there is always a strange underside of looking for an apartment in New York. Picking up the want-ads a newcomer will read things like this:[2]

> 40's W. Furn or unfurn studio. Wd deck gdn, full ceramic tiled kit, full bth, lndry rm, a/c, fpl, wd flrs, hi ceils, wndws w/ beautiful vu. No fee. $1000/mo.
>
> 18 St. E. Best block in Gramercy, 1 BR w/DA; quiet, overlks gdn; prewar features. Possible share. Drmn bldg; $1375.
>
> CHELSEA 2BR
> LR, DR, EIK, lg closets, a/c, fpl, $1550 mo. no fee.

Yet all the while, the new arrival will also be hearing and reading stories about a whole separate class of tenants who seem to have been in their apartments forever and who pay rents that would be remarkably low even in a small town. For example:

In October 1986, *The New York Post* reported that John Balfour Ker, a 74-year-old "inventor-philosopher" and distant relative of Alexander Graham Bell, was blocking the construction of a block-long apartment complex by refusing to leave a four-room flat he had occupied for 41 years. Ker paid $45 a month in rent for his apartment. He had refused a relocation offer of $110,000 from the developer.[3]

In January 1987, *The Daily News* reported that the Marquis Bernard-Alexis Poisson de Menars, who traces his ancestry to Charlemagne, was refusing to leave a $103.50-a-month, five-and-a-half-room duplex on Manhattan's posh Upper East Side. His landlord, who wanted to take over the apartment for his ailing mother-in-law, had offered the Marquis an almost identical apartment three blocks away for only $50 a month. The Marquis refused on the grounds that the new location was unsuitable for "someone of my class and social standing." "With my name, you cannot be a proletariat," he told the newspapers. The Marquis had another home in France and had frequently sublet the apartment for as much as $1,000 a month.[4]

In April 1987, Rita Ebenhart, a 55-year-old, self-described off-off-Broadway actress, was forgiven $17,000 in unpaid back rent by an appeals court. Ebenhart argued that her previous landlord, Abraham Hirschfeld, had promised her in 1974 that she would not have to pay rent until he rewired the building. Hirschfeld vigorously denied ever making such a promise and said he had tried to evict Ebenhart for years. Her rent on the one-bedroom, Riverside Drive apartment—in which she has lived since 1957—is $286.15 a month. Ebenhart, whose last stage appearance was ten years ago, listed her other occupation as "tenant activist."

Shortly after Judge Jay Stuart Dankberg was appointed to the New York City Housing Court in 1980, it was revealed that he had been on a personal rent strike at his own two-bedroom apartment near Gramercy Park for almost seven years. Judge Dankberg had refused to pay rent because: 1) his kitchen sink didn't drain right, 2) the floorboards squeaked, and 3) there were cockroaches in the apartment. The rent on his rent-controlled apartment was $75.15 a month. Judge Dankberg went on to become the most fearsome pro-tenant judge on the housing court during his eight-year tenure.

As an entering point to the wonderland of New York housing, let us introduce Elzie Robinson. An 86-year-old former janitor, somewhat slowed with age but still strong and vigorous, Elzie Robinson is a Harlem landlord who spent a month in jail in 1986 for not providing heat to *squatters* who had moved into one of his apartment houses after the building was half-destroyed by a fire.

Robinson was born in the South but moved to New York City during the Depression. He worked for the National Recovery Administration (NRA) for 50 cents a day from 1932–33, then signed on with the WPA. After the war he worked as a building superintendent for $15 a week plus a room. He trained as a plumber and became an all-purpose handyman.

In 1956 he began working for I. G. Maloof, a Harlem landlord who owned over a dozen large apartment buildings. Maloof liked Robinson and eventually put him in charge of repairs in all the buildings. During the 1960s and 1970s, Robinson worked three jobs—his duties with Maloof, some outside plumbing work, and as a night security guard. His wife worked as a registered nurse. Together they saved a considerable amount of money and bought a house in Teaneck, N.J., where they raised several children. Robinson went on working past retirement, until insurance problems forced Maloof to drop him at age 75.

Shortly afterward, Maloof died. He liked Robinson so well that he left him $12,000 in his will. Then when Maloof's family did not want to take over the business, a second will was drawn up giving Robinson title to twelve buildings.

When he and his wife became landlords in 1978, they had managed to save $80,000.

The buildings were not in great shape. In fact, all of Harlem is no longer in great shape. Over the years, tenant-landlord wars have raged through the once-beautiful buildings so that *70 percent* of Central Harlem has now been taken over by the city government. These properties, the majority of them empty, are managed by HPD—the Department of Housing Preservation and Development—a vast, sprawling bureaucracy that runs most of New York's housing programs. In fact, Robinson's buildings were some of the last few that had not fallen into the hands of the city government.

Robinson set about trying to keep the buildings afloat. At age 78, he continued to do all his own repair work and spent winter nights sleeping next to boilers to make sure nothing went wrong. All Robinson's tenants were either "rent-controlled" or "rent-stabilized" (the distinction will be explained a little later), paying from $72 to $250 for virtually identical apartments, with the average around $145. By some strange rule of human behavior evident everywhere in New York, the tenants with the cheapest rents were always the most difficult about paying.

For six years, Robinson subsidized the buildings, watching his savings dwindle to about $40,000. HPD, responding to occasional tenant complaints, began writing up Robinson for a series of building-code violations. Soon Robinson was spending a great deal of his time in housing court.

Then, in the winter of 1984, one of his buildings was burglarized and the boiler stolen. Robinson had a new one installed four days later, but it wasn't quick enough for HPD. He was fined $1,000 for the four days his tenants were without heat and hot water. Robinson didn't know where to pay the fine and when he missed the deadline the levy was doubled and he was sent to jail for 20 days. Now branded a "slumlord," Robinson was subjected to ever-increasing inspections and fines from HPD.

Hemorrhaging money, Robinson and his wife tried to unload some of the buildings but soon found no one would take them at any price. Neither would any bank loan them money on a rent-controlled Harlem building. Instead, the banks wanted the Robinsons to put up their Teaneck home as collateral. They refused. By 1985, they had lost eight of the twelve buildings to HPD for fines and back taxes.

In November 1985 the Robinsons suffered another burglary at one of their remaining buildings. The thieves stole some copper plumbing, then set the basement on fire. The whole heating system was knocked out and the back half of the lower floors severely damaged.

Robinson had no money left to fix the building. On the other hand, he was reluctant to turn his tenants into the street in the dead of winter. So he moved most of his long-term tenants onto the upper floors and told them he would collect only enough rent to buy oil to keep the hot-water heater running. He also rewired the building and bought electric heaters for all the rooms.

The arrangement might have worked except that squatters moved into the vacant apartments on the lower floors. Soon *they* began complaining to HPD that the main heating system wasn't working. HPD—willing to back any tenant in any situation—began sending out inspectors. Soon Robinson was back in housing court, on trial for failing to provide heat and hot water to his *illegal* squatters.

The trial was held before Housing Court Judge Lewis Friedman. Jane Del Bianco, staff attorney at HPD, acting as prosecutor. Ralph Accoo was Robinson's attorney. Two long-term tenants, Dorothy Bing and Horace Brown, came to testify on Robinson's behalf. They told the court that, after the fire, Robinson had continued to collect enough rent to run the hot-water boiler and had provided them with space heaters to heat their rooms. Del Bianco savaged both witnesses, arguing that they were not qualified to determine what constituted "adequate heat and hot water."[5]

DOROTHY BING: Before the fire, we had heat and hot water—OK? And after the fire, Mr. Robinson made it possible for us to have hot water—because I have four children and my kids go to school, and before I'll pay Mr. Robinson a dime I've got to have some kind of proof that he's going to—you know, help me out before I give him my rent because my children have to go to school. But we—before the fire we had heat and hot water and after the fire we've been having hot water. . . .

JANE DEL BIANCO: Do you know what temperature—do you—is this your thought, that he's just supposed to provide you with *some* heat and hot water? . . .

BING: Well, I feel like—long as I can get up in my house from a certain time I have to—long as I can get up in the morning and put my children in school and have heat and hot water to provide them to go to school, I have no problem with my landlord. . . .

DEL BIANCO: Do you have any idea what degrees the landlord is required to provide you for in the daytime between 6 A.M. and 10 P.M. when it's lower than 55 outside?

BING: No, I have no idea. . . .

When Robinson took the stand, Accoo asked him about his financial situation.

ACCOO: Do you have any cash?

ROBINSON: No, I ain't got a nickel.

ACCOO: Are you collecting any rents?

ROBINSON: No, I don't collect no rents. From none of 'em. 'Dis day I had to take the money dat I—my retirement check, I took dat to pay you wit'—I couldn't give dat 'til I come into court dis mornin'.

On cross-examination, Del Bianco tried to establish that Robinson had income from other buildings he owned in the area.

DEL BIANCO: Mr. Robinson, isn't it true that on the street where this building is that you own several other buildings? Quite a few, as a matter of fact? . . .

ROBINSON: Yes.

DEL BIANCO: And can you give us those addresses?

ROBINSON: No ma'am, why should I? You have dem.

DEL BIANCO: Because you're instructed to answer.

ROBINSON: You've got judgments against all my houses, so what is the difference?

FRIEDMAN: Mr. Robinson, just answer the question.

ROBINSON: 259, 219–229.

DEL BIANCO: Any others?

ROBINSON: No, that's all—yes, I own two more. 247. Dat building is empty. You-all done took dat away from me. . . .

DEL BIANCO: What about 535 West 144th Street?

ROBINSON: I did own dat building at one time. Five years ago.

DEL BIANCO: What about 537 West 144th Street

ROBINSON: Five years ago.

DEL BIANCO: What about 539 West 144th Street?

ROBINSON: Five years ago. You-all own dose buildings now. I don't own 'em. Never did.

Immediately after the testimony, Friedman reached a verdict, apparently based on a confused notion that Robinson had been collecting rents to run the *heating* boiler, not the hot-water boiler, and then pocketing the money.

FRIEDMAN: Mr. Robinson's description of why he did not provide the heat is certainly less than clear as far as I'm concerned. It seems to me the defendant is depending on the grounds that he didn't have the money to afford it. And yet there is obviously ample—according to his words there is ample rent money to be received that the tenants could afford the oil to provide the heat. That's a contradiction on its face. If the money were there, if it were collected, then it's obviously sufficient to provide as an asset of Mr. Robinson. Mr. Robinson's testimony that he can't afford it I think has to be taken with an enormous grain of salt, under the circumstances of his ownership of property in the area. . . .

The law is clear that everyone is entitled to adequate heat and hot water *whether they are lawful tenants or otherwise*. . . . It is not a defense that rent is not collected. . . .

I will therefore impose a civil commitment by which the respondent Mr. Robinson will be committed to jail until such time as heat and hot water are provided at the premises. In addition, and concurrently, the court will impose a criminal jail sentence of 20 days. . . . Mr. Robinson's age is a factor in this case, but it is not under the circumstances an affirmative shield behind which one can hide in not providing services. [Emphasis added.]

Robinson was immediately taken to the Bronx House of Detention. He served ten days before his health began to fail and he was released.

I began following Elzie Robinson's case about a month later, after I met both him and his wife at a meeting of the Harlem Taxpayers and Property Owners' Association. Mr. Robinson's health was still weak and he was unable to speak. His wife took the podium and gave an emotional account of their experiences. "Sometimes I think I'm going out of my mind trying to deal with these housing people," she told the audience.

For several months previously, I had been running a contest in the newspapers offering $50 prizes for the best stories about rich and famous New Yorkers with rent-controlled apartments. Reporters had been calling regularly looking for more news on celebrities. Having become familiar with some of them, I began offering them the story about an 86-year-old black Harlem landlord who had been jailed for 20 days for not providing heat to squatters in his building.

Each reporter responded in the same way. They would listen to the entire story, then give what soon became a familiar little chuckle, and say: "That's a pretty good story, but, ah, I don't think we're going to be able to use it." And none ever did. The reason is simple. Writing a story in New York that is sympathetic to a landlord is like writing sympathetically about polio. It would force readers to confront an idea that most have never encountered before—that all landlords might not be oppressors and all tenants might not be oppressed. Only *Insight* magazine, published by *The Washington Times,* ever did a story on the Robinsons.[6]

In pursuit of the Robinsons' story, I began going to housing court, the arena in which most tenant-landlord battles end up being fought. Housing court is a necessary part of rent control, since tenants and landlords are now adversaries and every little issue can be turned into a major confrontation. Boston now has a housing court, as do San Francisco and Santa Monica. In other rent-controlled cities like Berkeley, Brookline, and Cambridge, the rent-control board itself sits in judgment on tenant-landlord cases. In fact, sooner or later, the rent-control administration becomes a government-within-a-government. Santa Monica's Rent Board has a $4.2-million budget, nearly all of it raised from fees to owners. The board was even forced to borrow an additional $350,000 from the city government recently. New York's HPD now has a $475 million administrative budget and a $640 million capital budget.

When originally set up in 1973, New York's housing court was supposed to deal only with rent disputes and evictions. But as the war over housing escalated and the law became ever-more complicated, the city was forced to extend its supervision into every minute aspect of tenant-landlord relationships. By 1986, the court was completely overwhelmed with cases.

"The issues become more complicated because people living in apartments can't find comparable apartments to move to, and we have to take this into account," Judge Jay Stuart Dankberg told the *The New York Times.*[7]

Judge Dankberg—the one with the $75 apartment—had only recently presided over a lengthy trial involving actress Ann Turkel, who paid $2,350 a month for a seven-room, four-and-a-half-*bath*room duplex on the East Side. (Although this rent may seem high, the monthly *maintenance* fee to apartments in the building that had recently been converted to cooperative ownership was $2,500. Identical apartments in the building were subletting for $6,500.)

Living on both coasts, Turkel wanted to keep her New York apartment, even while spending most of her time in California. The housing law says, however, that a regulated apartment must be the tenant's "primary residence." Legally, this means that the tenant must live in the apartment two years out of every four.

Evidence at the trial made it clear that Turkel barely spent two months a year in the apartment. After 28 days of testimony, however, Judge Dankberg decided in her favor, concluding that, "Her residence was in California, but her domicile was in New York City." Dankberg noted that Turkel had never removed her furs, jewelry, furniture, or works of art valued at $200,000. "It was a case of the state of mind of the person," Dankberg said in his ruling. "In this case I had to conclude that she thought she lived in that apartment regardless of where she actually was."[8] (Dankberg's decision was later overturned on appeal and Turkel lost the apartment.)

For the most part, though, the denizens I encountered at housing court were a much sorrier lot. Everyone seemed poor and it is impossible to tell the tenants from the landlords. The only recognizable figures were the lawyers. They were the ones with the nice clothes.

On the first day I attended, the Robinsons answered a 10 A.M. calendar call and were told to wait in the halls until their case was called. Accoo, their attorney, was with them. A tall, nattily dressed, black man, he hadn't sounded too persuasive on the trial tapes but was much more impressive in person. "Your big mistake was letting your tenants stay in the building in the first place," he told Robinson as we stood in the hallways. "You should have kicked them all out right after the fire. Once you conform with one regulation, you've got to conform with them all."

As the waiting began, the Robinsons ran into a friend of theirs, Jerry Oxford, another Harlem landlord who had also spent time in jail. Oxford was small and wiry, about 50, dressed in a threadbare tweed jacket. A mechanical engineer by training, Oxford had gotten into the business of repairing dilapidated two- and three-family buildings. Working mostly in Queens, he would line up buyers, secure them mortgages, even make the down payment and closing costs for them. It was a pretty good living and he had rehabilitated more than 30 buildings.

Then he tried to move into Harlem—a territory that HPD virtually considers its personal domain. "They were all over me from the first day," he said. "They dragged me into court, charging me with trivial violations. They called me a 'speculator' and told my tenants not to pay rent. I swear if I had been out on a streetcorner selling drugs I think they would have given me less trouble."

HPD finally put Oxford in jail for a few months. They also took eight of his 14 buildings. Still, he considered himself lucky. "I know another landlord who spent six months in jail.

"I try to work on my own," he added. "I never asked the city government for any money. I think that's why they hate me, because I won't play ball with them."

Trying to get both sides of the issue, I went looking for tenants. One gray-haired lady with pink cheeks and a coat that put her a step-and-a-half above a bag lady, looked as if she were a likely prospect. I asked if she was a tenant.

"Yes, but I can't tell you my name. I'm afraid of what they'll do to me."

Was she here fighting her landlord?

"No, we're fighting the city. We're supporting the landlord."

HPD, it emerged, was taking over the building for back taxes. Both the landlord and the tenants were opposing it. HPD—which handles many of the homeless—was taking people out of the shelters and moving them into the building. Most of them were drug addicts. "They're terrorizing us," she said. "I'm afraid for my life."

She had no phone so I gave her my number and told her to keep in touch. She called twice from a pay phone, but I missed her both times. She told my wife she was still afraid for her life. I never heard from her after that.

The next person I encountered was a tall, well-dressed man just emerging from the courtroom. He was carrying a briefcase. Tenant or landlord? I asked him.

"Tenant. It's just ridiculous, man. I've been coming down here ten years now and all they do is give you the runaround. They never fix a damned thing. We've had water leaking, ceilings falling down, and nothing ever happens. You can spend all your whole life in court, get all the judgments you want, and they still don't do anything about it."

He gave me the address of his building. I checked later and found it was The Century, a truly magnificent old building on Central Park West. The building houses such rent-regulated tenants as Theodore Sorensen, President John Kennedy's speechwriter, and Barbara Fife, David Dinkins' long-time aide, who was appointed deputy mayor after Dinkins was elected mayor in 1989. At the time,

Sorensen paid $1,393 for a seven-room apartment and also owned a home in Westchester Country. The Fifes had two apartments in the building—a ten-room, four-bathroom apartment for $2,193 and another two-and-a-half-room apartment for $681. (Although such prices may once again seem high, they are probably less than half their market value.)

Tenants at The Century had been on a rent strike for ten years, during which the 58-year-old building—considered an Art Deco masterpiece—had nearly gone to ruin. Arguing they could not carry the building on low rents, the owners had withdrawn such services as individual mail delivery and a 24-hour doorman. Tenants went to court and received rent reductions. This set off another round of service cutbacks, another round of rent reductions, and on and on until the building was falling apart.

"The Battle of The Century" did not end until 1989, when 229 of the 346 residents bought their apartments under a condominium conversion. (The Sorensens and Fifes both bought.) The remaining 117 residents stayed on as rent-regulated tenants. Those who bought their apartments paid special "insider" prices that are usually less than half the market price. Several long-time residents immediately sold their apartments at market rates—called "flipping"—and realized overnight windfalls of $1 million or more.

Next I encountered another Harlem landlord named Mary Peterson. She was black, about 45, dressed in tight-fitting jeans and stiletto heels. Her eyeglasses were thick as coke bottles. Her hair was drawn back severely and her eyebrows were penciled blue.

"I own a brownstone in Harlem," she said. "I've been there about 10 years. I'm the only one left on my block. Every other building is in the hands of the City. They've driven out every landlord around."

What was her problem? I asked.

"Rents. They don't pay you nothing. I'm not allowed to collect more than $100 for any of my apartments. Yet I'm supposed to supply them with heat, hot water, pay insurance, you name it. Then half of them don't pay anyway."

One of her tenants, it turned out, was the daughter of a woman who worked for HPD. She hadn't paid rent in five years.

How close was she to losing her building?

"Any day. I ain't got no money left. I've put $100,000 into that building over the last ten years. I work full time to support it and I still can't make it. Every time you come down here the City is here supporting the tenants. If it's not HPD, it's legal aid. If a tenant doesn't pay rent for a year—for five years—there's still nothing you can do about it. I'm supposed to support them. So what's going to happen if I lose my building? Who's going to take care of me?"

I didn't have any answers so I started talking to another woman who had responded as a tenant on another case. She was about 30, rather nicely dressed in an African motif. What was she doing down here? I asked.

"Oh, HPD asked me to come down and testify against my Jew landlord," she said. "They're trying to get him out of the building and they want me to say some things against him."

She told me her name was Shabazz, but wouldn't give her first name. She lived on East 124th Street and paid $281 a month for six rooms. "It's cheap. I love the apartment. But the damned landlord won't fix a thing. We're not poor people, you know. My husband and I make $30,000 a year."

Why did she stay there? Making $30,000, she could probably afford a co-op or move to New Jersey.

"Well, we talked about it. But when you buy a co-op, you've got to talk to banks and they want to look at your income and everything."

So?

"We don't pay taxes, you see. We're street vendors. So if we bought a place and had to start dealing with the government it would cost us a lot of money."

Mary Peterson, who had been standing nearby, now strolled over to join the conversation.

"You know, I heard you say something just a minute ago," she said. "I heard you say your landlord was a Jew. Well let me ask you something. How do you know he isn't fronting for a Chinese? Or an Arab?"

Shabazz knew she was being called down but didn't give an inch. "Well, I just said it, that's all," she shot back. "We had a Jew lady in there who owned the building, and then she sold it to a Jew man. And that's what happened."

"Well, what difference does it make? Why bring it up in the first place?"

Mrs. Shabazz might have answered, but the bailiff called her case and she disappeared into the courtroom.

Finally, about 4:30, the Robinsons were called. The HPD lawyer was Carol Steinberg, one of the thousands of eager attorneys struggling for housing justice in New York. Dressed in a powder-blue suit with matching pearl necklace and earings, she moved easily behind the bar, laughing and joking with Judge Friedman.

The hearing was brief. Steinberg and Friedman agreed that Robinson was making a satisfactory effort to remedy the situation. He would be excused from completing his jail sentence for another two months. "Come in next time prepared to show that you are either going to repair or sell the building," Friedman said.

As we stood outside again, Steinberg came rushing down the hall and ran straight into the group. I had introduced myself to her earlier and now she realized I was with the Robinsons.

"Have you applied for a City loan?" Steinberg asked Robinson cheerfully. Robinson said he had already been turned down. "Well, keep trying. The City wants to help you, you know."

Then her curiosity overcame her. "How did you happen to get the building in the first place?" she asked, obviously puzzled to find someone like Mr. Robinson dabbling in real estate.

"Show her your hands, Elzie," said Accoo, Robinson raised his hands. They were swollen and arthritic, every third fingernail a lump of discolored tissue. Steinberg smiled bravely.

"That's how he got the building," said Accoo. "With those hands."

Chapter 18

A Temporary Wartime Measure

New York's rent controls are an extension of World War II price controls. In 1943, the entire country was put under wage-and-price controls as a wartime measure. Congress lifted New York's controls in 1950 and all other cities were phased out during the early 1950s. But New York continued rent control as a state program. As a result, the city essentially missed the postwar boom in housing construction. More than 60 percent of New York's housing is now more than 60 years old. This makes it easy to understand why the preservation of older housing is so crucial to New York's housing market.

What was life like before rent controls? Until 1945, New York developed like any other city. The earliest residential areas were centered in Lower Manhattan, moving north from the original settlement in the Wall Street area. By 1850, Greenwich Village and Chelsea were fashionable districts. On the Lower East Side, tenements sprouted and old homes were being turned into apartment houses. Most of midtown was built after the Civil War. Theodore Roosevelt grew up in a house on East 20th Street. J. P. Morgan built his mansion on 36th and Lexington and continued to live there long after most of society moved north. When a developer put up a magnificent 26-story apartment building at 72nd Street and Central Park West in 1884, it seemed so far out of town that people called it "The Dakota." John Lennon was living there when he was shot in 1980.

Beginning in 1858, land north of midtown was purchased to form Central Park. The 840 acres of glacially scarred terrain was landscaped by Frederick Law Olmstead and Calvin Vaux. The area was dotted with pig farms, among which poor people had begun building squatters' shacks. All had to be evicted. The Park soon became the focus of what are still the two most famous residential districts of Manhattan, the Upper East and Upper West Sides.

In 1883, the Brooklyn Bridge connected Manhattan to Brooklyn, then a separate city. The two had long been linked by as many as 17 ferries, but Brooklyn remained mostly rural, with the suburban development limited to Brooklyn Heights, overlooking the East River. Now the Flatbush Avenue streetcar lines started carrying the suburbs out to Prospect Park—Olmstead and Vaux's second great project. As trolleys, bridges, and ferries knit the city together, Brooklyn, Queens, and Staten Island joined Manhattan and the Bronx, after an 1898 referendum, to form Greater New York.

Then in 1904, the Interborough Rapid Transit subway line was dug beneath Broadway, from Wall Street to Morningside Heights, linking Manhattan from end to end. Other lines quickly tunneled into Brooklyn and the Bronx, where Eastern Parkway and the Grand Concourse—the "Champs-Elysees of America"—became centers of affluent development. Before the automobile started influencing urban patterns, most of New York was laid out as it is today.

All that remained now was to fill in the gaps. This was done in what may qualify as the greatest outburst of housing construction in American history. From 1900 to 1930, developers put up a stunning 80,000 housing units per year in New York. Nor was this shoddy, fly-by-night construction. The luxury housing that festoons Upper Broadway is still almost beyond belief—huge ocean-liners of buildings like the Bel Nord, the Ansonia, the Apthorp, and Astor Court. Apartment houses were built to last for centuries and a level of elegance was achieved that has probably never been equalled in America.

A favorite device was the interior courtyard. A huge residence 15 to 20 stories high would often fill half a square block. From the street it appears to be a solid and imposing wall of granite. But the building itself is only about 50 feet deep. Inside, it opens up into a small interior park, opening up every apartment to light and air and offering solace and retreat from the din of city life.

Yet it was not only the luxury buildings that were built to last. The New

Tenement Law resulted in the construction of extremely sturdy brick structures that still line hundreds of city blocks. Even many Old Law tenements are being renovated today into contemporary housing. The lots were small (40′ × 100′) and the apartments often crowded (six to a floor), but they have offered housing to generations. From the passage of the New Law in 1901 until 1930, thousands and thousands of these four-to-five story walk-ups rose all over Manhattan, Brooklyn, and the Bronx.

Along elegant avenues like the Grand Concourse and Eastern Parkway, builders were more ambitious. Large apartment buildings housed anywhere from 50 to 200 apartments. In areas like Harlem, a familiar pattern developed. Nineteenth century brownstones already lined the cross streets, producing neighborhoods like "Strivers' Row," a famous stretch of middle-class housing between 137th and 139th Streets near Eighth Avenue. Now, on the corner of each block, a 10- to 15-story apartment house containing 100 or more units was added. Within each square block, about half the housing was in townhouses and half in large apartment buildings.

In 1916, New York City invented the nation's first zoning law. The object was to keep midtown residential districts from being invaded by the burgeoning garment industry. Still, the impulse to stop new housing had not yet developed. The huge building boom of the 1920s took place within the context of the city's zoning ordinance.

A major blow came during the Depression. Between 1930 and 1940, construction nosedived to only 5,000 units. One problem was the low demand for housing. With thousands unemployed, few people could pay rent. The marriage rate fell, birth rates tumbled, and people moved in with relatives. Rents dropped and landlords begged the banks to renegotiate their mortgages.

Although it is often believed that the need for a large number of apartment buildings has doomed homeownership in New York, cooperative ownership was already being introduced in the 1930s. Many luxury buildings along Park Avenue were originally marketed as cooperatives. With the economy in collapse, however, owners were forced to convert them back to rentals and give them away at bargain prices. (These rents were later frozen in place by rent control.)

In 1933, at the depth of the Depression, the vacancy rate in New York had stood at a remarkable 17.3 percent. By 1940, it was still at 10.8 percent.[1] Each year, landlords anxiously awaited the "Fall renting season," when people who had been away for summer vacations returned to Manhattan to look for apartments. Housing was so cheap and abundant that people found it easier to put their furniture in storage over the summer and rent a new apartment in September. Worried landlords, bankers, and civic leaders had organized a "Live in Manhattan" campaign, urging people to take advantage of the city's low rents and high vacancy rates.[2]

All this changed very little with the outbreak of World War II. In manufacturing cities like Detroit, Chicago, and San Diego, the rapid influx of workers to new defense industries created gigantic housing problems. With their high salaries, defense workers could often outbid existing residents for rental apartments. In order to avoid a backlash of resentment against defense workers, the Office of Price Administration (OPA) began imposing rent controls in key defense cities in 1941.

New York, however, did not have that problem. Without any large defense plants, the city actually *lost* population in the early 1940s as draftees headed for boot camp and skilled workers migrated to other cities. Housing was so abundant that in 1942, the Commerce and Industry Association of New York sent a plea to President Franklin Roosevelt urging him to move several Federal agencies to New York in order to relieve overcrowded housing conditions in Washington. The Association cited the city's high vacancy rates—still over 6 percent—as "proof for Washington officials that proposed transfers of certain government bureaus to this city would find adequate and comfortable living quarters available here for the personnel of these bureaus."[3] Washington soon complied by transferring several offices.

Naval bases in Brooklyn and Staten Island made housing tight in those boroughs, but by 1942 New York's overall vacancy rates were still at acceptable levels. In March, *The New York Times* reported that vacancies in "cheaper living quarters" around the city had actually *risen* from 8.6 percent in 1941 to 9.9 percent in 1942. In April, a complete survey found vacancy rates at 5.2 percent, with Manhattan the highest at 7.9 percent and Staten Island the lowest at 2.0 percent.[4]

By 1943, New York remained the last major metropolitan area in the country where the OPA had not imposed rent controls. Chicago, Boston, San Francisco, Jamestown, in New York, and Scranton, Pennsylvania, all had rent controls. More than 75 percent of the nation's population was living under emergency regulations. Yet New York still had adequate housing.

Mayor La Guardia and New York's tenant organizations were infuriated at OPA and openly pleaded for the agency to intervene in New York's "crisis" of rising rents. Yet in mid-September 1943, *The New York Times* reported:

> An authoritative source in the OPA . . . explained that New York had not acquired rent control largely because it was not a manufacturing war center, had a conspicuous out-migration of workers, and a comparatively high vacancy ratio.
>
> The Bureau of Labor Statistics, whose figures help the OPA in its studies of rent

> control, reported that between March and June the average price of rents in New York rose one-tenth of 1 percent. The bureau's cost-of-living index shows that in June the average rental in New York was only 3.3 per cent higher than the average price during the five-year-period 1935–39.[5]

In an effort to avoid rent controls, the Real Estate Board of New York had voluntarily pledged to freeze rents at the levels of March 1942. This effort had held for more than a year and was primarily responsible for the OPA's reluctance to extend rent controls to New York. (Congressional criticism of the administration of rent controls in other cities and a reluctance to impose the cumbersome system on New York's vast rental market also played a part.)

Yet by late 1943, the grinding effects of the wartime economy finally took their toll. Because of the diversion of resources to the war effort, almost no new housing—except defense-related housing—had been built anywhere since 1941. In the fall of 1943, newcomers to Manhattan suddenly found it very difficult to find housing. Vacancy rates fell below three percent and landlords were criticized for leaving up "For Rent" signs on buildings where no apartments were available. Landlords found their fall rentals filled up by early September and some even started charging "lease renewal fees" to their old tenants.

As vacancies ground down, the voluntary system started to crack. A few landlords in Queens began refusing to renew leases under the belief that they would not be violating the voluntary system by charging higher rents to new tenants. Other small owners started raising rents. By September the OPA had reports of over 100,000 proposed rent increases. On September 28—three days before New York's traditional "moving day" of October 1, (when thousands of leases expired)—the OPA finally brought New York under wartime controls.

In making the announcement, Chester Bowles, director of the OPA, said, "We have found it necessary to take this step in spite of the remarkable record of those New York landlords . . . in holding down rents on a voluntary basis. Their achievement is best expressed in the fact that New York has remained the last major city in the country in which it has been necessary to introduce Federal rent controls." But the recent reports of 100,000 rent increases had finally made it necessary. "In all justice we cannot deny these 100,000 tenants the protection of rent control. Nor can we expect cooperating landlords to hold their rents in line voluntarily while others are getting increases."[6]

Within six months, New York's housing market was in the "state of wartime emergency" from which it has never really recovered. Studies by both the Mayor's Committee on Rents and the Real Estate Board placed vacancies at about two percent. *The New York Times* reported that "it becomes easy to understand why some families are searching so frantically for living quarters here, why members of the armed forces are appealing for aid in finding rooms, and why realty agents report that some prospective tenants even have been scanning the obituary columns of newspapers for 'leads' on possible new vacancies."[7] The situation continued until the end of the war.

As everywhere else, rent controls were never intended as anything but a temporary wartime measure. Once in place, however, they proved remarkably difficult to remove. While general wage and price controls were lifted in 1947, the effort to phase out rent controls did not begin until 1950. Boston had rent controls until 1952, Chicago had them until 1956.

Once again, New York's housing situation was not regarded as serious at the Federal level. New York was among the first cities to be phased out of rent controls in 1950. Well before that, however, New York's tenant organizations and politicians had geared up to make rent control a permanent institution.

In 1947, tenant activists marched on Albany and persuaded the New York State legislature to continue rent controls at the state level. The law was quickly overturned by the New York State Court of Appeals on the grounds that it was an unjust extension of government power. But the legislature came right back with another attempt when Federal controls were lifted in 1950. This time, the courts, growing increasingly reluctant to defend property rights, let it stand.

By extending rent controls, city officials understood, of course, that they would be discouraging new housing. As a result, anything built after 1947 was exempted from regulation. Still, builders remained wary—and with good reason. Several large projects completed after 1947 were brought under special regulations that essentially duplicated rent control. Tenant power was consolidating and anti-landlord sentiment was on the rise.

Despite these self-imposed handicaps, New York City came out of World War II with the world's most magnificent housing stock. True, the problem of the slums remained (although buildings regarded as slums in New York would often be considered solid housing anywhere else). Older housing was always deteriorating and needed to be maintained. But in terms of solidity and total availability, no city in the world had a better housing stock.

Then came the effects of rent control.

To get an idea of what post-war housing might have been like in New York, we can look at two major post-war projects, Stuyvesant Town and Peter Cooper Village. Both were built by the Metropolitan Life Insurance Company, which, like other cash-rich insurance companies, was expected to become a major investor in rental housing after World War II.

Both projects were originally proposed in 1943. Stuyvesant Town (known as "The Town") contains 7,000 units in 89 buildings covering an 18-block area just north of East 14th Street. Peter Cooper Village ("The Village") contains 4,000 units in a seven-block area just north of The Town. The Village, with air-conditioning and slightly larger apartments, has always been considered a little more luxurious.

Construction was postponed by the war, and the projects were not completed until 1947 and 1948. A controversy immediately arose over whether they should be brought under rent control. City officials were reluctant to blindside Met Life, which promised to become a major builder in New York. Yet it was also difficult to ignore 10,000 tenants. In the end, officials compromised by setting up a special board that would supposedly raise rents in the two projects according to an independent financial criterion—a kind of early "second-generation" system. The board was soon overwhelmed by tenant activism and Stuyvesant Town and Peter Cooper Village effectively became rent-controlled. The process was formalized in 1971 when both projects were brought under the new "rent stabilization."

The tenants at Stuyvesant Town and Peter Cooper Village are all distinctly middle class. Several prominent television personalities, many Wall Street brokers and bankers, plus a whole cadre of Metropolitan Life executives live there. Yet after decades of regulation, rents have fallen far below market. In 1986, they averaged only $550 for one-bedroom apartments and $650 for two-bedroom apartments—$300 to $400 below market levels.

Just like every regulated housing market, both Stuyvesant Town and Peter Cooper Village have become essentially closed communities. In 1986, The Town had a waiting list of 9,700 people for 7,000 apartments, while The Village had 5,300 applications for 4,600 units. Annual turnover rates are only 3 percent. In 1985, only 384 tenants left their apartments—124 unwillingly because they had violated lease agreements.[8] A person applying today will have to wait 22 years for an apartment in The Town and 100 years for one in The Village.

As with all such communities of protected tenants, the problem of illegal subletting has become rampant. Taking advantage of the huge gap between regulated and market rents, tenants have become landlords themselves, renting their apartments at market rates and pocketing the difference. Apartments that rent for only $600 can easily be sublet for $1,200. (Such prices, however, shouldn't be taken to represent free-market values. They are actually a bit above market because of the severe housing shortage. The best way to calculate the real value of a regulated apartment is to average the sublet price and the regulated rent.)

In 1983, Met Life officials canvassed both projects and found that 40 percent of the apartments were being occupied by illegal subtenants. Many prime leaseholders had retired to Florida and upstate New York, using their sublet income as a retirement pension. The company started cracking down—bringing a chorus of protest. "The issue is simply whether big corporate landlords should be the only ones allowed to make money in the rental business," wrote one tenant-landlord to *Town and Village,* the community newspaper.[9]

What is most interesting is that Stuyvesant Town and Peter Cooper Village have produced a perfectly controlled experiment for measuring the distribution of rent control's benefits. Peter Cooper Village, always slightly more luxurious, started with rents that were 25 percent higher in 1949. After 40 years of rent control, however, *rents are now higher in less luxurious Stuyvesant Town.*

The reason—according to Met Life officials—is that the more affluent tenants in Peter Cooper Village have been more skillful in taking advantage of the regulations. Turnovers in The Village are *nine times lower* than they are in Stuyvesant Town. More affluent people, because of greater foresight or greater flexibility in their lives, seem to be able to parlay rent regulations into much lower rents. This 40-year turnaround in Stuyvesant Town and Peter Cooper Village perfectly illustrates what might be called the Golden Rule of Housing Regulations—affluent people always tend to end up with more benefits.

Needless to say, except for the 13,000-unit Parkchester complex in the Bronx (finished before the war), Metropolitan Life never built any other housing in New York. Nor have any other large insurance companies or major investors. While the rest of the country was going through a housing explosion during the 1950s, New York limped along, producing only 15,000 new housing units a year. And so, life in New York City settled down to a permanent housing crisis.

In 1954, Robert F. Wagner, Jr., the son of the sponsor of the Housing Act of 1937, became the first in a long line of mayors to be elected on the promise of "solving the housing crisis." Wagner's first proposal was that the city government be allowed to take over the administration of rent control from the state. (It has since bounced back and forth three more times.) Second, he promised a "city without slums by the year 2000," calling for more urban renewal. Third, Wagner became one of the principle sponsors of a state effort to extend subsidized housing to the *middle* class.

The quest for middle-class housing led to the Mitchell-Lama Act of 1955, the first of many city and state efforts to "keep the middle class in the city" by offering it housing subsidies. Since 1955, more than 135,000 Mitchell-Lama units have been constructed in New York City (including most of Roosevelt Island). Another 30,000 have been built elsewhere in New York State.

Mitchell-Lama works as follows. Private developers contract to build an apartment house and rent it to middle-income people at low rents. In order to keep down construction costs, builders are offered low-interest state loans. The municipalities also grant property-tax exemptions up to 95 percent. The arrangement holds for the life of the mortgage—usually 20 to 30 years. When the mortgage is fully paid, the builder can withdraw his building from the program and rent it at market rents.

The program, once again, is limited to *middle*-income tenants. There are *minimum* income requirements as well as maximum. As of 1988, the minimum was $15,000, the maximum was $50,000. Once tenants are in a building, however, their incomes can rise as high as $75,000—although even this limitation is rarely enforced.

As a result, the same pattern of closed-club membership, widespread subletting, and amateur landlording has emerged in Mitchell-Lama housing. Building owners have almost no incentive to enforce maximum income limits, since their only real concern is collecting rents. Thus, people go on living in Mitchell-Lama housing even though they are making huge amounts of money. In addition, owners are not too diligent about preventing subletting, since they can't raise rents to prime tenants anyway. There are no hard figures, but the widely accepted estimate is that 15 to 20 percent of the prime tenants in Mitchell-Lama apartments are actually living elsewhere while profitably subletting their apartments.

Another predictable result of Mitchell-Lama has been tenant immobility. In 1988, Mayor Koch announced that 3,500 Mitchell-Lama apartments—more than five percent of the population—contained one or two people who lived in units of two bedrooms or more. He asked these tenants to exchange their apartments for smaller units in the same building. "We've got single people living in four-bedroom apartments and families with three and four kids living in one-bedroom apartments," complained Abraham Biderman, Commissioner of HPD. Even Robert Hayes, then head of the Coalition for the Homeless, supported the effort.

It came to naught. Koch's motivations came under fire when it was revealed that one tenant who would be affected was David Dinkins, Koch's principal rival for mayor in 1989. Although Dinkins' children are grown, he and his wife still occupy a three-bedroom Mitchell-Lama co-op near Riverside Drive, where they have lived since 1964. They pay a maintenance fee of $711.99 a month.[10] State legislators from all over New York City opposed Koch's proposal and by mid-1989, the effort was abandoned.

The other notorious aspect of Mitchell-Lama buildings has been the obvious favoritism in tenant selection. Mitchell-Lama buildings offer a virtual lifetime subsidy and waiting lists usually average ten years. Since there are no fixed standards for tenant selection—and since the program is very little supervised—nepotism abounds.

One of the most notorious examples is a Mitchell-Lama building on 23rd Street and Second Avenue, owned by Robert Seavey, former chairman of the Battery Park City Authority. As it happens, Seavey is a close friend of Governor Mario Cuomo, who appointed him to the Battery Park City job.

In 1983, only a few months after graduating from college, Cuomo's youngest daughter, Maria, secured an apartment in Seavey's building, paying $650 for a one-bedroom apartment. At the time, people had been waiting for apartments since 1979. Maria Cuomo's cousin also had an apartment in the building, as did Rosemary Breslin, daughter of newspaper columnist Jimmy Breslin, also a close friend of Cuomo's. Tenants in the building call it a "haven for Queens politicians' daughters." Maria Cuomo lived in the subsidized apartment until she married in 1987.[11]

Mayor Robert Wagner's efforts to solve New York's housing crisis in the 1950s and 1960s produced tens of thousands of subsidized units, both for the poor and middle class. Large sectors of Harlem were cleared by urban renewal programs and replaced with high-rise public housing. But a lack of private development kept the city's vacancy rate low. By the early 1960s, national vacancy rates were above six percent. In New York, they were below four percent.

Toward the end of Wagner's twelve-year reign, the city government embarked on another campaign—a drastically tightened zoning law. In 1960, the city's zoning ordinance was completely overhauled, "up-zoning" almost every residential and commercial category. Building setbacks were increased, side yards widened, and floor-area ratio—the amount of floor space permitted in relation to the size of the lot—drastically reduced. The idea was to eliminate the bulky apartment houses that anchored the corners of innumerable blocks and replace them with smaller buildings surrounded by plazas and open spaces. It was precisely the kind of residential tower surrounded by "keep off the grass" signs that Jane Jacobs was criticizing in *The Death and Life of Great American Cities,* published the same year.[12]

When the new law was finally adopted in 1961, developers were given a three-year grace period in which they could build under the old ordinance. Owners who had been hanging back for decades suddenly found themselves facing a 25 percent reduction in the size of the building they could put on their property.

The up-zoning set off something New York had not seen for over 30 years—a building boom. Everywhere, developers were suddenly throwing up apartment houses to beat the deadline. By 1965, the market was glutted with new housing. Whole floors stood vacant as builders gave away three months rent and vacations to the Caribbean to get people to sign two-year leases. (One of the problems of marketing new housing in New York has always been to persuade affluent people to move out of their rent-controlled apartments.) Rents in all these new buildings—still unregulated—were remarkably low.

Then, just as quickly, the boom ended. By 1967, new construction was back to Depression-era levels. Vacancies plummeted. When the two-year leases signed in 1966 came up for renewal in 1968, tenants found landlords were asking for 100 percent rent increases. And so, for the first of many times, tenants in new, unregulated apartments marched off to City Hall and Albany demanding they be regulated.

The problem confronted Mayor John Lindsay just as he began a difficult 1969 re-election campaign. Lindsay was always rumored to be personally opposed to rent control (although no politician has ever admitted to such a thing in public). But election pressures proved too much. In 1969, he persuaded the state legislature to modify the old rent-control law and adopt a new "rent stabilization."

Thus, there are actually two kinds of rent control in New York. (Understanding the difference is the mark of being a real New Yorker.) The old post-war "rent control" now only applies to about 150,000 of the city's 1.9 million apartments. These rents are usually from 40 to 90 percent below market. Trying to phase out the old system, the 1969 law provided that rent-controlled units, when vacated, would take a one-time run-up to market value and then come under rent stabilization, if they were in buildings with more than six units. (The new rent stabilization applied only to buildings with six or more units, while the old rent control had applied to everything.)

Under the 1969 law, the Rent Guidelines Board would meet every year to determine how much rents should go up. Once again, all *new* construction was exempted.

In Albany, meanwhile, Governor Nelson Rockefeller had decided to take matters into his own hands. Intensely opposed to rent control, Rockefeller pushed through "vacancy decontrol," which provided that whenever a rent-controlled apartment became vacant, it would be completely deregulated.

Vacancy decontrol is often proposed as the best way to phase out rent control. (Boston and Los Angeles have what they call "vacancy decontrol," but in neither case do vacant apartments become completely deregulated. They are allowed a one-time run-up to market value and then re-regulated.) As things turned out, vacancy decontrol is probably the *worst* way to get rid of rent control. The glacially slow process of deregulation did almost nothing to open up new housing. Yet it did give landlords an enormous incentive to get rid of their tenants. Emptying a rent-controlled apartment meant increasing rents by 100 to 1,000 percent. (If all apartments had been deregulated simultaneously, on the other hand, the upward pressures would not be nearly as great.)

Landlords started hiring thugs to drive tenants out of their buildings. Families were thrown out of their homes, elderly widows cast into the street. A whole new set of "landlord harassment" laws were rushed onto the books, providing huge fines and jail sentences for intimidating tenants. (Tenants also learned to take advantage of these laws by turning every minor dispute into a "harassment" proceeding.) New York's jaundiced vision of landlords had become a self-fulfilling prophecy. Landlords were really as bad as everyone said they were.

All these unfortunate developments were soon swept aside by the Arab Oil Embargo. Faced with skyrocketing fuel costs, landlords began to warn city officials they could no longer maintain their buildings on regulated rents. A special fuel-adjustment allowance was tacked onto rent-controlled apartments (although it rarely exceeded $15 a month). In all, the city and state's familiar response was to protect tenants. Mayor Lindsay's administration openly advised landlords to practice "deferred maintenance" in order to offset rising oil prices.

Long insulated from reality, New York tenants simply were not prepared to cope with the 1970s. One of the most spectacular rebellions was a "rent strike" in Co-op City, a 30,000 unit, state-subsidized, city-within-a-city in the north Bronx. Constructed in the 1960s on the site of old Freedomland amusement park, Co-op City emptied the Grand Concourse of elderly tenants fleeing before the influx of Puerto Ricans and blacks. The 80,000 Co-op City residents *owned* their own apartments—albeit with generous assistance from the state and city governments. Yet when rising 1974 oil prices forced a $15 increase in the monthly maintenance payment, the new owners went on a "rent strike," withholding maintenance and mortgage payments. Since the underlying mortgage was held by the state-funded Urban Development Corporation, the state itself had to swallow the losses. After nine months, the state legislature caved in and voted more subsidies so that maintenance fees would not have to be raised.

The panic over rising fuel costs and Governor Rockefeller's vacancy decontrol program led to the Emergency Tenant Protection Act of 1974. Vacancy decontrol was repealed. Rent stabilization was extended into Nassau, Suffolk, Westchester, and Rockland Counties, where suburban renters were clamoring for protection.

Once again, the state legislature reneged on its promise to exempt new housing. All buildings constructed since 1969 were now regulated. The first promise had lasted 22 years. The second lasted only five. Once again, the legislature promised that new construction would be exempt from rent regulations.

The real story of the 1970s, however, turned out to be housing abandonment. Landlords had long warned New York City officials they could not go on subsidizing their tenants. During hearings on the rent-stabilization bill in 1969, Edward Sulzberger, chairman of the Metropolitan Fair Rent Committee, told the city council, "If you don't get rid of rent control we're going to have people sleeping in Central Park." His comments were met with derisive laughter.

In the early 1970s, these warnings finally came full circle. Beginning around 1972, landlords began to "walk away" from formerly sound apartment buildings. (The process is not as easy as it sounds, since the owner remains liable for damages and injury incurred on the property. That is why failing owners hide their identity under layers of dummy corporations.) Between 1972 and 1982, owners abandoned an annual average of 30,000 apartments—a stunning ten-year total of 300,000 units, almost two percent of the housing stock. By 1980, New York City had three percent of the nation's housing and ten percent of its "dilapidated" housing.

Nor was this older housing stock at the end of its life cycle. Defenders of rent control always argue that other cities have suffered housing abandonment and the phenomenon should not be tied to rent control. Detroit is often cited for its high rate of vacant housing. One of the country's most severe rates of abandonment turns out to be in Lynn, Massachusetts.

Yet there is a crucial difference. Abandoned housing in other cities is usually older housing that has completed its usefulness. A typical abandoned building in Detroit or Lynn is a wooden-frame house built around the turn of the century. This kind of housing has obviously outlived its life cycle.

But in no other city except New York has housing been lost *during a housing shortage.* Abandonment is usually a sign of *surplus* housing, as George Sternlieb discovered in Newark in 1966. In New York, however, the housing lost during the 1970s was some of the most beautiful and solid housing ever built in this country. Huge brick and granite apartment houses in the Bronx and Upper Manhattan that had barely lived half their useful life were leveled to the ground. Whole moonscapes were created. As Assa Lindbeck, the *left*-wing Swedish economist put it: "Next to bombing, rent control seems to be the most efficient technique so far known for destroying cities."[13]

Despite the new assurances that post-1974 buildings would remain unregulated, even the most slow-witted politician in New York knew that rent controls had poisoned the well. And so, it was necessary to come up with a new subsidy program to encourage new construction. Predictably, these subsidies went to extremely affluent tenants. Predictably, the promise was broken and the new buildings were eventually brought under permanent regulation. (The word city officials use to describe this process is "recapture," a term with a distinctly Orwellian flavor. Although the buildings were always unregulated, the implication is that they never really belonged to their owners in the first place.)

The new subsidy program was called "421-a," after a section of the Emergency

Tenant Protection Act. Builders were granted an initial 100 percent property-tax exemption on new apartments. In exchange, they were temporarily put under rent stabilization. The tax exemption would be phased out over ten years, the builder paying 20 percent of the tax bill the second year, 40 percent the fourth, and 100 percent the tenth. At that point, the building would be taken out of stabilization and the owner could charge market rents.

Once again, a handful of developers went for the bait. Over ten years, 30,000 new units went up, most of them in "superluxury" buildings like the Bristol and the Greenthal on the Upper East Side. Property taxes were phased in and, when 1984 rolled around, the first buildings were scheduled for deregulation.

The tenants, of course, objected. Soon they were in Albany demanding their buildings be kept under rent stabilization. The legislature capitulated and the 421-a program fell apart. It was phased out in 1986.

Just to complete the cycle, the 30-year mortgages on the first Mitchell-Lama buildings constructed in the 1950s also started coming up for expiration in the mid-1980s. Under the 1955 law, owners could withdraw their buildings from the program and rent them at market prices. Naturally, the tenants protested. As of 1989, both Republicans and Democrats in the state legislature had agreed to a 15-year moratorium on the withdrawal of buildings from the Mitchell-Lama program, although the bill had not been adopted because of disputes over other landlord-tenant issues.

Thus, since 1947, the state and city governments have reneged on almost every promise ever made to allow new housing to remain outside rent regulations. HPD officials constantly point out that rent stabilization is still a "voluntary" program and any new, unsubsidized apartment house can be built free of rent controls. "You can put up anything you want and charge anything you want," said Abe Biderman, Commissioner of HPD. "It's right in the law."

But as with "Welcome stranger" assessments, the policy only works as long as new people don't understand the system. As soon as they catch on, they run to the legislature to have their buildings "recaptured."

As a result, in the midst of the nation's worst housing shortage, very little new housing is ever built in New York. Certainly there is a trickle of about 12,000 new units a year, but Dallas, with one-seventh the population and 15 percent vacancy rates, puts up the same amount. When a new apartment complex was opened in mid-town Manhattan in 1986, *The Daily News* ran the headline: "Rarity: Manhattan Gets New Apartments."[14]

All the major developers have long since departed. Sam Lefrak, builder of the 5,000-unit, middle-income Lefrak City in Queens (now decaying under rent regulations), has decamped for New Jersey. When builder Dan Rose, of the Rose

Brothers Corporation, was asked by a reporter what he had learned from rent regulations, he replied: "I learned to get on an airplane and build my apartments in other cities." Harry Helmsley, the largest private owner of rental housing in New York (with 3 percent of the market) announced in 1985 that he was selling off his apartments. He could no longer live with rent regulations. His departure left the city government unchallenged as New York's largest landlord, with nine percent of the market. When New York almost went bankrupt in 1975, the erosion of its real-estate tax base and its huge volume of uncollected property taxes were cited as a principle source of the financial failure.

All this has certainly protected tenants from their landlords. It has only failed to protect buildings from their tenants. The thousands of skeletal remains of buildings that sit with the legend, "Property of the City of New York, Department of Housing and Urban Development" stenciled on their walls, the bombed-out sections of the South Bronx (often compared to Dresden after the war), the thousands of homeless who sleep in vacant lots and doorways—all these are only the visible results of rent regulations. Forty-six years of rent control in New York have produced something that is impossible in a free market—homeless people and peopleless homes.

Chapter 19

The Best Deal in Town

The outcome of rent control is that long-tenured or affluent tenants get reduced rents. In New York, the remarkable result has been that some of the best deals are held by the city's cultural and political luminaries.

Former mayor Edward Koch himself is one of the biggest winners. He has a rent-controlled apartment on Washington Street in Greenwich Village. Koch pays $441.49 a month for a large, one-bedroom apartment with an outer terrace that would probably be worth $1,200 in an unregulated market. Koch kept the apartment the entire twelve years he lived in Gracie Mansion.

Supermodel and actress Lauren Hutton and her husband, Robert Williamson, have title to a rent-controlled chalet in the rear of a small apartment building in Greenwich Village. They pay $469.70 a month. (Rent-controlled rents are always calculated to the penny, since they are raised by annual percentages.) The chalet, built as an artist's studio in the 1920s, has floor-to-ceiling mahogany paneling, a fireplace, and a loft. The couple also own a home in California and oceanfront property in the Hamptons on Long Island. Williamson has another rent-controlled apartment in the neighborhood that he uses for storage. Strangely, both his landlords independently sued Williamson for non-primary residence without realizing he had two apartments. Williamson won both cases.

Arnold Scaasi, fashion designer for Barbara Bush, Elizabeth Taylor, and Mary Tyler Moore, pays $1,109.53 for a seven-room duplex at 100 Central Park South that has 14-foot ceilings, a fireplace and terrace. Donald Trump is his landlord. When the apartment was featured in *Architectural Digest* in 1988, columnist Liz Smith wrote, "Scaasi can live in his too-small apartment, where he has resided for twenty-six years, because he doesn't spend much time there."[1] He has another home on Long Island. Scaasi and five other tenants fought off a six-year effort by Trump to raze the building and replace it with a hotel. Trump says that Scaasi is regularly seven months behind on his rent.

Television personality Alistair Cooke has a rent-controlled apartment on Fifth Avenue, overlooking Central Park. For eight rooms, Cooke pays $1,357.66, plus a $35 fuel adjustment left over from the oil crisis. Cooke, who has held the lease for 39 years, once told a British newspaper he kept the apartment because it was cheaper than renting hotel space when he came to New York. In recent years, he has used it as his principal residence.

In the same building, William Shawn, long-time editor of *The New Yorker* (now retired) also pays $1,340.12 for eight rooms overlooking Central Park. Phillipe De Montebello, head of the Metropolitan Museum of Art, pays $1,833.90 for nine rooms overlooking the park. The building is also filled with successful Wall Street bankers and brokers. One owns two other homes in Jamaica and Florida. Another tenant is the son and daughter-in-law of a world-famous architect. All pay less than $1,000 for apartments of six or more rooms.

On Central Park West and 73rd Street sits a veritable oceanliner of a building containing an all-star cast of rent-regulated tenants. Actress Mia Farrow pays $2,272.43 for an eleven-room apartment overlooking Central Park (probable market value about $6,000). The apartment was featured in the movie, "Hannah and Her Sisters." Farrow also has a home in Connecticut.

Carly Simon pays $2,683.63 for ten rooms overlooking the park. Whitney Ellsworth, publisher of the *New York Review of Books,* pays $1,928.47 for ten rooms overlooking the park. Jean Stein, heir to the MCA fortune, pays $1,508.28 for ten rooms overlooking the park. Warren Rubin, owner of the Workbench chain of hardware stores, pays $1,811.48 for ten rooms overlooking the park. Anna Strassberg, widow of Lee Strassberg, world-famous acting coach, pays $1,965.86 for eleven rooms overlooking the park. Phillip Langner, a Broadway producer, pays $1,453.58 for six rooms on the park. James Levine, musical director of the Metropolitan Opera, pays $1,405.15 for six rooms on the park. Manfred Ohrenstein, Democratic minority leader in the New York State Senate (and an avid supporter of rent controls) pays $2,070.67 for eleven rooms overlooking the park.

Back on the East Side, William vanden Heuval, President Jimmy Carter's ambassador to the United Nations, owns a co-op on Park Avenue but also keeps a six-room, rent-stabilized apartment in a building on East 72nd Street for only $671.55 a month. Vanden Heuval (who was once married to MCA heiress Jean Stein) admits the apartment is not his primary residence but considers it a "family residence." The head of a blue-chip law firm, vanden Heuval has used procedural tactics to fight off eviction for years. "It is wrong, but I'm not taking advantage of the landlord," said vanden Heuval. "The law permits it."[2]

In the same building is Alice Mason, New York City's premier real-estate broker. (As one gossip columnist put it, "If your apartment cost more than $4 or $5 million, you probably bought it from Alice.") Mason is famous for the parties she gives two or three times a month in her vast apartment, which includes a living room, dining room, library, full kitchen, butler's pantry, two maid's rooms, and three bathrooms. Jimmy Carter is said to have launched his Presidential campaign in Mason's apartment, where he first met Zbigniew Brzezinski, vanden Heuval, and other New York illuminati. A typical write-up of a Mason party goes like this:

> Alice Mason . . . gave one of those dinner parties of hers that snap, crackle, and pop because so do the guests. **Jean Claude Nedelec** of Glorious Food always comes in to prepare a fine, hot meal for the more than 50 stars and satellites scattered through the living room, dining room and library of her apartment. . . .
>
> Who was there? To name a few—**Malcolm Forbes,** who arrived on his motorcycle. . . . **Countess** (Aline) **of Romanones,** whose navy blue windbreaker over a long, bare, black dress was as chic as any mink or sable, **Barbaralee Diamonstein-Spielvogel** and **Carl Spielvogel, Helen Gurley Brown** and **David Brown; [Elie and] Mrs. Elie (Marion) Wiesel. . . . Frances Lear** of the Lear's magazine Lears. . . . (etc. etc. etc.)[3]

The apartment is rent-stabilized. Mason pays only $1,001.88. Her landlord, Eugene Martin, said that Jean Claude Nedelec and Glorious Food once overloaded the elevator with so much food that they overrode the brakes, costing him $5,000 in repairs.

Back on the West Side, Suzanne Farrell, principal dancer of the American Ballet Theater pays only $1,167.27 for a fourteen-room rent-controlled duplex within walking distance of Lincoln Center.

Barry Farber, a popular radio talk-show host, pays about $1,575 for a five-bedroom apartment in The Athol, an old luxury building on Broadway. Writer Nora Ephron is in the same building and has a similar deal. CBS sportscaster Brent

Musburger also had a $900-a-month regulated apartment on the West Side but skipped owing $6,000 in back rent.

Television actress Tracy Scoggins long held the lease on a $772.20-a-month rent-stabilized apartment in Lincoln Towers, near Lincoln Center. Scoggins was finally evicted in 1987 for being seven months behind in the rent. Her press agent, Sue Patricola, told *The New York Post* that it was all a mistake—she hadn't lived in New York since 1981.[4]

For many years, Shelley Winters had a rent-controlled apartment near Central Park, paying only $839.93 for two bedrooms. She also owned a home in Beverly Hills. She finally bought her apartment in 1987—four years after the building went co-op—when the new management board proved in court that the Beverly Hills home was her primary residence. Farley Granger, another old-time actor, remains in a rent-controlled apartment in the same building, paying $916.75 for a two-bedroom apartment.

Another regulated tenant who eventually lost her apartment was supermodel Kim Alexis. She had a cheap, rent-stabilized apartment on East 27th Street, which she used while visiting the city on business and to run the New York Marathon. The owner challenged her residence in 1987 when he spotted a spread on her million-dollar Florida home in *Vogue.* Alexis eventually agreed to leave after finishing her two-year lease.

Frank Lorenzo, president of Eastern Airlines, had a three-bedroom, rent-stabilized apartment on the Upper East Side, for which he paid $1,172. When Lorenzo moved to Houston to take over Texas Air, the landlord sued him for non-primary residence. In 1986, Lorenzo signed a court stipulation agreeing to pay the market rent—$2,500. Two years later, however, the landlord became concerned that the arrangement might be regarded as an attempt to evade rent regulations and Lorenzo was forced to give up the apartment.

Politicians in New York make out equally well under rent control. On the City Council, many of the most outspoken advocates of rent regulations are beneficiaries themselves. Of the seven representatives from Manhattan (where most of the best rent-controlled deals are located), three have benefited substantially from rent control.

Councilwoman Carol Greitzer pays $769.45 a month for a two-bedroom, rent-stabilized apartment in Greenwich Village. The building has gone co-op, but Greitzer has elected to remain a tenant. Those who bought are now paying a monthly maintenance fee of nearly $1,000—meaning that Greitzer, like so many other regulated tenants, isn't covering the basic utilities, common expenses, and property taxes. Greitzer owns a vacation home on Fire Island.

Councilwoman Miriam Friedlander has a rent-controlled apartment on the

Lower East Side. The owner, an elderly retired woman in Brooklyn, would not reveal her rent, but it is probably no more than $300 per month. The building is remarkably rundown—locks broken and the mailboxes vandalized—and neighbors said that Friedlander had not even been seen in the building in recent years (although it is still listed as her address in the Manhattan phone book). The rumor on the Lower East Side is that Friedlander has another apartment in the neighborhood but is hanging on to her rent-controlled apartment in the expectation that the building may one day go co-op.

Councilwoman Ruth Messinger—who wants to extend rent control to commercial spaces—owns her own co-op on Riverside Drive. But her childhood home was a rent-controlled apartment on Central Park West. Until 1988, her parents still rented the apartment, paying only $851.25 for eight rooms. They finally bought when the building went co-op. Messinger's parents also list their Westport, Connecticut, home in the Manhattan directory.

At the state level, Manhattan politicians are also well protected by rent regulations.

In the New York State Assembly, representative William Passannante, of Greenwich Village, pays $405.31 for a two-bedroom apartment on Barrow Street. Assemblyman Alexander "Pete" Grannis—probably the most outspoken proponent of rent controls in the Assembly—pays about $892.43 for a two-bedroom apartment on the Upper East Side. Assemblyman Jerry Nadler pays $804.31 for a two-bedroom apartment on the Upper West Side. Assemblyman Brian Murtaugh pays $523.73 for a stabilized apartment in Upper Manhattan.

In the State Senate, Democratic minority leader Manfred Ohrenstein—as already mentioned—has an eleven-room rent-controlled apartment on Central Park West. Senator Marty Conner, who represents Lower Manhattan and Brooklyn, has a two-bedroom-and-dining-room stabilized apartment in Brooklyn Heights, for which he pays $553.41. When asked to justify his regulated status, Conner responded, "I only make $57,000 a year," which means he pays 15 percent of his income in rent.

One of the most interesting stories in Manhattan politics is State Senator Franz Leichter, who represents the Upper West Side. Since 1975, Leichter has sublet a three-bedroom apartment on Riverside Drive from Priscilla Ryan, widow of former Congressman William Ryan. Mrs. Ryan has since moved to Washington. Her rent is $885.79 a month. Leichter sends her a check and she forwards the money to the landlord, Columbia University. The arrangement is of questionable legality (the law on whether rent-controlled tenants can sublet has never been completely clarified). Nevertheless, Columbia does not challenge the arrangement—for obvious political reasons. At age 59, senator Leichter still has not found his own apartment.[5]

Columbia is also landlord to another ex-Assembly member, Marie Runyon, a housing activist who served one term in the early 1970s. Runyon, now in her 70s, achieved fame in 1968 when Columbia attempted to demolish her building in order to relocate its school of pharmacology from Midtown. Runyon was one of a handful of rent-controlled tenants who refused to move. She eventually won and the school of pharmacology closed down. Today Runyon still pays $94.09 a month for an eight-room apartment. She has long rented out rooms to Columbia students. "I used to charge them, but now I just ask them to walk my dog," she said.[6]

At the Federal level, Congressman Theodore Weiss, who represents the 17th District in Upper Manhattan, also has a rent-controlled apartment.

As can be seen, New York has evolved what might be called a "tenant aristocracy." For more than a generation, most of the political, social, and cultural leaders have been permanent beneficiaries of rent control.

The situation was actually much worse in the 1970s, before many major buildings were converted to cooperatives. Writing about New York's bankruptcy crisis in 1978, Ken Auletta found people like Arthur Leavitt, Jr., chairman of the American Stock Exchange, living in rent-controlled apartments on Central Park South for less than $700 a month.[7] Arthur Ochs Sulzburger, owner of *The New York Times,* also had a rent-controlled apartment. When Auletta asked Nat Sherman, the owner of a gilt-edged tobacco store on Fifth Avenue, whether the $400-a-month he paid for six rooms on Central Park South was a fair price, he replied: "I use the apartment so little, that I think it's fair." Sherman spent most of his time in Florida.

Yet it is not just the rich and famous who make out well under rent control. Throw a rock in Manhattan and you are likely to hit someone who has a friend of a friend who has a great rent-controlled apartment.

In 1986, for example, a moderately successful novelist published a memoir in *The New York Times,* called "Once A New Yorker," in which he described his days as a struggling writer. "I found a nice place on 79th Street near Madison," he wrote, "in the days when your rent check wasn't as big as your telephone number. It was a glorious and captivating time for a young man." After a period of "books, and movie deals," in which "I found myself wearing a tuxedo a little too often," he "sold his apartment [sic] at an indecent profit and moved to a bigger one, encountering my share of glamorous women, and the evening routine became three-parties-a-dinner-and-a-dance." After a decade of this, he decided to return home to Alabama.

> "But the truth is, I never really left. . . . I still keep my apartment in the city and return every month or so like an old alumnus, and a lot of my friends do the same; New York is still the gathering place, the matrix that holds our varied worlds intact."[8]

The apartment was rent-stabilized.

A few years ago at a party, I was introduced to a free-lance writer who was doing articles for small magazines. After a few minutes he started talking about his vacation home in upstate New York. When he told me his income was $21,000, I said it sounded as if he had a rent-controlled apartment. Sure enough, he paid only $81 a month for four rooms. "We wanted to invest in property, so we bought something upstate," he explained.

Another couple I know has two rent-stabilized apartments on different floors in the same building, which they tried to use as one apartment. (Having multiple apartments, in one building—or even separate buildings—is common in New York. Among the tenants that Donald Trump tried to evict from 100 Central Park South, one stockbroker had five apartments, four of which she had combined into one palatial unit.)

A young graduate student who helped me research this book (and who spent two unsuccessful years hunting an apartment) became quite alert to rent-control stories. One day she was standing in a liquor store and heard the clerk talking about taking an extended vacation in Spain. She asked how he could afford it on his salary. He had a rent-controlled apartment that cost only $80 a month. His savings had enabled him to buy a home in Spain. He didn't think he had such a great deal—another tenant in the building paid only $40.

Another couple she met had two small rent-controlled apartments in adjoining buildings. Unable to live in either apartment and tired of running back and forth, they finally punched a hole through the walls and connected the two apartments with a large pipe, through which they crawled from building to building.

Overall, the benefits of rent control have generally filtered up to the affluent. In a 1988 study, the Arthur D. Little Corporation found that 71 percent of the apartments in affluent neighborhoods were regulated, while only 47 percent were regulated in lower-income neighborhoods. The biggest differential between regulated and market rents were on the Upper East and West Sides and in Greenwich Village. On the Upper East Side, the city's most affluent neighborhood (average income, $43,000), 82 percent of the apartments are regulated, the highest concentration in the city. The average rent discount was also the largest—$474 below market.

On the other hand, among districts with the lowest rent discounts, eight of ten were in lower- and lower-middle-income areas. In most low-income neighborhoods, regulated rents are barely below market levels and in some cases are actually *above* market.[9] Harlem landlords have occasionally called the Rent Stabilization Association complaining that they can't get the legal rents.

Rent control has also influenced affluent tenants against moving up to home ownership. Among people making over $75,000 in New York, only 63 percent own their own home, as opposed to 89 percent for the whole Northeast. In fact, above $100,000, home ownership actually *declines* in New York City.[10] The rule-of-thumb has been you "rent in the city and buy in the country."

When confronted with these obvious inequities, most New Yorkers usually shrug and say, "What difference does it make? Do you really think if Mia Farrow gave up her rent-controlled apartment today that some homeless person from Grand Central Station would end up living in it?"

As we have seen, the most important factor in providing housing to low-income people is the *circulation* of housing. Because of its astonishing benefits for long-term incumbency, New York has the slowest rate of circulation in the nation. In most cities, between 26 to 38 percent of rental units turn over annually. In New York, only 11 percent turn over. In most cities, only about 5 percent of renters have lived in the same apartment for 20 years. In New York, the figure is 12 percent.[11]

All this adds up to what another Arthur D. Little report called "Housing Gridlock in New York."[12] The study found 175,000 apartments in New York where one person is occupying four or more rooms. These are largely elderly tenants who have become "stranded" in rent-controlled apartments. Over one-third of these tenants had been living in the apartment for more than 16 years and two-thirds were paying less than $300 a month. Meanwhile, there were 112,000 households in which three or more people were living in three rooms or fewer and 9,000 in which five or more people were living in three rooms or fewer.[12]

Even more significant is the remarkable mismatch of incomes to rent. While the median New Yorker pays only 26 percent of his income in rent, the figure fluctuates wildly among income groups. For people at the poverty level, 50 percent pay more than 50 percent of their income in rent. Meanwhile, 87 percent of the highest income group pay less than 20 percent of income in rent and *41* percent pay less than 11 percent. For all groups, 17 percent pay more than 50 percent of income, while 8 percent pay less than 11 percent.[14]

In a remarkable thought experiment, the Arthur D. Little study simply reallocated existing rents among existing incomes, matching the highest rents with the highest income groups and the lowest rents with the lowest income—and found a much more equitable distribution! After reallocation, *no one* paid less than 11 percent of their income in rent and only 1.4 percent paid more than 50 percent of income. Instead, all the rents were bunched toward the middle, with 30.3 percent of the population paying 11 to 20 percent of income, 30.3 percent paying 21 to 30 percent, 28.7 percent paying 31 to 40 percent, and 9.3 percent paying 41 to 50 percent.

The problem in New York is not a lack of affordable housing. It is the *distribution* of housing. As Manhattan developer-philosopher Seymour Durst puts it: "We've got plenty of low-income housing in New York. We've just got upper-income people living in it."

Perhaps the strangest thing about rent control and housing immobility is the weird, often leisurely, lifestyles it encourages people to lead.

Gail Kammerer, a Chicago native, owns a small, three-family brownstone in Greenwich Village. Kammerer occupies a one-bedroom apartment on the first floor herself and a childless young couple pay $1,800 for the third floor.

On the second floor is a 63-year-old NBC executive, his wife, a telephone-company manager, their two teenage children, and a dog. They have lived in the same one-bedroom apartment for 18 years. "The boy sleeps in a nine-foot closet and the girl sleeps in the dining room," said Kammerer. "They spend all their money on clothing and vacations. A delivery from a department store arrives at my door every day. I offered them $50,000 to move but they said they wanted $300,000."

"My experience is that most tenants with great deals tend to be underemployed underachievers," added Kammerer, who has several neighbors with rent-controlled tenants. "Once they get that apartment, they're set for life."

Judy Seigel, who owns a brownstone in Greenwich Village, has a rent-controlled tenant in his 50s who lived in her building for 25 years. He pays $297-a-month for four rooms. "I knew him when I was growing up in the neighborhood," said Seigel. "I actually rented him the apartment as a favor, thinking he would only stay a few years." Instead, the tenant quit his job as a teacher and tried an acting career. "He's never really made it—only a few jobs in summer stock. But he's been able to convince himself he's an artist all these years because I've been supporting him."

Victoria Ross is a successful television and off-Broadway actress who bought a six-unit brownstone in Greenwich Village in 1984, hoping to give both herself and her two daughters a place to live. She soon discovered that none of her rent-controlled tenants was about to budge. "One is about 50 and has a Ph.D. from Columbia. He sits in his room all day and listens to classical music. His apartment is stacked to the ceiling with newspapers. The windows are painted yellow.

"The other is a woman in her 30s whose brother is a well-known philosopher.

She has rooms full of scholarly books and occasionally sells them at book fairs. She also works a few days a month in a rare book store." Both tenants pay $111 a month in rent. "There's a garage across the street where people pay $300 a month just to park their car."

Yet when Ross tried to evict another tenant in order to move into the building herself, all hell broke loose. "All these people who hadn't done anything in years suddenly sprang to life," she said. "They were filing petitions with HPD, holding organizational meetings, plastering the hallways with bulletins and Marxist slogans. I think it was the most exciting thing that ever happened to them." The tenants easily won their case in housing court. After five years, Ross has never been able to get an apartment in her own building.

Sigmund Rothschild, a descendent of the real Rothschilds, is another Manhattan artiste who has built a career around a rent-controlled apartment. An art appraiser with a modest reputation, Rothschild has what both *The New York Post* and Fox Television's "A Current Affair" called "the best deal in town."[15] The 73-year-old Rothschild is the sole tenant of an eight-room duplex, featuring a 2,000-square-foot living room that has a 22-foot ceiling, plus handcarved woodwork and cathedral windows, all in an ornate building just off Central Park West. He pays $568.24 a month.

Divorced three times, Rothschild said he is fairly certain his last wife married him in the hope of eventually getting the apartment. "When I die," he added, "I just want to be cremated and have my ashes buried right here under my living-room floor."

Even in death, New Yorkers rarely want to give up their rent-controlled apartments.

Chapter 20

"I Didn't Know It Would Be Impossible"

Rent control and tight zoning create a situation where entrenched people do very well, protecting their own interests while making housing difficult to find for others. But what does the situation look like for those outside the system?

Take Robert B, a native of New Jersey, who graduated from NYU in 1984 with a degree in economics. Robert immediately landed a job with a major investment firm and has worked there ever since. His salary has gone from $18,000 to $29,000 over five years. In most respects, he is a successful college graduate making a career in New York. However, he still hasn't found his own apartment.

Immediately after graduating he checked *The New York Times* and found a listing for a one-bedroom apartment on York Avenue. He liked the place and started paying $1,100 a month with no lease. After three months, the person who had rented him the apartment told him he had to leave. For the first time he realized that this person was not the landlord but another tenant. He later found the tenant was rent-controlled, paying only $400.

Next he found another sublet from a lawyer. This was a legal arrangement (no more than 10 percent over the prime tenant's rent), costing him $900. He stayed for a year, then the prime tenant returned.

Robert started hunting the papers again. He read an ad for a rental on the Upper East side that mentioned a "fixture fee." He saw the apartment and liked it. The husband was not at home but the wife said it would require a $1,000 deposit. He wrote a check on the spot. As he handed it to her, the wife said that there would also be "a $6,000 fixture fee." (Like key money, fixture fees are bribes attached to the transfer of an apartment.) Robert asked for more details. The woman said he would have to talk to her husband.

By the time he got a hold of the husband, his check had cleared. The man informed him that the "fixtures" consisted of the mantle piece and two small wooden cabinets. Robert said he didn't want to pay and asked for his money back. The man said he would have to deduct several hundred dollars for his time and expenses in advertising the apartment. Robert argued. The man hung up the phone. Robert later did some investigating and found the tenant was the son of a senior partner in one of New York's most prestigious law firms. He never saw his $1,000 again.

Turned out of his sublet, Robert began living like a vagabond. "I was beginning to realize it was going to be very difficult to find a permanent place to live." He stayed with friends, slept on couches, and lived with his parents in New Jersey. He lost some of his possessions, gave away most of his furniture, and started living out of his car. Once, when he left the windows open during a rainstorm, he lost 150 books to water damage.

Finally, he met a man named Ken Matthews who actually owned a few buildings on the Upper East Side. "That man is a saint," he said, "probably the fairest person I've ever dealt with in New York housing. I would recommend him to anybody who was looking for an apartment."

Unfortunately, while Matthews had several buildings, he never had any vacancies. Instead, he started shuffling Robert around among apartments as tenants left on sabbaticals or long vacations. "One of his tenants was a snowbird who spent the winter in Florida. Others took extended vacations during the summer. He had good relations with all of them and they let me stay in their apartments."

Finally, during one period when Matthews had nothing available, Robert moved in with his aunt and uncle, who own a co-op on the East Side. Then he heard that an acquaintance from NYU had an apartment she wanted to sublet on 58th Street. She was moving, but, like thousands of other New Yorkers, wanted to hang on to the lease in anticipation that the building would go co-op—at which point sitting tenants can buy at discount prices. Meanwhile, she was moving to West 22nd

Street. Robert agreed to pay $900 a month with the understanding he would leave whenever she requested.

In June 1988, he moved in. In mid-October, the tenant called and said she wanted the apartment back at the end of November. She asked him to pay the November rent early so she could settle with her landlord on 22nd Street. Robert decided he had had enough and left immediately without paying. He went back to his aunt's apartment.

Once again, after making subsequent inquiries, Robert found that the apartment hadn't belonged to his friend at all. The prime tenant was one of her friends who lived two floors above. He was hanging onto the lease, waiting for the building to go co-op, and had allowed Robert's friend to live there rent-free for seven years. The $900-a-month she had had been collecting from Robert was clear profit.

"I've been apartment-hunting for six years and never had my name on a lease," said Robert in 1989. "It took me a while to realize that I'd never even met a landlord—except for Ken Matthews, who is the only decent person I've ever met in New York housing. I've never made less than $18,000 and have still spent many nights sleeping in my car. It's easy for me to see how people end up homeless."

For anyone hunting an apartment in Manhattan today, the situation ranges from desperate to hopeless. Writes Michael deCourcy Hines, of *The New York Times*:

> Finding a decent, affordable rent-regulated apartment in New York City is like trying to recover a contact lens from a subway platform at rush hour. . . .
>
> Statistically, the frustration is suggested by the city's unofficial vacancy rate of *minus* 1 percent—the official rate of 2 percent minus the 3 percent of housing that is dilapidated.[1] [Emphasis added.]

Or as another frustrated apartment-hunter told *The Times* after six months of fruitless effort, "I knew it was going to be hard, but I didn't know it would be impossible."

In a 1987 cover story in *New York* magazine entitled, "How to Find an Apartment (Seriously)," Jane Goldman warned newcomers:

> Otherwise reasonable people are considering—and renting—apartments with rats in the bathtub. Or tiny studios with view of an air shaft. Or apartments in neighborhoods they're afraid to walk through. After weeks of looking for an affordable one-bedroom apartment, one man walked up the stairs to one last dark, cramped "spac 1BR, newly renov" flat and cried.[2]

Goldman warned readers they would be looking at studios for $900, one-bedrooms for $1,200, and two-bedrooms for $1,600—if they were lucky and diligent.

> If you *don't* want to look hard—if you just like to walk into an attractive, sunny, two-bedroom, two-bathroom flat in a doorman building in a pleasant neighborhood—expect to pay $2000 a month. . . . Are you insisting on a place with big rooms, lots of light, and maybe even a small terrace? Raise the rent to $3000. . . .[3]

When Jon Etra, a writer who has a synthetic heart valve and a heart murmur, finally found a $650-a-month, fifth-floor walk-up in Manhattan, he rented it—even though his doctor strenuously warned against it. "Death is a small price to pay for an apartment in New York," he told *The Daily News*.[4]

Nor are these things without consequence to the city's future. New York has always been a mecca for ambitious young people, yet high housing prices now make this migration extremely difficult. A study by the Center for Social and Demographic Analysis at the State University of New York at Albany found that 40 percent of the people who moved out of New York between 1975 and 1980 were young people between ages 10 and 34. "There is a potential for danger to the city," said Richard D. Alba, the director of the center. "It is possible that as housing becomes more expensive or hard to get in the city, it will choke off potential immigration."[5]

The problem, of course, is that regulated apartments, which comprise half the city's housing stock, almost never come on the market. In the rare instance that a tenant does move, the apartment quickly passes to family or friends. Everyone hunting an apartment ends up being funneled into the unregulated sector, where the short supplies and overwhelming demand have pushed prices higher than market levels.

"Very little of our listings come from actual building owners," said Nancy Packes, a former Federal prosecutor who runs The Feathered Nest, one of New York's biggest rental agencies. "About 80 percent is from individual co-op or condominium owners who are renting their apartments.

"Frankly, I think the prices people are getting are a little ridiculous—$1,000 for a studio, $1,500 for a one-bedroom," she added. "But that's what the market will bear. With over half the market locked up in rent regulations, everybody is forced into a very narrow portion of the market."

Looking in the papers or filing with apartment brokers, however, is not the best way to go about the task. Much better is having good connections.

As Michael deCourcy Hinds put it:

> [A]nother, seemingly contradictory, housing statistic [is that] [e]very year, tenants vacate about 135,000 rent-regulated units. . . .
>
> The numbers raise troubling questions about the rent-regulated market. Could there really be that many turnovers each year in a city with a negative vacancy rate? Where are all these vacant apartments and why are they so hard to find? . . .
>
> Most of the . . . vacant apartments are snapped up by the former tenants' friends or friends of friends. Apartment hunters who are not plugged into this sort of tenant network generally have to develop one.[6]

Jane Goldman suggested one possible strategy to her *New York* readers:

> Alan Ross, a writer and teacher, found his East Village apartment by staking out the few blocks on which he wanted to live. [One of] Ross's techniques was to hang around when cars were being moved to the other side of the street [for alternate-side-of-the-street parking regulations]. "There's a whole community of people out there who move their cars every day. . . . If you talk to them, you can find out what's going on."[7]

Luella Adams, who teaches a course entitled "Finding an Apartment" at the Discovery Center on West 72nd Street, recommends "going to church or synagogue," and "mingling with the congregation" in order to get tips on apartments.[8]

Just how elaborately these networks can function for people who are finally plugged into them is illustrated in this lengthy but enlightening anecdote from *The Village Voice*.

> It is February, 1978, and I've been in New York for two months when I take over the apartment from Sarah, who has been subletting from Graham, an actor away on location in L.A. It is one room, five flights up, and the rent is $212, which I am told is a steal. Since in L.A. I was paying $165 to share a four bedroom house with a view of the beach and a bathroom three times as big as the new apartment's kitchen, it does not seem like a steal to me. . . . Graham will be back in six weeks, but. . . I have nowhere [else] to go.
>
> After two months, Graham calls from California to say I might as well stay on. After seven months, the landlord grows restive, but that is all right, because Graham, who is back in New York, has decided to move in with his girlfriend Annie. I sign a lease. . . .
>
> When summer comes, I am unemployed and want to go West. I sublet the apartment to April, a 19-year-old from Queens, who cuts my hair. The summer goes well for me, but not for my neighbor, Jack, an unemployed actor who has sublet his apartment to spend the summer with his family in Hawaii. When he comes back, his tenant has changed the locks on the door. . . .

By next summer, I have bought a new bed and . . . sublet the apartment to Nikki, an editor, who is divorcing her husband, and go to L.A., where I sublet an apartment from Ginger [and] fall in love with Dan. . . .

I decide to move to L.A. to be with Dan. The rent on the apartment is now $326.72, which is such a steal I can't even think of giving it up. Instead, I . . . sublet to Karen, a copywriter, who is being evicted from a downtown sublet. . . .

In the fall, I spend a month in the apartment. I sign a new two-year lease, then sublet to Jeffrey, a writer who lives in New Jersey and needs a pied-a-terre. Jeffrey stays four months [and] bounces three checks. . . . He is followed by Leann, a filmmaker, who comes via Pat, a childhood friend who now lives in New York, moving from sublet to sublet. She stays a year. . . .

I interview many people to take Leann's place. I chose Jose, a reporter whose girlfriend is kicking him out. Jose stays five months . . . and leaves . . . an unpaid phone bill. . . .

At first there is no one to take the apartment, but then Pat, who is a photographer, decided she can no longer live with the lover who has put her up since her last sublease ended. . . . I sign another two-year lease, even though I am still living with Dan in L.A. The apartment floor has begun to warp and slope, the formica in the kitchen is cracked, the stairs outside have not been painted in years. The rent is now $372.45. It is a deal for which one might kill. I spent a month there and remembered how much I love it. The Con Edison bills come addressed to Graham. Letters arrive for Leann, who lives in Brooklyn. Phone calls in Spanish come for Jose. . . . Graham has become a successful actor. Dan wears his shirts.[9]

While such arrangements may be benign, they can also become highly duplicitous. Friends exploit friends, lovers exploit lovers. *The Daily News* recounts how "[o]ne young woman sharing a rent-controlled penthouse with a doctor was shocked when she mistakenly opened his rent statement and discovered she was paying not only the entire rent each month, but several hundred dollars more."[10] Another gentleman discretely enquired of *The New York Times*' real-estate page: "I rent a room in my stabilized apartment for $330 a month. My renter found out the whole apartment rents for $300. Can she sue?"[11]

George Wen, an editor at *New York* magazine, reports being awakened by his prime tenant at 9 A.M. one Saturday morning and being told he would have to leave his sublet apartment that afternoon. After living on the West Coast for several years, hanging on for the building to go co-op, the prime tenant suddenly found she was being sued for non-primary residence. Wen spent all day frantically phoning friends before finding a place to sleep that night.[12]

Nick Bogos, a 24-year-old lawyer who arrived from Florida in 1984, read an ad in *The Times* and visited a small real-estate agency, where he rented a one-bedroom, East-Side apartment for $1,000. Shortly afterwards, the owners announced the building would be sold as a co-op. Having seen hundreds of condominiums for sale in Florida, Bogos was unimpressed and did not consider buying.

Then people in the building began telling him that his rent seemed high and that he was probably being overcharged. Bogos went back to visit the rental agency. When he mentioned the overcharge, the manager—a man named Evan Seplow—became irritated and told him he would have to leave the apartment immediately. When Bogos refused, Seplow told him he might be visited by underworld enforcers.

"I had never even heard of rent control when I came to New York," said Bogos. "I thought rent stabilization had something to do with stabilizing neighborhoods. Now here I was sitting across from a guy who's telling me he's going to break my legs."

Bogos hired an attorney, who soon discovered that Seplow was one of Manhattan's most notorious "illusory landlords"—a tenant who accumulates regulated leases and rents the apartments at market prices. Seplow controlled dozens of apartments (he bragged to Bogos it was "hundreds") and had his name on New York's first illusory-landlord court case, *Vann vs. Seplow*. Business was so good that he had set up his own rental office.

By the time Bogos had sorted out the situation, Seplow had already bought the apartment. Next, Seplow went into state supreme court (the lowest branch) and got an eviction notice. But Bogos went to housing court and got a delay. The case dragged on for two years, during which time Bogos paid no rent. He was finally evicted in 1986.

"I got two years' free rent and a real education," said Bogos. "But it didn't do much good. Dealing with New York housing doesn't prepare you for anything, except maybe organized crime." He eventually moved back to Florida.

Illegally subletting apartments at market rents has become a whole underground industry in New York. "What New York has done is create a whole class of pseudo-landlords," said George Sternlieb. "The only responsibility they don't have is maintaining their buildings."

When Dustin Hoffman came to New York to shoot "Tootsie" in 1981, he rented a penthouse apartment on West 72nd Street for $7,000 a month. After only a few weeks, Hoffman discovered he wasn't getting enough heat and hot water. The prime tenant, one Paul Brine, told Hoffman he couldn't do anything about it—that was the landlord's problem. Hoffman did some investigating and found Brine was only paying $948.62 a month. He moved out and spent four years trying to collect damages.[13]

Even more enticing than the profits of capitalizing on rent differentials, however, is the bonanza that falls on long-term tenants when a building is converted to a co-op. This windfall is the bribe the owner must pay tenants for giving up their rental status, or, alternately, the profit tenants earn by remaining for years in their regulated apartments.

When a building is converted to co-operative ownership in Chicago, for example, nothing much happens. The selling price is already pro-rated against the rental price. The only decision is whether the tenant wants to rent or make a long-term investment. Buildings that have been marketed as condominiums are often switched to rentals if the market proves soft, then back to ownership if it firms up.

In rent-controlled cities, however, a landlord must offer his regulated tenants huge discounts in order to persuade them to give up their regulated status. These "insider" prices are usually 50 percent below market. The profit comes from selling the other, unoccupied apartments. This creates another incentive, not only to empty apartments of their tenants, but to keep them empty for long periods of time in preparation for a co-operative conversion. (This "warehousing" of apartments is yet another absurd consequence of rent control.)

If tenants can be persuaded to buy, they may choose to live in the apartment. Equally attractive, though, is to turn around and sell the apartment immediately at market price. This "flipping" of an apartment brings the tenant a huge windfall.

Michael deCourcy Hinds, of *The Times,* told of one professional couple living in the high-priced Lincoln Towers who bought their apartment for $178,000 in April 1987, and sold it in June for $400,000—a staggering $222,000 profit. They used the money to buy a $500,000 home in Westchester. Said another couple: "We made $40,000 selling something that was never ours; we were very lucky."

> This kind of profit involves no risk, little effort and even the taxes can be deferred if the money is properly channeled into the purchase of a primary residence. Tenants use their windfalls to start businesses, buy cars and country homes, move to the suburbs, or even abroad, and as a financial cushion for retirement.
>
> Real-estate professionals say the tenant profits probably ranged between $50 million and $100 million last year.[14]

In fact, the profits have become so staggering that even the government boards of co-ops and condominiums have secured a cut of the action. Since 1982, they have been allowed to impose a special "flip tax," whereby the other owners in the building share some of the windfall.

What is most remarkable is that, even with these enormous incentives, the majority of tenants still turn down the insider price and stay on as regulated renters. As Hinds explains:

> In many ways, rent-regulated tenants in New York already have many ownership rights since current law allows them to pass on their apartments within their

immediate family at regulated rents. . . . For this and other economic reasons, two-thirds of the tenants in conversion plans give up the potential for making enormous short-term cash gains to keep their protected status as rent-regulated tenants."[15]

Even those who do flip tend to see themselves as victims. After flipping their one-bedroom Greenwich Village apartment and buying a two-bedroom co-op, Larry Steinhorn and Gay Green, who own their own textile company, told Hinds:

"Yes, we made money on the flip, but we plunked it right down into this co-op and wound up spending more. If we had been able to get a two-bedroom rental in the building, we could have bought a weekend house instead of this co-op.

"These deals are great for people like us who don't need it or if you're moving to Ohio," Mr. Steinhorn said. "It's sort of like the rich get richer and the poor get nothing. For people who are not as fortunate as we are—older people on fixed income or younger people just starting out—it's not such a great deal when the building goes co-op. Tenants are buying something that they, in effect, already own—rent-stabilized apartments."[16]

Another bizarre way in which tenants sometimes cash in on their regulated status is when buildings are being demolished for new construction.

The refusal of property owners to sell small parcels to large developers has always been a thorn in the side of urban redevelopers. (Urban renewal was, in large part, designed to overcome this difficulty.) Several Manhattan skyscrapers have been built around three- and four-story brownstones whose owners refused to sell.

But owners are at least negotiating over something they own and can replace. Tenants are negotiating only their regulated status, which they know they can never replace. While some tenants deliberately play the game for large cash winnings, others refuse to move at any price. These hold-outs often become folk heroes.

At any one time, there are at least a dozen major projects being held up in New York while the developer negotiates with rent-regulated tenants. Developer Peter Kalikow, who owns *The New York Post,* has spent five years trying to relocate 1,200 regulated tenants from a square-block area near the Queensboro Bridge in order to build 1,600 high-rise units. Despite generous relocation arrangements, half the buildings sit empty while the last few tenants vie for higher and higher payoffs.

A few blocks away on East 60th Street, Jean Herman, a 55-year-old free-lance writer, has held up development of a 30-story office tower since 1985 by refusing to give up her $168-a-month rent-controlled apartment in which she has lived for 31 years. "Everyone in the neighborhood seems to be relishing Miss Herman's determination," reported *The New York Times* in an article that characterized her as an "urban pioneer."[17] Herman has turned down an offer of $500,000 to vacate.

In 1983, Paul Brine—the same man who sublet Dustin Hoffman his apartment—became the last holdout in a development on the corner of Third Avenue and East 53rd Street. Brine turned out to have leases on three rent-controlled apartments. The one on Third Avenue cost him $90.14 a month. The developer, Sterling Equities, obtained an eviction by showing it was not Brine's primary residence. But when Brine threatened a lengthy appeal, Sterling capitulated and paid him $1 million to leave. (Delays on such projects can cost a developer $200,000 a month.) Brine, who also claimed to be a writer, told *The New York Times* he had donated all the money to a Tibetan charity.[18]

Even Anthony Gliedman, former commissioner of HPD, admitted that such holdouts are becoming a major impediment to new housing in New York. "In Manhattan, it increases the cost of building, but in the other boroughs, the project is not going to happen," Gliedman told *The New York Times.* "We have empty and nearly empty buildings sitting on Ocean Avenue and Eastern Parkway [in Brooklyn] and I think this problem is definitely a piece of it."

But Peter Marcuse, the principal academic spokesman in New York for rent regulations, disagreed, saying that if regulatory complexities discourage new development, so much the better. "The right of tenants to stay put protects housing," said Marcuse.[19]

With the circulation of housing so completely clogged, everyone's strategy becomes to opt *out* of the market and into one's own sheltered arrangement.

Universities and hospitals, for example, are all buying and erecting their own buildings, desperately trying to provide housing for students and employees. In recent years, Cornell Medical Center, Memorial Sloane-Kettering Cancer Center, New York University, and Rockefeller University have all built housing complexes—often with special zoning variances due to their non-profit status.[20]

Still, housing remains the number-one problem in trying to recruit out-of-town employees. One study by the New School of Social Research estimated that between one-third and one-half of all out-of-town recruitments fail because of the problems in finding housing. In 1988, Richard L. Durbin, the executive director of Bellevue Hospital, recruited after a six-month, nationwide search, quit his job and returned to Texas after three weeks of living at the hospital, because he and his wife could not find satisfactory housing.

Both Columbia and New York University have long rankled neighborhoods by buying up property for faculty and student housing. Columbia, New York's third largest landlord (behind the City and the Catholic Church) owns 155 buildings containing 6,200 apartments.

The problem is that when an institution buys a building, it usually comes filled with regulated tenants. About one-quarter of Columbia's apartments are occupied by non-university tenants at regulated rents. Although Columbia charges its affiliated tenants break-even rents, its regulated tenants still pay much lower. Predictably, there is always a move afoot among graduate students and faculty to have their apartments put under rent regulation as well.

Another difficulty is getting students and faculty to leave once their salaries start to rise. David Shaeffer became briefly famous during the Columbia students' rebellion in 1968 when he was photographed with his feet propped up on President Grayson Kirk's desk while smoking one of his cigars. Shaeffer eventually became an instructor at Columbia. He got into faculty housing in 1973 and didn't leave until 1986, shortly after he turned 40.

In February 1987, 30 students and faculty members were arrested while demonstrating on behalf of Susana Jaafar, who was being evicted from Columbia housing. Jaafar had moved into the apartment in 1969 when it was occupied by her brother, a Columbia employee. The brother left in 1974, but Jaafar managed to stave off eviction for thirteen years. Several people were arrested during the unsuccessful protests.[21]

Presbyterian Hospital, in Upper Manhattan, has an almost medieval system of employee housing. The hospital owns about 1,000 apartments in the neighborhood. Half the apartments are still tied up with older controlled and stabilized tenants, but the other half are available to staff members. They are not offered on a rental basis. Instead, employees hold apartments as part of their job contract. Their "rent" is deducted directly from their wages. In this way, Presbyterian avoids problems with evicting tenants after they have left their jobs.

Such insulated arrangements are constantly being set up by other institutions as well. One of the favorite tactics is to set up a limited-equity cooperative, in which apartments are sold very cheaply but cannot be resold at market prices. Such ventures are usually given large property-tax abatements by the city government. Several unions have built such co-ops and others have been set up by neighborhood and volunteer organizations. Turnover is excruciatingly slow and units change hands almost entirely through affiliation and inside information.

One of the most famous of these limited co-ops is the Westbeth artists' complex in Lower Manhattan, which opened in 1970. The project received more than $2 million in seed money from the National Endowment for the Arts and the J. M. Kaplan Fund, plus a 75 percent property-tax abatement. Still, when costs climbed in the 1970s, tenants went on a rent strike and the building finally defaulted. HUD now holds the mortgage. An attempt to co-op the building and retire the $2.9 million in mortgage debt was blocked by activist tenants.[22]

For large institutions that don't want to get into the real-estate business, on the other hand, one of the few alternatives is to refer employees and affiliates to one of Manhattan's many thriving roommate agencies.

"When I started this business in 1979, I thought I would be dealing with college students," said Michael Santomauro, owner of Roommate Finders. "Most of my customers turn out to be young professionals between 25 and 35."

Santomauro has handled referrals from Citibank, ITT, Merrill Lynch, Goldman Sachs, Price Waterhouse, American Express, Texaco, and Exxon. Transferees to Manhattan can end up paying $600 to $700 to share an apartment or $400 to $500 to sleep on a stranger's living-room couch. "I see people with $30,000 incomes all the time," said Santomauro.

In April 1989, Linda Carrol's Roommates made headlines by placing Justin Martin, a $25,000-a-year public relations editor, in a "commuter share" with a New Jersey advertising artist. Pierre Pezzella owned a Manhattan co-op that he used as his studio. Under the arrangement, Martin paid $600, with the understanding that he would be gone from 9 to 5 each day when Pezzella came to work. "It's a fairly common arrangement," said Martin, who just arrived from Kansas City. "I know people who share apartments where they have to be gone on the weekends."[23]

Linda Carrol reported that 90 percent of the people offering to share their apartments are rent-stabilized tenants. "We don't ask how much they're paying," said Carrol. "All we know is it's legal. Obviously, some of our roommates are going to be paying more than half the rent—maybe even the whole thing. But we don't get involved in that."

Another set of entrepreneurs that has emerged is the people who will find you an apartment for a large fee, no questions asked.

"I found myself dealing in this whole underworld where people wouldn't even tell me their names." said one NYU graduate who spent two years looking for an apartment. "One person promised to get me into a Mitchell-Lama building for $5,000 up-front. I decided it was too creepy."

In her *New York* article, Jane Goldman told the story of a woman who was sitting in her living room, lamenting her son's inability to find an apartment, when a window-washer stuck in his head and promised to find him an apartment for $500. She anted up the money. Months later her son hadn't heard anything, but she still considered it a good investment.

Werner Magars, a retired hardware-store owner who owns one building on the Upper West Side, came to work one Monday morning and found two dozen people milling in the lobby. All claimed to have rented one of his apartments.

Two women tenants, it emerged, had gone on a week's vacation. During that time, a young man had advertised the apartment in a neighborhood newspaper and "rented" it to eight different people, collecting a $3,000 cash deposit from each—a cool $24,000. Then he disappeared. The two women claimed to have no idea how he got into the apartment.

Three days before Christmas in 1987, *The Daily News* told of the same scam in Brooklyn:

> A Brooklyn woman and her eight children may be homeless for the holidays because of a cruel housing scam in which another woman allegedly bilked nine families of at least $15,000 by "renting" them the same apartment. . . .
>
> Police said suspect Iris Sheffield, 36. . . took a $625 security deposit and a month's rent of $625 from most of the victims, giving them a phony signed lease in return. The money has not been recovered.[24]

Most of the people depicted here, of course, are basically middle class. But that is the problem. With middle-class people fighting so desperately over marginal housing, nothing ever circulates down to the poor. Low-income people, with their lack of network connections, cash deposits, or key money, don't even stand a chance. As one resident of a Harlem homeless shelter put it: "Paying rent for me is no problem. My big problem is finding an apartment in the first place."

Does any rationality ever penetrate this mass insanity? Occasionally, it does. In 1985, a woman named Karen Wilson wrote the following letter to *The New York Daily News*:

> I recently moved to New York and I pay almost $1,000 a month for a nice little apartment on the lower East Side. The landlords have been reasonable, and the building is clean. Still, when I found out at a tenants' meeting that 30 of the building's 34 apartments rent for below $200 and that most of the tenants in those cheap apartments make more money than I do, I was a bit outraged. I understand protecting the old people, but protecting fellow yuppies with bargains?
>
> In Texas, $300 will pay rent on a two-bedroom apartment with air conditioning, washer/dryer, swimming pool, fireplace and garage. The vacancy rate is over 30 percent [actually nearer 20 percent]. There are no rent controls, and the tenants hold all the cards. And landlords are not a hated breed. If New Yorkers are so smart, why can't they see that what exists now is more than unfair? It's stupid.[25]

Within a week, several reader responses were printed. All of them said the same thing: "Why don't you go back to Texas!"

Chapter 21

The Destruction of the Landlord Class

Perhaps the best way to illustrate the popular conception of landlords in New York City is to report a rumor that circulates—and is widely believed—among tenant activists and politicians. The rumor is that the small property owners who regularly show up at hearings of the Rent Stabilization Board or legislative hearings to argue the case against rent control are actually actors hired to impersonate aggrieved landlords.

This rumor has such broad credence that it is often introduced into the political debate. When state senator Franz Leichter was asked about the problems of small landlords on the "Morton Downey, Jr., Show," he replied, "Those are actors. They aren't landlords."[1]

Even John Gilbert, head of the Rent Stabilization Association, the landlords' principal lobbying group, says he suffered a bad scare his first week on the job when he noticed the Association was making monthly payments to Actors' Equity.

> My blood froze in my veins. Had RSA really been hiring actors and actresses [to impersonate landlords]?

"What are these payments to Actors' Equity?" I asked the Comptroller.

"They are our monthly rent payments," he said. "We sublet our offices from Actors' Equity."[2]

Anyone attending these hearings, however, would be tempted to the same conclusion. New York City landlords are simply one of the most frayed, unsophisticated groups of people that can be assembled in this country. They speak dozens of different languages and hail from all parts of the world. There are so many different nationalities that I have often been left with the impression that there are signs posted on trees all over the Third World reading, "Make big money as New York City landlord! Buy this building!"

These impressions were dramatically confirmed in a 1985 study by Arthur D. Little, Inc. In a random survey of 1,252 buildings (producing 730 responses) the study once again turned up the familiar pattern of widely decentralized ownership, with the field dominated by immigrants and people from the lower-middle-class.

> Fully sixty percent of New York City's building owners own only one building. Forty-four percent of owners owned a total of 10 apartments or less, and 77.8 percent of owners owned 40 units or less. Less than 10 percent of owners owned 100 units or more.[3]

Incredibly, *53.5 percent of the landlords were born outside the United States.* Over one-quarter (26.2 percent) were born in Southern and Eastern Europe. Another 5.6 percent were from English-speaking Caribbean countries and 10.6 percent from Latin America and Puerto Rico. Moreover, the pattern of immigrant ownership is on the rise. Among landlords who had bought in the previous five years, 61.6 percent were born outside the United States.[4]

Once again, rental housing is clearly a field dominated by small operators who frequently enter the profession to provide themselves and their families with housing. Thirty-seven percent lived in their own buildings, while 71 percent lived in the same borough. Only 16 percent lived outside New York City.

> This pattern of relatively small property owners is confirmed when we look at the income sources of building owners. Fully 61 percent of all building owners are making only one-quarter of their income or less from the rental buildings which they own. Only 5.1 percent said that they receive all their income from ownership of rental housing.[5]

The majority of owners (54 percent) had incomes between $10,000 and $40,000. Thirty percent had incomes of less than $20,000 and 9 percent had incomes of less than $10,000. Thirteen percent had incomes of over $75,000.

Concluded the study: "While many building owners are clearly part-time landlords (largely because of their interest in living in their building), they are not wealthy as a group."[6]

I hadn't been working on New York housing very long when I found all this out first-hand. I was writing for *Manhattan, Inc.*, a glitzy publication that was seeking to become the *People* magazine of New York's financial establishment. For their inaugural issue they wanted a story on rent control. I arranged a meeting in their offices with a group of representatives from New York's various landlord organizations.

I walked into the meeting expecting to encounter a few Donald Trumps and Sam Lefraks. Instead, I knew immediately that the whole story was a disaster. They were, quite simply, the most forlorn group of middle-aged people I had encountered in a long, long time. I couldn't believe it. These were some of New York City's dreaded landlords? The idea of putting any of these people into the pages of *Manhattan, Inc.* was utterly ridiculous.

Most of them were so nervous that they could not bear to be interviewed. Instead, "with trembling hands," they preferred to read lengthy statements scrawled or typed on dog-eared pieces of paper.

One woman—a professional in her mid-30s—seemed a bit more at ease than the others. I decided to leave her for last. As we went around the room, she became progressively more anxious. When it finally came her turn to tell her story, someone interrupted and I was distracted for a moment. When I turned back, she had completely broken down. She put her head on a table and sobbed for several minutes. In ten years of newspaper work, I had interviewed many people in very difficult situations—parents whose children had just died, wives who had lost their husbands, people whose homes had just burned down. Yet I had never had anyone so completely fall apart in an interview. (When I finally heard her story, I realized she had good reason to cry—she was being sued by her low-paying tenants for tens of thousands in back rent because of procedural oversights by the previous landlord.)

So it went, through months of meeting New York landlords. Several people urged me to attend meetings of the American Property Rights Association, a landlords' group in Brooklyn. ("You'll think you're in the Third World," they said.) The group is run by Lee Sterling, a huge, overweight, publicity hound (kind of a third-rate Howard Jarvis) who is regularly dragged from meetings shouting things like: "It's worse than Watergate!"

Before his small assembly of landlords in the basement of a Brooklyn YMCA, however, Sterling was much more intelligent and benign. "The city will be around asking you to rent to welfare tenants, but we recommend against it," he began.

"You'll find they stop paying rent after three months and you'll never get rid of them."

The group was a remarkable congregation of Second and Third World peoples. There were Haitians, Egyptians, Malaysians—nationalities I had never met or heard in all my years in New York. Halfway through the meeting, an emaciated, elderly woman with a thick Eastern European accent stood up and started talking almost incoherently. She sounded crazy. Surprisingly, Sterling made no attempt to stop her, but sat down and gave her the floor. I looked around, expecting to see yawns of exasperation, yet everyone was respectful and listened politely. Whatever it was she was saying (and I'm sure they understood no better than I), it seemed to express their frustrations exactly.

What all these people had in common, I finally realized, is that they had come to landlording with an overwhelming faith in free enterprise. For all of them, buying a building had been the fulfillment of the American dream. Some had emigrated from cotton fields in Alabama. Others had fled oppressive regimes in backward or totalitarian countries. Most had arrived in New York kissing the earth and proclaiming, "At last, we're in a free country." They had worked hard and put their life's savings into the first building they could afford. Six months later, they found themselves staring in open-eyed wonder, saying, "Wait a minute! This is the same system we just escaped from!"

There are very few "big landlords" in New York, at least in the residential sector. Commercial real estate is indeed highly concentrated. About 50 percent of the market is controlled by only a dozen major firms and five of *Forbes* magazines' ten richest Americans are New York City *commercial* landlords.

The overwhelming number of residential landlords are carpenters and immigrants—meaning, generically, people who enter housing either through the building trades, to provide themselves with a home, or as a retirement investment. Even those who end up big usually started small. Sheldon Solow, the owner of several luxury buildings and estimated to be worth $435 million by *Forbes,* started as a general contractor. His father was a mason who emigrated from Russia. Donald Trump's father, who built the empire, was the son of a Swedish immigrant who started his own contracting business by building a neighbor's garage at age 16.

This lack of an aristocratic landlord class is confirmed by the frustrations of tenant activists, who constantly find themselves dealing with the people they call "those crazies."

The New York State Tenants and Neighborhood Coalition argues in a broadside:

> The fact is that the landlords who own the vast majority of apartments are . . . names like Trump, Sulzberger, Lefrak, Kalikow, DeMatteis, Durst—well-known as

> the city's largest landlords with untold billions of dollars in holdings. These landlords never come out to claim losses for the simple reason that they are making large profits. Instead, they trot out alleged small landlords as a smokescreen for their financial position.[7]

"The real-estate industry is diabolically clever in using small landlords," says Michael McKee, director of the Coalition.

At a 1986 Rent Guidelines Board hearing, I interviewed a nattily dressed young man in his late 20s who had just spoken on behalf of some tenant organization. Only a few moments before, a woman had been dragged semi-hysterical from the microphone, screaming, "My parents walked away from a building in Warsaw in 1945 because the Communists were taking over and now the same thing is happening here!"

What did he think of the debate? I asked the young man, who turned out to be a law student.

"The trouble is the big guys never show up," he said, echoing a constant complaint of tenant activists. "All you see are these people who are scruffing out a petty bourgeois existence. Half of them are refugees from the 'captive nations.' "

What should be done with such people? I asked in a way that probably didn't hide my annoyance.

"Well, I suppose they have a perfect right to scrap out a living from buying a building," he said. "It's just that they inject such an element of global politics into New York housing."

Such are the people who provide New Yorkers with housing. Here are a few of their stories.

Paul Goedig grew up in a four-story brownstone owned by his parents, right across the street from Mt. Morris Park in central Harlem. The family lived in the basement while renting out the top three floors. Goedig grew up and married, moved to California and became a hospital technician. His father died in 1981 but his mother continued to run the building.

Then his mother's health began to fail and she asked a man from the neighborhood to manage the building for her. The man turned out to be a crook. He stole the rent money and filled the building with friends, some of whom were drug dealers. In 1984, a serious operation left Goedig's mother unable to walk. She went into a nursing home.

In early 1985, Goedig came back to deal with the situation—a job he thought would take about a month. The thieving manager had fled, but the building was infested with drug dealers. Given free rein, the tenants had ravaged the upper floors, ripping out plumbing fixtures, selling off the furniture. The building was a shambles.

In fact, the whole neighborhood was rapidly deteriorating from a combination of drug dealing and landlord-tenant disputes. All up and down West 120th Street, beautiful brownstone buildings, once owned by striving middle-class families like Goedig's, stand with their windows boarded up by sheetmetal and cinder blocks, the ominous message, "Property of the City of New York, Managed by the Department of Housing Preservation and Development" stenciled everywhere.

Goedig tried to evict the tenants. They appealed to HPD, which started representing them. When the case came to housing court, the tenants said they weren't getting any services. They were right, of course—the plumbing and heating systems had long since been plundered. The court sided with the tenants. Goedig would have to restore services before taking action for non-payment of rent.

By this time, Goedig had spent several months sleeping on a friend's couch. It was obvious he wouldn't be going back to California for a while. He borrowed $3,000 to have the plumbing reinstalled. The tenants ripped it out again. He installed it again and started sleeping in the kitchen to protect the pipes. The tenants waited until he left during the day, then stole them once again.

Goedig changed tactics. He shut down the heat, turned off the electricity, and tried to starve the tenants out of the building. The tenants retaliated by building cooking fires and stealing electricity from neighboring buildings. Every time Goedig went back to housing court, HPD and the court ruled he still wasn't providing adequate services.

I met Goedig one frozen February morning in 1987. He showed me through the building—including a glimpse of one of his tenants through a chain-locked door. The inside was a shambles, although traces of its former elegance shone through. Crack vials littered the upper bedrooms. For the third time, Goedig confiscated fifty feet of heavy-duty wire that the tenants were using to steal electricity from a neighboring basement.

Goedig took me downstairs, into his family's old apartment. The tenants had broken through the lock and were using the bathroom to store sinks stolen from a nearby construction project. Goedig's mother's old wheelchair stood in the center of the living room. Sifting through the debris in one bedroom, I found a picture of Goedig when he was eight years old. He betrayed little emotion but took it with him.

Sitting in a neighborhood bar an hour later, I asked Goedig why he persisted. He had been fired from his job, lost touch with his career, and—although not much was said—seemed to have watched his marriage go down the drain as well.

"Everything my mother and father spent their lives working for is wrapped up in that building," he said. "As it stands now, that building isn't worth $50,000. Fixed up it could be worth a quarter-million. I could fill it with good tenants in five minutes—people who would pay the rent on time and never give me any trouble.

"But the city government doesn't want that. They say they want to save housing, but first they want to destroy small owners so they can take all the buildings for themselves. Everything my tenants know about dodging rent they learned from the Department of Housing Preservation and Development. They actually train tenants to destroy their landlords down there."

It was a miserably cold day. Trying to find a more cheerful subject, I asked him how he liked California.

"Beautiful," he said. "It's relaxing. The sun shines all the time."

"It must seem like coming back to the Old World to be back here."

He gave a wry little smile. "Brave new world," he said.

Brian Jevmerov left Yugoslavia when he was fourteen. His parents helped him escape because they wanted him to have a career. He has not seen them since.

Trained as a carpenter, Jevmerov did an apprenticeship for ten years, then founded his own business doing customized woodwork interiors. He built a reputation and soon had his own shop with a dozen employees. He rented commercial space for a while, then decided to buy his own building.

In 1983, at the age of 28, Jevmerov purchased an old, five-story industrial structure in Lower Manhattan. The building is part of the "loft district," an old industrial sector that once housed hundreds of small factories, including the nation's first electrical industry.

The industries had long since departed, but for decades the city government refused to rezone the area, in order to keep up the pretense that they might some day return. Eventually, whole blocks of buildings, characterized by their distinctive cast-iron facades, stood vacant. In the 1960s, desperate landlords started illegally renting whole floors to artists at bargain rates. The artists made of them what they could, often spending their own money to transform them into working residences. Out of this transformation grew the Soho art district.

In the early 1970s, the city government finally decided to acknowledge these developments. It rezoned the area for residences. All this left tenants and landlords in a delicate situation. Tenants had often spent thousands of dollars remodeling their lofts. But with residences now legal, landlords could start charging market rents. On the other hand, most of the artists' studios still did not meet building-code standards. Rather than let the parties work things out themselves, the city government set up the Loft Board, a new regulatory agency that has provided yet another form of rent control to loft tenants.

Jevmerov had two such artist-tenants in his building. One was a fairly successful painter and his wife, who rented the entire third floor for $450 a month. Above him was an artist from New Zealand who had the same arrangement. Neither had a lease but both claimed to have a verbal agreement from the previous landlord to keep the rent at $450 in perpetuity.

Jevmerov set up his workshop on the first floor, built an apartment for himself on the second floor, and used the fifth floor for a warehouse. Carrying a $3,000 monthly mortgage, however, he asked his tenants to pay $1,000 a month rent. The third-floor artist immediately went to the Loft Board for protection.

The Loft Board officially set the rent at $450 and put the apartment under rent stabilization. It also told Jevmerov he would have to bring the building into compliance with the residential building code. Jevmerov was forced to borrow $150,000 to install plumbing, wiring, and central heating for the entire building.

Jevmerov soon realized that his fourth-floor tenant wasn't using his apartment at all. He was living in New Zealand, apparently maintaining the New York address to avoid New Zealand's high income taxes. Jevmerov went to housing court for an eviction. Predictably, the tenant flew in from New Zealand to fend off eviction. He claimed to be living temporarily with his parents while studying art. The housing-court judge let him keep the apartment.

Jevmerov's business was going well—he had 30 employees—but now the third-floor tenants began to complain about having a woodworking operation in the building. They said it created too much dust. The couple complained to the EPA. Jevmerov was required to spend another $200,000 to comply with dust-control regulations. He borrowed more money and made more renovations. The artist couple still wasn't satisfied and the EPA eventually forced Jevmerov to pay $15,000 in fines.

In 1985, two years after he had bought the building, Jevmerov went into chapter 11. "The building was sucking me dry," he said. He was forced to lay off most of his employees.

Jevmerov offered the third-floor couple $25,000 to vacate. They demanded $100,000. In 1986, Jevmerov lined up a buyer for the building who agreed to pay the couple $100,000. The couple raised their demand to $150,000. The buyer backed out. No one else would buy the building because of the problem with the tenants. In 1988, Jevmerov went into liquidation and lost everything.

"I worked eighteen years to make something for myself and now I have nothing," said Jevmerov. "These people cry poverty but they make much more money than I do. They think the world owes them a living because they're artists. Well, I'm an artist too. The difference is I also work for a living."

Audrey Brumskine emigrated with her family from Liberia in 1978. She and her sister both bought buildings on the same street in the Brownsville section of Brooklyn. They all moved into an apartment in her sister's building, then tried to evict one tenant in her own building so she could take an apartment for herself.

Four of the tenants were rent-stabilized, paying between $220 and $300 a month. The other two were rent-controlled, one paying $112.15, the other $96.20 for four-and-a-half rooms. Brumskine made a common mistake of trying to evict the tenant with the cheapest rent. The tenant stopped paying rent, claimed code violations, and soon had the building on a rent strike. The housing-court judge told her she could not collect rent until the violations were corrected. When she tried to make repairs, the tenants wouldn't let her in their apartments. One tenant threatened to burn down the building if she tried to collect rent. Meeting her operating costs absorbed her entire nurse's-aide salary.

Five years after buying the building, Brumskine had still not been able to move into one of her apartments. "I don't understand," she said. "My mother owned a building in Liberia and it was nothing like this. She maintained the building, collected rents, and everyone got along fine. Here the tenants tear down the apartment right in front of your eyes and there's nothing you can do about it."

Claudette Rubin is a tough woman—a Chinese immigrant, about 50, with jet-black hair and a guttural voice. Members of her family once operated a hotel in Szechwan Province. The building was confiscated during the Cultural Revolution and half her family was murdered. Rubin had escaped with her parents in 1959 and settled in the United States, where she studied architecture and married an American.

Later divorced, Rubin ran her own contracting business, rehabilitating old housing in New Jersey. After a decade, she decided to try New York. "I admit I was bored in New Jersey," she said. "There are so many beautiful old buildings in New York. It was a challenge."

She started with an old loft building on the Lower East Side. Rubin took the bottom floor and had tenants on the top three. It was another illegal arrangement, with each tenant providing his own heat. For one 2,000-square-foot floor, Rubin collected $500.

In 1985, one of Rubin's tenants moved elsewhere and quit paying rent—but didn't want to give up the loft. When Rubin went for an eviction, the tenant told the housing court that he hadn't been getting any heat. Rubin said the tenant had agreed to provide his own heat. The tenant admitted this was true—he had operated his own kerosene heater. The judge asked the tenant what time he usually turned it on. The tenant said around 8 A.M. The judge told Rubin the law demanded the heat be turned on at 6 A.M. Since the tenant had not turned on his own heater until 8 A.M., she was in violation of the housing law. The tenant was forgiven $5,000 back rent and got to keep the apartment. Rubin sold the building.

She bought another one in Harlem. The building had 20 virtually identical apartments, renting anywhere from $76 to $450 a month. It also had 402 housing-code violations. Borrowing $100,000, Rubin installed new sewer connections, heating, plumbing, and sidewalks, and whittled the violations down to 189.

Her main problem was a tenant who lived on the second floor, directly above her office. The man was a drug addict, on welfare, and never paid rent. He lived with two large dogs. When Rubin asked for the rent, he slashed her tires. When she went to court, he threatened to kill her.

Finally, after two years in housing court, Rubin succeeded in getting an eviction. The day after the court notice came through, the tenant firebombed her office, nearly burning down the building.

Rubin filed a complaint in criminal court for attempted murder. The criminal court judge looked at the case and said, "This isn't really a criminal case, it's a housing case." He sent it back to housing court.

The housing court judge reviewed the case and decided to overturn the eviction. The tenant got to keep the apartment. The firebombing charges were eventually dropped. He is still in the building.

In 1987, Rubin said she was considering going back to China. "The government has offered me the chance to take back my family's old hotel," she said. "I may do it.

"In China, when they want to take your property, they just kill you and get it over with," she said. "Here they torture you first. I think I prefer it the old way."

Maurice Mann is one of the few landlords I met in New York who seemed successful. The owner of a thriving hair-transplant business, Mann had used his profits to buy seven buildings on Central Park West, Central Park North, and in East Harlem.

Mann's tenants are mostly black and Hispanic, many of them thoroughly middle class. "I have about 125 units in all, with 50 rent controlled. Almost every rent-controlled apartment overlooks the park. The tenants are all very nice, leisurely people. They've been there forever and they know they're not going anywhere. Their only real concern is passing their apartments on to their grandchildren.

"I have one elderly black woman in the building on Central Park North who pays $300 for nine rooms. She has four boarders, each with a padlock on her own door. She charges them all $50 a week and makes $500 a month on my apartment. I don't care that she takes in boarders but it's insulting to have someone else making more money on your apartment than you do."

The key to his success, Mann said, has been to admit right away he can't make money on the *operation* of his buildings. "The whole rent control system—the whole city—is working against you. But if you can afford to stay in the game at a loss for a few years, you can make money in three ways—by selling, by co-oping, or by refinancing. If you have the staying power, it can be done."

On one of his buildings in Spanish Harlem, for example, Mann paid $325,000, using a $50,000 down payment and a $275,000 private mortgage with the previous owner. The rent roll was about $211,000 a year with only $145,000 of it collectable.

"We immediately started pouring money into the building," said Mann. "We've found that above all that tenants want two things from their buildings—safety and cleanliness. We started by installing a very expensive, high-security lock system on the building. We also made the place immaculate. We add a little cosmetic schmaltz to spruce the place up and make it look nice. Then we start trying to collect rent."

After establishing good relations with the tenants, Mann began to cull the rent roll, evicting people who wouldn't pay. "We were very patient in housing court," he said. "Basically, the judges will do everything they can to avoid evicting someone. But we get the tenants into a position where they will consider a payoff to move. Usually they'll settle for about $5,000. In four years, we got the rent roll up from $211,000 to $450,000—with 99 percent of it collectable."

This was still barely enough to make the building break even. But it enabled Mann to use the building as collateral to borrow money and start the same thing with another building. "I just finished refinancing that building with Freddie Mac [the Federal Home Loan Mortgage Corporation] for $1.5 million," said Mann. "The building itself has been assessed at $2.4 million. We've turned it around. But I had to take out a $150,000 mortgage on my Easthampton home to do it."

Mann had one extremely difficult "professional tenant" whom he has tried to evict for five years. "The guy knew all the angles," he said. "I never once collected a rent check from him without taking him to court. He played the violations game to the hilt. He'd take down a smoke alarm, break a doorknob or a window latch, and then call the housing inspectors. Then we would go to court. The judge would order us to fix the violations. When we'd send people around, he wouldn't let them in. Then it's back to court to start all over again." Throughout the proceedings, the tenant—who made $25,000 a year—was represented by the Legal Services Corporation, the Federal program that provides legal services to the poor. (In fact, 75 percent of the Legal Services' work in New York involves representing tenants against landlords.)

"Basically, the housing court judges don't believe in private ownership," said Mann. "They rule against landlords whatever the circumstances. In my case the judge finally told my tenant that he wouldn't have to pay rent until the violations were corrected to *his* satisfaction. Naturally, I never collected any rent."

Mann finally solved the problem by making videotapes of his workmen doing repairs. "After we're done, we hold up a copy of today's newspaper to show when it was finished. Then we bring the tapes and play them in court."

Mann did not feel that his efforts could be easily duplicated. "I've had some success, but only because I've worked excruciatingly hard and because I have access to other funds that I can keep pouring into my buildings. All the profits from my surgical implant business go into my properties. It's very easy for me to see how any landlord can be destroyed by New York City. Basically you're up against a system that doesn't believe in private property.

"I drive around and see all these empty shells and I say to myself, 'Everybody says the owner "walked away" from that building. But I know different. Every one of those buildings was torn from some owner's bleeding hands.' "

When Otto Teitler was 15 years old in Austria in 1942, he saw his parents taken away to a concentration camp. They never came back. Friends helped him escape through Yugoslavia and he eventually joined the British Navy. Coming to America in 1952, he was adopted by the Children's Fund of Hadassah and eventually graduated from Harvard Business School. As an international economist, he travels the world, often spending two or three years in a developing country.

In 1968, he invested his life's savings in a six-story building just down the street from Gracie Mansion, the mayor's official residence. The building contained 11 apartments. Teitler borrowed $350,000 and did a "gut rehab," completely rehabilitating the interior. He also installed an elevator. On the top floor he created a 2000-square-foot apartment, adding a small penthouse on the roof. He planned to occupy it himself.

When the renovation was complete in 1976, Teitler was scheduled to spend two years in India. On a reference from a friend, he rented the top-floor apartment to a successful lawyer and his artist wife who were having their co-op renovated. The couple only wanted the apartment for six months. He even added a clause that would allow them to leave before the end of their one-year lease. The rent was $900.

During the six months, however, the couple divorced. The husband got the co-op. When Teitler returned from India he found the artist still occupying the apartment. She refused to leave.

Teitler went to housing court to have her evicted. The tenant responded by citing building-code violations. She organized the other tenants into a rent strike.

The striking tenants presented the usual laundry-list of complaints. They said the building should have a live-in superintendent (the super lived down the block). They claimed the building had roaches and the halls were dirty.

In addition, the top-floor tenant claimed she wasn't getting any heat in the small penthouse. The room had a single steam radiator, which didn't seem to work properly. Over the course of several years Teitler hired half-a-dozen heating experts to deal with the problem, but none were able to figure out why the radiator wouldn't work. It eventually became obvious that the tenant herself was sabotaging it in some way.

After three years of deliberations, Housing Court Justice Ralph Waldo Sparks decided the rent strike was legitimate. The tenants could withhold rent. Teitler appealed into Civil Court, where—as often happens—the housing court decision was reversed. The tenants were ordered to pay $350,000 in back rent.

One first-floor tenant—a wealthy lawyer—moved to Connecticut owing Teitler $42,000. Another tenant decamped to her second home on Long Island, although she kept up a long series of appeals. The top-floor tenant resumed paying rent, but fought the back payments on the grounds that the penthouse still wasn't getting any heat.

On a windy afternoon in March 1987, I visited Teitler's building. There was a certain tension to the encounter. Besides being broken financially, Teitler has suffered three nervous breakdowns over the ordeal. The first time he tried to tell me his story over the phone he became so emotional that we had to stop after about five minutes.

The building was a beautiful structure, immaculate outside and in. Almost all the apartments were empty, since Teitler refused to take any more tenants. In the front part of the building were a pair of tiny duplex apartments that Teitler occasionally rented to foreign medical students for $1,200 on a month-to-month basis. (The top-floor artist had immediately claimed she was being harassed because Teitler was filling the building with "people who don't speak English.")

As we started upstairs a delivery boy arrived. He was bringing lunch to the penthouse tenant from a neighborhood deli. During the two hours I spent in the building, two more deliveries arrived. "She never leaves the apartment," Teitler told me.

On the third floor Teitler showed me a vacant, six-room apartment that ran the entire length of the building. It had been occupied by an aspiring young playwright whose family owned a plumbing factory in Cleveland. The tenant had joined the rent strike, then left owing $40,000.

On the second floor was Teitler's sole paying tenant, a young businessman and his family who had recently moved from Ohio. Like all newcomers to New York, they were paying an eye-popping rent—$2,400 a month for a six-room apartment. The tenant's family was visiting from Ohio and we all collided in the hall.

After some friendly banter, I pulled the tenant aside and asked him how he felt about his high rent. "Everything else we saw was the same price," he said genially. I asked him about the woman in the penthouse. He rolled his eyes. "She's kind of a pain in the neck," he said. "She leaves her garbage out in the hall and it stinks the place up something terrible."

Teitler later told me that the woman regularly dumped her garbage in the hallway, insisting the superintendent carry it down for her. When one bag sat outside for three days, she filed for a rent reduction. He also noted she had just bought a new Mercedes.

Later we strolled around Gracie Mansion Park, gazing at the East River and trying to catch a glimpse of Mayor Koch.

"You know this may sound like a horrible thing to say, but this whole experience has really affected me worse than losing my parents in the concentration camps," he said. "That only ruined my childhood. This has ruined my adult life."

"I've seen totalitarian governments all over the world and know about injustices," he said. "But I never expected to encounter something like this in America. When the Nazis invaded Vienna in 1939, we at least had a sense of injustice. We knew we were right and they were wrong. But being a landlord in New York, you're not even allowed a sense of injustice. Everywhere you go you are surrounded by people who hate you and tell you that it's your own fault."

Eric Blair is a former city-employed laborer who lost his sight to glaucoma at age 50. Forced into early retirement, he moved in with some cousins in Bedford-Stuyvesant. Then someone said there was a building for sale in the neighborhood. Blair, who has a good head for figures and a remarkable memory, decided he could do the job. He got a bank loan and purchased the 10-unit structure. His tenants—

all rent stabilized—paid $150 to $200 for four-room apartments. Blair got a vacancy and moved into a first-floor apartment himself.

Over the first three years he put $25,000 of borrowed money into the building—"not counting my own labor." He put in a new boiler, hot water heaters, and painted the fire escapes himself. When he got another vacancy a year later, he was approached by a pregnant young woman in the neighborhood about to go on welfare. Feeling sorry for her, he gave her an apartment for $225. A short time later, she asked if he could find an apartment for her sister, and then brought in another friend as well. All three were on welfare. Blair rented them apartments.

After a year, the first tenant started working her way off welfare. She went to secretarial school and then landed a job with the Legal Services Corporation.

"She came home after the first week and announced she wasn't paying any more rent," said Blair. "She said the whole building needed repairs and I wasn't entitled to collect anything." The three welfare mothers called the building inspectors and Blair was written up for a series of violations. Windows needed caulking, a latch didn't work, some tiles had peeled in the bathroom.

Blair tried to make the repairs, but the women wouldn't give him access to their apartments. "I started by giving them 24-hour notice, then I sent certified letters. They didn't have telephones, so I eventually had to spend hundreds of dollars in mailgrams. Still, they would never be there when the repairmen arrived." The women also filed a complaint with the state Department of Housing Conservation and Renewal (DHCR) claiming they were being overcharged in rent. Blair had to put down a $1,000 retainer with an attorney. He also filed to evict the tenants on the grounds of non-payment of rent.

In May 1986, I went to Brooklyn Housing Court for one of many appearances by Blair and his tenants. Blair was seated at the front of the bar wearing dark glasses. With him was an attractive young woman he introduced as his cousin, Theresa Hutchins. Blair's attorney was an older man with disheveled gray hair and a rumpled suit. The three welfare mothers sat at the opposite table, all nicely dressed. They were represented by a Legal Services attorney—a young woman in a business suit who was a head taller than Blair's attorney. The judge was Robert Jackson, a young black man with wire-rimmed glasses who looked about 22 years old.

The case was called and Blair's attorney presented the papers on the building. The Legal Services attorney took one look and said, "Your honor, I move for dismissal on the grounds that this is not Mr. Blair's signature. I've seen his signature many times and this is not his handwriting." Judge Jackson sat considering the authenticity of a blind man's signature. Nobody batted an eye. He finally said something inaudible that apparently decided the case in Blair's favor.

Without a moment's hesitation, the Legal Services rattled on, "Your honor, I move for dismissal on the grounds that registration on this building has not been renewed as of April 1, 1986. The building is out of compliance and no rent is due."

Blair's attorney was stunned. He made a few weak arguments and a long conference ensued. Judge Jackson stared into space, obviously trying to simulate contemplation, then again said something inaudible. Both attorneys packed their briefcases. The case was over.

"Apparently they forgot to send us the building registration form this year," Blair explained in the back of the courtroom. "Now we have to go back and start over again."

Next to us, the three tenants awaited the Legal Services attorney. She strode back, made a jaunty gesture of clapping dust off her hands, and said, "Let's go to lunch." The group dissolved in laughter.

Blair's attorney had already disappeared. Ten minutes later, when we found him in the hall, I asked him what happened. "They're supposed to re-register the building every three years," he shrugged. "They just didn't do it. It's a procedural matter but it'll cost us two months." His manner clearly suggested client ineptitude.

"Well, what should they do now?"

"Go up and register it. We'll probably get another trial date by July." Then he disappeared again.

The rest of the afternoon was spent shuttling through the city clerk's offices, right above the courthouse. It turned out that the buildings department usually sends out re-registration forms in March, but this year they were already six weeks late. (It also became clear that the Legal Services attorney had probably known this.) When Blair asked to register, the clerks told him to go home and wait for the card in the mail.

"But I just lost a case in court because the building isn't re-registered," said Blair.

"Well, then, you should have come in and registered it," said the clerk.

"But how were we supposed to know?"

She shrugged. "That's your responsibility, not ours."

She then allowed him to register. The process consisted of listing the owner's name, address, and insurance carrier. Theresa Hutchins filled out the forms.

Then a thought struck me. "You know, the next time they come into court, the judge is probably going to rule that the building was out of compliance because it wasn't registered for two months and he can't collect back rent. Could you just give us a note saying the city is late in sending out the forms?"

The clerk looked at me in horror.

"We can't give you anything."

"But you just told us this."

"If you want anything in writing, you'll have to see the supervisor's office."

The next two hours were spent roaming the building, trying to find someone willing to put in writing what everyone would admit—that the city was six weeks late in sending out the forms. One administrator wouldn't even tell us his name. Finally, we ended up in the office of the director of housing inspections. He told Blair the problem was his own fault. "The city only sends out the forms as a courtesy. It's the owner's responsibility to register the building." He suggested we go to the printing offices in the Bronx where the forms were being printed if we wanted anything in writing.

Finally, we ended up back in the registration clerk's office in a fruitless search for another supervisor. As we stood there another owner came in asking to register his building. The clerk sent him home, telling him to wait for the form in the mail.

Fred Schuman was the last person to speak at the Rent Guidelines Board Hearings of May 22, 1986. By the time he stood at the microphone at 10 P.M., there were few people left in the audience.

"I'm a landlord in the Bronx," he began. "I used to be the superintendent of the building. I run a candy store on the first floor and live in the back. I bought it when the former owner got sick and gave up on it.

"My tenants have been on a rent strike for two years. They never paid much rent before that, but now they don't pay anything. There's nothing I can do about it. Whenever I fix something, they wreck it the next day. They know that if they destroy something, it just means they don't have to pay rent."

After the meeting, I caught him outside and rode uptown with him on the subway. He was a gaunt, angular man, about 50, with one eye. He wore tattered sneakers. Had I seen him on the subway, I would have thought he was homeless.

"I started out in this business wanting to help my fellow man," he said as we swayed back and forth with the car. "I was going to fix a place up, provide decent housing. But my tenants think anything they do against me is justified. There's a hatred for landlords out there—it's just unbelievable."

When I finally got off at 42nd Street, I passed a store displaying a set of fashionable sweatshirts sold everywhere in Manhattan. The message on one of them caught my eye. It said: "Live cheap. Marry your shrink and screw your landlord."

* * *

As the years went by, I tried to keep up with several landlords to see how their cases were doing. Eventually, I found it wasn't easy. When I called Howard Jevmerov a year later, his phone had been disconnected. The number where I usually reached Paul Goedig rang for days with no one answering. When I tried to contact Mary Peterson, the woman who called down the tenant about her "Jew landlord," her phone had also been disconnected.

All had disappeared into the black hole that New York City reserves for people who provide housing.

Chapter 22

The Government Takes Over

Once a municipal government has stifled private enterprise in housing, the other shoe drops. The government must now become the "supplier of last resort." The private sector can no longer provide housing, so the government must. The process can be observed in England, where rent controls were first imposed during World War I. By 1980, almost 80 percent of Great Britain's housing was owned by the government. Only Prime Minister Margaret Thatcher's well-received policy to sell public housing to its tenants has begun to reverse the process.

New York City is going through the same transition. "Private developers can't even build middle-income housing in New York," said Abe Biderman, commissioner of HPD. "The numbers just aren't there. By the time you factor in land costs, construction costs, and property taxes, you're already up to $800 to $900 a month rent. If we're going to have low-income housing in New York, the city itself is going to have to build it."

Just how seriously the city government is taking this charge can be gleaned from a report by Ken Auletta, columnist with *The New York Daily News*. After being badgered for months by Biderman to do a story about the wonderful things HPD is doing for New York housing, Auletta took a tour of Harlem and the South Bronx with Biderman as his guide.

> [I]n the front seat, Biderman started belching numbers—this year he will build or renovate 17,000 apartments, twice what private developers are doing in all of Manhattan; in 1983 only 1 percent of the city's capital budget was devoted to housing versus 17 percent today. . . .
>
> With Biderman in the front seat, half turned around like a Disney tour guide, the car passes Manhattan Ave., where apartments are being renovated for 33 single, female ex-addicts and their children, who have been in foster care. We pass 104th St., where the entire block between Manhattan Ave. and Central Park West has been restored with middle-income condominiums. The city, says Biderman, subsidizes about one-quarter of the cost of the $90,000 apartments, and these attractive three- and four-story buildings are among the 23,000 apartments the city and business leaders from the Private Partnership will manufacture.
>
> Heading north on Adam Clayton Powell Boulevard [Central Harlem], nearly every abandoned building is already under city construction or padlocked, waiting for renovation bids. Reaching 140th St., the eye settles on seven whole blocks under construction, and Biderman explains, "We are creating a little city" of 740 apartments, one-third set aside for homeless families, 45 percent for families with incomes under $19,000, and the rest for those with incomes between $19,000 and $25,000. "The commitment is to rehabilitate every vacant building in the city by 1993." At this point, Biderman pulls out a black looseleaf book with a computer printout of the 5,000 vacant buildings the city controls. "We own these neighborhoods," he declares, sweeping his right arm up and down the boulevard and toward the South Bronx. "What was a blight has become an opportunity."
>
> The car reaches the Bronx and Biderman has become almost possessive, announcing, "There is not a vacant building left on the Grand Concourse." We pass restored buildings, construction trucks, cement mixers, carpenters and plumbers all along the Concourse. Who owns these? "There is no private rehabilitation in these neighborhoods," announces the city's major landlord. "If you see construction, it's us."
>
> In the car going toward the South Bronx, which also now sprouts gardens of new city-financed homes, Abe Biderman puts the scope of the building in an even more majestic light: Once the entire program is complete, he says, the Koch administration will have provided new housing for 350,000 people, a population equal to that of the state's second-largest city, Buffalo.[1]

What Biderman is describing is the first stirrings of the 10-year, $4.2 billion program of housing construction and rehabilitation unveiled in April 1986 by Mayor Edward Koch. (The figure has since been raised to $5.1 billion.) The plan specified the following goals:[2]

LOW INCOME HOUSING ($2.7 billion) 126,000 units
(Annual family income up to $15,000)

In addition to the continued production of 3,000 units a year of housing for the homeless, the new program will:
—Reconstruct 16,000 units in vacant buildings.
—Preserve 74,000 units from abandonment.
—Rehabilitate 36,000 occupied units of city owned housing.

MODERATE INCOME HOUSING ($900 million) 93,000 units
(Annual family income of $15,000–$25,000)

—Provide 17,000 units of additional housing including 10,000 reconstructed units in currently vacant *in rem* buildings and 7,000 newly constructed units in homeownership programs.
—Support upgrading of 76,000 private units.

MIDDLE INCOME HOUSING ($600 million) 33,000 units
(Annual family income of $25,000–$48,000)

—Remove barriers to private construction.
—Reduce taxes and fees on private building.
—Provide government support for 33,000 new units in homeownership program.

TOTAL PROGRAM ($4.2 billion) 252,000 units

Where will the $5.1 billion come from to accomplish all this? The answer is easy: out of taxpayers' pockets.

City officials always try to disguise the process by saying the money will come from somewhere else. In this case, the bulk of revenues are said to be coming from the "unexpected profits" the state government will achieve from the commercial rents collected on the new Battery Park City at the lower tip of Manhattan.

Battery Park City, built on state-owned land created by filling the Hudson River, will indeed be bringing in a handsome economic rent. In fact, there are not many major developments anywhere in New York City today where the state, the city, or some public agency like the Metropolitan Transportation Authority or the Port Authority is not the landowner or a principal partner in the development.

The city and state collect economic rent on all these projects, as any good landlord should. Yet instead of using these rents to lower New Yorkers' crushing tax burden, the city and state siphon them off into new projects. Housing is now the favorite form of government activity. If all goes well with the Mayor's program, by 1996, New York City and its political affiliates will be landlords to one out of every 20 New Yorkers.

Koch's program was immediately criticized by housing activists, who argued it would provide much housing for middle- and moderate-income groups and very little for the poor. This is quite accurate. The actual number of *new* units subsidized for each income group looks like this:

Low income	16,000 units
Moderate income	17,000 units
Middle income	33,000 units

Half the new units will be going to people with incomes 10 to 110 percent *above* the city's median income of $22,000. The general redistribution of income will be upward.

True enough, the new housing created for people with higher incomes will soon filter vacancies down to the poor. But *why is it necessary for the government to build this housing in the first place*? Private builders are more than willing to build housing for people with incomes between $22,000 and $48,000 almost everywhere else in the world.

Perhaps the most interesting question, though, is this: Where is the city government ever going to get all the vacant and half-vacant buildings that will be reconstructed and rehabilitated into low- and moderate-income housing? We have already heard the answer. It is to be "torn from landlords' bleeding hands."

As we have seen from the history of urban renewal, the major impediment cities face in implementing their ambitious plans for government-sponsored development is the acquisition of land. Condemnation can be extremely expensive, even when the government sets the price unilaterally. New York City has solved the problem through a kind of "rolling condemnation," whereby the Department of Housing Preservation and Development is constantly organizing tenants and encouraging community and neighborhood organizations to drive landlords off their property. Once the landlord has been financially crippled, the building is taken *in rem* (meaning "as a thing") for back taxes.

Properties are routinely taken *in rem* all over the country. The numbers are usually small, though, and the foreclosed buildings are quickly sold back to the public at auction. Boston, for example, rarely owns more than 75 *in rem* buildings at a time and recycles them back into private ownership within six months.

In 1986, New York City owned 9,000 buildings, containing 50,000 vacant and 50,000 *occupied* apartments—9 percent of the city's housing stock. *Seventy percent of Central Harlem is now owned by the city government.* Only about 100 buildings are auctioned back to the public each year, all of them very small structures with only one to four units. The remainder are being held as a war chest for the city government's future housing programs.

The Mayor's ten-year program, in fact, is nothing more than a blueprint for taking more buildings out of the hands of private owners and turning them over to the growing legions of politically connected non-profit organizations that are going to be the city's new landlords. *Half the money* in the $5.1 billion will go to non-profits—church groups, community groups, and the increasingly powerful "neighborhood preservation companies," which are already subsidized out of city, state, and Federal money.

"The big advantage of the non-profits is that they won't be paying any mortgage debt," said Catie Marshall, public relations director at HPD. "We're giving them the building for $1 and providing them with the money for rehabilitation. That will enable them to keep the rents down. They'll start around $300 a month and will be under rent stabilization."

The non-profit organizations range from the Catholic Archdiocese of New York to the neighborhood preservation companies that now operate in almost every neighborhood of New York City. Subsidized both with government funds and with grants from banks and other private corporations, the neighborhood preservation companies are staffed almost entirely by full-time political activists. For more than a decade, they have been organizing rent strikes, driving landlords out of their buildings, and taking over management of buildings. Companies like Good Old Lower East Side (GOLES) now manage as many as 20 buildings and the competition for buildings has become so intense that turf wars have broken out. Buildings all over the Lower East Side (where a dozen neighborhood companies operate) are festooned with signs proclaiming ownership by one organization or another.

The history of one neighborhood group, although not typical, gives an idea of the way political activism has become the road to real-estate ownership in New York. In 1979, the Maoist Communist Workers' Party (CWP) achieved notoriety when five of its members died in a gun battle with Nazis and Ku Klux Klansmen while staging a "Death to the Klan" march in Greensboro, North Carolina.

Deciding it could not win a war of attrition, the CWP regrouped and decided to become active in New York neighborhood politics. It changed its name to the New Democratic Movement and set up several affiliates, including one entitled "Asian Americans for Equality" (AAFE). For a while the two organizations shared the same office and telephone and Margaret Chin, a former leader of the CWP, became a principal of AAFE.

In the early 1980s, AAFE entered the ring of New York's housing wars. Working closely with city councilwoman Miriam Friedlander (who has a rent-controlled apartment and is a former member of the Communist Party herself), AAFE soon had members appointed to Community Planning Board 3 and the Lower East Side Area Planning Board, which controls the distribution of anti-poverty funds.

Within a few years, AAFE was out organizing rent strikes and taking over buildings with the help of a $2 million grant from the state Department of Housing and Community Renewal (DHCR) and a $1.25 million grant from HPD—typical allotments for neighborhood preservation companies. In 1989, Asian Americans for Equality was prominently featured in *The New York Times* as one of the many enterprising non-profit groups that will soon be providing the bulk of New York's poor people with their housing.[3]

Another much more mainstream, non-profit organization has been the South East Bronx Churches' Organization (SEBCO), run by Father Louis Gigante, an activist priest. SEBCO has been the main developer of *in rem* housing in the South Bronx, now owning and operating over 2,000 apartments. HPD has awarded the organization more than $200 million in grants and has steered more than 1,500 section-8 certificates into SEBCO's projects. "Father G" is generally considered to be a saint by his South Bronx parishioners.

In March 1989, *The Village Voice* published a lengthy investigation of SEBCO, revealing that Father Gigante annually collects $450,000 in management fees through SEBCO Management, of which he is the sole principal. *The Voice* also disclosed that almost all his rehabilitation work had been contracted to Mafia-dominated construction firms run by Father Gigante's brother, Vincent "The Chin" Gigante, the reputed boss of the nation's second-largest Mafia family.[4] SEBCO is expected to play an even larger role in housing the South Bronx under the ten-year housing plan.

To illustrate how completely the program constitutes a transfer of property ownership from private landlords to politically dominated community organizations, let us look more closely at the housing that is to be provided for people with low incomes.

The poor are to be provided with 125,000 housing units—16,000 "reconstructed" apartments in vacant buildings, 36,000 "rehabilitated" units in occupied city buildings, and 74,000 units to be "preserve[d] . . . from abandonment."

The 52,000 "reconstructed" and "rehabilitated" units, of course, are all in *in rem* buildings that were owned and operated by private landlords only a few short years ago. Thus, they do not really represent any long-term addition to the city's housing stock. The truly remarkable figure, though, is the 74,000 units to be "preserve[d] . . . from abandonment." *These are apartments that the city PLANS to take over from private landlords during the next ten years.* In the Orwellian jargon of New York housing, a property is "preserved from abandonment" when it is confiscated by the city government. All these apartments are now occupied, almost entirely by low-income tenants. The 74,000 units will become "new housing" only in that the city government itself or some community organization will be the new landlord.

The principal means by which property is taken out of private hands is the 7a administration program, named after section 7a of the 1974 Emergency Tenant Protection Act.

The 7a program was based on the idea that landlords are a naturally unscrupulous breed of individuals who prefer to run down their own buildings. New York housing could only be saved, it was argued, by getting property into the hands of upstanding people—lawyers, realtors, and other professionals.

The 7a statute authorized housing court judges, upon the request of only two or three tenants, to appoint a special administrator to manage the building under trusteeship. The administrator is authorized to collect all the rents and use the money to make repairs on the building. The landlord is not even allowed on the property. If he wishes to get his building out of 7a administration, he must keep up all his mortgage and tax payments and eventually convince a housing-court judge that he has reformed and is worthy of running his building.

In taking over the management of the building, the 7a administrator faces a considerably lighter load than does the landlord. He does not have to make either mortgage or property-tax payment. Even the insurance premiums remain the landlord's responsibility.

Yet remarkably, even relieved of taxes and mortgage payments, which usually make up 60 to 80 percent of a landlord's routine expenses, *the 7a administrator often finds it impossible to run the building out of the rent rolls.* As a result, HPD often allows the administrator to *raise* the rents—called "restructuring"—in order to cover *minimal* expenditures. "We like to get the rents up to about $35 or $45 a room," said Ned York, of HPD's Division of Alternate Management, which runs the program. "We feel that's what we need to make a building work."

Despite all these advantages, 7a administrators are rarely successful. In more than 90 percent of the cases where a 7a administrator is appointed, the building is turned over to the city for back taxes within two years. From there, HPD may try to put the building into one of its various "alternate management" programs—"tenant management," "community management," even a "private ownership management program" (called "POMP") where the building is turned over to politically favored individuals. But success in these programs has been spotty and often limited to buildings that are distinctly middle class. (Otto Teitler's tenants tried to have his building put in 7a.)

Altogether, the 7a program has become just another form of organized looting of the housing stock. Instead of lawyers and realtors, most administrators have turned out to be tenant organizers, housing activists, or friends of the housing-court judges. HPD also runs a training program in which people are invited off the street to become 7a administrators. There is an overflow of applications. The chief attraction is that 7a is widely regarded as, at best, an investment-free way to enter the real-estate business, at worst, a license to steal.

In 1986, the New York City Department of Investigations published a lengthy report on the administration program. It found that more than half the money collected by 7a administrators had disappeared.[5]

On a cold day in February 1986, I was walking down West 125th Street on the edge of Harlem when I passed a storefront marked "Harlem Restoration Project." Curious, I entered and discovered a huge second-hand store. "Is this how Harlem is being restored?" I asked. No, I probably wanted to see the offices on the second floor.

At the top of the stairs, I was met by a heavy-set black woman. When I said I wanted to interview someone with the Harlem Restoration, she gave me a strange, wordless look and disappeared. A few moments later, another heavy-set black woman appeared from a back room. I repeated my request, she gave me the same wordless stare, and led me through a series of partitions to a spacious office at the front of the building. Without saying a word, she left. At desks on opposite sides of the room sat two professional-looking white women. My inner sense of irony told me I had finally reached the nerve center of the Harlem Restoration Project.

The older woman was on the phone, talking with a lilting southern accent. I introduced myself to the other, whose name was Dorothy Keller. She was quiet and demure, one of those well-bred, well-spoken Westchester women who seem essential to any good cause.

"We're working with HPD, managing two buildings under the 7a administration program," she explained. "We're putting both buildings through the Tenant Interim Leasing Program [called "TIL"]. The tenants pay one dollar to lease the building from us for a year. During that time, we train them to run the building by themselves. If they're successful, they're allowed to buy their apartments for $250 as a limited-profit cooperative."

"How long will it be before they take over?" I asked.

"Well, it's supposed to be one year, but actually this one building has been in the TIL program for seven years."

"What happened?"

"Well, the problem was that the rents were too low," she said. "When we started in 1978 a lot of people in there were paying only $50 for four-room apartments.

The highest anybody was paying was around $125. It just wasn't enough to make repairs and get the violations off the building. The tenants can't take over until all the violations have been cleared. We kept putting pressure on HPD, but it wasn't until 1985 that they finally restructured the rents up to $200. After that, we were able to get the building up to code."

"Do people pay the rents?"

"Yes. In this one building they've been pretty good."

"You don't make mortgage payments or pay property taxes?"

"No."

"How did the previous owner lose the building."

"He didn't pay his taxes."

"Did anyone seriously expect him to be able to run the building and pay his taxes on those rents?"

"Well, it's different. You see, the landlord has to make a profit. We don't have to take any profit so we can run it more cheaply."

"It sounds to me as if he must have been taking a huge loss."

"Not necessarily. Landlords usually have other resources. Or else they hold a building for speculation, waiting to sell it at a profit."

It did emerge that Harlem Restoration was taking an eight percent "management fee" that it collected right off the top of the rent roll.

Keller continued to talk about how difficult it was to work with HPD and other city agencies. "We tried to get section-8 money for some of our tenants," she said. "It took them years to come through. The welfare department is the same way. Several of our welfare tenants have applied for $250 grants so they can buy their apartments. They filed months ago and we still haven't heard anything."

The Restoration, she said, operated on a budget of $200,000 a year. Half of this came from the thrift shop downstairs, one-quarter from private donations, and one-quarter from the New York State Department of Housing and Community Renewal. "People give the thrift shop all kinds of things—cars, appliances, it's all tax deductible." None of the Restoration's $200,000 budget was spent on operating the buildings. "We believe they should be run right out of the rent rolls and the money HPD gives us," she explained. "We also try to get loans from HPD. We don't have to repay them. They become a lien against the building if the landlord ever wants to get it back."

The other building that was in 7a management was a much larger and more troublesome project—a 42-unit building on Amsterdam Avenue, across from City College. The building was half-empty when the Harlem Restoration was appointed 7a administrator in 1985. The landlord had stopped collecting rents and there had been no heat for over a year.

"Most of the tenants were stabilized and were paying around $185 for six rooms," said Keller. "That was much too low. HPD allowed us to charge the new tenants $300 and we eventually got the older tenants up to $300 as well."

"Does everybody pay?"

"No, we've had a lot of trouble with the tenants in this building. We've had to evict a few." The Restoration had evicted six of the original 23 tenants for non-payment. Two of these were tenant leaders who had opposed the Restoration's takeover of the building. "We felt they were in cahoots with the old landlord," she said confidentially.

"Who was the previous landlord?"

"The Willing Workers Baptist Church," she said.

"Does Willing Workers want the building back?"

"They're trying, but we don't think they're going to be able to get it. Once we get the building through the TIL program, that will be the end of it. The difficulty is there's another tenant who is now trying to get the building away from us. She's started a tenants' group and is trying to have us replaced. HPD is backing her up."

"So HPD is now working against you?"

"HPD doesn't seem to like community groups like ours much anymore," she said. "They're making a strong push for tenant management. I think it's because we do such a good job—it shows them up and makes them mad. They think the TIL program should be easy—you just hand the building over to the tenants and let them run it. But we feel they're pushing the tenants into something they're not really capable of handling yet.

"HPD just doesn't seem to have very realistic notions of what it means to run a building," she continued. "They say to us, 'What's the big deal? All you do is collect the money, put it in the bank, and pay the bills.' I tell them, 'You ought to come down to our office and see what we have to go through trying to collect rents, especially when you're in an eviction proceeding.' You wouldn't believe the problems. Really, HPD is very naive. They never managed a building in their lives."

At this point the other woman got off the phone. She was Marie Runyon, executive director of the Restoration and the former Assemblywoman whose successful fight for her $80-a-month apartment had closed down the Columbia School of Pharmacology. (At this point, I knew nothing about her.) A flinty woman of about 70 with white hair and glasses, she had the regal manner that often seems to go with a Southern accent.

Runyon started off by recounting her epic battle with Columbia. The incident had made her into a folk hero among tenant organizers on the Upper West Side. It also launched her own career as a housing activist, in which she eventually participated in more than 50 rent strikes. She showed me a recent feature on her in *City Limits*, a monthly New York newspaper devoted entirely to housing activism.

I asked her about her problems in running the two buildings.

"Let me tell you," she said, "I've worked in over 50 to 60 buildings in New York over the last ten years and I've never found a building where there was not at least one troublemaker. It's the nature of the beast. There is always one tenant who is never satisfied and who will use the system just as an excuse not to pay rent."

"Do you mean your tenants are going to housing court and complaining about *you?*"

"Certainly they are."

"What do you do?"

"Well, luckily, we have Judge Friedman [the one who jailed Elzie Robinson]. Although he is very pro-tenant, he is also very pro-7a. He tells these people they just have to pay their rent. I'm not saying that people shouldn't have the right to withhold their rent when they are not receiving services," she added. "But I think there is one exception and that is when the building is being run by a 7a administrator. A landlord has other resources he can draw upon. But for a 7a there is nothing else except the rent rolls. If you're going to run a building, people just have to pay their rents."

I asked Runyon if I could see the records on her buildings. She pulled out two long, hand-lettered charts on construction paper. Paid-up rent was marked in black, delinquencies in red. There was a lot of red. In the smaller building, half the tenants were in arrears for a total of $9,000. In the larger one—the Willing Workers building—seven tenants were up to date but 14 were in arrears for a total of $15,000.

"I really didn't believe these stories about people not paying their rent before we began this project," she said. "Now I'm starting to realize that there is some truth to it."

Was she having any trouble evicting people for non-payment? I asked.

"We certainly are. It is absurd how much trouble we have to go through with the courts and everyone else to evict these people. Believe me, if there were any way at all to get rid of these people, we would do it in a minute. I think it is ridiculous that you can't do anything about people who just won't pay rent."

I said she was starting to sound an awful lot like a landlord herself.

"I think I have more sympathy for some of the small owners than when I started," she said. "But there are still landlords out there who do terrible things to people."

Didn't the opportunity to buy their apartments for $250 make these people want to pay their rent?

"You'd think so, wouldn't you?" she said. "That is the really frustrating thing. Here we are offering these damned fools this golden opportunity—this *golden opportunity*—and they won't take it."

All this was making her Southern accent sound even more interesting.

"Why is that?" I asked.

"Oh, you know these welfare people. They say, 'I ain't never had nothin' from nothin'. What the hell do I want my apartment for?' They feel they're better off not owning things. The welfare system teaches them that—they know welfare will take care of them."

It had been a long interview and all of us were getting tired. I sincerely thanked both Mrs. Keller and Mrs. Runyon. It had been a wonderful afternoon.

Just how far New York City will go to replace private ownership with city ownership can be seen from the fate of the Federal voucher program in New York.

Section-8 vouchers have been notoriously difficult to spend in rent-controlled cities. This is often taken to be a fault of the vouchers, rather than rent control. As Jacob V. Lamar wrote in *Time*:

> The Reagan Administration's approach to housing was another version of the supply-side experiment: instead of subsidizing low-cost construction, as Washington had done since the 1930s, the Reaganites decided to subsidize tenants. Give cash vouchers directly to the poor to help them pay their rent, went the theory, and the market would respond by supplying more housing.

In fact, vouchers have worked well where the market is left free to operate.

> Vouchers have had some success in the Southwest, where prices are depressed and vacancy rates relatively high. But in much of the country, as housing prices have increased by 43 percent in the past eight years, voucher recipients have been unable to find apartments with affordable rents that also meet federal quality standards. In New York City, where rent control, high taxes and land prices discourage the construction of modestly priced housing, three out of four vouchers were returned to the Government last year after futile apartment searches by the recipients. Supply-side housing, like supply-side economics, has had drastic, unintended consequences.[6]

In New York City, however, the problems go beyond rent control. In 1987, city government officials refused even to *distribute* the vouchers because of ideological objections. HPD, which handles more than half the vouchers, *will not give them to tenants who live in privately owned buildings*. Instead, it has tried to steer all the Federal money into *in rem* buildings that are being rehabilitated by the city itself or by non-profit organizations.

As Anthony de Palma reported in *The New York Times*:

> Joseph D. Monticciolo, [HUD] administrator of Region II, which includes New York, New Jersey, and the Caribbean, said that as of last June [1987], Puerto Rico had reached almost 150 percent of its assigned goal and Newark about 135 percent. New York City, which had been assigned more than 7,000 of the region's 11,500 [vouchers], on the other hand, had not reached even 40 percent. . . .
>
> Because of New York City's poor performance, it became obvious that the region would not meet its goal. Mr. Monticciolo said he met with city officials to clear the air. "We had philosophical differences. . . ," Mr. Monticciolo said. "But I told them that since Congress had already appropriated the money, it was incumbent on us to make the program work. Then I told them that if they couldn't guarantee lease-up of the vouchers that had been reserved for them, we were going to give them to those who could."
>
> Region II was the last region in the country to meet its voucher goal. To do that by the end of the fiscal year on Sept. 30, officials directed that no other subsidies be offered until regional goals were met. They also threatened to take back up to 4,300 of the 5,500 unused vouchers for tenants in rehabilitated buildings in New York City unless they are used by next April.[7]

The problem is that HUD has designated that the vouchers be spent in buildings that have been partially rehabilitated with Federal section-8 funds. In most cities, these rehabilitations are done in privately owned buildings. In New York, however, little of this money goes to private owners and most is funneled into city-owned projects. But HUD said the vouchers could not be spent in publicly owned housing.

Casting around for ways to distribute the vouchers, HPD finally decided to give them to *middle*-income tenants in Mitchell-Lama housing.

> So far, [HPD] has used fewer than 400 of the [5,900] vouchers in the rehabilitation program, applying them to several city-subsidized Mitchell-Lama buildings in which the roofs and heating systems have been repaired. Federal officials do not consider this to be the kind of rehabilitation for which the program was designed. In their eyes, New York City has yet to lease even a single unit with a voucher—even though the first ones were reserved for the city in the 1984 fiscal year.[8]

Finally, HPD decided that if it could not distribute its vouchers to tenants in its own buildings or in Mitchell-Lama housing where the city would get the credit, then it would not distribute them at all. Eventually, it convinced HUD to go along.

> The city, meanwhile, was focusing on its own buildings. After months of negotiations, the city's housing agency convinced Washington that the city's tax-foreclosed buildings would eventually be sold to tenants and therefore qualify as privately owned. But until then, the city will pay for the renovations of some 3,000 apartments and be reimbursed when the buildings are sold to tenants. At that time, qualifying tenants will receive vouchers to help them pay the higher rents necessitated by the improvements.[9]

All this has led New York City officials to condemn unanimously the voucher program.

"In places like New York, where there clearly is not enough housing, this stuff ain't going to help," said Joseph Shuldiner, general manager of the New York City Housing Authority.

"The problem with the concept as conceived by the Reagan Administration is that it does not address the real housing problems," said Paul Crotty, then commissioner of HPD. "They've cut the housing budget from $35 billion to $7 billion. They may think this program covers the shortfall, but it doesn't."

Charles Schumer, a Democratic Congressman from Brooklyn, argued that vouchers are "nothing but a fig leaf [that] allows the Administration to gracefully exit from the housing stage without admitting they're naked."[10]

Even the newspapers seemed to acquiesce. In any other city, the story of HPD's refusal to distribute its vouchers unless they went to tenants in city-owned buildings might have run under the headline, "City hoards housing vouchers while thousands go homeless." But in *The New York Times*, the headline read: "New York City Finds U. S. Subsidies System Fails to Meet Its Needs."

In 1986, I got my own guided tour of the South Bronx. My mentor was not Abe Biderman but Frank Marrero, a member of the Area Policy Board and now a committee member of Community Planning Board 2, which oversees the district. Marrero had been recommended by several people as someone who knew all the ins and outs of South Bronx housing.

I met him at his Bronx home, a four-story walk-up with abandoned buildings on both sides. Marrero looked about the way he sounded over the phone—friendly, mature, a little scholarly with his horn-rimmed glasses. A "New York-a-Rican" (Puerto Rican living in New York), he spoke both Spanish and English with a humorous lilt. His apartment was long, dark, and comfortable. On one wall was a Puerto Rican pin-up calendar. On another, a tennis racket had been hung for decoration.

Marrero makes a living as a consultant on building management and maintenance. Born in Puerto Rico, he has lived in the building since he was seven years old and now owns it. "It went through a bunch of owners until the last guy went bankrupt in 1973. I said to my mother, 'What the heck, let's buy it.' I was only 23 at the time but it seemed like a good idea. I live in one apartment, my mother has another and my sister has a third. We rent five others."

When they bought the building, it was filled with rent-controlled tenants paying between $65 and $100 for four- and five-room apartments. "We gradually persuaded people to move out. Then one guy got mad and started a fire and that got rid of everybody. Now we get about $300 a month. I'm like everybody else, I'd love to charge $600 for these apartments but where am I going to find people to pay that much in this neighborhood?"

Marrero also had one top-floor, six-room apartment with a stabilized rent of only $120. He had kept it vacant for ten years. "I can't in good conscience rent that apartment," he said. "The money I'd get wouldn't even pay the utilities."

In 1984, on the recommendation of a planning board member, Marrero took the seven-week, 7a administrator's training course given regularly by HPD. "It's completely tenant-oriented," he said. "They give preference to people who 'bring a building with them'—meaning they already had a rent strike going. That way they don't have to organize the building themselves."

Marrero did well in the course and struck up a friendship with Sol Schwarz, the director of the program, who eventually hired him as deputy director. "Most of what they were teaching people was how to get the building away from the owner," said Marrero. "I started showing people how to do plumbing and electrical work. I even found a couple of people jobs as superintendents." HPD objected, saying it was a conflict of interest for a landlord to be teaching the 7a course, but Schwarz stuck by him.

Marrero set up his own small realty company and started getting involved with individual cases. But when HPD finally caught him trying to help a 25-year-old Bronx landlord get his building out of 7a administration, he was fired on the spot. "It's incredible," he said. "They'll do anything to get a landlord but they'll let a tenant get away with anything. It's like being down in the Old South and watching segregation."

Marrero came away from the 7a program believing it is utterly corrupt. "The majority of people are in that class simply because they've heard it's an easy way to steal money. And it's all done under the watchful eyes of those housing-court judges. At HPD, I once made a report to a judge that the administrator had stolen $2,000 out of a building. The judge looked at me and said, 'What am I supposed to do about it?'

"Basically, neither HPD nor the judges really care whether the administrators steal or not. The whole purpose of the program is to get buildings into the city's hands. From the city's point of view, it makes sense. The sooner they take over a building, the less they have to spend in fixing it up before they turn it over to one of these community organizations."

After a while, Marrero took me for a tour of the neighborhood. "This is the famous South Bronx," he said, swinging his beat-up Dodge out into the broad, deserted streets. "You won't believe what you're going to see. It isn't really a city anymore. We're like a little frontier town here just starting out. We've torn everything down and now we're trying to start over again."

The streets were indeed eerily reminiscent of a mining town or frontier village. Once upon a time, the signature of the South Bronx was the large elevator apartment building, one of the sturdiest structures ever built in this country. Today the most common sight is a brick-strewn lot the size of several football fields. The only sign of life was boys turning graceful somersaults on trampolines made out of piled-up bedsprings.

"The community planning board is big on demolitions," said Marrero. "After one of these buildings sits vacant for a while, the junkies and rats get in it and ruin what's left of the neighborhood. Whenever we get permission to knock down a building, it's as if we've made a big accomplishment."

Scattered among the ruins, looking like little props on a movie set, were little two- and three-story townhouses, still occupied. These smaller structures have been exempt from rent controls.

We drove through what must have once been a 12-block area, now completely levelled. "It's strange to have such a long view in New York, isn't it?" said Marrero. "You're not used to being able to see that far." The community planning board was trying to convert the area into a park. "We might as well," he said cheerfully. "We've got plenty of room around here."

The few apartments that remained were, without exception, being run by some HPD-sponsored organization. Marrero catalogued the history of each one in bewildering detail.

"Most of these nice buildings you see are in section-8," he said. "HPD channels all that Federal money into these projects. Most of them are being run by community organizations. In fact, if HPD sees anything up here with the word 'organization' on it, they'll throw money at it.

"There are two main groups, SEBCO and the Mid-Bronx Desperados. SEBCO stands for Southeast Bronx Community Organization—that's Father G's group [Father Gigante]. That man is a saint. He's done wonders up here. Usually, HPD will get title to a building through 7a, then turns it over to SEBCO. They set them up with section-8 money to make sure they're financially sound.

"SEBCO is allowed to be very selective about tenants," he added. "They don't rent to people who don't have good credit records and they certainly don't rent to tenant organizers. They don't even rent to welfare much. SEBCO also gets very favorable treatment in housing court. If SEBCO wants a tenant out, that tenant is gone in a few weeks.

"The Mid-Bronx Desperados is another community group, although they don't have the church connection. They're basically a political organization, with strong ties to the Puerto Rican faction of the Democratic Party. They do the same thing. The city gives them a lot of abandoned buildings and section-8 money and they fill them with their own tenants."

Marrero drove us past the latest, widely heralded solution to New York's housing problems—a row of aluminum-sided, single-family homes recently built by Father Gigante with city funding. They looked like a third-rate motel outside Atlantic City.

"Beautiful, aren't they?" he said, ironically. "The one good thing about them is they won't have landlords."

"The key thing to remember up here is that everything is political," he went on. "The Mid-Bronx Desperados can deliver 4,000 votes in a primary—every tenant out of every one of their buildings. You either vote for their candidate or you're out. SEBCO is the same way. They can deliver every one of their tenants in an election.

"And after all, you really can't blame the people, can you? I mean, what's a vote as long as they give you a place to live?"

Standing on a South Bronx subway platform an hour later, surveying the moonscape before me, I realized a city is really nothing but its buildings. New York or San Francisco or Baltimore or New Orleans is not a harbor or a downtown shopping district or an intersection of highways or a baseball team, or even the people living in it at any particular time. What is most enduring about a city is its architecture and physical structure—its buildings.

What was going on up here in the Bronx had nothing to do with the New York I and millions of others once loved and admired. It wasn't New York at all—the majestic apartment buildings, the vibrant street life, the vaunted skyscrapers. The city government was now replacing these majestic landmarks with forlorn little rows of suburban cottages whose only virtue was that they didn't have landlords.

The city's vast armies of homeless, I realized, are really a population in transition. One day—Federal subsidies willing—the city government may indeed be able to provide housing for everyone. Every affluent tenant will have his own rent-regulated apartment, every middle- and moderate-income tenant will have his own Mitchell-Lama building, every low-income tenant will have some non-profit neighborhood organization for a landlord. It may all eventually happen. But in the meantime, the homeless will have to wander the streets while the housing wars continue all around them.

Standing on the platform, I was struck by the same feeling I had had in Berkeley. "So this is what it's like to live in Rumania or East Germany." All those stories of dispirited lives, completely stifled by an overwhelming bureaucracy, that you hear about but never quite believe—they are all true. Nor is it really ever imposed completely by force. Socialism is the fate of people who are unwilling to trust their fellow man.

Enterprise is the best system, not only because it produces the finest material goods, but because it produces the best *freedom*—the ability to live one's life without being supervised by a moralistic bureaucracy intent on driving every imaginary evil from the world.

But then, what's freedom as long as they give you a place to live?

Part III

CONCLUSIONS

"The effects of rent control have in fact been exactly what can be predicted from the simplest type of supply-and-demand analysis—"housing shortage" (excess demand for housing), black markets, privileges for those who happen to have a contract for a rent-controlled apartment, nepotism in the distribution of the available apartments, difficulties in getting apartments for families with children, and, in many places, deterioration of the housing stock. In fact, next to bombing, rent control seems in many cases to be the most efficient technique so far known for destroying cities, as the housing situation in New York City demonstrates."

—Assa Lindbeck, chairman of the
Nobel Prize Committee for Economics

Chapter 23

Homelessness in Other Countries

The dynamics of the housing market—and the consequences of interfering with that market—are by no means unique to the United States. They are the same all around the world. It might behoove us to take a brief look at how government housing policies work in different parts of the globe.

Japan is an excellent example of a country where government land-use and zoning laws have lowered the general standard of life for the majority, to the benefit of only a small minority.

Japan is a tightly packed little island, with half the population of the United States living in an area smaller than the size of California. The land is also very inhospitable. Mountains are common and level terrain is fairly rare.

Historically, most of the accessible land has been used for rice farming. With Japan's industrial development, however, much of this agriculture became outdated. Japan could import rice much more cheaply, while the level land could have been used to accommodate the growing population.

For political reasons, however, the Japanese government has decided that the country must remain self-sufficient in rice production. Therefore, elaborate zoning laws have been adopted that keep most of the country's hospitable land permanently in agriculture. During the nationalistic period of the 1930s, this may have made some sense. But as Japan has joined the international trading economy since World War II, its indigenous rice production has become a luxury. Nevertheless, farmers are so politically powerful (despite being only 4 percent of the population) that they have maintained their zoning protection and live entirely subsidized lives while occupying more than 70 percent of the hospitable land.

As a result, the Japanese population remains cooped up in cities, living at densities that most Americans would find difficult to imagine. The average Japanese family lives in a 500-square-foot apartment—about the size of the average American living room. While American homes are frequently sited on quarter-acre lots (about 1200 square meters), Japanese yards are advertised in square meters, with 125 square meters a common figure. James Fallows, Asian correspondent for *The Atlantic Monthly*, has speculated that it is the microscopic living space of the Japanese that makes them run such a high trade surplus. They collect foreign currency rather than foreign goods because they have no place to put things at home.[1]

Still, the Japanese do not have a serious homeless problem. The reason seems to be threefold: 1) the strong nature of family life; 2) a willingness to deal with antisocial and deviant behavior; and 3) a lack of strict urban zoning or rent control.

The extreme ethnic homogeneity of Japanese society has made it possible to enforce cultural norms in a way that no longer appears possible in the United States. Crime is quickly punished, confessions and conviction rates averaging about 95 percent. Involuntary commitment to mental hospitals is a regular procedure. People who attempt to sleep outdoors are quickly taken to institutions that are the equivalent of poor houses.

The lack of severe building and zoning restrictions or rent control, however, is perhaps the most important factor. With such limited terrain, the Japanese obviously cannot be very demanding about space requirements. Nor is there room for exclusionary zoning. Visitors to Japan often note how rich and poor live together in close proximity without tension or anxiety. The low crime rate and the general social consensus seem to make this possible. And Japan is the only industrial country in the world that has not adopted rent control.

The payoff for all this is that everyone finds a place to live. This mutual toleration means that space is not wasted creating buffers between rich and poor. Even though Japan's land resources are severely—and artificially—limited, the efficient use of space has produced almost non-existent rates of homelessness.

In contrast to Japan, Europe and Canada have had experiences with housing regulation much more similar to the United States. Canada, with vast amounts of land, has practiced strict zoning for many decades. The tradition is stronger in the English-speaking provinces, which more closely imitate the United States, than in French Canada.

The most notable example is the Province of Ontario, which has practiced strong interventionist housing policies since the early 1970s. Ontario and Toronto have both instituted exclusionary zoning practices and have flirted with no-growth ordinances. In 1975, the entire Province of Ontario adopted rent control as a temporary measure during an intense election campaign. The strongest impact has been in Toronto. Typically, Ontario exempted new construction from rent regulations and typically, this exemption lasted only so long as new tenants remained politically naive. In 1986, after eleven years, all units built since 1975 were "recaptured" and the exemption on future housing construction repealed.

"By 1986, the impact of rent control had been to lower prices on pre-1976 buildings but raise them on post-1976 construction," said Lawrence Smith, professor of economics at the University of Toronto. "Since controls have been extended to new construction, the result has been a reduction of all new apartment construction. Key money and bribes have become crucial to finding an apartment."

Vacancy rates have fallen to a microscopic one percent and American-style homelessness is on the rise. More than 23,000 people used the city's 2,500 shelter beds in 1988—a rate comparable to most American cities.

Most of Europe was built long before the concept of zoning became relevant. Medieval transportation conditions made it difficult to put great distances between rich and poor. Since the time of the Romans, affluent city dwellers have retreated to their country villas. But in the cities, the economic classes have generally lived side-by-side.

What people did instead was to practice a kind of inverse zoning—the walled family compound. Not for nothing did Romeo and other Medieval lovers scale high walls in order to visit their sweethearts. Since the Middle Ages, people of any wealth in European cities have surrounded their houses with enclosures. The practice extends to almost every other part of the world. Arab cities like Tunis and Algiers are like beehives, with the narrow public streets dwarfed by the honeycombs of private passageways inside the walled compounds. The same practice is used in cities from Bombay to Mexico City.

In 1988, I was in the company of some Italian visitors on a drive through a Long Island suburb. They were utterly amazed at the open, unprotected lifestyle of the affluent residents. "You mean you can actually walk on these people's lawns?" they said with amazement. In Italy (where the kidnapping for ransom of wealthy people is still commonplace), affluent people still live behind high walls.

As the United States becomes more crowded and crime becomes more random, we have initiated some of the same practices. Detroit's Renaissance Center is a tightly guarded suburban shopping compound located in the downtown area. Suburban homes in Houston and Dallas are now being built with enclosing walls and private streets, and are marketed for their security arrangements. On the whole, though, the spread to the suburbs has made possible a more open and secure lifestyle.

As far as actual land-use planning is concerned, most European cities and villages have practiced it for centuries. Municipal governments have always had considerable authority to control local development through a general permit process.

The rights of private property, as elaborated in the writings of John Locke, have never really gained much foothold in European society. In America—for a long time, at least—ownership of private property was regarded as a prior claim to the government's control of the land. The right to use one's private property was considered one of the founding principles of America.

In Europe, on the other hand, all land implicitly belonged to the king, or his contemporary successor, the state. There is no sense that private property can be developed "as of right." Developing one's own land in Europe means securing elaborate permission from the government, the success of which is by no means certain.

As a result, many small European towns and villages rarely grow at all. This produces a quaintness that is always so appealing to tourists. It also accounts for the extremely low rates of homeownership among Europeans—averaging only 45 percent in France, 33 percent in Germany, 29 percent in Britain, and 26 percent in The Netherlands. Consequently, Europe is even more dependent upon rental housing than is America. With tenants such a large part of the housing market, European countries have almost all established rent control.

Just as rent control began in New York as a temporary measure during World War II, so it was introduced in European countries as a temporary measure during World War I. As always, once controls were imposed, they proved almost impossible to remove. Coupled with a rising acceptance of socialist principles, rent controls have led to almost complete government domination of most nations' housing markets. The list of countries with rent control includes: Great Britain, Ireland, France, Germany, Luxembourg, The Netherlands, Belgium, Denmark, Norway, Finland, Sweden, Italy, Greece, Spain, and Portugal. Only Switzerland lacks it.

Because they have been in place so long, rent controls have often lowered prices for sitting tenants even beyond the levels found in New York. E. Jay Howenstine, a researcher at HUD, reported after a survey of European rent controls in 1977: "The proportion of family expenditure devoted to rent declined in all Western European countries [after World War I]; in fact, housing approached in some instances almost the status of a free good. In 1947, average rents in Italy and France fell to 0.5 and 1.3 percent of average family income, respectively."[2] It is often said that the French laborer pays about the same price for a month's rent as he pays for a pack of cigarettes. In Lisbon, older rent-controlled apartments often rent for as little as $2.00 a month.[3] Howenstine noted that rent-controlled apartments are "often the largest and choicest in the central city."

In some countries, this extreme pressure on private landlords has led to an almost complete disappearance of the private rental sector. In Britain, until recently at least, government "council housing" accounted for 80 percent of the new rental housing in the country. In Sweden, public and subsidized housing make up 62 percent of the market, in West Germany about 20 percent.

Where private ownership does persist in Western Europe, the pattern seems to be identical to that discovered in this country—small, decentralized holdings among small property owners. As Howenstine discovered:

> In the United Kingdom, more than half of old [rent-] controlled tenancies in 1967 were owned by 400,000 small landlords, two-thirds owning only one property each. A 1960 study of rental housing in the fairly representative city of Lancaster showed that 70 percent of the landlords had inherited their property and that 90 percent planned to sell out at the earliest opportunity, that is, as soon as the property became vacant.[4]

Unwilling ownership by inheritance is usually a sign that a property has become so devalued that it is essentially unsellable.

In Eastern Europe, on the other hand, rent controls have been avoided because private property itself is illegal. Only in the last decade have Hungary and Yugoslavia allowed the ownership of two-family homes. (In New York, I met two Yugoslavian landlords who both said it was easier to be a landlord in Belgrade than New York.)

Hungary forms an interesting amalgam of socialist and free-market ideas. Surprisingly, 80 percent of housing construction is done by small builders operating on bank loans.[5] The liberalization of the 1970s that allowed ownership of two-family homes has been so successful that the government is planning to expand the limits to three- and four-family units. It would be impossible to permit this much housing without some kind of government regulation, however, and in 1986, Hungary dispatched a representative to New York to consult with housing officials there about setting up rent controls.[6]

With so much housing regulation in Europe, the question naturally arises: Why haven't they experienced serious problems with homelessness?

The answer is that, in some instances, Europe *has* developed problems with homelessness. Both West Germany and The Netherland have had housing riots, mainly among young, middle-class people unable to find housing. Squatting in abandoned buildings—even the forceful takeover of occupied buildings—is common in The Netherlands, Great Britain, West Germany, France, Italy, and Portugal. In The Netherlands, the *kracken*, middle-class squatters, have become famous for breaking into houses—sometimes empty, sometimes not—and taking up residence. Many countries give great latitude to squatters and prevent building owners from evicting them after they have occupied a home for a few days. In most major cities of Europe, it is regarded as risky to leave your home unoccupied while on vacation. You may return to find an unevictable stranger living there.

What seems to protect Europe from American-style homelessness is its strict immigration policies. European countries simply do not have the large populations of immigrant poor or indigenous minorities that make up a sizable portion of America's homeless populations. Where these populations do exist—Arabs in Paris, Turks in Germany, and Jamaicans in London—both intense squalor and homelessness have developed in American portions. Among the East Germans who have recently escaped to West Germany, a few have ended up homeless.[7]

For the most part, indigenous Europeans, rich and poor, deal with the housing shortage by staying put, generation after generation. The major manifestation of rent control in Europe is not homelessness but what is called "labor immobility." Quite simply, almost everyone in the country is a prisoner of rent control. The problem is so serious that by the 1980s it was considered the major impediment to modernization of the economy in almost every Western European country. As one French manufacturer in a small outlying city told *The Wall Street Journal*, "If we moved across town, we'd lose half our work force."

E. Jay Howenstine noted:

> In Vienna, one authority attributed the doubling of the volume of public transportation between 1913 and 1928 at a time of diminishing population mainly to inhibited mobility caused by rent control; another investigator estimated—admittedly with some exaggeration—that additional fares squeezed out of the Viennese public by rent controls accounted to two-thirds of the annual outlay on new building in the city.[8]

The legendary difficulties of finding an apartment in Paris almost rival the tales of New York. As *The Financial Times* reported in 1987:

> Anyone who has ever looked for somewhere to live in Paris will remember the experience with mixed feelings. . . .
>
> For although the stunningly beautiful city is full of elegant, comfortable homes, they all tend to be occupied. Rented accommodation is in such short supply that in a recent issue of the weekly guide for homeseekers by the *Figaro* newspaper, only one page was devoted to property to let in the city centre and two in the suburbs. . . .
>
> There are no short cuts . . . and the successful househunter always needs both time and luck. Add to this contacts and cash and you might find somewhere in Paris within three months. . . .
>
> [One young woman reported,] "The only way I could find somewhere was to move in with a boyfriend and then get rid of him."[9]

Similar situations exist all over Europe. Americans moving temporarily to Spain or Italy may have an easy time finding an apartment, because—as in New York and Berkeley—landlords are anxious to rent to visiting foreigners because they probably won't stay long and may be unfamiliar with rent regulations.

A far more typical European experience was the dilemma of a 56-year-old hospital worker in rent-controlled Mantova, Italy, who made news in 1980 when he placed the following ad in a newspaper: "I will gladly donate one of my eyes or kidneys, or both an eye and a kidney, to anyone who will help me find a non-luxury rental apartment in this city."[10]

All this has made many Western European officials extremely anxious to get rid of rent controls, particularly as the Common Market countries move toward economic unification in 1992. Any country with extreme labor immobility, or any large city where newcomers cannot find housing, is likely to be at a disadvantage in the newly competitive economy.

The French government has already instituted plans for getting rid of all rent controls by 1996. The task may prove difficult, though, because—as always—the affluent and well-connected have become the principal beneficiaries. When the first stages were implemented in the 1980s, it emerged that the city government itself had become Paris's principal "illusory landlord."

> Indeed, up to 100,000 flats in the historic heart of the city are said to belong to the Ville de Paris (the city government) which uses them as "grace and favour" residences for long-serving civil servants and political friends.
>
> Others, such as those in the picturesque Palais Royale, belong to the Banque de Paris. Again, these tend to be occupied by privileged tenants such as "*inspecteurs des finances*."[11]

In 1987, an international conference on rent control was convened at the John Deutsch Institute for the Study of Economic Policy in Ontario. Papers were presented reviewing rent controls in Los Angeles, Ontario, Great Britain, Sweden, and Israel. At the outset, most of the economists were somewhat sympathetic toward rent controls. As Richard J. Arnott, professor of economics at Boston University, who chaired the conference, said in his opening remarks:

> Ten years ago, almost all North American economists smugly regarded rent controls as the folly of the unenlightened; if all citizens were required to take a course in introductory microeconomics as part of their civics training, rent controls would disappear. Recent developments in economic thought have shaken, though not destroyed, this general belief. . . .
>
> Most experts on the subject, while not advocating controls, are now considerably more guarded and qualified in their opposition, and some believe that a well-designed rent control program can, on balance, be beneficial.[12]

Arnott attributed the smugness of traditional economists to an overreliance on theory and a "casual empiricism" about the real-life benefits of rent control.

It came as something of a shock, then, when researchers from all five countries reported unanimously that rent control had all but devastated their countries' housing markets. Said Arnott in his closing remarks:

> Despite the revisionism referred to earlier . . . the various jurisdictions' experts were unanimous in their opinion that rent controls have been harmful. . . .
>
> The experts were . . . unanimous on the qualitative impacts of control: reduced maintenance and accelerated deterioration of the rental stock; shrinkage of the private rental housing stock due to demolition, abandonment, conversion, and a fall in the rate of private rental construction; relatedly, a switch towards owner-occupied and public rental housing; mismatch of households to housing units; excess demand phenomenon—low vacancy rates, keymoney and other black and grey market activities; and reduced mobility, which has caused significant distortions in the labour market. . . .
>
> The "old lady who swallowed the fly," while not so-named, played a role in all the [countries]. To offset the problems induced by controls, government intervention in the housing market becomes increasingly extensive, incursive, and Byzantine, until, in some jurisdictions, the rental housing *market* is essentially replaced by government allocation. [Emphasis in original.][13]

Once again, the experts unanimously agreed: rent controls ruin housing markets.

The Soviet Union forms an interesting test case for homelessness and housing policies, since American housing activists have often noted that "there are no homeless people on the streets of Moscow." The Russians' system of widespread housing subsidies is also cited frequently by housing activists. In 1985, Michael McKee, one of New York's most frequently quoted tenant activists, told *The New York Times,* "In an ideal situation, like the Soviet Union, you would pay [rent] according to your income, but we're not going to have anything like that."[14]

In reality, the situation turns out to be much different. The Soviets have indeed made a gigantic effort in public housing, as Hedrick Smith reported in 1976:

> Westerners . . . marvel at the rows of panelled prefab 9-story, 11-story, and 14-story apartment houses that dominate the outskirts of Moscow and other large cities. The monotony of their architecture and their inhuman size are numbing and their interiors are much humbler than their grand facades. But the scale of the effort is impressive. Almost everywhere that I went, I encountered scholars, engineers, workmen, teachers boasting about their new apartments. They might be modest by Western standards but they were bright and airy enough to produce a new outlook on life for those who previously had been crammed into communal flats, sharing kitchen, bath, and toilet with four to six other families. "You cannot imagine how important a change that is for people," a middle-aged teacher asserted.[15]

What must be recognized, though, is that these impressive public housing projects are reserved for essentially *middle-class* people who would be served by the private sector in a free-market country. The occupants are scholars, engineers, workmen, and teachers—people important enough to merit first consideration in a socialist regime. The *dachas*—country estates for weekend use—are also generally reserved for people in high party echelons and are considered the prized perquisite of office.

For the people in the lower reaches of Soviet society, however, the reality is quite different:

> [S]o massive and aching is the housing shortage that Western economists like Gertrude Schroeder still reckon that the Soviet Union is "the most poorly housed of any major country in Europe. . . ."
>
> More than 25 percent of [the population] still live in communal apartments [two or more families sharing the same quarters]. Soviet officials concede and Western specialists think the figure may be closer to one-third. In 1972, the national average was 7.6 square meters of living space per person [eight feet by eight feet] in Soviet urban areas—or about one-third the space of American city-dwellers and one-half the space of people in Western European cities.[16]

The Russians, of course, have always been much poorer than Western Europeans and the Soviet system cannot be faulted simply because they have not caught up. What these statistics fail to convey is the price in personal freedom the Soviet system has extracted in achieving even these minor accomplishments.

No one is allowed to move to Moscow without permission. The same restrictions apply to other large cities and centers of employment. The Soviet controls on *internal* migration are essentially the same as those that exited between European countries during the most hostile periods of the 19th and 20th centuries.

The reason is simple. The Soviet system can provide cheap, subsidized housing only to certain select groups—educated and employed scholars, teachers, engineers, and factory workers. Everyone else must be forcibly prevented from taking advantage of these subsidies. It requires an extensive application procedure (including proof that one can find housing) in order to get government permission to live in Moscow.

As might be expected, a whole culture has also evolved for avoiding these restrictions. One of the most common ploys is for young people from the country to move to Moscow without permission in the hope of finding a boyfriend or girlfriend with whom to live. Moscow girls are warned to beware of country boys proposing marriage. As in New York and Paris, they may just be looking for an apartment.[17]

What does the view of housing look like in those countries usually referred to as the Third World? Once again, it is all too familiar. Housing regulations are pursued perhaps even more diligently in these countries than in the industrial nations of Europe and North America.

The roster of countries that practice some kind of rent control runs as follows: Algeria, Antigua, Argentina, Bangladesh, Barbados, Bolivia, Brazil, Burma, Chile, Columbia, Costa Rica, Cyprus, Dominican Republic, Ecuador, Egypt, El Salvador, Guatemala, Honduras, Hong Kong, India, Indonesia, Iran, Iraq, Jamaica, Kenya, Lebanon, Libya, Malaysia, Malta, Mexico, Monaco, Pakistan, Panama, Peru, Philippines, Singapore, Sri Lanka, Sudan, Syria, Tunisia, Turkey, Uganda, Uruguay, Venezuela, Zaire, and Zimbabwe. Israel, Australia, and South Africa also have it. The only major countries without rent control are Morocco, New Zealand, Nigeria, Taiwan, and Thailand.

To be sure, such systems are often limited to small urban areas and may not be very strictly enforced. International Property Consultants, Ltd., of New York, is currently completing a survey of rent control in 80 countries. "Systems differ quite a bit around the world," said Rene Frank, author of the study. "Mexico City has a horrible system of rent control. As you might expect, both Bombay and

Calcutta have rent control. But believe it or not, we found the most punitive system in the world is right here in New York City."

In 1989, North Vietnam attracted international attention when it announced that it would try to abandon rent control after ten futile years. Nguyen Co Thach, foreign minister of North Vietnam, told a crowded news conference in New Dehli that a "romantic conception of socialism" had led his country to ruin much of its housing stock. "The Americans couldn't destroy Hanoi, but we have destroyed our city by very low rents," he said. "We realize it was stupid and that we must change policy."[18]

Rent control, of course, cannot be blamed for all the beggary and homelessness in the Third World. Burgeoning populations, extreme poverty, and general government restriction on the economy are partly to blame. Yet it is often easy to overlook the role rent control has played in creating absurd inequities and housing shortages.

In 1989, Alan Cowell, of *The New York Times*, filed a report from Cairo, telling how entrepreneurs had begun to remodel old mausoleums in an ancient cemetery called "The City of the Dead," in response to Cairo's housing shortages.

> [T]he City of the Dead has become a repository for those who cannot find a home elsewhere in Cairo's urban tangle and an emblem of one of Egypt's anomalies: In a land where millions live in slums and one-room apartments, in shanties built on rooftops or in the rooms once reserved for the guardians of the tombs, upward of a million apartments stand empty.[19]

The cause of this Egyptian anomaly turned out to be a familiar one:

> Rents controlled by official decree in the 1940's and 60's to protect the tenants have never been raised, so a wealthy family can pay the equivalent of a few dollars for a 2,000-square-foot apartment. The rent controls also protect some less wealthy tenants.
>
> But in the City of the Dead, a poor family has to pay up to $40—a month's wage for some people—for a small apartment in the new rentals where controls are circumvented. . . . Like many other areas of the city, the necropolis has no protection from the entrepreneurs who build 90 percent of the city's new housing in disregard of zoning, safety and many other laws to meet the growing demand for low-cost homes.[20]

As usual, landlords in Cairo have found it advantageous to rent to transients and foreigners, rather than to natives who will stay on forever.

"I have an interesting situation," said a landlord in the relatively prosperous Mohandeseen area across town. He rents out two spacious apartments above his own.

"Directly above me, I have an Egyptian family paying $8 a month in rent, and that figure is controlled," he said. "The Germans on the top floor pay $2,000 for the same size apartment, uncontrolled. And it's not even the nicer of the two apartments."[21]

Although always crowded, Cairo did not experience an intense housing shortage until many Egyptians began to migrate to Persian Gulf countries as temporary workers during the Oil Boom of the late 1970s. Paying absurdly low rents, the emigrants hung on to their unoccupied apartments. Milad Hanna, former chairman of the Egyptian Parliament's housing committee, reported:

> In 1976 . . . Egypt had 6.94 million households in 7.3 million housing units of all categories, leaving a surplus of 360,000 units. A decade later . . . the surplus had risen to 1.8 million, one million of them in Cairo.
>
> The vacant properties are in varying categories.
>
> They include the homes of Egyptians working abroad and homes bought by those who can afford what Mr. Hanna called, "stored flats for future generations," or as other investments. . . .
>
> "A lot of marriages are postponed for long periods because the groom can't afford an apartment," a Western expert said. "The very poor," Mr. Hanna said, "marry and live in one room in the family house. So you have a return to the extended family unit."
>
> "What we have today," he said, "is houses without tenants and tenants without houses."[22]

Or, as they would call it in New York, Boston, Washington, San Francisco, Los Angeles, and a growing roster of American cities, "homeless people and peopleless homes."

Chapter 24

Homelessness and the Constitution

The conclusion of this book, as is already clear, is that regulation of the housing market is primarily responsible for homelessness—at least that portion which can be attributed to housing shortages and affordability, which is probably itself about half of all homelessness. Deregulation of the housing market is the solution. The American housing industry is an awesomely powerful engine capable of providing enough housing for everyone. The problem is that the majority has kept this housing from being built.

This conclusion is contrary to most popular wisdom. The conventional view, put forth by housing activists and accepted almost uncritically by the press, is that homelessness has been caused by the failure of the Federal government to provide low-income housing. The solution is that the government must build more housing, at a cost of tens of billions of dollars, to solve the problem.

There are several things that should be said in response to this analysis.

First, as illustrated in chapter one, there has been no reduction in Federal housing assistance. Much more money is being spent today, many more poor people assisted—and fewer middle-class people going along for the ride—than was the case at the beginning of the 1980s.

The only significant trend has been the efforts by two successive Republican administrations to switch Federal assistance from a cumbersome process of building and maintaining housing to a far more efficient system of giving housing vouchers directly to the poor. Since vouchers cost only about $4,500 a year while a new unit of public housing costs $9,000 a year to build and maintain, it is axiomatic that twice as many people can be helped for the same amount of money through a voucher system.

All the complaints about "cuts in housing spending" focus on a single figure—the reduction in annual spending *authorizations* from $35 billion to $8 billion over the last eight years. But, as illustrated before, this has no bearing on the actual money being spent, but merely indicates a change in the time over which money is being committed. The almost complete unwillingness of any more than a few members of the press to understand this distinction is one of the mysteries of the era.

Second, it should be noted that the unfolding scandals over HUD's distribution of section-8 certificates—although certainly reprehensible and indicative of vast corruption—has little bearing on the overall housing problem. Given the normal tenor of the debate, it probably will not be long before someone is charging that the political favoritism in distributing section-8 certificates has been the principal cause of homelessness. This is hardly the case.

Whatever inefficiencies the Reagan administration may have created in its award of section-8 certificates are essentially the inefficiencies of the program itself. As we have already seen, city governments have long pursued the same practices in distributing housing vouchers. The City of New York has refused to distribute section-8 vouchers at all, rather than allow them to be passed through to private landlords. A lengthy exposé by *The Chicago Tribune* found the leaders of several neighborhood political organizations, who spent all their time opposing private development in poverty-stricken areas, living comfortably on section-8 certificates.[1] The City of Berkeley has used section-8 certificates to subsidize city-constructed housing projects that have been filled with activists and affiliates of the dominant Berkeley Citizens Action.[2]

Thus, it has made only a small difference whether section-8 15-year housing certificates have gone to a Republican-connected builder in Essex, Maryland, or a Democratic-connected builder in Ypsilanti, Michigan. The poor in one city may be just as deserving as the poor in the other.

The important thing is that distributing Federal money to the *builder* of housing, rather than the poor themselves, has been eminently inefficient and corruptible in the first place. Ironically, the moderate rehabilitation programs that are the focus of the scandal are the very programs that the Reagan administration continually tried to eliminate, only to be thwarted by Congress. Even more ironically, the scandals have given HUD Secretary Jack Kemp the opportunity to end several of the programs despite Congressional objections.

Last, it must be said that the universal impulse to call upon the Federal government to solve the homeless problem only seems to serve as a way of distracting attention from the real locus of the problem—the universal hostility of local and municipal governments to new housing and development.

Exclusionary suburbs that wouldn't think of allowing a two- or three-family house to be built within their borders all chorus for the Federal government to "solve the housing problem" by building housing somewhere else. Rent-controlled tenants, who are essentially devouring a city's housing stock, all self-righteously demand the Federal government spend money to undo the damage they are steadily inflicting.

Such situations are familiar to all students of Constitutional history. They constitute something that is commonly called a "tyranny of the majority."

As all Constitutional scholars know, the Constitution was not written to establish unlimited democracy. It was written essentially to *curb* democracy, particularly the kind of majoritarian tyranny that was being practiced in the Colonial and state legislatures. Popular majorities were voting for the cancellation of all private debts, the payment of state debts through worthless paper money, and a variety of other short-sighted policies that were ruining the possibilities for viable commercial enterprise.

It is always with a great deal of embarrassment that we learn that the "minorities" that the Constitution was originally designed to protect were *commercial* minorities, rather than racial, ethnic, or sexual minorities. "[T]he most common and durable source of factions has been the various and unequal distribution of property," wrote Madison in *Federalist X*. Yet "the protection of different and unequal faculties of acquiring property" is "the first object of government."

Today, most of our concerns are for "civil" rights that apply to non-commercial behavior. People want to be left free to engage in whatever behavior they choose without interference from the government or a disapproving majority.

Groups engaged in unusual, but non-harmful, behavior are certainly deserving of basic civil protections from the passions and persecutions of the majority. But why can't people engaged in commercial behavior have the same protections as well? After all, their actions are just as likely to be immediately unpopular but beneficial to the long-term health of the society as are the actions of those who test the *mores* of a community through freedom of speech.

It was a common, widespread belief of the 19th century that the protections of the Constitution had ensured the nation's prosperity. In *A Machine That Would Go of Itself: The Constitution in American Culture* (1987), Michael Kammen, professor of history at Cornell, notes:

> The first schoolbook to discuss the Constitution appeared in 1796. Called *A Plain Political Cathechism*, it assured American youngsters that the Constitution provided for the happiness and prosperity of their country. In 1922 a basic civics text stressed exactly the same point. During the intervening 126 years, no connection was more commonly made. Not until the Great Depression began in 1929 did it begin to wither. . . .
>
> Even such a sophisticated man as James Madison, writing his will in 1835, could not resist incorporating this conventional formulation, referring to the Constitution's favorable "effects during a trial of so many years on the prosperity of the people living under it. . . ." Madison, like the rest of his countrymen, had accepted this nexus as a given.[3]

Yet Kammen, like so many contemporary academic historians, dismisses this long-held belief as a quaint bit of folk wisdom. Critiquing Noah Webster's *History of the United States* (1832), Kammen writes:

> Webster's chapter on the Constitution is seventeen pages long. Its opening sentence is a dilly: "In Asia the governments are all despotic." Then European absolutism gets slammed. The second paragraph defines republican government, and the next its distribution of governmental powers. After that the constitution is epitomized in five and a half pages. . . . Most of it narrates what the new government did in 1789, and then concludes: "From that time commenced the prosperity of the United States, which, with little interruption, has continued to this day." That is the equivalent, in American constitutionalism, of affirming that they all lived happily ever after. No causal link is really needed. It's a given.[4]

The failure of contemporary scholars to appreciate the *economic* accomplishments of the American Constitution only indicates how far we have come from understanding our own origins. The basic principles of minority rights enshrined in the Constitution are fundamental to the working of any successful economic system. The reason is simple. *Under the division of labor, everyone is a commercial minority.* There will always be more buyers than bakers of bread, more patients than dentists, more clients than lawyers, more rodeo fans than rodeo riders.

Economics cannot run on the principles of democracy. "Economic democracy," as quasi-socialists like Tom Hayden like to call it, does not work. The simple reason is that consumers will always outnumber producers. (If everyone were his own producer, there wouldn't be any need for commercial transactions.) The workings of an economic system rest, not upon majority rule, but upon the *restraint of the majority in NOT taking advantage of the minority*. Any one of the professions—doctor, lawyer, carpenter, plumber—could be permanently disabled if consumers were allowed to vote "democratically" on the terms of trade. It is only through voluntary restraint and the uninhibited transactions between producers and consumers that commercial life continues to exist.

The Constitution, for the better part of two centuries, made America safe for commercial prosperity. Producer minorities generally felt safe to pursue their professions, even in the face of vast consumer majorities. Majorities generally restrained themselves and the courts were willing to uphold the rights of commercial minorities, even when the task proved unpopular.

The threat of majority tyranny is never entirely erased, however, and it can always reassert itself. More often than not, it will take place under the banner of some kind of "progressivism." Price controls, government planning of the economy, partnerships between government, business, and labor—all are basically attempts by the majority to gain domination over commercial transactions by the power of the vote. During the economic crises of the 1930s, the courts wearied of the unpopular task of protecting property rights. They have now essentially abandoned it altogether.

All this might spell disaster for the economy, except that we have now outgrown national boundaries so that it is futile for the Federal or state legislatures to try to inhibit commercial minorities within our borders. The oil price controls of the 1970s were such a fiasco, not because Congress wasn't diligent in trying to exercise majority power, but because so much of the oil economy now lies outside our national boundaries.

One place where majorities can still exercise almost absolute economic power, however, is in housing. The building, selling, and renting of housing is still a local matter over which local majorities can exercise raw political power. We have a housing crisis precisely because so many of these majorities have been so successful in abridging the rights of people who build and maintain housing.

The case of zoning is particularly curious, since it reverses the common historical pattern and pits an affluent *majority* against a less affluent minority. Homeowners are more affluent than tenants and the people already established in a community are usually more affluent than people trying to get in. By voting to exclude rentals and other cheap housing, the majority constricts the *property rights* of a less affluent minority who would be able to secure housing under normal market conditions, as the case of Takoma Park so clearly illustrates.

Rent control is only slightly different. Tenants always outnumber landlords, but they do not always outnumber homeowners, who may be a majority in the community. Still, homeowners usually support rent control under the mistaken impression that they are helping the poor. In either case, rent control is a majority tyranny that leads to a breakdown in commercial transaction and makes housing scarce and unaffordable. The solution to this problem is to protect landlords and let the housing market work.

What immediate and practical strategies does this analysis suggest?

First, the legislative privileges that majorities have voted themselves in the housing market should be curbed. The U.S. Supreme Court has already taken a step in this direction by outlawing "welcome stranger" assessments. If property taxes were equalized and administered in an even-handed way, communities would be much more receptive to new development. Although there is some underlying logic to impact fees, they should not simply be used to load general costs onto newcomers in the community.

Zoning is a thicket that only the most courageous dare enter. The powers of local governments to determine land use are so well entrenched—and governments themselves so diligent in resisting challenges to these powers—that it is very difficult to imagine zoning being curbed on a case-by-case basis. The long ordeal and meager results of the Mt. Laurel case in New Jersey only underline the difficulties.

A far more useful approach is the concept of "takings," built on the Fifth Amendment, which states, once again, "nor shall private property be taken for public use without just compensation."

In 1987, the U.S. Supreme Court ruled that a decision by Los Angeles County to prohibit the First Evangelical Lutheran Church of Glendale, California, from rebuilding a structure in a floodplain constituted a taking of the property and must be financially compensated. In the majority opinion, Chief Justice William Rehnquist acknowledged that the decision would "lessen to some extent the freedom and flexibility of land-use planners." Commented *Time* magazine: "[C]itizens trying to limit development in their localities may find themselves at a disadvantage."[5]

The decision curbed a complete prohibition against any new building, but the principle could easily be applied to zoning itself. Sooner or later, some court is going to have to look past the fiction that zoning is aimed only at protecting the "health and safety" of the community and admit that the privacy, solitude, and property values of people within the community are also at stake. In addition, someone is going to have to acknowledge that a community's responsibility to future and potential residents is just as important as its responsiveness to the contemporary majority.

Anyone who values a free economy must dread the prospect of a nationwide, New-Jersey-style system of quotas for housing units in each community. The prospects of trying to administer such a plan are horrifying. What would be far easier to implement would be a system in which it is acknowledged that, when a municipality "downzones" a piece of property, it is taking part of the property for public use just as surely as if it were to condemn a portion of the property for a public cemetery. A system of compensation that reimbursed property owners for the losses inflicted by zoning restrictions would form an effective curb on the majority's unbridled powers of municipal zoning.

There is nothing wrong with a community trying to exclude unwanted uses and create a clean, quiet, exclusionary environment *as long as people are willing to pay the price*. To date, however, exclusionary zoning has been a free good—more than a free good, in fact, since exclusionary zoning raises property values. Compensating the losers in this process would not only curb excesses, it would also work toward social justice.

Finally, the question remains, what to do about rent control? The benefits of rent control are so ludicrously distributed while the disadvantages are so obvious and so general, that it is hard to imagine such a system has survived so long in a nation dedicated to the preservation of basic civil order. But of course there is no sense in trying to tell that to tenants in a rent-controlled community. They gain most of the advantages while pushing the disadvantages onto outsiders and future residents of the community.

The natural recourse against rent control would seem to be through the courts. Permanent rent controls would have been dismissed out of hand by the Federal judiciary 50 to 60 years ago. In more recent years, however, the Supreme Court has been more than willing to tolerate majority tyrannies and has refused several times to outlaw local rent control.

It would be easy enough to imagine that a Federal or state judiciary might some day rediscover property rights and look at rent control in its proper perspective. But is this to be preferred? And is it worth waiting for?

The Reagan administration took absolutely no initiatives in repudiating rent control. Satisfied with the task of reducing the scope of the Federal government, the administration took a very tolerant attitude toward economic regulation at the state and local level. Any attempt at dealing with rent control at the national level might be seen as contrary to the principles of the "new Federalism."

As homelessness becomes a national problem, however, the Federal government may soon be forced into a choice between dealing with the municipal origins of the housing problem, or awarding those same municipal governments billions of dollars in pursuit of housing programs that will not solve the problem. All things considered, a legislative approach at the national level seems preferable.

If I were Secretary of Housing and Urban Development, I would propose an omnibus anti-homelessness act that would do three things:

1) double the number of housing vouchers issued by the Federal government each year (cost about $5 billion);

2) require municipalities that exclude apartments or multi-family homes to compensate property owners and support the construction of multi-family housing in other communities;

3) abolish rent control except for national wartime emergencies.

Such a bill would be likely to meet with fierce local resistance. Abolishing rent control in New York, for example, would probably elicit the kind of mass public protest that characterized the South's response to school desegregation.

There are many things that cities like New York could do to help themselves in abolishing rent control. In Europe, for example, funds have been set up to help tenants readjust to a normal housing market. This usually means compensating tenants for the difference between their regulated rent and market rent over a number of years. In New York, the average regulated tenant has a rent differential of about $250 a month. This adds up to $3,000 a year.

If the city government reimbursed half these claims for two years, the two million regulated tenants could claim $6 billion. This compares favorably with the $5.1 billion the city is already planning to spend on a program that will do nothing more than take buildings out of the hands of private owners and turn them over to community organizations. For virtually the same price, New York could resolve its 45-year-old housing crisis and obviate forever the need for massive new housing programs.

Perhaps even more important than any legislation, though, will be the need for a national change in attitude toward developers and landlords. Housing is housing, and the only way to have enough of it is to build it. Developers are people who build housing. Landlords are people who maintain housing and make it available to people who can't afford to buy their own homes. Each is operating in a time-honored tradition of American entrepreneurship. If we can honor people who create prosperity in other fields, we can certainly honor the people who create prosperity in housing.

Conversely, we will also need to recognize that the person who draws the line around his property and tries to use the law to prevent others from getting what he already has is *not* a civic hero. It is difficult not to be envious and want to emulate the person who has achieved the isolated splendor of a country estate or suburban enclave. And admiration is certainly due where people have paid for it.

But where this kind of exclusiveness is achieved only by manipulating the law and exercising majoritarian tyranny, it should be seen for what it is—not a benign effort to "protect the environment" but a popular form of snobbery that has grave social consequences. If we are going to make room for each other in a more crowded America, we are all going to have to be a little more tolerant of each other's presence.

Taken together, all these measures should be sufficient to create enough room in this country for all Americans. It will certainly be enough to rescue those people who have been pushed to the fringes of our society and beyond—America's homeless.

Epilogue

Grand Central Station, February 28, 1989

It is two years to the day since I made my first sojourn among the homeless. The weather is cold. The newspapers say the homeless situation is still growing worse. It seems appropriate that I go back.

Frankly, I am not enthusiastic. The stories about the homeless have become more violent. The press coverage is exhaustive. Only three weeks ago, CBS's "48 Hours" did an extensive story about the homeless living in the bowels of Grand Central Station. The thought of a cold floor is no longer appealing. This time I have experience, though. I take a folded cardboard box with me when I leave home.

Arriving earlier in the evening, I catch the end of the commuter rush. The station is filled with people. At the center of the floor, a man plays haunting melodies on some kind of African flute, collecting money from a small crowd. The more disheveled people are against the walls. I take up a place at the end of a long row of homeless men under the Kodak mural. The man next to me is a huge Puerto Rican whose bloated body looks like that of a drowned man. He sleeps fitfully, waking every once in a while to scratch himself furiously, then sleeps again.

After getting settled I realize there is a television crew near one of the gates. They are taking pictures of homeless people. A cameraman wanders over in our direction and casually places his camera on the floor. Without being too obvious about it, he pans the camera from left to right, filming the row of sleeping men. The camera ends up pointing straight at me. I resist the temptation to wave into its dark eye and stare straight ahead.

Once again, it is only a short journey to the realization that nothing much is going to happen. With my cardboard mattress and my knit cap pulled down far over my head I apparently look right for the part. The few stares I get from commuters reflect the frightened curiosity the homeless must see every day. In fifteen minutes, the only interesting thing that has happened is a wiry, gray-haired homeless man in a jogging suit who has wandered by several times talking to himself.

I decide to talk to the television crew. I wander over and engage a cameraman on the edge of the group. "What network is this?" I ask.

"CBS," he says, obviously startled to find himself being quizzed by a homeless man.

"You just did a show about the homeless a few weeks ago, didn't you?"

"Oh, that was '48 Hours.' This is 'Sixty Minutes.' " Now he is in on the game and eager to talk. "We're doing a whole story on the permanent residents of Grand Central Station. You wouldn't believe all the people who live in here. They're upstairs, downstairs, everywhere. It's going to be great. You should see it."

Not wanting to get too far out of character, I wander back to my post against the wall. After a few more minutes, the skinny little man with the jogging suit comes wandering by again, still talking loudly to himself. For lack of anything better to do, I jump up and fall in beside him.

"Where's a good place to sleep around here?"

"Ah, it ain't no good up here anymore," he says, suddenly rational. "I'm going downtown. Just follow me. I'll show you where to go." Then he spots my cardboard. "Oh, you've already got your sleeping bag." He is impressed.

Almost immediately, he leads me out past the ramp where I slept the last time. It is already much more crowded now, with people huddled together on both sides of the wall, like patients in a hospital emergency room. We carefully pick our way through the crowd. People eye us curiously. Nearly all the faces are black.

"This place ain't no good anymore," my companion whispers conspiratorially as we head down the subway stairs. "I'll show you somethin' much better."

We come to an isolated turnstile. On the other side, a lone transit worker mops the floor. My friend gives an exaggerated sense of alarm and sneaks back up the hallway to hide behind a post. "Don't let him see us," he whispers. He is definitely of the old school.

Finally, the mop-wielder moves off to another sector. We sprint from our post and duck under the turnstile. "You got to be smart about these things," he winks at me as we head down the stairs.

On the downtown train, he regales passengers with Irish drinking songs. As my eye wanders, I spot a new subway poster showing Mayor Koch gesturing expansively toward the Manhattan skyline. "Who says you can't find an affordable apartment in New York?" the mayor asks riders. "The City of New York is providing thousands of affordable 1–3 bedroom apartments for low-, moderate-, and middle-income New York families." Torn from bleeding hands.

At the first stop, my friend jumps up. "This is it. Let's go." We are at 34th Street. We wander upstairs and become completely lost. I have no idea where he wants to go. Finally, he wanders over to some late-night construction workers. "Hey, which way is it to Penn Station?"

"What are you going to do, run the marathon?" they shout over the clatter of jackhammers.

"Ah, go to hell," my friend mutters and walks away.

"I think it's over this way," I suggest, pointing toward the West Side.

"Nah, I know where I'm going," he says, starting down the slope toward the East River. Not wanting to be impolite, I go along. After half-a-block he changes his mind and wordlessly reverses direction. "I know where I am now," he says.

"My wife always carries a compass," I say. He is unimpressed.

"I was married for twenty years, you know. I got two sons older than you. I used to be a bricklayer. Had a house on Staten Island. I been on the streets for twenty years now. It ain't a bad life, once you get used to it. I go home every once in a while, see my family."

"Why'd you leave in the first place?"

"Liked to drink too much, I guess. Drank all my money away, then everybody else's too. They were glad to see me go."

"Do you ever think of going back to bricklaying?"

"Nah. I'm too old now. Anyway, I like it out here. It's easy enough, once you know the ropes. You got to watch out about getting robbed, though. These kids get meaner all the time."

We are approaching Penn Station. After a few more wrong turns, we wander into the subway station. About two dozen homeless men are congregated in a small waiting area behind the turnstiles. We pass through the gate, walking right past two nodding policemen. It is like entering a men's club. "Hey, Mickey, how you doin'?" says a dignified black man in a Russian fur hat, greeting my companion. Mickey introduces me all around. "Hey, you already got your own bed!" says the man in the Russian hat, eyeing my cardboard. "Pretty smart." I feel like a veteran.

It is an odd setting. Most of these men seem rational, comfortable, only a bit seedy. Quiet conversations buzz all around. On the floor behind us, a dormitory row of about 20 men lie sleeping. At worst, it feels like an army barracks or a senior citizens' center. Yet we are all homeless in the bowels of Penn Station.

It doesn't last for long. In a few minutes, a cleaning crew arrives and begins shooing everyone away. "Come on. Let's go, you guys. On to the next stop." Sleeping bodies drag themselves awake. The pungent odor of ammonia fills the air. The crews slap their mops back and forth in neat, wet rows.

Mickey disappears, so I follow the other men on to the next way station. It is occupied by a younger crowd, with vague overtones of suburban drug-dealing. A group of cops stand engaged in a long conversation with a couple of kids with sleeping bags. A middle-aged black man hovers over an older man in a wheelchair. I realize that the shuttered book-store in front of me is a place where I have shopped many times.

Once again, I take a seat on the floor. The station lights burn brightly overhead. A listless man next to me asks other homeless men for spare change. A rookie cop wanders among the rows, giving civics lessons. "Can't any of you guys find a job? What the hell's the matter with you, anyway? I work, don't I? You don't see me sitting around on my rear end."

I move once more to get away from the glare and commotion. Wandering past a row of stores I find a narrow passageway that serves three automatic bank tellers. It is warm and the floor is covered with bodies. There is room for just one more at the end. I take the last place and survey the other residents. Few are asleep but no one says a word.

After a while, I notice a man about three bodies away. He is young—probably only about 34—with a face ravaged by years of hard living. His hair is long, his chin covered with stubble, yet he wears the wrinkled remains of a business suit. There is something vaguely respectable about him. He looks like a stockbroker who went on a drinking binge a couple of years ago and hasn't called his wife yet to tell her what happened.

In another minute, the seedy stockbroker stands up and walks over to the automatic teller machine. Slowly he undoes his pants and starts to urinate into a small wastepaper slot beneath the video screen. Everyone holds their breath.

"Why you filthy PIG!" A nightstick slams the wall inches from my head. The rookie cop has caught him just as he finishes. "All right, all of you, out of here, right now. Let's go. See this guy—he spoiled it for the rest of you. Remember that.

And you—I never want to see you in this station again." The stockbroker shows only animal resentment. Not much enlightenment in that face after all.

So again we move on. I shuffle from place to place, following the general drift of the crowds, without much expectation. The cops are always moving people to make way for the cleaning crews, yet the station is open all night and apparently everyone is allowed to stay. Later, I see the stockbroker lurking behind a post. He hasn't left the station after all and there will probably be another confrontation.

By 4 A.M., I have had enough. I take the subway home, leaving without any regrets. Whatever knowledge is going to come of this, I have probably achieved it.

In two years of studying homelessness, I feel I have grasped some of the basic issues. Still, the problem sometimes seems almost overwhelming. Some of the people I have met could probably survive in seedy hotels or boarding houses, but for others, some kind of social services are obviously necessary.

Despite the force and confidence with which people put forth their arguments, I wonder if anybody really knows what is causing homelessness. Building more housing and getting rid of rent control are my favorite solutions, but other things are obviously going to be needed as well.

In a sense, homelessness remains an enigma that the homeless themselves must live out. I doubt if anyone completely understands the problem. Despite all we can do, there are probably many long nights left ahead in Homeless America.

Appendix

Source of Statistics for the Regression Analysis

The homeless figures for 35 cities are from the 1984 *Report to the Secretary of Housing and Urban Development on Emergency Shelters and Homeless Populations.* Figures for the remaining 15 cities were compiled from local estimates.

The complete list of cities added to the study is: St. Louis; Santa Monica; Newark; Yonkers; Dallas-Fort Worth; Denver; Charleston, West Virginia; Atlanta; San Diego; New Orleans; Albuquerque; Tucson; Burlington; Milwaukee; Providence; and Lincoln, Nebraska.

The only reason for eliminating the six smaller cities was the great difficulty in securing a reliable figure for the rental vacancy rate.

In only three cities—Cleveland, Baltimore, and New York—did HUD's estimates seem unrealistic. Cleveland had a per-capita rate of only 0.8, Baltimore 0.9, and New York 4.0. For Baltimore I used another report that doubled HUD's "highest estimate," giving a per-capita rate of 2.4. For Cleveland and New York I used figures well below the "highest estimates" but slightly higher than the "most reliable range." Given the high visibility of the homeless in New York, the per-capita figures still seem low.

Hartford was counted as a rent-controlled city even though the government does not fix the price of every apartment. Hartford and several other Connecticut cities practice "rent review," whereby a city board can lower a tenant's rent on request. Given the high visibility of rent regulations in both nearby New York and Boston, this kind of rent regulation appears to be an incipient form of rent control.

HUD's estimates of the number of homeless were made for the year 1984. The other figures are from the following sources:

Population figures are from the 1984 Census Bureau report. Unemployment figures are an average of 1985 and 1986 figures from the U.S. Department of Labor. Poverty rates are from the 1980 census. Public housing figures are from HUD's records published February 27, 1987. Population growth figures are from the 1970 and 1984 census. The temperature and rainfall figures were compiled by the National Oceanic and Atmospheric Administration (NOAA) from 1951 to 1980. Rental vacancy rates are from the Bureau of Census for 22 major cities (averaging the figures from 1981 to 1985), plus a wide variety of 1986 estimates from local sources. Median rents and median home prices are both from the 1980 census. Rents are for the city itself, while home prices are for the entire Standard Metropolitan Statistical Area (SMSA).

The actual regressions were performed by Dr. Jeffrey Simonoff, professor of statistics at New York University.

Notes

Chapter 1 The Paradox of Homelessness (I)

1. James Hughes and George Sternlieb, *The Dynamics of America's Housing*, Piscataway: Center for Urban Policy Research, 1987, p. 177.
2. The United States Conference of Mayors, *A Status Report on Hunger and Homelessness in America's Cities: 1988*, January, 1989.
3. Sarah Glazer, "Affordable Housing: Is There Enough?", *Editorial Research Reports*, January 6, 1989.
4. Conference of Mayors, *op. cit.*, p. 25.
5. Source: U.S. Bureau of Labor Statistics.
6. Source: U.S. Bureau of the Census, Incomes Branch.
7. Conference of Mayors, *op. cit.*, p. 62.
8. Kim Hopper and Jill Hamberg, *The Making of America's Homeless: From Skid Row to the New Poor*, New York: Community Service Society, 1984.

9. *Ibid.*, p. 12.
10. Peter Rossi, *Without Shelter: Homelessness in the 1980s,* New York: Priority Press Publications, 1989, p. 40.
11. George Sternlieb and James W. Hughes, *Future of Rental Housing,* Piscataway: Center for Urban Policy Research, 1981, p. 10.
12. *Ibid.*, pp. 9–10.
13. Source: U.S. Bureau of Census, Incomes Branch.
14. William C. Apgar, Jr., and H. James Brown, "The State of the Nation's Housing," Cambridge: Joint Center for Housing Studies of Harvard University, 1988, pp. 14–15.
15. Rossi, *op. cit.*, p. 19.
16. Fund-raising letter, Community for Creative Non-Violence, 1989.
17. Edgar O. Olsen, "Housing Subsidies Rise for the Needy," *The Wall Street Journal,* December 12, 1988.
18. R. Allen Hays, *The Federal Government and Urban Housing,* Albany: State University of New York Press, 1985, p. 169.
19. Source: U.S. Department of Housing and Urban Development.
20. William Celis III, "Public-Housing Units Are Rapidly Decaying, Causing Many to Close," *The Wall Street Journal,* December 15, 1986.
21. Source: U.S. Department of Housing and Urban Development.
22. Bonita Brodt, "The Chicago Wall, Part IV," *The Chicago Tribune,* December 3, 1986.
23. Rick Atkinson and Chris Spolar, "D.C. Public Housing: A Legacy of Despair," *The Washington Post,* March 26, 1989.
24. Spolar and Atkinson, "Maintenance System Needs Fixing," *The Washington Post,* March 27, 1989.
25. Anthony de Palma, "Newark Suit Would Keep High-Rises," *The New York Times,* March 30, 1989.
26. Apgar and Brown, *op. cit.* p. 17.
27. Source: U.S. Department of Housing and Urban Development.
28. Apgar and Brown, *op. cit.* pp. 17–18.
29. Interview with author.
30. *The Report of the President's Commission on Housing,* Washington: U.S. Government Printing Office, 1982.

Chapter 2 The Paradox of Homelessness (II)

1. Gina Kolata, "Twins of the Streets: Homelessness and Addiction," *The New York Times,* May 22, 1989.
2. Hopper and Hamberg, *The Making of America's Homeless,* p. 53.
3. Sternlieb and Hughes, *The Future of America's Housing,* p. 7.
4. "Affordable Housing: Is There Enough," *Editorial Research Reports,* January 6, 1989.
5. Source: U.S. Bureau of Census, Housing Starts.
6. Source of multi-family figures: Daniel O'Connor, *Rent Control in the United States: A*

Declining Phenomenon, Emeryville, California: Johnstown Institutional Advisors, Inc., 1987; source of vacancy figures: U.S. Bureau of Census.

7. John I. Gilderbloom and Richard P. Appelbaum, *Rethinking Rental Housing,* Philadelphia: Temple University Press, 1988.
8. Apgar and Brown, "The State of the Nation's Housing," p. 1.
9. *Ibid.,* pp. 4, 7, 8.
10. Anthony Downs, *Rental Housing in the 1980s,* Washington: The Brookings Institution, 1983, p. 27.
11. Apgar and Brown, *op. cit.,* p. 5.
12. *Ibid.,* p. 8.
13. Gilderbloom and Appelbaum, *op. cit.* p. 23.
14. Source: U.S. Bureau of Labor Statistics.
15. Martha R. Burt and Barbara E. Cohen, "Feeding the Homeless: Does the Prepared Meals Provision Help?" Washington: Urban Institute, 1988.
16. E. Fuller Torrey, *Nowhere To Go,* New York: Harper and Row, 1988.
17. Charles Krauthammer, "Billie Boggs Revisited," *The New York Daily News,* December 27, 1988.
18. Ellen Bassuck, "The Homeless Problem," *Scientific American,* July 1984.
19. David Whitman, "Finally, Hope for the Homeless," *U.S. News & World Report,* February 29, 1988.
20. Michael R. Sosin, "Homeless in Chicago," *Public Welfare,* Winter, 1989, pp. 22, 28.
21. *Ibid.,* p. 27.
22. *Ibid.,* p. 25.
23. Rossi, *Without Shelter: Homelessness in the 1980s,* p. 28.
24. *Idem.*
25. *Ibid.,* p. 40.
26. Martin Morse Wooster, "The Homeless Problem: An Adman's Dream," *Reason,* July 1987.
27. Thomas J. Main, "The Homeless of New York," *The Public Interest,* Summer 1983.
28. Howard Bahr and Theodore Caplow, *Old Men Drunk and Sober,* New York: NYU Press, 1974.
29. Anna Kondratas, "The Homeless," *The Sovereign Citizen,* Summer 1987. Quote is from Alice W. Solenberger, *One Thousand Homeless Men, A Study of Original Records,* New York: Charities Publication Committee, 1911.
30. Rossi, *op. cit.,* p. 19.

Chapter 3 What Causes Homelessness?

1. Mitch Snyder and Mary Ellen Hombs, *Homelessness in America,* Washington: Community for Creative Non-Violence, 1982.
2. Fund-raising letter, Community for Creative Non-Violence, 1989.
3. Personal interviews.

4. Rossi, *Without Shelter: Homelessness in the 1980s,* p. 4.
5. Peter H. Rossi, James D. Wright, Gene A. Fisher, and Georgianna Willis, "The Urban Homeless: Estimating Composition and Size," *Science,* March 13, 1987.
6. *A Report to the Secretary on the Homeless and Emergency Shelters,* U.S. Department of Housing and Urban Development, 1984.
7. See appendix for complete explanation of method.

Chapter 4 A Housing Model for Homelessness

1. Ellen Bassuck, "The Feminization of Homelessness: Homeless Families in Boston Shelters," unpublished monograph, quoted in Thomas Main, "The Homeless Families of New York," *The Public Interest,* Fall, 1986.
2. Kolata, *op. cit.*
3. Hopper and Hamburg, *The Making of America's Homeless,* pp. 60, 62.
4. John Atlas and Peter Drier, "The Phony Case Against Rent Control," *The Progressive,* April 1989.
5. Downs, *Rental Housing in the 1980s,* p. 36.
6. Thomas Geoghegan, "America's Greatest City," *The New Republic,* March 25, 1985.
7. M. Bruce Johnson, ed., *Resolving the Housing Crisis,* San Francisco: Pacific Institute for Public Policy Research, 1982, p. 2.
8. Bernard Frieden, *The Environmental Protection Hustle,* Cambridge: The MIT Press, 1979, p. 37ff.
9. *Ibid.,* p. 45.
10. *Ibid.,* p. 46.
11. Asra Q. Nomani, "Buyers' Panic Sweeps California's Big Market In One-Family Homes," *The Wall Street Journal,* June 1, 1988.
12. Thomas J. Lueck, "Citizens Gain in Anti-Development Wars," *The New York Times,* May 14, 1989.
13. Carter B. Horsley, "Pinching the Popsicles: Civic Groups Campaign for Major Downzoning," *The New York Post,* June 29, 1989.
14. Diana Shaman, "A 307-House Proposal for the Pine Barrens," *The New York Times,* May 14, 1989.
15. "The City's Low-Rise Side Stands Up," *The New York Times,* May 21, 1989.
16. George Sternlieb, *The Tenement Landlord,* New Brunswick: Rutgers University Press, 1966, p. 93.
17. Anthony Downs, *Opening Up the Suburbs,* New Haven, Yale University Press, 1973, pp. 116–17.
18. "Bringing the City Back to Life," *Time,* November 23, 1987.
19. George Sternlieb and James W. Hughes, "The Changing Demography of the Central City," *Scientific American,* August 1980.
20. *Report of the National Housing Task Force: Hearing before the Subcommittee on Housing and Urban Affairs of the Committee on Banking, Housing, and Urban Affairs, United State Senate, April 12 and 13, 1988,* p. 40.

21. Herb Jaffe, "New Home Prices Hitting the Roof," *The Newark Star-Ledger,* January 8, 1989.
22. Hughes and Sternlieb, *The Dynamics of America's Housing,* p. 134.
23. Jack Lail, "Braking the Mobile-Home Industry Skid," *The New York Times,* November 11, 1988.
24. This point is made throughout Hughes and Sternlieb, *The Dynamics of America's Housing.*
25. Downs, *Opening Up the Suburbs;* Michael N. Danielson, *The Politics of Exclusion,* New York: Columbia University Press, 1976.

Chapter 5 How the Housing Market Works

1. All figures provided by Motor Vehicle Manufacturers' Association.
2. John B. Lansing, Charles Wade Clifton, and James N. Morgan, *New Homes and Poor People,* Ann Arbor: Institute for Social Research, 1969.
3. *Ibid.,* p. 68.
4. *Ibid,* pp. 42ff.
5. *Ibid.,* p. 32.
6. Sternlieb and Hughes, *The Future of Rental Housing,* pp. 10, 71–73.
7. Lansing, Clifton, and Morgan, *op. cit.* p. 48.
8. *Ibid.,* p. 49.
9. *Ibid.,* p. 66.
10. Downs, *Opening Up the Suburbs,* p. 50.
11. Patrick Reardon and Bonita Brodt, "The Chicago Wall, Part Six: CHA Finances Falling Apart as Quickly as its Buildings," *The Chicago Tribune,* December 5, 1986.
12. Reardon and Brodt, "The Chicago Wall," *The Chicago Tribune,* November 30, 1986.
13. Lewis G. Watts et. al., *The Middle-Income Negro Family Faces Urban Renewal,* Waltham, Massachusetts: Brandeis University, 1964.
14. Herbert J. Gans, *The Urban Villagers,* Glencoe: The Free Press, 1962, p. 20.
15. Sternlieb, *The Tenement Landlord,* p. 70ff.
16. Michael Dorman, *The Making of a Slum,* New York: Delacourt Press, 1972.
17. *Ibid.,* p. 1.
18. *Ibid.,* p. 13.
19. *Ibid.,* p. 3.
20. *Ibid.,* pp. 28–29.

Chapter 6 The Housing Market in Action

1. Source: National Association of Realtors.
2. Patricia Ewing Pace, *Kansas City: The Spirit, The People, The Promise,* Northridge, California: Windsor Publications, 1987, p. 71.
3. *Idem.*
4. Constance McLaughlin Green, *American Cities in the Growth of the Nation,* New York: Harper Colophon, 1965, pp. 41ff.

5. *Cincinnati: The Queen City,* Cincinnati: Cincinnati Historical Society, 1988, p. 133.
6. Walter Muir Whitehill, *Boston: A Topographical History,* Cambridge: Harvard University Press, 1968, pp. 52, 47.
7. Oscar Handlin, *Boston's Immigrants,* Cambridge: Belknap Press of Harvard University, 1959, p. 94.
8. John P. Marquand, *The Late George Apley,* quoted in Whitehill, *op. cit.,* pp. 119–120.
9. Albert Benedict Wolfe, *The Lodging Housing Problem in Boston,* Cambridge: Harvard University Press, 1913.
10. Whitehill, *op. cit.,* p. 164.
11. Sam Bass Warner, Jr., *Streetcar Suburbs: The Process of Growth in Boston, (1870–1890),* Cambridge: Harvard University Press, 1978, p. 37.
12. *Ibid.,* p. 26.
13. *Ibid.,* p. 33.
14. *Ibid.,* p. 66.
15. *Ibid.,* pp. 75–76.
16. *Ibid.,* p. 40.
17. Whitehill, *op. cit.* p. 193.
18. Howard Husock, "With Kemp In, How Will Housing Make Out? Boston, San Diego Show the Way," *The Wall Street Journal,* January 18, 1989.

Chapter 7 Exclusionary Zoning

1. Richard F. Babcock, *The Zoning Game,* Madison: The University of Wisconsin Press, 1966, p. 3.
2. Quoted in Carl J. Dahlman, "An Economic Analysis of Zoning Laws," in Johnson, ed., *Resolving the Housing Crisis,* p. 221.
3. *Village of Euclid v. Ambler Realty Co.* 272 U.S. 365, 47 S. Ct. 114, 71 L. Ed. 303 (1926.)
4. *Ibid.*
5. *Ibid.*
6. *Ibid.*
7. Babcock, *op. cit.,* p. 17.
8. "On L.I., Bias Case Looks At Zoning and the Poor," *The New York Times,* September 5, 1988.
9. Virginia Postrel, "Tapping the Shadow Housing Market," *The Wall Street Journal,* March 13, 1987.
10. "Suburb of Washington at Odds Over Evictions," *The New York Times,* February 21, 1988; "Eviction of Renters Begins in Maryland Town," *The New York Times,* May 1, 1988.
11. Asra Q. Nomani, "Buyers' Panic Sweeps California's Big Market In One-Family Homes," *The Wall Street Journal,* June 1, 1988.
12. "Campers Wait Days on Condo Trail," *The New York Times,* April 26, 1987.
13. *Ibid.*

14. George Gilder, *Wealth and Poverty,* New York: Bantam Books, 1981, pp. 210–211.
15. Personal communication, March 13, 1989.
16. Dahlman, *op. cit.,* p. 218.
17. Bernard H. Siegan, *Land Use Without Zoning,* Lexington: D.C. Heath, 1972.
18. Thomas Hazlett, "Private Blueprint for Houston's Boom: Doing It Without Zoning," *Reason,* November 1983.
19. Steve Frazier, "Housing-Market Bust in Houston Is Creating Rash of Instant Slums," *The Wall Street Journal,* February 2, 1987.
20. Hazlett, *op. cit.*
21. Source: San Diego city government.
22. Robert Reinhold, "In San Diego, the Developers Profit As Homeless Get Low-Cost Housing," *The New York Times,* September 6, 1988.
23. *Village of Belle Terre vs. Boras,* 416 U.S. (1974), p. 1.
24. Dahlman, *op. cit.,* p. 236.
25. Ernest Erber, "The Road to Mt. Laurel," and Herbert M. Franklin, "The Most Important Zoning Decision Since Euclid?" *Planning,* November 1985.
26. Excerpts from decision, *The New York Times,* January 21, 1983.
27. *Ibid.*
28. Robert Hanley, "Affordable Housing in Jersey Is Still An Elusive Goal," *The New York Times,* October 24, 1988.
29. Downs, *Opening Up the Suburbs,* p. 44.
30. Jerome G. Rose, "Questions Remain in the Wake of Mt. Laurel," *Planning,* November 1985.

Chapter 8 Who Pays the Piper?

1. This account is taken almost entirely from Robert Kuttner, *The Revolt of the Haves,* New York: Simon and Schuster, 1980, pp. 31ff.
2. Henry J. Aaron, *Who Pays the Property Tax?,* Washington: Brookings Institution, 1975, p. 60.
3. Michael Winerip, "Howdy, Stranger, Have a Big Dose of Realty Taxes," *The New York Times,* April 11, 1989.
4. George Sternlieb, *The Garden Apartment Development: A Municipal Cost-Revenue Analysis,* New Brunswick: Bureau of Economic Research, Rutgers University, 1964.
5. Danielson, *The Politics of Exclusion,* pp. 58–59.
6. *Ibid.,* p. 73. First quote is from Morton Lustig, *Hearings before the National Commission on Urban Problems,* 1967; second is from brief of plaintiffs-respondents in *Southern Burlington County NAACP v. Township of Mt. Laurel,* 1972.
7. Robert C. Wood, *1400 Government: The Political Economy of the New York Region,* Garden City: Doubleday Anchor, 1961.
8. *Ibid.,* p. 62.
9. *Ibid.,* pp. 53–56.

10. Terry Schwadron, editor, *California and the American Tax Revolt,* Berkeley: University of California Press, 1984, p. 4.
11. Aaron, *op. cit.*
12. *Ibid.,* p. 93.
13. Arthur C. Roemer, "Classification of Property," in C. Lowell Harriss, ed., *The Property Tax and Local Finance,* New York: The Academy of Political Science, 1983, pp. 115ff.
14. Kuttner, *op. cit.;* Schwadron, *op. cit.;* James Ring Adams, *Secrets of the Tax Revolt;* New York: Harcourt Brace Jovanovich, 1984.

Chapter 9 Controlling Growth

1. Frieden, *The Environmental Protection Hustle,* p. 12.
2. *Ibid.,* p. 97.
3. *Ibid.,* p. 150.
4. *Ibid.,* p. 5.
5. Allan R. Gold, "Governor Offers Vermont a Plan on Controlled Growth," *The New York Times,* January 13, 1988.
6. Cornelius F. Foote, Jr., "Fauquier, Faced with Growth, Moves to Control It," *The Washington Post,* February 28, 1987.
7. "Slow-Growthers Regroup After Election Losses," *California Planning and Development Report,* December 1988.
8. *Ibid.*
9. Paul Clancy, "California City Votes on Population Limits," *USA Today,* April 20, 1987.
10. Robert Reinhold, "The New California Dream: Closing the Door," *The New York Times,* June 12, 1988.
11. *Ibid.*
12. *Ibid.*
13. Frieden, *op. cit.,* p. 9.
14. Quoted in Herb Jaffe, "Bureaucrats blame 'the other guy' for home building woes in Jersey," part nine, *The Newark Star-Ledger,* January 15, 1989.
15. Jon Sonstelie and Alan Gin, "Residential Development and the Cost of Local Public Services," in Johnson, ed., *Resolving the Housing Crisis,* p. 113.
16. Wood, *1400 Governments,* p. 53.
17. Herb Jaffe, "Builders say some municipalities reap a windfall from their excessive fees," part ten, *The Newark Star-Ledger,* January 18, 1989.
18. Richard W. Stevenson, "Debate Grows on Development Fees," *The New York Times,* February 16, 1989.
19. *Ibid.*
20. Alan S. Oser, "Innovator in Suburbs Under Fire," *The New York Times,* March 28, 1971.

21. Robert A. Hamilton, "A Lottery (and Other) Affordability Deals," *The New York Times,* January 10, 1988.
22. Michael Winerip, "D'Amato, His Village and Favoritism in Housing," *The New York Times,* June 8, 1989; Winerip, "Village Facing Suit on H.U.D. Deals," *The New York Times,* June 20, 1989.

Chapter 10 Municipal Rent Control

1. Richard J. Devine, *Who Benefits from Rent Control?,* Oakland: Center for Community Change, 1985, p. 63.
2. *Ibid.,* p. 64.
3. Anne Morgenthaler, "Santa Monica rent board takes an aggressive turn," *The Outlook,* September 25, 1988.
4. Sticks and Stones, "Missing Units Found!" *The Berkeley Express,* October 21, 1988.
5. "Missing Houses," *The San Francisco Chronicle,* October 3, 1988.
6. Tom Bethell, "Why Berkeley Is Turning Into a Commuter School," *The Wall Street Journal,* October 11, 1988.
7. Anne Morgenthaler, "Would-be SM tenants need luck landing unit," *The Outlook,* April 8, 1989.
8. Tracy Wilkinson, "Santa Monica: A House Divided by Rent Control," *The Los Angeles Times,* April 29, 1989.
9. Mark E. Kann, *Middle Class Radicalism in Santa Monica,* Philadelphia: Temple University Press, 1986, p. 176.
10. Devine, *op. cit.*
11. Marty Shiffenbauer, Letter to the Editor, *The Wall Street Journal,* July 9, 1985, quoted in *Ibid.,* p. 32.
12. Peter Collier and David Horowitz, "Slouching Toward Berkeley: Socialism in One City," *The Public Interest,* Winter 1989, p. 65.
13. Marcia Chambers, "Tolerant Policy on Homeless Divides Santa Monica," *The New York Times,* March 28, 1986.

Chapter 11 Housing Reform (I)

1. Jacob Riis, *How the Other Half Lives,* New York: Hill and Wang, 1957.
2. *Ibid.,* pp. 43–46.
3. *Ibid.,* p. ix.
4. Riis, "The Clearing of Mulberry Bend, *Review of Reviews,* 12 (1895) 172, 177.
5. Lawrence Friedman, *The Government and Slum Housing: A Century of Frustration,* Chicago: Rand McNally and Company, 1968.
6. Riis, *op. cit.,* p. 5.
7. *Ibid.,* pp. 5–6.
8. *Ibid.,* p. 6.
9. *Ibid.,* pp. 11–12.

10. Downs, *Opening Up The Suburbs,* pp. 6–7.
11. Octavia Hill Association, "Annual Report for the Year 1986," "Annual Report for the Year 1987."
12. Friedman, *op. cit.* p. 75.
13. Riis, *op. cit.,* p. 27.
14. Friedman, *op. cit.,* p. 87.
15. Woody Klein, *Let in the Sun,* New York, Macmillan, 1964, p. 69.
16. James Ford, *Slums and Housing,* Cambridge: Harvard University Press, 1936, vol. 1, p. 205.
17. Chapter 635, Section 44, Massachusetts Acts, 1912.
18. Prescott Hall, "The Menace of the Three Decker," *Housing Problems in America,* Proceedings of the Fifth National conference on Housing, 1916, p. 133.
19. Hall, *op. cit.,* quoted in Howard Husock, "The Case for Three-Deckers," *The Public Interest,* forthcoming.
20. *Ibid.*
21. *Ibid.*
22. Edith Elmer Wood, *Housing for the Low-Income Wage Earner,* New York: The Macmillan Company, 1919.
23. *Cincinnati: The Queen City,* p. 111.
24. Klein, *op. cit.* p. 95.
25. *Ibid,* p. 96.
26. *Ibid,* p. 97.
27. Quoted, *Ibid.,* pp. 102–103.
28. Iver Peterson, "Tenements of 1880's Adapt to 1980's," *The New York Times,* January 3, 1988.
29. Friedman, *op. cit.,* p. 114.
30. Jane Lang McGrew and Ana Fabregas, "The Housing Act of 1937: Legal Origins," *Journal of Housing,* September/October 1987.
31. Quoted in Friedman, pp. 109, 139.
32. Bonita Brodt, "The Chicago Wall, Part 4: Dream of Progress Died Quickly at Taylor Homes," *The Chicago Tribune,* December 3, 1986.
33. Harrison Salisbury, *The Shook-Up Generation,* New York: Harper and Row, 1958, p. 75.
34. Jane Jacobs, *The Death and Life of Great American Cities,* New York: Random House, 1961.
35. Friedman, *op. cit.* p. 143.

Chapter 12 Housing Reform (II)

1. Robert Moses, "Slums and City Planning," *The Atlantic Monthly,* January 1945, p. 63.
2. " 'Federal Bulldozer's' Fallacies identified in NSHRO's detailed examination of book" *Journal of Housing,* No. 4, 1965.

3. Bernard J. Frieden, "Housing and National Urban Goals: Old Policies and New Realities," in James Q. Wilson, ed., *The Metropolitan Enigma,* New York: Doubleday Anchor, 1970, p. 200.
4. *Citizens Housing and Planning Council News,* New York, July 1950, p. 1, quoted in Klein, *Let in the Sun,* p. 110.
5. Roger Starr, *The Living End: The City and Its Critics,* New York: Coward-McCann, 1966, p. 131.
6. Martin Anderson, *The Federal Bulldozer: A Critical Analysis of Urban Renewal Policies, 1949–1962,* Cambridge: MIT Press, 1964.
7. *Ibid.,* p. 60.
8. *Ibid.,* p. 46.
9. *Ibid.,* p. 58.
10. "Bringing the City Back to Life," *Time,* November 23, 1987.
11. Allen J. Matusow, *The Unravelling of America: A History of Liberalism in the 1960s,* New York: Harper and Row, 1984, p. 232.
12. *Ibid.,* pp. 233–234.
13. HUD, "Report on Audit of Section 236 Multi-family Housing Program," 1972.
14. Matusow, *op. cit.,* p. 236.
15. Hays, *The Federal Government and Urban Housing,* p. 151.
16. Clifford B. May, "How H.U.D. Helped Many Make Money From Poverty," *The New York Times,* June 25, 1989.
17. Michael Carliner, "Homelessness—A Housing Problem?" in Richard D. Bingham, Roy E. Green, and Sammis B. White, eds., *The Homeless in Contemporary Society,* Newbury Park, California: Sage Publications, 1989.
18. Michael H. Lang, "Measuring Economic Benefit Streams Occasioned by Gentrification," paper presented at seminar, "Gentrification: Alternative Explanations and Polar Policies," American Association for the Advancement of Science, annual meeting, March 24–29, 1984.
19. *Ibid.*
20. Raymond L. Flynn and Joseph P. Kennedy III, "Decent, Affordable Housing for All," *The New York Times,* January 25, 1988.
21. Gilderbloom and Appelbaum, *Rethinking Rental Housing,* p. 68.
22. Community Ownership Organization Project, *The Cities' Wealth: Programs for Community Economic Control in Berkeley, California,* Washington: Conference on Alternative State and Local Policies, 1976, p. 21.
23. Philip Shanon, "Why H.U.D. Has Been So Inviting To So Many," *The New York Times,* June 4, 1989.

Chapter 13 Landlords

1. Klein, *Let in the Sun,* pp. 144–145.
2. Gilderbloom and Appelbaum, *Rethinking Rental Housing,* p. 58.
3. *Idem.*

4. *Ibid.*, pp. 60, 64.
5. *Ibid.*, p. 89.
6. Sternlieb and Hughes, *The Future of Rental Housing*, p. 9.
7. Downs, *Rental Housing in the 1980s*, p. 34.
8. *Ibid.*, p. 35.
9. Riis, *How the Other Half Lives*, pp. 3–4.
10. *Ibid.*, p. 48.
11. *Ibid.*, pp. 32–33.
12. Friedman, *Government and Public Housing*, pp. 32–33.
13. Mary B. Sayles, *Housing Conditions in Jersey City*, Philadelphia: Supplement to Annals of American Academy of Political and Social Science, 1903.
14. Friedman, *op. cit.*, pp. 40–41.
15. *Ibid.*, pp. 39–40.
16. Sternlieb, *The Tenement Landlord*, pp. 124–128.
17. *Ibid.*, p. 128.
18. *Ibid.*, pp. 138–139.
19. *Ibid.*, p. 143.
20. *Ibid.*, pp. 143–145.
21. Quoted in Paul Ciotti, "Socialism . . . On The Street Where You Live," *Reason*, April 1981.
22. Quoted, *Ibid.*

Chapter 14 The War Between Tenants and Landlords

1. Brian Hill, "Singing the Housing Blues," *The Daily Californian*, August 29, 1988.
2. Irving Welfeld, *Where We Live*, New York: Simon and Schuster, 1988, galley p. 218.
3. Hill, *op. cit.*
4. Helen Machado, "Rent Board Study Tells Great Deal About Berkeley Tenants," *The Daily Californian*, date unknown.
5. Michael Freeman, "Rent Control Blamed for Housing Decay," *The Daily Californian*, May 12, 1989.
6. Personal interview with author.
7. Dan Walters, "Even Liberals Shudder at Berkeley Now," *The Wall Street Journal*, December 13, 1985.

Chapter 15 The Paperworking Class

1. Thomas F. Fox, "Morrison Protest," *The Berkeley Voice*, September 19, 1984.
2. Dan Walters, *op. cit.*
3. Anne Morgenthaler, "Santa Monica rent board takes an aggressive turn," *The Outlook*, September 25, 1988.
4. John C. Dvorak, "Rich Get Richer," *The San Francisco Examiner*, May 13, 1985.
5. Nikki Rexroat, "Landlord Can't Evict Activist Tenant," *The Daily Californian*, December 6, 1985.

6. *Ibid.*
7. "101st Street Horror Story," KTVU, Channel 2, Oakland, broadcast February 27, 1988.
8. Carolyn Jones, "Neighbors Ask City to Evict Homeless Group," *The Daily Californian,* February 2, 1988.
9. Laura Fraser, "Squatters Rights," *The Berkeley Express,* February 6, 1987.
10. Paul Rauber, "Nightmare on 10th Street," *The Berkeley Express,* March 18, 1988.
11. Dave Linn, Letter to the Editor, *The Daily Californian,* February 2, 1988.
12. Roya Camp, "Evicted Homeless Confront City Council," *The Berkeley Voice,* March 10, 1988.

Chapter 16 Landlords and Economic Rent

1. Adam Smith, *The Wealth of Nations,* New York: The Modern Library, 1937, p. 248.
2. *Ibid.,* p. 49.
3. David Ricardo, *Principles of Political Economy and Taxation,* Middlesex, England: Penguin, 1971, p. 91.
4. *Ibid.,* p. 93.
5. *Ibid.,* p. 392.
6. S. Leon Levy, *Nassau W. Senior, 1790–1864,* Newton Abbot: David & Charles, 1970.
7. Robert Nozick, *Anarchy, State, and Utopia,* New York: Basic Books, 1974, pp. 161ff.
8. Henry George, *Progress and Poverty,* New York: The Modern Library.
9. Garrett Hardin, "The Tragedy of the Commons," in Garrett De Bell, ed., *The Environmental Handbook,* New York: Ballantine Books, 1970.
10. Herman Daly, *The Steady-State Economy,* San Francisco: W. H. Freeman, 1977, pp. 90, 110.

Chapter 17 Moscow on the Hudson

1. Deirdre Carmody, "Hard to Find, Harder to Afford: A Decent Manhattan Apartment," *The New York Times,* July 19, 1984.
2. *The New York Times* real-estate ads, July 2, 1989.
3. "Bell No, I Won't Go, Says $45 Tenant," *The New York Post,* October 18, 1986.
4. Alex Michelini, "His 'castle' besieged," *The New York Daily News,* January 9, 1987; Michelini, "Marquis rents and raves over evict plan," *The New York Daily News,* January 10, 1987.
5. All quotes are from trial transcript.
6. "Protracted Rent Control War Takes Toll On Housing Stock," *Insight,* April 13, 1987.
7. Richard D. Lyons, "Complex Cases Swamp Housing Court," *The New York Times,* August 17, 1986.
8. *Ibid.*

Chapter 18 A Temporary Wartime Measure

1. "Vacancy Ratio Increases," *The New York Times,* March 10, 1941; "Realty Men

Oppose Rent Control Here," *Ibid.,* March 21, 1941; Lee E. Cooper, "Population Down, Apartments Full; War Paradox Here Stumps Experts," *Ibid.,* February 16, 1944; "City's Apartments Virtually Full," *Ibid.,* April 14, 1944; also, Savings Bank Association, State of New York, *Association News Bulletin,* February 9, 1940.

2. "Apartment Groups Well Filled as Renting Season Nears Peak," *The New York Times,* September 6, 1942; "Live in Manhattan Commission Reports More Lease Renewals During Past Season," *Ibid.,* December 6, 1942.
3. "Report Surplus of Housing Here at Low Rentals," *The New York Times,* November 16, 1941.
4. "Cheaper Suites Show Vacancies of 9.9 Per Cent," *The New York Times,* May 1, 1942; "5% of Apartments in City Are Vacant," *Ibid.,* April 1, 1942; also, "Realty Board Reports Sharp Increase in Vacancies for Tenement Districts," *Ibid.,* March 17, 1943.
5. "Rent Decision Due Soon, Says Mayor," *The New York Times,* September 23, 1943.
6. "OPA Orders Rents Frozen Here On March 1 Level Starting Nov. 1," *The New York Times,* September 29, 1943.
7. "City's Apartments Virtually Full," *The New York Times,* April 14, 1944.
8. Michael deCourcy Hinds, "The Elusive Rent-Regulated Apartments," *The New York Times,* February 16, 1986.
9. Michael deCourcy Hinds, "Landlords Move To Halt Illegal Sublets," *The New York Times,* November 17, 1985.
10. "City's Putting the Squeeze on Mitchell-Lama Tenants," *The New York Daily News,* March 1, 1989.
11. Wayne Barrett, "The Cuomo Sleaze Team," *The Village Voice,* August 16, 1988.
12. Jacobs, *The Death and Life at Great American Cities.*
13. Assa Lindbeck, *The Political Economy of the New Left: An Outsider's View,* New York: Harper and Row, 1977, p. 39.
14. "Rarity: Manhattan Gets New Apartments," *The New York Daily News,* May 30, 1986.

Chapter 19 The Best Deal in Town

1. Liz Smith, "Arnold Scaasi: An Exuberant Collection Overlooking Central Park," *Architectural Digest,* September 1988.
2. Paul Schwartzman, "Palaces for Peanuts," *The New York Post,* April 9, 1989.
3. Cindy Adams, *The New York Post,* February 2, 1989.
4. "Page Six," *The New York Post,* date unknown.
5. Owen Moritz, "Apple Sauce," *The New York Daily News,* December 12, 1986.
6. Personal interview with author.
7. Ken Auletta, *The Streets Were Paved With Gold.* New York: Vintage Books, 1980, pp. 41ff.
8. Winston Groom, "Once a New Yorker . . .", *The New York Times Magazine,* (Special Supplement: "The World of New York"), November 9, 1986.
9. "Rent Regulation in New York 1987: To Have or to Have Not," Cambridge: Arthur D. Little, 1988, p. 27.

10. *Ibid.*, p. 17.
11. Arthur D. Little, Inc., "Housing Gridlock in New York," Cambridge: Arthur D. Little, 1987, pp. 1, II–2.
12. *Ibid.*
13. *Ibid.*, p. 3.
14. *Ibid.*, pp. VI–1—VI–5.
15. Schwartzman, *op. cit.;* "A Current Affair," Fox Television, WNEW-TV, New York, August, 1986.

Chapter 20 "I Didn't Know It Would Be Impossible"

1. Hinds, "The Elusive Rent-Regulated Apartments."
2. Jane Goldman, "How to Find an Apartment (Seriously)," *New York,* June 22, 1987.
3. *Ibid.*
4. Sheila Anne Feeney, "Un-Real Estate Tactics: The crazy things that people will do to find a New York apartment," *The New York Daily News,* January 10, 1988.
5. William R. Greer, "Price of City Life Hard on the Young in Arts, Theater," *The New York Times,* date unknown.
6. Hinds, *op. cit.*
7. Goldman, *op. cit.*
8. *Ibid.*
9. Sally Dayan, "Shall We Be Released? Le Ronde de Real Estate," *The Village Voice,* July 21, 1987.
10. Feeney, *op. cit.*
11. "Q/A: An Expensive Room," *The New York Times* Sunday Real Estate Section, January 26, 1986.
12. Goldman, *op. cit.*
13. Paul La Rosa, "It's a sub, sub world," *The New York Daily News,* June 23, 1986.
14. Michael deCourcy Hinds, "The Windfall Profits in Insider Flips," *The New York Times,* August 30, 1987.
15. *Ibid.*
16. *Ibid.*
17. Esther B. Fein, "A Rent-Control Holdout Showing Her Gumption," *The New York Times,* February 13, 1986.
18. Michael deCourcy Hinds, "Holdouts Battle Developers in Site Wars," *The New York Times,* September 1985.
19. *Ibid.*
20. Gene Rondinaro, "Institutions Taking on Developer's Role," *The New York Times,* October 14, 1984.
21. Linda Stevens, "30 Arrested at Columbia Tenant Rally," *The New York Post,* February 24, 1987.
22. William G. Blair, "Artist-Housing Tenants Are Split on Co-op Plan," *The New York Times,* November 24, 1985.

23. Hope MacLeod, "Time-share apt. tenant clicks by clocking in," *The New York Post,* May 6, 1989.
24. "Christmas Cruelty," *The New York Daily News,* December 22, 1987.
25. "Rent control: A lease on stupidity," Voice of the People, *The New York Daily News,* June 17, 1985.

Chapter 21 The Destruction of the Landlord Class

1. I appeared on the same show.
2. John J. Gilbert III, *Unreal Estate,* New York: Full Court Press, 1987, p. 1.
3. "The Owners of New York's Rental Housing: A Profile," Cambridge: Arthur D. Little, Inc., May 1985, p. 2.
4. *Ibid.,* pp. 4–5.
5. *Ibid.,* p. 2.
6. *Ibid.,* p. 3.
7. "Who Owns New York's Housing?" New York State Tenant and Neighborhood Coalition, June 1, 1985.

Chapter 22 The Government Takes Over

1. Ken Auletta, "Bricks back up Biderman boast," *The New York Daily News,* April 9, 1989.
2. Remarks by Mayor Edward J. Koch at the housing-capital funds press conference, April 30, 1986.
3. Harvey Klehr, "Maoist nose enters Democratic tent," *The New York Post,* August 12, 1987; Thomas J. Lueck, "The Tenant-as-Landlord Movement," *The New York Times,* July 2, 1989.
4. William Bastone, "The Priest and the Mob," *The Village Voice,* March 7, 1989.
5. Thomas McDonald and Judith Frost, "An Analysis of Corruption Vulnerabilities in New York City's 7a Administrator Program," The New York City Department of Investigation, March 1986.
6. Jacob V. Lamar, "The Homeless: Brick by Brick," *Time,* October 24, 1988.
7. Anthony de Palma, "Are Government Rent Vouchers a Boon or a Bust?" *The New York Times,* November 1, 1987.
8. *Ibid.*
9. *Ibid.*
10. All quotes, *Ibid.*

Chapter 23 Homelessness in Other Countries

1. James Fallows, "Tokyo: The Hard Life," *The Atlantic Monthly,* March 1989.
2. E. Jay Howenstine, "European Experience with Rent Controls," *The Monthly Labor Review,* June, 1977.
3. "Rent-a-ruin," *The Economist,* July 12, 1986.
4. Howenstine, *op. cit.*

5. Marcia Kramer, "Housing Headache Hobbles Budapest," *The New York Daily News,* January 30, 1988.
6. Rene Frank, International Property Consultants, Ltd., personal communication.
7. Terence Roth and Thomas F. O'Boyle, "East German Refugees Face the Reality of Life As Familiar Strangers," *The Wall Street Journal,* October 4, 1989.
8. Howenstine, *op. cit.*
9. Pamela Readhead, "Rents to Raise the roof," *The Financial Times,* April 11, 1987.
10. "Eyes or Kidneys Offered for Apartment," *The Los Angeles Herald-Examiner,* September 3, 1980.
11. Readhead, *op. cit.*
12. Richard J. Arnott and Jack M. Mintz, editors, *Rent Control: The International Experience,* Kingston, Ontario: John Deutsch Institute for the Study of Economic Policy, 1987, p. 4.
13. *Ibid.,* pp. 9–10.
14. "Metropolitan Report," *The New York Times,* June 3, 1985.
15. Hedrick Smith, *The Russians,* New York: Ballantine Books, 1977, pp. 97–98.
16. *Ibid.,* p. 98.
17. Cathy Young, author, *Growing Up in Moscow: Memoirs of a Soviet Girlhood,* personal communications.
18. "Rent Control: It's Worse Than Bombing," *Fortune,* February 28, 1989, excerpted from an article in *The Journal of Commerce.*
19. Alan Cowell, "Apartments Sit Empty While City of Dead Booms," *The New York Times,* May 29, 1989.
20. *Ibid.*
21. *Ibid.*
22. *Ibid.*

Chapter 24 Homelessness and the Constitution

1. John McCarron, "Chicago on Hold, Part I, 'Reformers' declare war on development in poor areas," *The Chicago Tribune,* special reprint.
2. Collier and Horowitz, *op. cit.*
3. Michael Kammen, *A Machine That Would Go of Itself: The Constitution in American Culture,* New York: Vintage Books, 1987, pp. 14, 70.
4. *Ibid.,* p. 82.
5. Alain L. Sanders, "No Taking Without Paying," *Time,* June 22, 1987.

Bibliography

Aaron, Henry J., *Shelter and Subsidies: Who Benefits from Federal Housing Policies?* Washington: The Brookings Institution, 1972.

______. *Who Pays the Property Tax?* Washington: The Brookings Institution, 1975.

Adams, James Ring. *Secrets of the Tax Revolt.* New York: Harcourt Brace Jovanovich Publishers, 1984.

Alcaly, Roger E. and Mermelstein, David. *The Fiscal Crisis of American Cities.* New York: Vintage Books, 1977.

Anderson, Martin. *The Federal Bulldozer: A Critical Analysis of Urban Renewal Policies, 1949–1962.* Cambridge: The MIT Press, 1964.

Apgar, William C., Jr., and Brown, James H. "The State of the Nation's Housing." Cambridge: Joint Center for Housing Studies at Harvard University, 1988.

Arnott, Richard J. and Mintz, Jack M. *Rent Control: The International Experience.* Kingston, Ontario: John Deutsch Institute for the Study of Economic Policy, 1987.

Aronson, J. Richard and Hilley, John L. *Financing State and Local Government.* Washington: The Brookings Institution, 1986.

Auletta, Ken. *The Streets Were Paved With Gold.* New York: Vintage Books, 1980.

Babcock, Richard F. *The Zoning Game: Municipal Practices and Policies.* Madison: The University of Wisconsin Press, 1966.

Bahr, Howard and Caplow, Theodore. *Old Men Drunk and Sober.* New York: NYU Press, 1974.

Baird, Charles W. *Rent Control: The Perennial Folly.* Washington: The Cato Institute, 1980.

Banfield, Edward C. *The Unheavenly City.* Boston: Little, Brown, and Company, 1970.

Bingham, Richard D., Green, Roy E., White, Sammis B., eds., *The Homeless in Contemporary Society.* Newbury Park, California: Sage Publications, 1987.

Block, Walter and Olsen, Edgar, eds. *Rent Control: Myths and Realities,* Vancouver, B.C.: The Fraser Institute, 1981.

Bradbury, Katharine and Downs, Anthony, eds., *Do Housing Allowances Work?* Washington: The Brookings Institution, 1981.

Burchell, Robert W., Beaton, W. Patrick, and Listokin, David. *Mournt Laurel II: Challenge and Delivery of Low-Cost Housing.* New Brunswick: Center for Urban Policy Research, 1983.

Burt, Martha R. and Cohen, Barbara E. "Feeding the Homeless: Does the Prepared Meals Provision Help?" Washington: Urban Institute, 1988.

Chinitz, Benjamin. *City and Suburb: The Economics of Metropolitan Growth.* Englewood Cliffs, Prentice-Hall, 1964.

Cincinnati Historical Society. *Cincinnati: The Queen City.* Cincinnati: The Cincinnati Historical Society, 1988.

Clinard, Marshall B. *Slums and Community Development.* New York: The Free Press, 1966.

Community Ownership Organizing Project. *The Cities' Wealth: Programs for Community Economic Control in Berkeley, California.* Washington: Conference on Alternative State and Local Policies, 1976.

Danielson, Michael N. *The Politics of Exclusion.* New York: Columbia University Press, 1976.

Daly, Herman, *The Steady-State Economy,* San Francisco: W. H. Freeman, 1977.

DeAngelo, Dory. *Voices Across Time: Profiles of Kansas City's Early Residents.* Kansas City: Tapestry Publications, 1987.

Dolce, Philp C. *Suburbia: The American Dream and Dilemma.* Garden City: Doubleday Anchor, 1976.

Dorman, Michael. *The Making of a Slum.* New York: Delacorte Press, 1972.

Downs, Anthony. *Opening Up the Suburbs: An Urban Strategy for America.* New Haven: Yale University Press, 1973.

———. *Rental Housing in the 1980s.* Washington: Brookings Institution, 1984.

———. *The Revolution in Real Estate Finance.* Washington: The Brookings Institution, 1985.

———. *Residential Rent Controls: An Evaluation.* Washington: The Urban Land Institute, 1988.

Edel, Matthew, Sclar, Elliott D., and Luria, Daniel. *Shaky Palaces: Homeownership and Social Mobility in Boston's Suburbanization.* New York: Columbia University Press, 1984.

Epstein, Richard. *Takings: Private Property and the Power of Eminent Domain.* Cambridge: Harvard University Press, 1985.

Erickson, Jon and Wilhelm, Charles, ed. *Housing the Homeless.* New Brunswick: Center for Urban Affairs, 1986.

Frieden, Bernard. *The Environmental Protection Hustle.* Cambridge: The MIT Press, 1979.

Friedman, Lawrence. *Government and Slum Housing.* Chicago: Rand McNally and Company, 1968.

Fulton, William. "Development Agreements in Santa Monica." Los Angeles: University of California, 1985.

Gans, Herbert J. *The Urban Villagers.* Glencoe: The Free Press of Glencoe, 1962.

George, Henry. *Progress and Poverty: An Inquiry Into the Cause of Industrial Depressions and of Increase of Want With Increase of Wealth.* New York: The Modern Library.

Gilbert, John J. III, with Alex York. *Unreal Estate.* New York: Full Court Press, 1987.

Gilder, George. *Wealth and Poverty.* New York, Bantam Books, 1981.

Gilderbloom, John I. and Appelbaum, Richard P. *Rethinking Rental Housing.* Philadelphia: Temple University Press, 1988.

Grant, George. *The Dispossessed: Homelessness in America.* Westchester, Illinois: Crossway Books, 1986.

Grant, R. W. *Rent Control and the War Against the Poor.* Manhattan Beach: Quandary House, 1989.

Green, Constance McLaughlin. *American Cities in the Growth of the Nation.* New York: Harper Colophon Books, 1965.

Hanlin, Oscar, *Boston's Immigrants,* Cambridge: Belknap Press of Harvard University, 1959.

Harriss, C. Lowell, ed. *The Property Tax and Local Finance.* New York: The Academy for Political Science, 1983.

Hawley, Peter K. *Housing in the Public Domain: The Only Solution.* New York: Metropolitan Council on Housing, 1978.

Hayek, F. A., Friedman, Milton, and Stigler, George J. *Rent Control: A Popular Paradox.* Vancouver, B. C.: The Fraser Institute, 1975.

Hays, R. Allen. *The Federal Government and Urban Housing.* Albany: State University of New York Press, 1985.

Hope, Marjorie and Young, James. *The Faces of Homelessness.* Lexington: D. C. Heath, 1986.

Hopper, Kim and Hamberg, Jill. *The Making of America's Homeless: From Skid Row to New Poor.* New York: Community Service Society, 1984.

Hughes, James W., and Sternlieb, George. *The Dynamics of America's Housing.* New Brunswick: Center for Urban Policy Research, 1987.

Johnson, M. Bruce, ed. *Resolving the Housing Crisis: Government Policy, Decontrol, and the Public Interest.* San Francisco: Pacific Institute for Public Policy Research, 1982.

Kammen, Michael. *A Machine That Would Go of Itself: The Constitution in American Culture.* New York: Vintage Books, 1987.

Kann, Mark E. *Middle Class Radicalism in Santa Monica.* Philadelphia: Temple University Press, 1986.

Kaplan, Harold. *Urban Renewal Politics: Slum Clearance in Newark.* New York: Columbia University Press, 1963.

Klein, Woody. *Let in the Sun.* New York: The Macmillan Company, 1964.

Koch, Edward, Mayor, City of New York. *The Mayor's Management Report: Preliminary, January, 1986.* New York: Citybooks, 1986.

Kozol, Jonathan. *Rachel and Her Children.* New York: Crown Publishers, 1988.

Kramer, Horace Z. *Assessment for Real Property Tax Purposes.* Garden City: Adelphi University Press, 1975.

Kuttner, Robert. *The Revolt of the Haves.* New York: Simon and Schuster, 1980.

Lansing, John B., Clifton, Charles Wade, and Morgan, James N. *New Homes and Poor People.* Ann Arbor: Institute for Social Research, 1969.

Lett, Monica. *Rent Control: Concepts, Realities, and Mechanisms.* New Brunswick: Center for Urban Policy Research, 1976.

Loewenstein, Louis K. *Urban Studies: An Introductory Reader.* New York: The Free Press, 1971.

Lowry, Ritchie P. *Who's Running This Town: Community Leadership and Social Change.* New York: Harper and Row, 1965.

Malthus, Thomas Robert. *On Population.* New York: The Modern Library, 1960.

Matusow, Allen J. *The Unravelling of America: A History of Liberalism in the 1960s.* New York: Harper Torchbooks, 1984.

Mayer, Martin. *The Builders.* New York: Viking, 1978.

Mayer, Neil S. *Neighborhood Organization and Community Development: Making Revitalization Work.* Washington: Urban Institute Press, 1984.

McCullough, David. *The Great Bridge: The Epic Story of the Building of the Brooklyn Bridge.* New York: Avon Books, 1972.

Minford, Patrick, Peel, Michael, and Ashton, Paul. *The Housing Morass: Regulation, Immobility, and Unemployment.* London: The Institute for Economic Affairs, 1987.

Mitchell, J. Paul, ed. *Federal Housing Policy and Programs.* New Brunswick: Center for Urban Policy Research, 1981.

Mushkin, Selma J., ed. *Proposition 13 and Its Consequences for Public Management.* Cambridge: ABT Books, 1979.

Muth, Richard F. *Public Housing: An Economic Evaluation.* Washington: American Enterprise Institute, 1973.

National Academy of Sciences. *Homelessness, Health, and Human Needs.* Washington: National Academy Press, 1988.

National Coalition for the Homeless. "The Homeless and the Economic Recovery." New York: National Coalition for the Homeless, 1983.

________. "The Homeless and the Economic Recovery: One Year Later." New York: National Coalition for the Homeless," 1984.

Nelson, Robert H. *Zoning and Property Rights.* Cambridge: The MIT Press, 1977.

New York State Division of Housing and Community Renewal. *Neighborhood Preservation and Rural Preservation Programs: Annual Report, 1984*. Albany: New York State Division of Housing and Community Renewal, 1984.

Nichols, James C., with Olsen, Mary C., Costomiris, Joyce, and Levesque, Adele. *State Regulation/Housing Prices.* New Brunswick: Center for Urban Policy Research, 1982.

Nozick, Robert. *Anarchy, State, and Utopia*. New York: Basic Books, 1974.

Pace, Patricia Ewing. *Kansas City: The Spirit, The People, The Promise.* Northridge, California: Windsor Publications, 1987.

Peterson, Paul E. ed. *The New Urban Reality.* Washington: The Brookings Institution, 1985.

Porter, Paul R. and Sweet, David C. *Rebuilding America's Cities: Roads to Recovery.* New Brunswick: Center for Urban Policy Research, 1984.

Ricardo, David. *Principles of Political Economy and Taxation.* Middlesex, England: Pelican Books, 1971.

Riis, Jacob A. *How the Other Half Lives.* New York: Hill and Wang, 1957.

Rossi, Peter. *Without Shelter: Homelessness in the 1980s.* New York: Priority Press Publications, 1989.

________. *Down and Out in America: The Origins of Homelessness.* Chicago: The University of Chicago Press, 1989.

Rossi, Peter H. and Dentler, Robert A. *The Politics of Urban Renewal.* Glencoe: The Free Press of Glencoe, 1963.

Salins, Peter. *New York Unbound*. New York: Basil Blackwell, 1988.

Sanjek, Roger. "Federal Housing Programs and Their Impact on Homelessness." New York: National Coalition for the Homeless, 1982.

Schuettinger, Robert L. and Butler, Eamonn F. *Forty Centuries of Wage and Price Controls.* Washington: The Heritage Foundation, 1979.

Schwadron, Terry, ed., Richter, Paul, principal writer, *California and the American Tax Revolt: Proposition 13 Five Years Later,* Berkeley: University of California Press, 1984.

Siegen, Bernard H. *Land Use Without Zoning*. Lexington: D.C. Health, 1972.

________. *Economic Liberties and the Constitution.* Chicago: University of Chicago Press, 1980.

Smith, Adam. *An Inquiry Into the Nature and Causes of the Wealth of Nations.* New York: The Modern Library, 1937.

Snyder, Mitch and Hombs, Mary Ellen. *Homelessness in America*. Washington: Community for Creative Non-Violence, 1982.

Starr, Roger. *The Living End: The City and Its Critics.* New York: Coward-McCann, 1966.

Stegman, Michael A. *Housing and Vacancy Report: New York City, 1987.* New York: Department of Housing Preservation and Development, 1987.

Sternlieb, George. *The Tenement Landlord.* New Brunswick: Rutgers University, 1966.

Sternlieb, George and Burchell, Robert W. *Residential Abandonment: The Tenement Landlord Revisited.* New Brunswick: Center for Urban Policy Research, 1973.

Sternlieb, George and Hughes, James W. *The Future of Rental Housing* New Brunswick: Center for Urban Policy Research, 1981.

Struyk, Raymond J. and Bendick, Marc, Jr., eds., *Housing Vouchers for the Poor: Lessons from a National Experiment.* Washington: The Urban Institute Press, 1981.

Thernstrom, Stephan. *The Other Bostonians: Poverty and Progress in the American Metropolis, 1880–1970.* Cambridge: Harvard University Press, 1973.

Torrey, E. Fuller. *Nowhere To Go.* New York: Harper and Row, 1988.

Turner, Margery Austin and Struyk, Raymond J. *Urban Housing in the 1980s.* Washington: The Urban Institute Press, 1984.

United States Conference of Mayors. *The Continued Growth of Hunger, Homelessness, and Poverty in America's Cities: 1986. A 25-City Survey.* Washington: United States Conference of Mayors, 1986.

________. *A Status Report on Hunger and Homelessness.* Washington: United States Conference of Mayors, 1989.

United States Department of Housing and Urban Development. *A Report to the Secretary on the Homeless and Emergency Shelters.* Washington: Department of Housing and Urban Development, 1984.

United States Government. *The Report of the President's Commission on Housing.* Washington: U. S. Government Printing Office, 1982.

Warner, Sam Bass, Jr. *Streetcar Suburbs: The Process of Growth in Boston (1870–1900).* Cambridge: Harvard University Press, 1978.

Watts, Lewis G., et. al. *The Middle-Income Negro Faces Urban Renewal.* Waltham: Brandeis University, 1964.

Welfeld, Irving. *Where We Live: A Social History of American Housing.* New York: Simon and Schuster, 1988.

Whitehall, Walter Muir. *Boston: A Topographical History.* Cambridge: Harvard University Press, 1968.

Whyte, William H. *The Last Landscape.* Garden City: Doubleday Anchor, 1970.

Wilson, James Q., ed., *The Metropolitan Enigma.* Garden City: Doubleday Anchor, 1970.

Wood, Edith Elmer. *Housing for the Low-Income Wage-Earner.* New York: The Macmillan Company, 1919.

Wood, Robert C. *Suburbia: Its People and Their Politics.* Boston: Houghton Mifflin Company, 1958.

________. *1400 Governments: The Political Economy of the New York Region.* Garden City: Doubleday Anchor, 1961.

Index

C

D

E